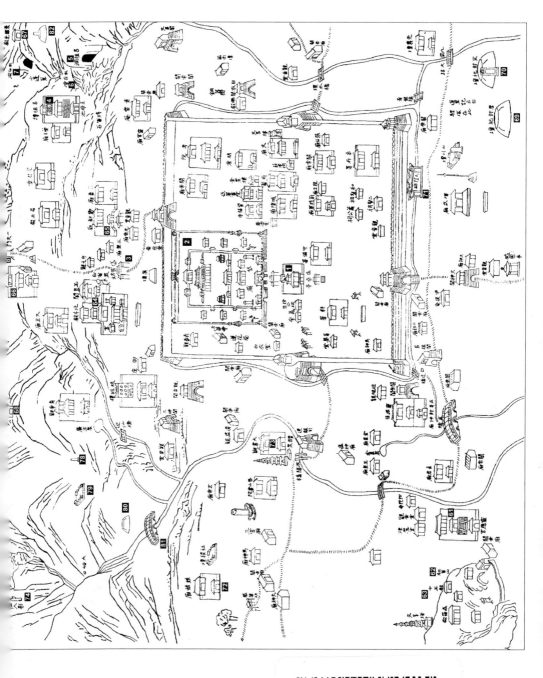

D1603742

Identity
Reflections

Pilgrimages to Mount Tai
in Late Imperial China

Harvard East Asian Monographs 244

Identity
Reflections

Pilgrimages to Mount Tai
in Late Imperial China

Brian R. Dott

Published by the Harvard University Asia Center
Distributed by Harvard University Press
Cambridge (Massachusetts) and London 2004

Printed in the United States of America

The Harvard University Asia Center publishes a monograph series and, in coor-
dination with the Fairbank Center for East Asian Research, the Korea Institute,
the Reischauer Institute of Japanese Studies, and other faculties and institutes, ad-
ministers research projects designed to further scholarly understanding of China,
Japan, Vietnam, Korea, and other Asian countries. The Center also sponsors projects addressing multidisciplinary and regional issues in Asia.

Library of Congress Cataloging-in-Publication Data
Dott, Brian Russell.
  Identity reflections: pilgrimages to Mount Tai in late imperial china / Brian R.
Dott.
      p. cm. -- (Harvard East Asian monographs ; 244)
   Includes bibliographical references and index.
   ISBN 0-674-01653-x (cloth : alk. paper)
   1. Social interaction--China--Tai Mountains. 2. Tai Mountains (China) 3. China--
Social life and customs--1644-1912. I. Title. II. Series.
   HMIIII.D68 2004
   306'.0951'14--dc22

                                                                2004020112

Index by the author

⊗ Printed on acid-free paper

Last figure below indicates year of this printing
14 13 12 11 10 09 08 07 06 05 04

For Alex

Acknowledgments

My research and writing for this work have benefited from a wealth of assistance. Evelyn Rawski provided exceptional guidance throughout the entire process, reading through many drafts. Always willing to talk through ideas with me, she has helped me to refine my arguments. Sally Bormann provided unflagging critical assessment, support, and editing. Susan Naquin has given me valuable advice from the inception of this project, including reading and commenting on an earlier version. I thank the Committee for Scholarly Communication with China for a Graduate Fellowship in 1994–95 through the United States Information Agency funding, which allowed me to conduct research in the People's Republic of China. The Qing History Institute 清史研究所 at Renmin University in Beijing hosted me during that year of research. My most recent trip to Mount Tai in 2000 was funded in part by an ASIANetwork Freeman Student-Faculty Fellowship. The Asian Studies program of the University of Pittsburgh generously supported my work with a travel grant in 1994 and a FLAS fellowship in 1996–97. The History Department at Whitman College funded a library research trip in 2003.

In Tai'an, Liu Hui 刘慧, director of the Tai'an Municipal Museum, and Zhao Guazhi 赵挂芝, the librarian at the museum, graciously facilitated my research. Jiang Fengrong 姜丰荣, who in

1994–95 was director of the Religion Department of the Mount Tai Scenic and Historic Site Administration Committee, brought his enthusiasm and expertise on matters about Mount Tai to our exchanges, liberally sharing materials and time.

In Beijing, Qin Baoqi 秦宝琦 of the Qing History Institute kindly advised me about sources of research materials in China. The staffs of the Beijing Library, the Number One Historical Archives, the Capital Library, the rare book room at the Beijing University library, and the library of the Academy of Social Sciences provided assistance.

In Taiwan I was assisted by librarians at the National Central Library, as well as the libraries in the Institute of History and Philology and the Institute of Ethnology, both at the Academia Sinica.

In North America, Cho-yun Hsu and Linda Penkower provided me with excellent advice as I was beginning to formulate my research and as I continued through the writing process. Kimberly Falk, who was conducting anthropological fieldwork in Shandong during my year of research in Beijing, generously exchanged findings and research materials with me at various stages of this work. Daniel Overmyer kindly sent me a copy of the first half of the precious volume about the Goddess of Mount Tai in the early stages of my research. My colleagues in the History Department at Whitman College provided key advice during the last stages of the revision. I am also obliged to the staffs of the East Asian Library of the University of Pittsburgh, the Asian Division of the Library of Congress, the East Asia Library of the University of Washington, and the C.V. Starr East Asian Library of Columbia University.

I am also grateful for the suggestions of two anonymous reviewers for the Harvard University Asia Center, particularly regarding the early imperial period.

B.R.D.

Contents

Tables
and Figures

Tables

Figures

Dates of Chinese Dynasties

Pinyin romanization is given first, followed (where different) by Wade-Giles romanization in parentheses.

Shang Dynasty	ca. 1766–1050 BCE
Zhou (Chou) Dynasty	ca. 1050– 221 BCE
Western Zhou	ca. 1050–771 BCE
Eastern Zhou	770–221 BCE
Spring and Autumn period	722–481 BCE
Warring States period	481–221 BCE
Qin (Ch'in) Dynasty	221–206 BCE
Han Dynasty	202 BCE–220 CE
Western or Former Han Dynasty	202 BCE–9 CE
Xin (Hsin) Dynasty (also known as Wang Mang interregnum)	9–23
Eastern or Later Han Dynasty	25–220
Period of disunity	220–589
Sui Dynasty	589–618
Tang (T'ang) Dynasty	618–907
Five Dynasties Period	907–60
Song (Sung) Dynasty	960–1279
Northern Song	960–1127
Southern Song	1127–1279
Yuan Dynasty	1279–1368

Ming Dynasty	1368–1644
Qing (Ch'ing) Dynasty	1644–1911
Republic of China (continues to present on Taiwan)	1911–49
People's Republic of China	1949–

Identity
Reflections

Pilgrimages to Mount Tai
in Late Imperial China

 Introduction

Mount Tai (Taishan 泰山) has long been sacred to believers of China's three major socio-religious traditions—Daoism, Confucianism, and Buddhism—as well as a center for popular religion and imperial ritual. The mountain is closely linked to filial piety, China's omnipresent social, moral, and religious driving force. The dominant peak on the North China Plain, Mount Tai has throughout its history been a magnet for Chinese from all walks of life—women, men, literati, villagers, religious leaders, lay believers, local officials, and emperors. Indeed, Mount Tai epitomizes China's religious and social diversity.

Emperors traveled to it to pray for the prosperity of the empire and the longevity of their dynasty. Literati combined more mundane desires, such as sightseeing and retracing the footsteps of celebrated philosophers, poets, and emperors, with the pursuit of moral rectification and spiritual enlightenment. For much of the past millennium, however, the vast majority of pilgrims were illiterate peasants who journeyed to its sacred heights in search of benefits for their deceased ancestors and to pray for heirs and for the health and fortune of their family. During the late imperial period (1500 to 1920),[1] various religions and traditions attracted throngs of worshipers and orchestrated dramatic spatial and ritual competitions that were played out upon, within, and against the sacred geography of Mount Tai.

Fig. 1   View of Mount Tai from the Dai Temple
(photograph by the author, 1994).

Different components of Chinese society approached this holy
and historic site with their own vision of its sacrality and history.
Each group's or individual's view of the world, interpersonal relationships, and ultimate goals or dreams—in a word, its identity—
was reflected in its interactions with this sacred site. James Watson
contends that "deities mean different things to different people,
depending on their [the people's] position in the hierarchy of

power. . . . The study of religious cults thus provides an opportunity to determine how values and symbols are transformed as they cross social boundaries."[2] The investigation of pilgrimages similarly gives us insight into people's mentalities, for "to study pilgrimage necessitates identification of what constitutes worship, the sacred, and the sphere of the religious more generally."[3] This book examines interactions with and interpretations of the sacred spaces of Mount Tai, as a means of better understanding the identities and mentalities of those who undertook the journey to the mountain during the late imperial period. It is the first to trace the social landscape of Mount Tai, to examine the mentalities not just of the prosperous, male literati but also of women and illiterate pilgrims, and to combine fiction, poetry, travel literature, and official records with the study of material culture and anthropology.

Part I, "Cultural Stratigraphy: Multiple Identities of a Sacred Site," traces the multivalent nature of Mount Tai. The human imprints on Mount Tai range from a few marks left on a stone to large temple complexes. This part begins by analyzing sites, historical events, and legends by categorizing them into six groupings or layers. Each of these groupings is a general rubric for one aspect of the drawing power of the mountain. Mount Tai has been a site for nature worship, imperial ritual, history, mysticism, death, and life. These separate facets delineate the diverse character of this sacred mountain. The majority of travelers to Mount Tai in the late imperial period, however, did not approach the mountain from just one perspective. They did more than appreciate the natural scenery or pray for a son. The sacred site of Mount Tai, like Chinese religion in general, reflects multiple belief systems and practices. All the beliefs, legends, and sacrality attached to this mountain blended to create contexts for the various groups who ascended Mount Tai in the late imperial period. Each group or individual emphasized and ordered the particular sites, events, and practices to fit personal goals and motivations. Part I turns to broader issues of what constitutes sacred space; how it is created and maintained; and how individuals, through ritual, use sacred space as a conduit for communing with the divine. It concludes with an analysis of the hierarchy of sacred space on Mount Tai.

Part II, "Late Imperial Pilgrimages," studies distinct groups of pilgrims in detail. Chapter 1, "Pilgrimage as Popular Agency: Women and Men Seeking Children and Heirs," examines gender differences in lower-class pilgrims' approaches to and interactions with the sacred spaces of Mount Tai. Although both men and women had the same primary motivation of family propagation, they had different expectations of what the birth of a son would accomplish. This chapter also explores some of the many ways in which women were able to circumvent written proscriptions pertaining to their lives. While on pilgrimage, women enjoyed a degree of freedom from some of the restrictions of their daily life. They were able to travel beyond their local area, they stayed overnight outside their own home, and they met people from other regions. Although women customarily played a minor role in rituals, they were the primary or sole actors in rituals associated with the Goddess of Mount Tai (Taishan Niangniang 泰山娘娘 or Bixia Yuanjun 碧霞元君). In addition to physical mobility, pilgrimages allowed women to exercise ritual authority and agency and to establish new identities as mothers and ritual experts.

Chapter 2, "Pilgrimage as Legitimation: Manchu Emperors in Chinese Sacred Space," analyzes Qing imperial pilgrimages to Mount Tai. Both the Kangxi and the Qianlong emperor made multiple pilgrimages to Mount Tai. Although on many levels the Qing emperors assumed the mantle of the Son of Heaven as the rulers of the territories once controlled by the Ming, or China proper, they were—especially during the seventeenth and eighteenth centuries— non-Han rulers of an empire that included non-Chinese peoples. Until recently much scholarship on the Qing dynasty asserted that the Manchus were successful because they adopted Chinese ways and culture, because they became "sinicized." However, "new scholarship suggests just the opposite: the key to Qing success, at least in terms of empire-building, lay in its ability to use its cultural links with the non-Han peoples of Inner Asia and to differentiate the administration of the former Ming provinces."[4] Investigation of interactions between these Manchu emperors and Mount Tai adds important dimensions to our understanding of the multifaceted nature of Qing rulership. Even on Mount Tai—a quintessentially

Chinese sacred site—they managed to manifest their Manchu identity. The actions of these two emperors on the mountain also reveal important differences in their personal styles of rulership and changes brought about by consolidation of Manchu authority.

Chapter 3, "Pilgrimage as Literature: Reading Oneself into the Past and Writing Oneself into the Future," examines the visits of literate men, the elite of late imperial Chinese society. At first glance, the differences between literati visitors to Mount Tai and pilgrims journeying to worship the Goddess of Mount Tai seem to far outweigh their similarities. The literati were apparently more interested in pursuing secular rather than sacred goals. This interpretation, however, is largely a product of the modern, Western dichotomization of the sacred and the secular. Although most of these men did not pray to the Goddess of Mount Tai, they still had spiritual motivations and aspirations. They went to admire and, in a sense, to worship nature. They sought self-cultivation and moral rectification. They connected to nature through poetry recitation and composition. They wrote themselves into long lineages of perfected persons through travelogues and inscriptions.

The religious professionals who resided on Mount Tai during the late imperial period are another obvious group for analysis. Unfortunately, extant sources do not provide sufficient information on them. Temple records would have been the best sources for examination of religious professionals, but regrettably all records for temples on Mount Tai were destroyed either by fires during the late imperial period or by the wars of the twentieth century.[5] In addition, the few biographies of Daoists or Buddhists found in the gazetteers are too short to allow meaningful analysis.

Historiography

The most important analytical work on Mount Tai to date is Edouard Chavannes's 1910 study, *Le T'ai Chan: essai de monographie d'un culte chinois*. Chavannes was especially interested in ancient and medieval history, and his thorough inventory of the sites on the mountain provides both historical references and descriptions of their condition in the early twentieth century. Much of Chavannes's work focuses on imperial visits to Mount Tai.

Other Western sources from the late nineteenth and early twentieth century are primarily descriptive or highly derivative of Chavannes.[6] Even G. E. Hubbard's 1925 article, "The Pilgrims of Taishan," although it provides some useful information, does little to explain the motivations of pilgrims.

Recent scholarly attention has focused on a particular genre or deity. Literary analyses include Paul Kroll's study of medieval poetry about Mount Tai, Wilt Idema's examination of thirteenth- and fourteenth-century dramas containing pilgrimages to Mount Tai to pray to the God of Mount Tai, Glen Dudbridge's translation and separate interpretation of a male literatus's representations of women pilgrims in a seventeenth-century novel, and Pei-yi Wu's reading of sixteenth- and seventeenth-century literati accounts of visits to Mount Tai.[7] Additional studies include Sawada Mizuho's account of the incense tax, Kenneth Pomeranz's article on the cult of the Goddess of Mount Tai, Susan Naquin's study of pilgrimages in honor of the Goddess of Mount Tai near Beijing, and Mei-hui Shiau's master's thesis on beliefs about Mount Tai during the Ming Dynasty.[8] Recent works on Mount Tai coming out the PRC, like Chavannes's, concentrate on the ancient and medieval periods or reprint primary sources. Liu Hui's book on the religions of Mount Tai includes a discussion of the late imperial period, but it looks more at religious institutions than at pilgrims.[9] Two new gazetteers of the mountain are quite thorough compilations of historical information and sources but offer little analysis of the pilgrims themselves.[10]

Methodology

Cultural studies continues to debate the contrasting concepts of culture as a system of beliefs versus culture as practice. In the introduction to *Beyond the Cultural Turn: New Directions in the Study of Society and Culture*, Victoria Bonnell and Lynn Hunt declare that a

focus on practice, narrative, and embodiment—whether of whole cultures, social groups, or individual selves . . . restore[s] a sense of social embeddedness without reducing everything to social determinants. [It is important to] . . . emphasize the relational process of identity formation, the conflict between competing narratives, the inherent tension between culture viewed as a system and culture viewed as practice, and the inevitable strain between continuity and transformation.[11]

Mount Tai was a multivalent symbol; how it was interpreted or appropriated depended on the social context of the individual. The present analysis hence falls mainly into the area of "culture viewed as a system." This study, however, also draws on practice as a means to understand identities. In this, it corresponds with William Sewell's conclusions that "system and practice are complementary concepts: each presupposes the other. To engage in cultural practice means to utilize existing cultural symbols to accomplish some end. . . . But it is equally true that the system has no existence apart from the succession of practices that instantiate, reproduce, or—most interestingly—transform it."[12] Interestingly, this view is similar to that held by many Chinese intellectuals during the late imperial period: "Confucians did not assume that belief preceded and was the stimulus for performance; they also understood that *performance* could lead to inculcation of belief. Rather than making a sharp distinction between belief and practice, therefore, Chinese ruling elites tended to see belief and practice as organically linked to one another, each influencing the other."[13] This study examines both the written, officially endorsed orthodoxy and actual practices. Analysis of how a practitioner's actions evaded proscriptions adds valuable insights into his or her culture and identity.

The paradigm for examining pilgrimages was developed by the anthropologist Victor Turner, who wrote several books either partially or primarily devoted to pilgrimages.[14] Despite Turner's claims of the universality of his model, it is only partially useful in analyzing pilgrimages to Mount Tai. The "Hierarchies of Sacred Space" section of Part I addresses some of the shortcomings of Turner and assesses some of the more recent theoretical approaches to pilgrimage. It is not a purpose of this book to refine a universal model for pilgrimage. Instead, it combines parts of Turner's model with the methods of many fields to explore the meanings of Mount Tai for different components of late imperial Chinese society.

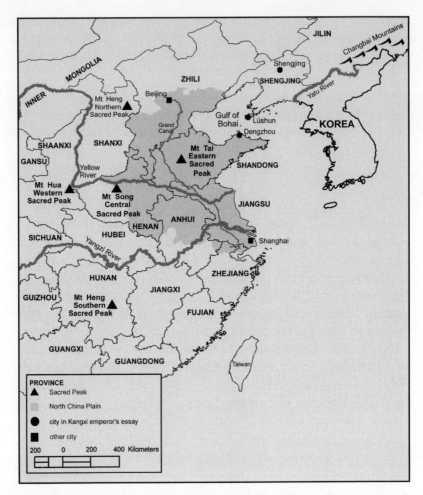

Fig. 2 Map showing the Five Sacred Peaks, the North China Plain, and places mentioned in the Kangxi emperor's essay, with 1820 boundaries (SOURCE: "China Historical GIS, Version: 2.0").

A multidisciplinary approach is needed if we are to understand the complex phenomena of pilgrimage. Simon Coleman and John Elsner emphasize the multiple layers of pilgrimage sites:

The image of landscape can be seen also as a powerful organising metaphor for examining pilgrimage cross-culturally and through time. . . . The "landscape" of any pilgrimage site consists not only of a physical terrain and architecture, but also of all the myths, traditions and narratives associated with natural and man-made features. . . . Physical and myth-historical landscapes provide the backdrop to movement, so that in progressing through the physical geography a pilgrim travels and lives through a terrain of culturally constructed symbols.[15]

Understanding such a rich layering of meanings, they contend, requires an interdisciplinary approach. James Preston argues even more explicitly for breaking away from a single-discipline approach, for "pilgrimage defies the kind of compartmentalized analysis associated with the present style of Western thought that organizes everything into discrete disciplines of inquiry."[16]

Only by using a broad spectrum of sources and methods can we attain an understanding of the variety of beliefs and motivations within a society. The vast majority of the sources used in this study were written by well-educated men. The potential and sometimes blatant biases of these sources make it imperative to balance such accounts with other types of sources, particularly when studying the illiterate majority and women. One way to circumvent this bias is through analysis of physical materials such as woodblock prints, ritual vessels and offerings, temple layouts, and the positioning of accreted structures such as arches. Religious scriptures written for a lay audience, often for women in particular, also supplement male literati writings. Stelae erected by peasant pilgrimage societies include texts that reveal their views of the mountain and various deities and provide as well a means of analyzing the membership of these groups, including their gender division. In addition, the judicious use of information gathered from fieldwork among contemporary pilgrims can shed light on earlier practices. The few works by male literati that discuss illiterate pilgrims usually caricature them. Despite this, such accounts do include apparently reliable descriptions of some of the rituals, clothing, expenditures, and attitudes of the illiterate pilgrims.

Pluralistic approaches and loci of study complement a theoretical concept integral to this study of groups within Chinese society: a single society can contain multiple cultures. For example, in "From 'Popular Religion' to Religious Cultures," Natalie Zemon Davis argues for a continuum of beliefs and practices, not just the dichotomy of popular and elite. In addition, she asserts that all cultures within a society mutually influence one another. Top-down or bottom-up models for the spread of cultural beliefs and practices, she posits, are not sufficient to explain the complexities of a given society.[17] Recent scholarship in a variety of fields supports this more pluralistic and flexible interpretation of culture. For example, William Sewell believes that cultures, as "distinct worlds of meaning," should be taken as "contradictory," "loosely integrated," "contested," mutable, and highly permeable.[18] Similarly, Susan Naquin, in her study of the role of temples in Beijing, assumes "that both individual and collective identities were multiple, fluid, and competing."[19] Richard Biernacki advocates making comparisons between different components and levels of a society as a means "for identifying signs and for exploring their meaning."[20]

A corollary of the multiplicity of cultures within a society is that individuals or groups can simultaneously have multiple identities. The anthropologist George Marcus argues:

The connotations of solidity and homogeneity attaching to the notion of community, whether concentrated in a locale or dispersed, has [sic] been replaced in the framework of modernity by the idea that the situated production of identity—of a person, of a group, or even a whole society—does not depend alone, or even always primarily, on the observable, concentrated activities within a particular locale or diaspora. The identity of anyone or any group is produced simultaneously in many different locales of activity by many different agents for many different purposes.[21]

This concept is important for the study of pilgrims to Mount Tai because it allows for multiple reasons behind an individual's or a group's journey to the mountain. In addition, studying pilgrimages can also inform us about the identity or identities of particular groups or individuals while they were at home.

This study moves beyond previous works to create a more complete picture of pilgrimages to Mount Tai. As David Johnson has noted:

By studying the . . . material that was specific to a given group, and discovering what the versions of various ideas or systems of thought intended for that group had in common, both in form and content, we will gradually achieve a deeper understanding of that group's collective

Fig. 3   Scroll of the God of Mount Tai as judge in the seventh court of the underworld (ca. 1930; author's personal collection).

mentality. And as in time our conception of the whole range of collective mentalities becomes clearer, our comprehension of what they had in common will improve as well, until at last we begin to see what made them all Chinese.[22]

Thus, through the analysis of mentalities and identities of specific groups within late imperial Chinese society, this book seeks to arrive at conclusions about characteristics common to all components of that society. Although these groups did not bind communally, they still belonged to the larger whole of late imperial Chinese society.

A number of the conclusions in this book address broader, more theoretical issues, which extend beyond the realm of Chinese studies. For example, it analyzes group identities as a means not only of distinguishing between different components of a society but also of demarcating characteristics common to all members of a society. In late imperial China, for example, the importance of oral culture for women contrasts sharply with male reliance on literacy, and the Manchus employed religion as one way of adapting their traditional nomadic culture to ruling a largely agrarian empire. Despite the many differences, tensions, and occasional conflicts among groups, at a basic level all the pilgrims shared certain practices such as reverence for filial piety, hierarchy, lineage, nature, writing, and ritual. In addition, this study examines the larger issue of how people interact with sacred spaces. In particular reference to literati visitors, this work raises criticisms of the Western sacred/secular dichotomy by demonstrating that labeling a particular group as either "pilgrims" or "tourists" offers little insight into the functioning of societies for much of the world and most of history.

One major criticism of cultural history has been that its practitioners often give so much priority to cultural phenomena that they exclude other important historical factors such as power and economics. This study, however, includes analyses of important political powerholders, such as male literati and two Qing emperors. In addition, it also discusses the economics of the site and economic factors as possible motivations for pilgrims.

Fig. 4 The Goddess of Mount Tai, Bixia Yuanjun. Statue in the Goddess Hall (Yuanjun dian) of the White Cloud Temple, Beijing. Used by permission (photograph by the author, 1995).

A focus on pilgrimage to Mount Tai also allows me to apply and test a number of trends in the study of culture. The variety of ways in which groups approached Mount Tai provides an excellent example of the argument that every society contains many separate cultures. In addition, the fact that each group journeyed to the mountain for several reasons demonstrates the multiplicity of individual and group identities. Finally, the best example that a balance can be achieved between analyzing culture as a system of beliefs and as practice is seen in women pilgrims. Contrary to legal and social restrictions, many of them not only went on pilgrimages but in some cases also established themselves as ritual experts.

This multidisciplinary focus on a site, which attracted a cross-section of society, as a means of analyzing how a culture operated, is transferable to other regions and periods. As this study of Mount Tai demonstrates, individual and group identities and their links to a larger entity can be investigated through the processes of accommodation, competition, and co-optation.

PART I

Cultural
Stratigraphy

Multiple Identities
of a Sacred Site

Mount Tai attracted a variety of people during the late imperial period because of its history, both real and mythical, and its
multifaceted meanings. Part I begins with an overview of various
types of structures found on the mountain and analyzes historical
events and legends relating to Mount Tai under six rubrics: nature
worship, imperial ritual, history, mysticism, death, and life. Each
of these groups is a general category for the drawing powers of the
mountain.

Types of Sites

Humans have left a variety of imprints on Mount Tai,
ranging from a few marks on a stone to large temple complexes.
The different types of monuments and inscriptions vary not only
in size but also in purpose. Because the Chinese terms for different
types of structures are often applied to more than one type, I use
English names to categorize them below. The numbers following
site names refer to the map of Mount Tai in Fig. 5 and to the
descriptive catalog of sites in the Appendix.[1]

Fig. 5 (*overleaf*)   Map of Mount Tai, adapted from Chavannes, *Le T'ai Chan*, frontispiece.
Chavannes derived his map from two Chinese maps dating from 1830 and 1902.

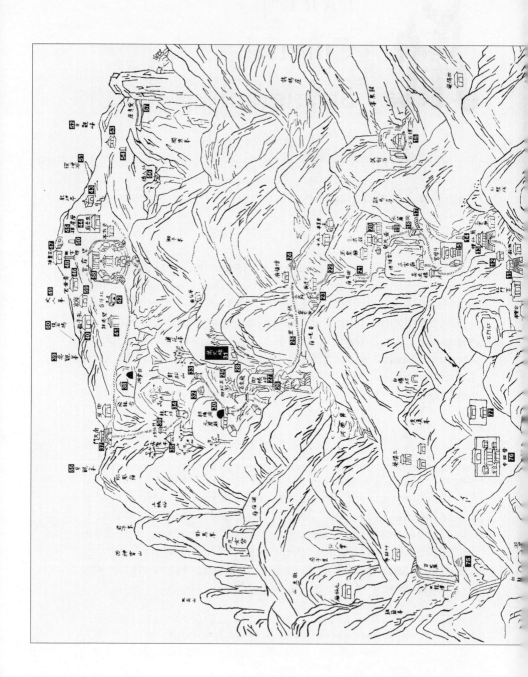

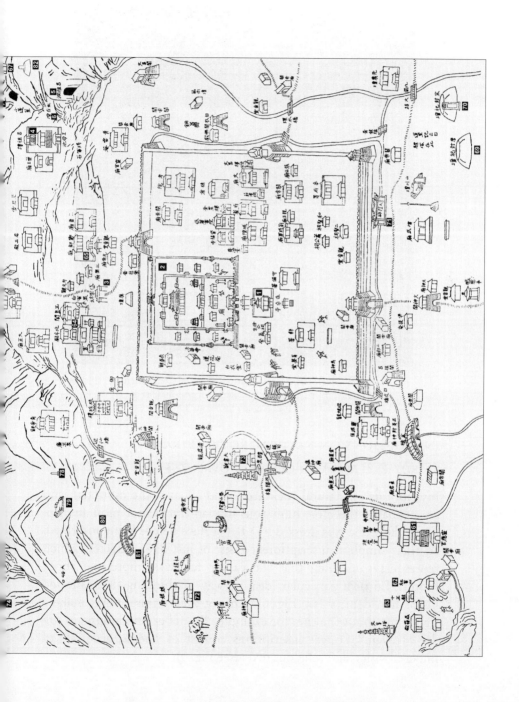

Fig. 6   Single character inscription in natural stone reflecting
the carver's faith. The character *fo* means Buddha or
Buddhism (photograph by the author, 1994).

INSCRIPTIONS ON NATURAL ROCKS (ZIRAN KE SHI 自然刻石) OR CLIFFS (MOYAI 摩崖)

Inscriptions on natural rock are found all over the mountain and are probably the most numerous human traces. For most inscriptions, the stone was dressed to a flat surface before being inscribed. At their simplest, inscriptions consist of just one character, which represents something that the carver felt was impressive about Mount Tai or a particular ideal or way of thinking that reflected his or her identity (see Fig. 6). An engraved phrase might make a statement about the site, for example, "Number one mountain under Heaven." Longer inscriptions consist of poems, accounts of imperial visits, and religious texts (see Fig. 7).

Fig. 7 Long cliff inscriptions. The largest one, on the right, is the Tang Cliff Inscription, composed by Tang Xuanzong in 726 (no. 45). The two large characters at the far left were written by the Kangxi emperor in 1684; the text underneath is poetry composed by the Qianlong emperor in 1748 (photograph by the author, 1995).

STELAE (BEI 碑)

These are inscriptions on fully dressed, usually rectangular stones, which were then erected on a base. The majority of stelae on the mountain are located inside temples and usually commemorate repairs or additions. Other stelae line the pilgrimage route up the mountain and include inscriptions in honor of various deities, accounts of pilgrimage societies, and poems (see Fig. 8).

ARCHES (FANG 坊)

There are two main categories of stone arches on Mount Tai: those associated with the entrance to a temple and those built over the pilgrimage route. All arches act as demarcations of space, much like the *torii* in Japanese shrine grounds. Both types usually consist

Fig. 8   A group of pilgrimage society stelae located along the pilgrimage path just above the
Red Gate (no. 11). The rocks placed on top of stone stelae are part of the *yazi* pun ritual (see
"Female Networking" section in Chapter 1). The women praying between the stelae created
their own ritual space by drawing a line in the dirt in front of the row of offerings because
they could not afford the fee to climb the mountain (photograph by the author, 1995).

of two pillars with a cap (see Fig. 9), forming an entrance; a few
arches are larger, with four pillars marking off three entrances (see
Fig. 10). The amount of decoration and inscription also varies. The
majority of arches on Mount Tai are of the smaller variety with
one entrance and few decorations.

Fig. 9   Arch of the Ridge Where the Horses Turn Back (no. 21).
This small arch is not connected with a temple and has few
decorations (photograph by the author, 1994).

PAVILIONS (TING 亭)

The *Hanyu dacidian* defines a *ting* as "a small structure built along-
side a road, in a garden, or at a famous scenic site as a place for
passersby to rest and admire the scenery. . . . Most have a roof but
no walls."[2] The pavilions on Mount Tai are usually square stone
buildings, 3 to 4 meters a side. Some of them are walled but with
open spaces for doorways and windows (see Fig. 11). Inside there
are often benches or stools.

Fig. 10   The Daizong Arch (no. 3). This large, decorated arch is located just
north of the old city wall (photograph by the author, 1994).

SHRINES (TING 亭 OR MIAO 廟)

In size and shape the shrines are the same as pavilions. Besides function, the biggest difference is that the shrines have no windows (see
Fig. 12). The entrances to shrines, like those to pavilions, do not
have doors. The interior is one small room. Shrines on Mount Tai
generally contain one image of a particular deity on a small altar.
The walls and altar are usually decorated with offerings from pilgrims (Fig. 13). Not all the shrines on Mount Tai are oriented along
the standard north-south alignment of Chinese temples. Instead,
many of them are built with the door facing the pilgrimage path.
This is probably an adaptation to the limited space along the path.

HALLS (DIAN 殿 OR MIAO 廟)

These buildings are rectangular and usually contain images of three
or more deities. Halls are two–three times wider than shrines. Like
shrines, they have only one room, no windows, door-less entrances,

Fig. 11 A nature-viewing pavilion: the Western Stream Stone
Pavilion on the Western Path up the mountain (no. 75)
(photograph by the author, 1995).

and are decorated with offerings. If Daoist or Buddhist nuns or
monks regularly tended the altars in a hall, they probably lived at
a nearby temple. The term *dian* is also applied to most individual
buildings containing altars in larger temple complexes (see Fig. 1,
p. 2). All the halls still extant in 1994 and 2000, and not within
temple compounds, face south.

Fig. 12   A small shrine. The east side and back (north side) of a small shrine to
the Goddess of Mount Tai (no. 12) (photograph by the author, 1995).

TOWERS (LOU 樓, GE 閣, OR MEN 門)

When not within a temple complex, towers are two-story structures built over the pilgrimage path (see Fig. 14). The path goes
through a tunnel in the base of the tower, and stairs, often at the
rear of the building, lead up to the second level. The upper story
consists of a hall, a rough square in shape, containing three or
more idols. Any attending monks or nuns, again, probably resided
in a nearby temple. Although the Chinese term *men* usually refers
to a gate, two towers on Mount Tai are called *men* (see Appendix,
nos. 11, 37).

Fig. 13   Interior of the Star of Longevity Shrine (no. 35). The
shrine is now dedicated to the Goddess of Mount Tai
(photograph by the author, 1994).

TEMPLES (MIAO 廟, SI 寺, GONG 宮, GUAN 觀)

Three main characteristics distinguish temples from shrines and
halls:

1. multiple buildings
2. a wall with closeable doors surrounding the entire complex
3. resident monks or nuns

Fig. 14   Southern Heavenly Gate (no. 37). This tower at the top of the steepest section of
the Pilgrimage Path has become a popular symbol of the mountain
(photograph by the author, 1994).

Among the Chinese terms in this category, *miao* 廟 is the most generic and ambiguous. On Mount Tai, the term *miao* is used for
buildings that range in size from small shrines all the way up to the
largest temple, the Dai miao 岱廟 or Dai Temple (no. 2 on Fig. 5)
at the foot of the mountain. *Si* 寺 are always Buddhist temples, and
gong 宮 and *guan* 觀 are used in the names of Daoist temples. The
structures in this study called "temples" range from the quite small
Confucian Temple (no. 40), which consists of three small buildings,
to the enormous Dai Temple, which has a circumference of 1.5
kilometers (see Fig. 1, p. 2).[3]

PILGRIMAGE PATH (PANDAO 盤道,
PANLU 盤路, PANDAO 磐道)

This path is the main route used by visitors to ascend the mountain. It lies on the south side of the mountain; as in a temple, one "enters" the mountain from the south. This main route goes up the center of the south face and runs for nine kilometers from the main Dai Temple (no. 2) to the Southern Heavenly Gate (no. 37; see Fig. 14), then to the main temple of the Goddess of Mount Tai (no. 58), and finally to the summit (no. 47).[4] It is marked with a series of dashes on the map in Fig. 5. The path ascends between the arms of two southern spurs of the mountain, a highly efficacious site according to Chinese geomancy theory. The path is stone paved; according to one source, there are 6,293 stairs (see Figs. 9 and 14).[5] The most common Chinese name for the path, *pandao* 盤道, means "winding path." It is sometimes called the *panlu* 盤路, "winding road," and occasionally the *pandao* 磐道, "stone path." It is also referred to as the "Central Path" (*zhonglu* 中路), because it begins at the center of the mountain's base, or as the "Eastern Path" (*donglu* 東路), due to its relation to the much less used Western Path (see Appendix, no. 74). It is also possible to climb the mountain from the north, but this route is far less traveled than, and not nearly as numinous as, the Central Path.

There was some sort of path up the center of the mountain at least by the Qin dynasty (221–206 BCE), for Qin Shihuangdi (秦始皇帝, r. 221–210 BCE), the First Emperor, ascended via the "chariot road" (*che dao* 車道).[6] Ma Dibo (馬第伯), writing in 56 CE, also refers to a path, but it is unclear whether it was paved at that time.[7] The paving of the path is traditionally dated to the Tang dynasty (618–907), but such claims are difficult to prove.[8] The path was certainly paved by the middle of the Ming dynasty (1368–1644), for there are references to its repair and to arches being built over it during that period.[9]

Nature Worship

In many societies around the world, mountains have been seen as dwelling places for deities or, because of their proximity to the heavens, as efficacious points for communicating with sky-dwelling deities.[10] Since their peaks are in contact with the clouds, mountains are often prayed to for favorable weather. Many mountains have become personified deities. Mountains appear as sites of worship in many of China's earliest writings, reflecting practices that had begun earlier, probably far earlier.[11] Mark Lewis notes that during the Warring States period (481–221 BCE) "mountains served as links between the human and the divine. [They acted as] an intermediate zone between Earth and Heaven."[12]

Mount Tai's location helps to explain its importance as a site for nature worship. The mountain physically dominates the North China Plain (see Fig. 2, p. 8). This plain contains some of the richest agricultural land in northern China, as well as the lower reaches of China's two largest rivers, the Yellow and the Yangzi. The only significant elevations lie in the center of Shandong province, and Mount Tai is the tallest peak in this range. Although Mount Tai is not an especially high mountain (1,545 meters), its height is amplified by the fact that its base is only 150 meters above sea level and it rises directly from this large plain. This made the mountain a logical political boundary. During the Zhou period (ca. 1050–221 BCE), for example, the state of Qi 齊 lay to the north, and Lu 魯, the home state of both Confucius and Mencius, lay to the south.

Its steepness and the contrast with the surrounding plain have been a theme of writings since the earliest written references to Mount Tai. A poem in the *Shi jing*, or *Book of Odes*, from around the seventh or eighth century BCE, praises Mount Tai as "towering high" (*Taishan yanyan* 泰山巖巖) above the plain.[13] The mountain's various names also express its stature. In its definition for *Tai* 泰, the *Hanyu dacidian* includes such superlatives as "big," "great," and "the utmost point."[14] Perhaps the earliest firsthand account of an ascent up Mount Tai also emphasizes its steepness: "Those in back could see only the soles of the sandals of the ones in front,

Fig. 15   Mountain symbol from a pottery vessel, ca. 2500 BCE.

while those in front could see only the tops of the heads of those in back—it looked like a picture of a stack of men."[15]

Because of its physical domination of the plain, Mount Tai was almost certainly worshiped as a nature deity in prehistoric times.[16] Possible evidence is found on a pottery vessel from the late Neolithic Dawenkou culture (ca. 3500–2200 BCE) dating from approximately 2500 BCE found near Mount Tai. A symbol engraved on this vessel resembles the sun sitting atop a mountain, with a third symbol between them (see Fig. 15). The center component has variously been interpreted as clouds, fire, and the moon.[17] Whatever the middle portion represents, however, the symbol implies sacrifices on top of a mountain (possibly Mount Tai itself), or an important connection between mountains (or a specific mountain) and the sun. Concentrating on the two identifiable components, the sun and a mountain, Liu Hui asserts that the drawing shows the important link between mountains and the sun—two of the most important objects of early nature worship in China. He speculates that this vessel may have been used in sacrificial ceremonies.[18]

In an agricultural society and economy like China's, an important characteristic of sacred mountains was their water-giving potential: "Not only were they sources for the water of rivers, but more important, they were sources of clouds which brought down the rain. Every time a drought took place, the emperor, in addition to praying at the Imperial Altar of Earth, dispatched special imperial messengers to the individual mountains to ask their favor."[19] The last such imperial messenger to Mount Tai was sent in 1829.[20] In particular, caves near the summit were "regarded as the dwelling places of the rain-giving clouds and mists."[21] Intrinsically connected with sacred mountains' power to provide rain was the belief that they could also grant relief from floods, as a number of imperial prayers sent to Mount Tai during the Ming dynasty attest.[22]

Chinese cosmology, reflected in early texts such as the *Shang shu*, or *Book of History*, and the *Li ji*, or *Book of Rites*, identified several mountains as more sacred and powerful than others. These mountains were called *yue* 嶽／岳, translated here as "Sacred Peak."[23] Initially there were four Sacred Peaks, located at the cardinal compass points. Kleeman convincingly argues that these four peaks represented the outer peripheries of the Zhou territory and "are analogues of the four regional hegemons . . . regional leaders who assume responsibility for managing the tribes of their region and acting as a bulwark against foreign invasion." Under this system, "the king is the center . . . , liegelord of the marchmount-hegemons, and as such, he must have had his own mountain. This central mountain would have been the acme of a pyramid of sacred peaks."[24] Thus, when the sage-ruler Shun visited the Four Sacred Peaks, he was touring the edges of his domain.[25] Sometime during the late Warring States period or the early Han dynasty (202 BCE–220 CE), "the central peak was added to the marchmounts, yielding a system of five. . . . All were defined within Chinese space and the central peak lost its primacy."[26]

Different sources assigned the status of sacred peak to different mountains. Within the set of the four, this was especially true for the Northern and Southern Sacred Peaks.[27] There is also a debate over which mountain was associated with the king, which later became the Central Peak, during the Zhou.[28] In all configurations, however, Mount Tai was the Eastern Sacred Peak (*dongyue* 東嶽),

and this term has been a widely used alternative name for Mount Tai. Since Han times the Sacred Peaks have been fixed at five and associated with the following mountains:[29]

Eastern Sacred Peak	Mount Tai (泰山), in modern Shandong province
Southern Sacred Peak	Mount Heng (衡山), in modern Hunan province
Western Sacred Peak	Mount Hua (華山), in modern Shaanxi province
Northern Sacred Peak	Mount Heng (恒山), in modern Shanxi province
Central Sacred Peak	Mount Song (嵩山), in modern Henan province

(See Fig. 2, p. 8, for the locations of these mountains.)

According to the ancient system of correlation based on the Five Phases (*wuxing* 五行, wood, fire, earth, metal, water; in English also called the Five Agents or the Five Elements), each phase was associated with, among other things, a season, a direction, a color, one of the five senses, and a body part. In this system Mount Tai, being in the east, was connected with wood, spring, green, vision, and the spleen.[30] In addition, because of its location, Mount Tai became associated with the sunrise. The mountain's connection with these creative forces or elements (spring, green, wood, sunrise) led further to associations with beginning and birth, and Mount Tai came to be seen as the source of all life (*wanwu zhi shi* 萬物之始).[31] Because of this link, Mount Tai became the most important, and thus the leader, of the Five Sacred Peaks (*wuyue zhi zhang* 五嶽之長).[32]

This leading position of Mount Tai within the Five Sacred Peaks is reflected in texts, inscriptions, and iconography. It is even found in another common name for the mountain: Daizong 岱宗. In ancient times *Tai* 泰 and *Dai* 岱 had the same pronunciation, and *Dai* meant Mount Tai.[33] The usual translation for *zong* is "ancestor," but the Han period commentary *Wujing tongyi* 五經通義 states that in this context it means "leader" or "chief."[34] Thus Daizong could mean "Dai, the ancestral mountain," or "Dai, the chief mountain." The Five Sacred Peaks were often portrayed as a group of personified gods in woodblock prints of the Chinese pantheon. In such groupings, the God of Mount Tai is either placed in the center of, or above the others (see Fig. 16).

The prominence of Mount Tai can also be seen in the earlier system of the Four Sacred Peaks. According to the *Book of History*, the sage-ruler Shun,

in the second month of the year, went on an eastern imperial tour (*xun-shou* 巡守) to Daizong (岱宗). He presented burnt offerings to Heaven and to the mountains and rivers according to their order. . . . In the fifth month, he went on a southern imperial tour to the Southern Sacred Peak (Nanyue 南岳). . . . In the eighth month, he went on a western imperial tour to the Western Sacred Peak. . . . In the eleventh month, he went on a northern imperial tour to the Northern Sacred Peak.[35]

In this passage, Shun practices nature worship in a manner that emphasizes the natural, spatial hierarchy believed to exist among Heaven, mountains, and rivers. This excerpt demonstrates the hierarchy within the Four Sacred Peaks as well. Shun visits Mount Tai before the other peaks, and Mount Tai is the only mountain given a name; the others are referred to by their geographical position. This passage also demonstrates that offerings to Heaven as well as to elements associated with the earth (mountains and rivers) were, from this early period, associated with Mount Tai.

The importance of Mount Tai as a channel between heaven and earth is seen explicitly in the fact that the hexagram in the *Yijing*, or *Book of Changes*, given the name "Tai" 泰 is a combination of the trigrams for heaven and earth.[36] Taken together with the mountain's position in the East, this particular association of Mount Tai with heaven and earth helps to explain its leading role among the Four and later the Five Sacred Peaks.

Nature worship on Mount Tai often involved human alteration or manipulation of nature. To understand this tendency, it is important to note that the Chinese did not view altering nature and honoring nature as contradictory. Indeed, this manner of approaching and interacting with nature is intimately connected with the Chinese concept of *fengshui* 風水, or geomancy (literally "wind and water"). This is the art of aligning cities, temples, houses, and tombs with the surrounding terrain and cosmic forces (*qi* 氣). The layout of a particular site is affected by the heavens as well as by the lay of the land, for the two are interconnected. Therefore *fengshui* masters also take into account the site's orientation in relation to the stars, planets, and constellations. The theory behind such careful placement is that the natural essence in all things flows in predictable ways and can be either beneficial or harmful. A *fengshui* master looks for a point where positive natural forces are concentrated as the ideal spot for a building or grave. The better the alignment and the stronger the concentration, the more efficacious the site will be for those living, visiting, or buried there. Intrinsic to the Chinese conception of *fengshui* is the possibility of increasing a site's efficaciousness. This can be accomplished through careful placement of walls, trees, and charms or by rerouting water in the vicinity. If correctly implemented, these alterations redirect and concentrate the flow of positive energy at the site. The idea is to create a balance that not only allows the site's natural energies to flow but also keeps them as concentrated as possible.

Fengshui masters always look for rises in the terrain, which represent concentrations of positive energy. These ridges, hills, or entire mountains are referred to as "dragons" or "veins of dragons" (*longmai* 龍脈).[37] Since the dragon veins manifest themselves as elevations, mountains are important centers of cosmic power. Shen Hao 沈鎬, a seventeenth-century *fengshui* master, emphasized the importance of dragons and mountains: "The beginning and end of geomancy is nothing more than the layout of mountain ridges, and all the authorities are alike in referring to them as dragons."[38]

At the macro level, the cosmic energy of Mount Tai as a whole is mapped out in Daoist texts such as the *Plans of the Ancient Origins of the True Forms of the Obscure, Numinous, Precious Caverns of the Five Sacred Peaks* (see Fig. 17).[39] These images reveal the underground and hidden aspects of the mountain's shape or essence. They strongly resemble *fengshui* charts or plans.[40] The "true forms" of the Five Sacred Peaks were also produced in simpler patterns

Fig. 16 Woodblock print showing the gods of the Five Sacred Peaks and five goddesses. The five mountain gods are the group on the left. The God of the Eastern Sacred Peak (Mount Tai) is in the center, above the others. On the right are the Goddess of Mount Tai (center) and four of her assistant goddesses. Detail from a print of a pantheon of Chinese deities purchased in 1931. (SOURCE: Columbia University, C. V. Starr East Asian Library, Goodrich Collection. Reprinted by permission).

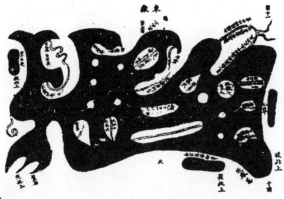

Fig. 17 (*above*)   Complex version of the "true form"
of Mount Tai (SOURCE: *Dongxuan lingbao* in the *Daoist Canon*, 6: 740–41).

Fig. 18 (*to left*)   Simpler version of the "true form"
of Mount Tai.

(see Fig. 18). Stelae with these patterns have been found in temples
at Mount Tai, at the Central Sacred Peak—Mount Song—as well as
in the collection in Xi'an known as the Beilin 碑林, or Forest of
Stelae.[41] Talismans in the shapes of these "true forms" were potent
protectors, especially when entering mountainous terrain.[42]

The influence of *fengshui* principles and of the Daoist concept of
the "true forms" of the Sacred Peaks is manifest in late imperial gazetteers. A simplified version of the "true forms" of the Five Sacred
Peaks can be found in Zha Zhilong's 查志隆 (*jinshi* 1559) *History of
Dai*, two sets of the "true forms" of the Five Sacred Peaks are included in Jin Qi's 金棨 *Gazetteer of Mount Tai*, and a simplified dia-
gram for Mount Tai is reproduced in Xu Zonggan's 徐宗幹 *Gazetteer of Tai'an County*.[43] Further evidence of the influence of *fengshui*
theories on authors of gazetteers can be seen in special maps devoted
to springs and rivers surrounding Mount Tai, called "spring sources
maps" (*quanyuan tu* 泉源圖).[44] In addition, some gazetteers also include maps of the stars especially important for that region.[45]

Besides revering the mountain itself, visitors also venerated
other natural phenomena such as the sunrise, springs, rocks, caves,

trees, and scenic vistas. In all cases, the particular natural feature was altered in some way during its associated ritual. Indeed, the very act of naming various parts of the mountain altered those sites. For example, Moon-Viewing Peak (no. 55) became accepted as the best place to view the moon, and natural rock formations such as Transcendents' Bridge (no. 56) and Transcendent's Shadow (no. 74) would ever after have a mystical aura. A site might have its name carved onto it (see Fig. 19), on a stele next to it (see Fig. 20), or it could be labeled on a map or identified in a gazetteer (one source for the map in Fig. 5 was an engraving on a stele).

Since Mount Tai is associated with the sunrise, watching the sunrise became an important aspect of visiting the mountain. Mount Tai is hardly unique in this respect; admiration of the sunrise from mountain tops is common throughout East Asia. The most famous example is Mount Fuji in Japan. As noted earlier, mountains have been endowed with supernatural powers in many cultures. Anyone who ascends to such a mystical place experiences some of these powers. The sunrise, in many cultures and certainly in East Asia, is correlated with birth, beginning, and renewal. The experience of climbing a sacred peak and viewing the sun at dawn augment each other, making witnessing a sunrise from a mountain top highly spiritual. Although the sunrise itself cannot be altered, the space from which it is observed on Mount Tai could be. Thus, on the eastern edge of the summit, the sunrise is viewed from the Sun-Viewing Pavilion (no. 53).

Springs in China, as elsewhere in the world, are often believed to have special healing powers. Because of their powers, temples were often constructed in their vicinity, taking advantage of the inherent attributes of the land. In *fengshui* practice, water is important for counteracting negative influences.[46] Given this importance, it is not surprising that four of the main temples on Mount Tai are associated with springs. The Queen Mother Pool (Temple) (no. 4) is, as the name implies, built around a spring-fed pool. The pool is surrounded by a stone balustrade—demarcating the space within. The main temple to the Goddess of Mount Tai on top of the mountain (no. 58) was built on that particular site because a statue

Fig. 19   The Rock That Came Flying Down (no. 28). The base of the stone has been black-
ened by years of incense and spirit money smoke. The movable altar is dedicated to the God
of Caves and Rocks. Behind the altar is the Fifth Rank Pine Tree Arch (no. 29). At the top
of the photo is a branch of one of the pine trees planted on the site where Qin Shihuangdi
sheltered from the storm when he ascended Mount Tai in 219 BCE (no. 29) (photograph by
the author, 1995).

of the goddess was found in a spring-fed pond adjacent to the temple. The Mother of the Big Dipper Temple (no. 15) was originally
called Dragon Spring Monastery, after a nearby spring.[47] Unlike
the natural springs associated with the other three temples, the
pool in front of the Dai Temple (no. 2) was added in 1880 to
heighten its alignment.[48]

Fig. 20 The Tang Acacia in the Dai Temple (no. 2). The two characters of the tree's name (Tang huai) are engraved on the stele on the left. The tree is set off from the surrounding space by a stone balustrade (photograph by the author, 1995).

Ancient trees are revered because of their longevity. Many of the most honored trees on Mount Tai were planted long ago in temple compounds. By the late imperial period, they had been set apart from the rest of the courtyard by terraces, fences, and low walls, creating a space like an altar for the trees (see Fig. 20). In a couple of instances, temple walls were built around tree branches in order to avoid damaging an honored tree. Medicinal herbs, roots, and fungi found on Mount Tai are believed to be especially efficacious because they grow in the soil of this sacred peak.

Fig. 21   The Wordless Stele (no. 48).
Above this stone megalith is the Jade
Emperor Summit Temple (no. 47).
The highest point on Mount Tai is lo-
cated just through the doorway (pho-
tograph by the author, 1994).

Several rocks on the mountain fit best into the category of nature worship. The Rock That Came Flying Down (no. 28; Fig. 19)
fell off the cliff above the pilgrimage path about three-fourths of
the way up the mountain in 1603.[49] Chavannes notes that the
phrase "came flying down" (*feilai* 飛來) implies a miraculous origin.[50] A small, cave-like space at the base of its south side bears the
stains of several centuries of smoke from burning incense and paper money. As noted above, the rock's name has also been carved
into it in large characters, further modifying it and emphasizing its
mystical nature.[51] The highest point on the mountain is located in
the courtyard of the Jade Emperor Summit Temple (no. 47). A

stone balustrade surrounds the peak, demarcating the space in the same way as the trees and pool described above. Tai'an native and author of the 1763 *An Itinerary of Mount Tai*, Nie Jianguang 聶劍光 (1715–ca. 1790), stated, and my own observations of contemporary visitors confirm, that visitors climbed (and climb) to the peak because it is the highest point, not because of the temple built around it.[52] Just below the summit is a dressed stone column known as the Wordless Stele (no. 48; see Fig. 21). It is quite likely that this is a megalith dating from prehistoric times and played a role in rituals conducted on top of the mountain. It may even have acted as an intermediary between heaven and earth in a manner similar to that implied in the symbol in Fig. 15.

One reason literati visited the mountain was to connect with nature in order to reflect on it and to cultivate themselves. Literati most often expressed their admiration for the scenic beauty, tranquility, and transcendental experience in poetry. Some also left more concrete markers of their appreciation in the form of small pavilions for future visitors to use as they contemplated their positions within the vast natural world (see Fig. 11). Here, as on the Sun-Viewing Peak, an edifice was deemed the best place from which to enjoy nature. In addition, these pavilions and nearby rocks were often engraved with poetic writings, further demonstrating the literati's desire to shape nature and to leave their own mark on the mountain.

Imperial Rituals

Mount Tai was an important site for imperial tours, rituals, and legitimation. Several ancient texts refer to the tour of inspection (*xunshou* 巡守) as an important duty of the ruler. According to David Keightley, as early as the Shang period, the "king displayed his power by frequent travel, hunting, and inspecting . . . mov[ing] through a landscape pregnant with symbolic meaning . . . receiving power at each holy place."[53] Howard Wechsler argues that on such tours "a new king tested the acceptance of his sovereignty throughout the land, and his acknowledgment as ruler by Heaven."[54] According to the *Book of History*, the sage-ruler Shun undertook a tour of inspection to the Four Sacred Peaks. The passage implies that imperial tours to Mount Tai and ritual offerings there were an expected, if not required, act of the ruler.[55]

Important legitimation rituals were also connected with tours to the Sacred Peaks. "When the foundation of a dynasty was secured, the emperor was supposed to visit these mountains, or at least Mt. Tai. He was to report to heaven through them and to receive the heavenly mandate for ruling the whole world."[56] The following passage from a Warring States text delineates the transferal of the Mandate of Heaven:

In [the sage-ruler Yao's 堯] fifth year, he made his first imperial tour of inspection of the Four Sacred Peaks (siyue 四岳). . . . In [Yao's] seventieth year in the first month of the spring, the emperor sent an emissary to the Four Sacred Peaks [to announce] the order conferring [rulership] upon Shun of Yu. . . . In [Yao's] seventy-fourth year, Shun of Yu made his first imperial tour of inspection of the Four Sacred Peaks.[57]

Proof of early royal sacrifices at Mount Tai was discovered in 1954 when seven bronze vessels were unearthed at the base of Mount Tai. The character for the state of Chu 楚 on two of the vessels suggests that they were part of the ritual paraphernalia from a sacrifice performed by the leader of that state in 589 BCE.[58]

The feng and shan sacrifices (fengshan si 封禪祀), a set of solemn and potent imperial rituals specifically associated with Mount Tai, developed at the time of China's unification under the Qin and early in the Former Han dynasty (202 BCE–9 CE). According to tradition, these sacrifices dated to the earliest legendary leaders of China. Chinese scholars and ritual specialists have debated their origins for centuries. Although Chinese classics, such as the Book of History, mention sacrifices at Mount Tai, none refers to the feng and shan. Sima Qian 司馬遷, in his famous Records of the Grand Historian (Shi ji 史記) from 87 BCE, accepted the ancient origin of these sacrifices, but he noted that their performance had "at times been separated by periods of as many as a thousand or more years, and at the least by several hundred years. This is the reason that details of the ancient ceremony have been completely lost."[59] Mark Lewis notes that "as early as the Liang Dynasty (AD 502–26) Chinese scholars began to argue that the sacrifices were created in the Qin and the Han."[60]

The exact meanings of the two terms have also been the subject of inquiry. In some sources, *feng* is glossed as "to seal up," as in sealing up a vessel containing the sacrificer's prayers or communications to the gods.[61] Lewis remarks that "there is no evidence of '*feng*' as the name of a ritual in the Shang or Western Zhou, but in later traditions it figured as the name for the rite of investiture, in which a noble was granted lordship over his realm."[62] He also observes that derivatives of early forms of the character on Shang oracle bones and early Zhou bronzes connote "earthen altar" or "to pile up earth for an altar."[63] This reading complements the most widely accepted meaning for *shan*, "clearing away earth" for an altar.[64] Lewis asserts that "these two glosses—'building up' and 'levelling down' as co-ordinate modes of preparing for a sacrifice— were easily linked with the dyad Heaven and Earth to define an all-encompassing pair of sacrifices appropriate to a universal polity."[65] Wechsler explains that "it was probably during the Ch'in [Qin] and early Han period that the Feng and Shan were first combined, linked primarily to Heaven and Earth, and centered on Mount T'ai."[66] The *feng* sacrifices were addressed to Heaven; the *shan* sacrifices, to Earth. As shown above, rulers had long journeyed to the Sacred Peaks to perform sacrifices. Since Mount Tai was considered the most important of these peaks and received special attention, the development of special rites solely connected with Mount Tai was a logical evolution.

One possible inspiration for this dual ritual at Mount Tai may be a famous passage in the *Mencius*: "When he ascended the Eastern Mount, Confucius felt that Lu was small, and when he ascended Mount T'ai, he felt that the Empire was small."[67] Throughout the centuries there has been much debate among scholars about the location of this "Eastern Mount." Many sources dedicated to Mount Tai place this eastern hill at the foot of Mount Tai. Other sources argue for a hill overlooking the capital of the state of Lu, Confucius' native Qufu.[68] In either case, the Confucian advisors to the first historical emperors to combine and locate these sacrifices at Mount Tai were aware of Confucius' connection with the mountain. In the account in the *Mencius*, Confucius' omniscient, cosmic ascent up Mount Tai was preceded by a more earthly vision upon climbing a smaller hill. Like the *shan* sacrifice, Confucius' first revelation had narrower, more earthbound focus. Like the *feng* ceremony, his second epiphany involved a more cosmic scale of removal, encapsulating the earth within a heavenly perspective.

Despite the doubts about the antiquity of the sacrifices, many rulers and scholars held on to a belief in their ancient origins, citing Sima Qian's reference to seventy-two venerable rulers who had performed the sacrifices.[69] Sima Qian attributed this account to Guan Zhong 管仲 (d. 645 BCE). Chavannes noted that when "in 651 BC Duke Huan [桓] of Qi proposed to perform the *feng* and *shan* sacrifices, his counselor, Guan Zhong, discouraged him from doing so by demonstrating that he did not have the requisite qualities; his principal argument was that these ceremonies were the privilege of the Sons of Heaven."[70] As a source and stage of power, prestige, and divinity, Mount Tai demanded appropriate observance. Similarly, Sima Qian argued that few rulers were virtuous enough to conduct the ceremonies and suggested that performance of the *feng* and *shan* rites could be seen as marking the high point of a monarch's rule.[71] This sense of reaching a pinnacle, with the implication of subsequent decline, may have motivated some advisors and rulers to defer performance of the rites.

Sima Qian quoted Guan Zhong's account of the ancient sacrificers at Mount Tai: "In antiquity, those who [performed] the *feng* sacrifices at Mount Tai and the *shan* sacrifices at [Mount] Liangfu 梁父 numbered seventy-two, but I, Yiwu, only [found] twelve of them in records. In former times, Wuhuaishi 無懷氏 [performed] the *feng* sacrifices at Mount Tai and the *shan* sacrifices at [Mount] Yunyun 云云."[72] The list continues with the commonly recognized legendary rulers: Fuxi 虙羲, inventor of writing and cooking; Shennong 神農, inventor of agriculture; Yan Di 炎帝; the Yellow Emperor 黃帝; Zhuanxu 顓頊; Diku 帝俈; Yao 堯, the sage-ruler who passed on his rulership not to his son but to the more appropriate and qualified Shun 舜; Shun, the sage-ruler who passed over his son in favor of Yu 禹; Yu, founder of the Xia dynasty; Tang 湯, founder of the Shang dynasty; and King Cheng 周成王, an early ruler of the Zhou dynasty. According to this account, all these rulers performed the *feng* sacrifices at Mount Tai, and most of them performed the *shan* sacrifices at Mount Yunyun, south of Mount Tai.[73]

Although modern scholarship, as well as Chinese evidential scholarship of the late imperial period, casts strong doubt on the authenticity of some of these early sources and the existence of legendary rulers, these ancient texts and rulers form an important part of the popular history of Mount Tai. The Yellow Emperor may be only a legend, and certain portions of "Zhou" texts may date to the first century CE, but by the late imperial period the history recorded or created by these texts and individuals had become an integral part of the foundation of the beliefs, legends, and sacrality surrounding Mount Tai. Although texts specifically on the *feng* and *shan* sacrifices often argued about their history, late imperial writings about Mount Tai, such as gazetteers and travelogues, often refer to the acts attributed to the legendary rulers not only as historical facts but also as a means of identifying particular geographic features. For example, in *Gazetteer of Tai'an Subprefecture, Tai'an-zhou zhi* 泰安州志, Ren Honglie 任弘烈 (fl. 1603) identified Mount Tingting 亭亭山 as being "50 *li* south of the subprefectural seat, the site of the Yellow Emperor's *shan* sacrifice."[74]

According to more historically reliable accounts of imperial pilgrimages to Mount Tai, Qin Shihuangdi ascended Mount Tai in 219 BCE shortly after the unification of China under his leadership. Sima Qian, writing some 130 years later, recorded that Qin Shihuangdi performed the *feng* sacrifice on top of Mount Tai and the *shan* sacrifice at Mount Liangfu.[75] All the stories surrounding Qin Shihuangdi's visit to Mount Tai derive from Sima Qian's account in the *Records of the Grand Historian*:

[Qin Shihuangdi] summoned seventy Confucian masters and scholars (*rusheng boshi* 儒生博士) from Qi and Lu to meet with him at the foot of Mt. Tai, where the scholars began to debate the proper procedure for carrying out the Feng and Shan sacrifices. "In ancient times when the Feng and Shan were performed," said some of them, "the wheels of the carriages were wrapped in rushes so as not to do any injury to the earth and grass of the mountain. . . ." But as the First Emperor listened to the debates of the scholars, he found that each of them expressed a different opinion and their recommendations were difficult to carry out, and with this he dismissed the whole lot.

Eventually he had a carriage road opened up, ascending from the southern foot of the mountain to the summit . . .[76]

[As Qin Shihuangdi was] descending, there was a fierce wind and rain storm, [and he] took shelter under a tree; because of this, he enfeoffed the tree as a *wudafu* (五大夫).[77]

. . . The Confucian scholars, who had been dismissed and were not allowed to take part in the ritual of the Feng sacrifice, hearing of the emperor's encounter with the storm, promptly used it as a basis to speak ill of him.[78]

In this account, the emperor rebuffs the Confucian scholars and charges up the mountain, presumably without observing the necessary rites. His treatment of the tree reinforces the power of the emperor to elevate and chastise counselors.

Conversely, the site on Mount Tai where Qin Shihuangdi took refuge from the storm became a popular point of interest (no. 29), especially for literati, because it represented to them a place where nature took revenge against an emperor often portrayed as a book burner and executor of scholars. Sima Qian emphasized how the unpopularity of Qin Shihuangdi was reinforced by nature's actions:

Thus the Qin dynasty fell just twelve years after the First Emperor performed the Feng and Shan sacrifices. The Confucian scholars loathed the Qin for having burned the *Book of Odes* and the *Book of Documents* and mercilessly [having] put to death the scholars who expounded them, while the common people hated its harsh laws, so that the whole world rose up in rebellion. At this time everyone began to speak ill of the Qin, saying, "When the First Emperor ascended Mt. Tai, he was attacked by violent wind and rain and thus was never really able to carry out the Feng and Shan sacrifices!" This is an example, is it not, of a ruler who, though he did not possess the virtue necessary to perform the sacrifices, yet proceeded to carry them out?[79]

The scholars felt vindicated when nature lashed out at Qin Shihuangdi; to them it demonstrated the danger of rituals being performed improperly or by improper individuals. Sima Qian pointed to the emperor's buffeting by wind and rain as proof of his unworthiness to perform the sacrifices—he had not reached the pinnacle of leadership. Sima also implied that improper performance of the *feng* and *shan* sacrifices contributed to the rapid collapse of Qin rule.

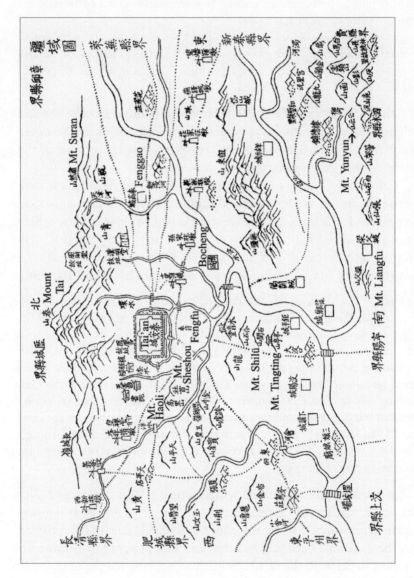

Fig. 22 Map of Tai'an county (source: modified from Huang Qian, *Tai'anxian zhi, juan shou, tu.*2b–3a).

Qin Shihuangdi's interest in performing these rituals at Mount Tai went beyond his desire to announce his successes to Heaven and Earth. He was obsessed with the highly personal goal of achieving immortality. Indeed, his ingestion of "pills of immortality" containing mercury may have been the cause of his death. In several places in the *Records of the Grand Historian*, Sima Qian described Qin Shihuangdi's dependence upon "magicians" (*fangshi* 方士) who claimed to hold the key to immortality.[80] These magicians made a direct connection between Mount Tai and the fabled island dwelling place of the immortals, Penglai 蓬萊.[81] Wechsler notes that "by traveling to P'eng-lai it was believed that one could obtain the elixir of immortality and become an immortal. . . . To the *fang-shih* T'ai-shan was the continental equivalent of P'eng-lai; it, too, was a mountain of immortals."[82] Thus, Qin Shihuangdi's sacrifices on Mount Tai were part of his search for immortality. Probably out of fear that the key to immortality would be revealed to others, "the directions for the ritual were sealed and stored away, being kept strictly secret."[83] Just as, according to Sima Qian, all records of the seventy-two ancient practitioners of the sacrifices had been lost, so too, the sacrifices of Qin Shihuangdi remained secret and unavailable as precedents for subsequent performances.

The next emperor to perform the *feng* and *shan* sacrifices at Mount Tai was Han Wudi 武帝 (r. 140–87 BCE) of the Western or Former Han Dynasty. At this point, the two rites were not completely linked. Wudi conducted the *feng* ceremony at Mount Tai five times, in the years 110, 106, 102, 98, and 93 BCE, and the *shan* ceremony only in 110, 102, and 93 BCE but not apparently on the other two occasions. Indeed, the account of the visit in 106 BCE mentions offerings to the Earth (Houtu 后土) but makes no reference to the *shan* sacrifice. In 109 and 105 BCE, Han Wudi performed rituals at Mount Tai, but not the *feng* or *shan* sacrifices. That Han Wudi did not see the *feng* and *shan* sacrifices as inseparable is further supported by the fact that he performed the *shan* sacrifice in 104 BCE at Mount Gaoli at the base of Mount Tai without making the *feng* sacrifice.[84]

Like Qin Shihuangdi, Han Wudi was interested in Mount Tai as a venue for activities other than the *feng* and *shan* sacrifices. He, too, sought to reach immortality from its summit. Again, his advisors connected Mount Tai with Penglai:

"With prolonged life you may visit the immortals who live on the island of Penglai in the middle of the sea. If you visit them and perform the Feng and Shan sacrifices, you will never die."

Master Shen told me, "The ruler of the Han shall also ascend the mountain and perform the Feng, and when he has done this, then he will become an immortal and will climb up to heaven!"

... A certain Master Ding of Qi, who was over ninety years old, stated, "The word *feng* indicates the concept of immortality."[85]

Just as with Qin Shihuangdi's visit, and almost certainly for the same reasons, there are no accounts of the ceremonies conducted by Han Wudi, who could be highly secretive about his ritual actions. In 110 BCE, he was accompanied up the mountain by only one trusted servant, who died shortly afterwards.[86] In his assessment of Han Wudi's secrecy, Lewis comments that "the hidden and mysterious nature of the performance is not a veil to be penetrated but a datum in its own right which contributes to our 'reading.'"[87] Sima Qian's chapter about the *feng* and *shan* sacrifices is usually seen as a critique of Han Wudi.[88] Sima was particularly critical of Han Wudi's reliance on *fangshi* advisors and his quest for immortality. Han Wudi's five repetitions of the sacrifices lend further support to the argument that his primary motivation in visiting Mount Tai was the search for immortality. Even though the earlier history of the ceremonies was clouded in mystery, there were no precedents for repeated performance of the *feng* and *shan* sacrifices by a single emperor, whereas examples of people repeating failed attempts to reach immortality are legion.

Ying-shih Yü, in his analysis of the evolution of this cult of immortality, notes that

as soon as the idea of hsien [*xian*] immortality attracted the attention of the worldly leaders, such as princes of the Warring-states period and emperors of the Ch'in and Han dynasties, it began to develop into a cult of a this-worldly character. Princes and emperors were not interested in transforming themselves into hsien immortals because they had suddenly developed a renunciatory attitude toward the honors and pleasures they enjoyed in this world. On the contrary, they were motivated by a strong desire to prolong their worldly pleasures forever.[89]

Thus, even when they were seemingly in pursuit of something mystical on the sacred summit of Mount Tai, both Qin Shihuangdi and Han Wudi probably had the longevity of their personal reigns and their dynasties foremost in their minds in the execution of the rituals they performed on the mountain.

Even though the exact rituals performed by Qin Shihuangdi and Han Wudi were not recorded, some of the rationales for their performances echoed those of the visits by Yao and Shun and added to the precedents for subsequent imperial visits. Confucian scholars during the early Han built on the tradition of imperial tours to Mount Tai in order to counter the influence of the magicians who urged the emperors to pursue immortality:

They linked T'ai-shan, the supreme peak in Eastern China, to the absolutist monarch—he who was highest. T'ai-shan thus became the symbol of kings. . . . "Going to T'ai-shan" assumed a powerful political meaning: It signified gaining possession over the empire. The Feng and Shan sacrifices performed at T'ai-shan were thus fashioned into a momentous religious and political ceremony, a potent symbolic vehicle for expressing the ruler's supreme position as the "one man" under Heaven, as well as his acknowledgment of Heaven's Mandate.[90]

Other recent scholarship has emphasized the close connections between political centralization and changes in imperial rituals: "The unifying force in these changes is a tendency toward integration. The mountainous regions of China were integrated into its cultural space, the gods of these mountains were integrated into the larger pantheon of popular worship."[91]

Lewis notes how political unification was reflected in spiritual practice by Qin Shihuangdi and Han Wudi:

As political authority had developed a radically new character through conquest and institutional reforms, the old religio-political order based on ancestor worship had been progressively supplanted by cults of natural divinities that created a power located in place and territory. At the same time, the powers of the spirit world and the forms of political authority emerging in the Warring States were increasingly patterned one after the

other. These developments culminated in the Qin unification. To mark
the unprecedented nature of his achievement and place the state under the
aegis of the eternal powers which offered both a model for his own su-
premacy and a foundation for his undying empire, the First Emperor of
Qin initiated a series of institutional and cultic reforms.[92]

After Han Wudi, only four other emperors journeyed to Mount
Tai to perform the *feng* and *shan* sacrifices. Unlike all the previous
actual and legendary visits, however, these final four performances
were well documented. They were performed in 56 CE by Guangwudi 光武帝 (r. 25–57 CE) of the Eastern or Later Han Dynasty (25–
220 CE), in 666 by Gaozong 高宗 (r. 650–83) of the Tang dynasty,
in 725 by Xuanzong 玄宗 (r. 713–55), also of the Tang dynasty, and
finally in 1008 by Zhenzong 眞宗 (r. 998–1022) of the Northern
Song Dynasty (960–1127).[93] As the existence of records of these performances suggests, they were much more public than those conducted by Qin Shihuangdi and Han Wudi. Indeed, Tang Xuanzong,
just prior to performing the sacrifices, declared: "Because [the rites]
We are performing today are all prayers for the sake of the people,
there is much less [reason] for Us to desire secrecy. Let the jade
tablets be taken out and shown to all the officials to let them know
Our intent."[94] Wechsler argues that the imperial search for immortality had decreased by the time of Han Guangwudi's visit. Thus,
these later emperors looked upon the *feng* and *shan* sacrifices "as an
announcement to Heaven and Earth of a change of dynasties and
of their personal achievements."[95] This view of the purpose of the
sacrifices is summarized in the Chinese phrase *shouming gaotian*
受命告天, an acknowledgment to Heaven of a dynasty's or emperor's reception of the Mandate of Heaven.[96] Chavannes offers a
similar interpretation of these four performances, stating that "the
essential object of the *feng* and *shan* ceremonies was to announce to
Heaven and to Earth the success of a dynasty. Having reached the
apogee of its [the dynasty's] glory, the emperor recalls the merits
of his predecessors and thanks Heaven and Earth for the support
they have given to his line."[97] In the same vein, Lewis argues that
Later Han scholarly interpretations "asserted that the *feng* and *shan*
sacrifices were offered to Heaven and Earth after a newly established dynasty had attained the state of 'Great Peace.'"[98]

Han Guangwudi refounded the Han dynasty in 25 CE after the Wang Mang interregnum (9–23 CE; styled the Xin or New Dynasty). When he performed the *feng* and *shan* sacrifices in 56 CE, one of his purposes was to solidify the connection with his family's dynastic lineage by performing the same rites of legitimation that his ancestor Han Wudi had performed.[99] Han Guangwudi quite consciously decided to disassociate these rites with the quest for immortality, which they had gained with Qin Shihuangdi and Han Wudi:

He explicitly denied the goal of attempting to "meet with Transcendents" and organized his rites according to the instructions of his Confucian officials instead of relying on the sort of *fangshi* who had advised the previous two emperors. . . . The purpose of Liu Xiu's [Han Guangwudi] rite was simply to announce to Heaven and to Earth his achievements as emperor and to ask their continued blessing for his dynasty. A result of this determination was that Liu Xiu performed the Feng and Shan openly before his assembled officials.[100]

Based on these four performances of the sacrifices, Chavannes compiled a detailed description of the ceremonies. I provide here a short summary of Chavannes's findings. The *feng* ceremony, the sacrifice to Heaven, was performed at two different locations. The first altar, constructed just south of the city wall of Tai'an, was less important than the second, and the ceremony conducted at it was a preliminary sacrifice, announcing the subsequent *feng* ceremony (see Appendix, nos. 69 and 70). The second, more important, *feng* sacrifice took place on an altar at the top of Mount Tai. Both of these altars were round, the symbolic shape of Heaven. Jade tablets engraved with an announcement of the successes of the dynasty were buried within the altar mounds.[101]

Although the *shan* sacrifice to Earth was not as ritually potent as the *feng* sacrifice to Heaven, it was nonetheless an essential complement and balanced the rite between the opposing forces of Heaven and Earth. The *shan* ceremony was quite similar to the *feng* ceremony, but the altar was square, the symbolic shape of the earth. It, too, involved buried messages engraved on jade tablets. Han Guangwudi conducted the *shan* sacrifice at Mount Liangfu. For the three performances conducted during the Tang and Northern Song dynasties, the *shan* ceremonies took place at a small hill southwest of Tai'an called Mount Sheshou (no. 62; see Fig. 22).[102]

The elaborate manner in which the jade tablets were sealed up was the same for the two *feng* sacrifices and the *shan* sacrifice. The jade tablets were encased on all six sides with additional pieces of jade, forming a box held together with gold cord. This jade box was then placed inside a stone box. This box was closed by sliding pieces of stone into notches along the side of the box, and these were sealed with a mixture of clay and gold dust. This box was placed in the altar mound and buttressed at each corner with long stones in order to keep it in place.[103]

In most sacrifices, prayers or messages were written on silk, bamboo, wood, or later paper and burned. The smoke carried the message to Heaven. In the *feng* and *shan* ceremonies, however, the messages were inscribed on jade and buried. Chavannes explains this difference by arguing that Mount Tai and Mount Sheshou were not the recipients of the prayers but intermediaries or messengers to Heaven and Earth, respectively.[104] Wechsler suggests that the use of the jade tablets could be a holdover of the earlier searches for immortality since it was thought that the durable tablets would last forever.[105]

After 1008, it was not until the Qing dynasty that another emperor visited Mount Tai. The Kangxi emperor (r. 1662–1722) visited the mountain three times, and his grandson, the Qianlong emperor (r. 1736–95), journeyed there nine times. Neither of them, however, performed the *feng* and *shan* sacrifices. For a discussion of their actions on the mountain and the rationale for not performing the *feng* and *shan* sacrifices, see Chapter 2.

History

One motivation for making the journey to Mount Tai in the late imperial period was to connect with China's long history. Many of the sites on Mount Tai, as well as legends about events that took place on its slopes, enabled visitors to experience this historical association. By visiting the sites discussed in this section, travelers could experience a connection with a particular event or person or with China's rich past in general. In the eighteenth-century novel *Dream of the Red Chamber* (also known as the *Story of the Stone*), the character Baoyu offers an insight into the Chinese respect for history: "To recall old things is better than to invent new ones; and to recut an ancient text is better than to engrave a modern."[106]

Although there are references to visits by rulers as far back as the Yellow Emperor, the earliest historic sites on the mountain identified with an emperor date to Qin Shihuangdi's ascent in 219 BCE. The site of the Fifth Rank Pine Tree (no. 29), the tree under which Qin Shihuangdi took refuge, was quite popular at least partially because it represented the power of nature over a despotic ruler. A stone arch, as well as pine trees planted periodically in subsequent periods, have helped keep this legend alive for those passing this spot (see Fig. 19).

The Wordless Stele (no. 48) on top of the mountain is another popular site sometimes connected with Qin Shihuangdi (see Fig. 21). This large, dressed stone stands just below the mountain's summit. Chinese sources continue to argue whether it dates from the Qin or Han dynasty (see Appendix, no. 48). Different sources connect the stone to either Qin Shihuangdi's visit or one of Han Wudi's visits. Both Zha Zhilong in the sixteenth century and Xiao Xiezhong 蕭協中 in the seventeenth century determined that the stone was erected by Qin Shihuangdi.[107] Most sources from the seventeenth century on, however, perhaps out of a desire to associate it with a more benign emperor, claim that it was erected in 110 BCE as part of one of Han Wudi's *feng* sacrifices. For example, after acknowledging the earlier view, Nie Jianguang noted that the famous seventeenth-century writer Gu Yanwu 顧炎武 (1613–82) believed that the stele had been erected by Han Wudi.[108] This uncertainty about the origin of this stone supports the idea that it is a prehistoric megalith. That this debate has continued for so long demonstrates the lack of textual proof. If the stone had been erected during either the Qin or Han, it seems likely that there would be some written record. Since the exact history of the stone was unknown, it was visited, especially by literati, primarily because of its age, not because of any particular story attached to it.[109]

Another site connected with both Qin Shihuangdi and Han Wudi was the Ancient *Feng* Sacrifice Terrace (no. 50), located near the mountain's summit. According to tradition, this was the site where these two emperors performed the *feng* sacrifice.[110] The only other physical remains purporting to date from the Han period are a number of cypress trees supposedly planted by Han Wudi. Several of these are still growing in the Dai Temple, and there is another in the God of War Temple (no. 66) near the mountain's base. In addition to being old, these trees represent a time considered to be a high point of Chinese civilization and a time of Chinese military expansion.[111]

Sites on Mount Tai dating from the Tang period are slightly more abundant. The Tang acacia tree in the Dai Temple (see Fig. 20) has attracted visitors because of its age and its association with a period considered by many to have been another peak of Chinese culture, particularly in the arts and poetry. The other Tang sites on the mountain are related directly to the two Tang emperors' visits in 666 and 725. Just south of the wall around Tai'an was the altar mound where the two Tang emperors performed the preliminary *feng* sacrifice (no. 69). This site is not mentioned in many late imperial guidebooks and probably was not commonly visited. The inscription known as the Tang Cliff Inscription (no. 45), however, has long been one of the most famous sites on Mount Tai (see Fig. 7). It consists of an impressive, gilt inscription on a cliff face on the top of the mountain (13.3 meters tall by 5.7 meters wide). The inscription, named "Eulogy Commemorating Mount Tai" ("Ji Taishan ming" 紀泰山銘), is an account written by Tang Xuanzong in 726 commemorating the accomplishments of the *feng* ceremony he performed the previous year.[112]

Since the sites connected with Song Zhenzong's visit in 1008 are nearly 300 years younger than those from the Tang, it is not surprising that they are much more numerous. These sites break down into three main groups. The largest group commemorates the arrival of the so-called Heavenly Text (*Tianshu* 天書). This text purportedly fell from Heaven at the base of Mount Tai in the middle of 1008.[113] Because of this auspicious event, the emperor's religious advisors convinced him to perform the *feng* and *shan* ceremonies at Mount Tai later that year. Zhenzong ordered a large hall to be built in the book's honor in the Dai Temple complex (no. 2). A stele in the Dai Temple grounds commemorates the construction of this hall. In addition, the emperor ordered the construction of a temple devoted especially to the Heavenly Text to the west of the city (no. 73). The emperor also wrote an essay thanking Heaven, which was inscribed in two separate places. One was carved into a cliff just to the East of Tang Cliff Inscription (no. 45). The other, called the Great Northward Facing Stele, was placed just south of the city wall (no. 71).

The second largest group of sites connected with Zhenzong relate to his performance of the *feng* and *shan* sacrifices. The altar where he performed the preliminary *feng* sacrifice (no. 70) was located adjacent to the one from the Tang Dynasty (no. 69). On top of the mountain, near where he performed the primary *feng* sacrifice, there was a small raised terrace with a stele in the middle commemorating his performance of the *feng* sacrifice. As noted above, he also engraved an account of his 1008 performance of the *feng* ceremony on a cliff face immediately to the east of the Tang inscription (no. 45). This inscription was much less impressive than its Tang predecessor and subsequently suffered the ignominy of having a later inscription carved across its face.[114]

One site connected with Zhenzong's visit commemorates the emperor himself, rather than the Heavenly Text or the *feng* sacrifices. According to tradition, when Song Zhenzong climbed Mount Tai he stopped and rested at the Esplanade of the Imperial Tent (no. 27). Several holes in the bedrock purport to mark the location of tent poles.[115] Dwight Baker speculated that the emperor's tent would have been placed at a perhaps more amenable spot higher up except that it then would have been too close to the place where the infamous Qin Shihuangdi took refuge from the storm (no. 29). As Baker noted, the Song emperor's "loyal annalists draw an invidious comparison between the royally perfect weather which their good emperor enjoyed and the storm of wind and rain which met the tyrant of Ts'in [Qin] at this place."[116]

A large number of sites are related to the two Qing dynasty emperors who visited Mount Tai. Both presented numerous temple plaques in the imperial hand and erected many stelae with their poetry. For example, just to the west of the Tang Cliff Inscription (no. 45) are two large characters meaning "Cloud Peak" (*yunfeng* 雲峰), written in the Kangxi emperor's hand in 1684 (see Fig. 7). Below these two characters is an inscription consisting of several poems written by the Qianlong emperor in 1748. The Qianlong emperor also had a cliff inscription carved into the mountain. His "Inscription of 100,000 Feet" quite consciously competed with the Tang Cliff Inscription (see Fig. 23).

Although some of the imperial sites are quite impressive, the figure who motivated most of those who visited Mount Tai for historical reasons was Confucius. There are many stories connecting Confucius and Mount Tai. These stories provided the names for a number of sites on the mountain: Point Where Confucius Began His Ascent (no. 9), Viewing Wu Peak (no. 39), Confucian Temple (no. 40), Place Where the Sage Saw Wu (no. 41), Pavilion of Heaven and Earth (no. 43). The sites and the stories mutually reinforced themselves in the minds of visitors. The most reliable and historically plausible of the stories involving Confucius is the passage from the book of *Mencius* quoted above. This passage helped form the image of Mount Tai in two ways. First, it created an association between Confucius and the mountain. This fact alone made the mountain an appealing site for literati in subsequent ages. In addition, it connected Mount Tai with a cosmic vision.

Another story connecting Confucius with Mount Tai is found in the *Book of Rites*:

Confucius was passing by Mount Tai, and [he heard] a woman crying and wailing beside some graves. The Master signaled [his group to stop] and listened. He sent Zilu to question the woman: "Madam, you cry as one who suffers great grief." She replied, "Yes, formerly my father-in-law was killed by a tiger, my husband also died in this way, and now my son has also died in this way." The Master asked, "Why did you not leave?" She replied, "The government [here] is not severe." The Master spoke, "My disciples, remember this, a tyrannical government is fiercer than tigers."[117]

Here we find, in association with Mount Tai, a key component of Confucius' moral, political philosophy: a virtuous ruler will draw

Fig. 23   The Qianlong emperor's Inscription of 100,000 Feet (no. 31), viewed from the Second Heavenly Gate (no. 23). The inscription is the whitish rectangle in the lower right. The Southern Heavenly Gate (no. 37) is visible at the top of the depression in the ridgeline of the mountain at the upper left (photograph by the author, 1994).

subjects to his lands, but corrupt or tyrannical rulers will drive people away. In this tale, Mount Tai is a space where justice rules over tyranny.

Poems written about the mountain added another layer of history and culture to Mount Tai. Many of China's most famous poets, including Li Bo 李白 (701–62) and Du Fu 杜甫 (712–70), visited the mountain and left their impressions behind in poems. In an article on poetry about Mount Tai from the third through eighth centuries CE, Paul Kroll demonstrates that the poets alluded to the religious as well as historical aspects of this sacred mountain in their poems. Literate visitors from the late imperial period would often recite these poems during their excursions, and in addition to appreciating the beautiful language and imagery of the poems, they would also be reminded of specific historical events, natural beauties, or the possibility of otherworldly ascendance within this sacred space.

Du Fu's "Gazing on the Sacred Peak" ("望嶽"), from 740, is a good example of a poem that fuses images of the power of nature with historic references:

> What is Mount Tai like?
> the unending verdant of Qi and Lu.
> A natural creation where all spirits flourish,
> northern and southern slopes divide dusk from dawn.
> Its vast bosom brings forth layering clouds,
> breaking through, [my] eyes follow the returning birds.
> Upon ascending its ultimate peak,
> in a glance how small are all other mountains.[118]

Du Fu's historical references note the mountain's position as a Zhou period boundary between the two states of Qi and Lu and recall Confucius' "finding the world small." His images of clouds and birds emphasize the peak's domination of the surrounding plains. The nature described by Du Fu also has mystical qualities. "Spirits flourish" on its natural slopes, and the view from the summit encompasses "all other mountains." The mountain is also associated with daily rhythms.

Mysticism

In addition to connecting visitors to China's past, stories about Confucius also tied the sage to the mountain's supernatural or transcendent powers. A story prevalent by the first century CE, which probably used the passage in the *Mencius* as a starting point, recounts an incident involving Confucius and his favorite disciple:

Yan Yuan and Confucius together climbed Mount Tai in Lu. Looking southeast, Confucius perceived a white horse tied to the Zhang Gate of the capital of the state of Wu [Suzhou]. He guided Yan, pointed to it, and asked him: "Do you see the Zhang Gate of the capital of the country of Wu?" Yan Yuan responded: "I see it." Confucius replied: "What is it before the gate?" Yan Yuan responded: "There is something in the shape of a silk cloth attached to it." Confucius touched his eyes so he could see in the correct manner, and [Yan] saw all below. But when the two descended, Yan Yuan's hair turned white, his teeth fell out, and following a sickness he died.[119]

The author of this version of the tale, Wang Chong 王充 (27–ca. 100), himself, as well as most subsequent writers who refer to this story, pointed out the impossibility of seeing Suzhou from Mount Tai. However, the story serves as a metaphor for Confucius' farsightedness and his abilities as a teacher. In the story the mountain is a site of extraordinary visibility and clarity. Furthermore, Yan Yuan's rapid decline after trying to perform at the level of his teacher echoes the dangers of performing rituals improperly or of lesser people usurping the prerogatives of others, as seen in examples of sacrifices at Mount Tai discussed above.

The idea that dangerous consequences can result from the improper performance of a ritual is also found in the only reference to Mount Tai in the *Analects*:

The Chi Family were going to perform the sacrifice to Mount T'ai. The Master said to Jan Ch'iu, "Can you not save the situation?"

"No. I cannot."

The Master said, "Alas! Who would have thought that Mount T'ai would suffer?"[120]

In the notes to his translation, D. C. Lau explains that "not being the lord of the state of Lu, the head of the Chi Family was not entitled to perform the sacrifice to Mount T'ai and it would be a violation of rites for Mount T'ai to accept the sacrifice."[121] Ge Hong 葛洪 (283–344), a Daoist and an "industrious collector of occult traditions," also expressed the dangers posed by mountains to the untrained:

Yet, those who are not aware of the procedures (法) for entering the mountains many times come to hazard and harm. . . . Mountains, whether large or small, are in all cases possessed of divine numina. If the mountain be large, then the divinity is a greater one. . . . Entering a mountain without being in possession of the [proper] technique (術), one is certain to find calamity and harm.[122]

A further example of the dangers of Mount Tai might be found in the history of the servant who accompanied Han Wudi on his first ascent of Mount Tai in 110 BCE and died only a few days after descending from the mountain.[123] This sudden death has often been attributed to Wudi's desire to keep his immortality rituals completely secret, but the story just as easily lends itself to the tradition of the dangers of this powerful site to the improperly initiated.

Another story involving Confucius blends Mount Tai's association with wisdom and Daoist principles:

Confucius was traveling by Mount Tai when he perceived Yong Qiji wandering in the region of Zheng. Yong was clothed in a stag skin tied with a cord, he played a lute and sang. Confucius asked him: "Sir, why are you so happy?" Yong responded: "The causes of my joy are numerous. When Heaven made the numerous beings, only humans were noble, and I am a human, this is happiness. In the distinction between men and women, men are esteemed and women are inferior, for this reason men are noble. Since I am a male, this is the second [cause of my] happiness. Among people there are those who do not live [long enough] to see either the sun or the moon, and who die before they leave their swaddling clothes. Since I have already lived to be 90 years old, this is the third cause of my joy. Poverty is the habitual [condition] of people, death is their [natural] end, since [I am in this] habitual [condition] and will have this [natural] end, why should I distress myself?" Confucius said: "Excellent! To be able to broaden oneself [in this way]."[124]

Here Mount Tai is a space where self-cultivation takes place. The aura of this sacred mountain is strong enough to make people understand their relationship with nature or the Dao, giving them both long life and happiness.

This sort of story about a sagely, ancient hermit living on a mountain was emblematic of the cult of *xian* 仙 immortality. Ying-shih Yü suggests that the prototype of a *xian* immortal is found in a passage from the *Zhuangzi*: "There is a Holy Man living on faraway Ku-she Mountain, with skin like ice or snow, and gentle and shy like a young girl. He doesn't eat the five grains, but sucks the wind, drinks the dew, climbs up on clouds and mists, rides a flying dragon, and wanders beyond the four seas."[125] An individual connected with Mount Tai who matched this description quite well was the Tang period hermit Lü Dongbin 呂洞賓, who was eventually apotheosized as one of the Eight Immortals.

Legend had it that Lü lived in a cave (Lüzu dong 呂祖洞, no. 5) across the small stream from the Wangmu Pool Temple (no. 4) during the Tang dynasty. A miraculous story arising from his residence in this cave gave names to another nearby cave and pool. Lü had written two poems on the wall of his cave. A young hornless dragon (*qiu* 虯) was in the habit of praying before these poems. One night the young hornless dragon came as usual, but this time Lü Dongbin, using his brush, painted a dot on its forehead. Immediately the young dragon was transformed into a full grown dragon (*long* 龍) and flew away.[126] Just north of Lü's cave are the Stream Bend Where There Is a Hornless Dragon (no. 6) and the Transcendent Hornless Dragon Cave (no. 7).

The magician or *fangshi* advisors to Qin Shihuangdi and Han Wudi, discussed in the previous section, promoted a connection between Mount Tai and the fabled Penglai, the island residence of the immortals alleged to be located off the northeast coast of Shandong. This connection carried over into the late imperial period as well. Between the Transcendent Hornless Dragon Cave and the Queen Mother Pool Temple is a twist in the stream called Little Penglai.[127] Although overt imperial pursuit of immortality on Mount Tai ceased with Han Wudi, others continued to connect the summit of this sacred mountain with immortals and the route to longevity. A bronze mirror dating from the Later Han dynasty (probably from the second or third century CE) echoes the earlier imperial desire for a balance between contact with the mystical world and success in this life: "If you climb Mount Tai, you will see the immortals. You can feed on the purest jade, drink from the sacred springs . . . [and] receive a long life that lasts ten thousand years, a fitting place in office, and protection for your children and grandchildren."[128]

Medieval poetry about Mount Tai was another genre that perpetuated the mountain's mystical aura. Xie Lingyun's 謝靈運 (385–433) poem about Mount Tai emphasizes its lofty heights and its role in the *feng* and *shan* sacrifices:

> Tai the Revered—flourishing is the Marchmount
>   [Sacred Peak, *yue*];
> Sublimely spiring, to pierce the cloudy heavens.

> Precipitous and acclivitous, both hazardous and high;
> Its jostled rocks, in every case luxuriant and lush.
> Ascending for the *feng*—interment at the exalted altar;
> Descending for the *shan*—a cache at Solemn State.[129]

Danger and death, luxuriance and life, are compounded in the poem about this traditional intermediary between Heaven and Earth.

Li Bo wrote a series of six poems about Mount Tai in 742. His poems, full of mystery, jade elixirs of immortality, encounters with immortals, and failed excursions into the clouds, are reminiscent of the ideal immortal from the *Zhuangzi* and the Han bronze mirror:

> Jade maidens, four or five persons,
> Gliding and whirling descend from the Nine Peripheries.
> Suppressing smiles, they lead me forward by immaculate hands,
> And let fall to *me* a cup of fluid aurora![130]
>
> Proceeding with the clouds, I trust to the lasting wind,
> Wafting on as though I'd spawned plumes and wings![131]
>
> Touching heaven, I pluck the Calabash Gourd;
> Confused and uncertain, I don't remember to go home.
> . . . .
> At bright dawn, as I sit, stars becoming lost in relation to each
>   other,
> I can only see five-colored clouds flying.[132]

At the beginning of Li Bo's sixth poem about Mount Tai, in a demonstration of the association between another mystical being and Mount Tai, he visits the Queen Mother Pool at the base of the mountain (no. 4). The Queen Mother of the West (Xi Wangmu 西王母) was the highest goddess in Han period religion and in the later Daoist pantheon. She was thought to dwell in the far west on the mythical Mount Kunlun, where she had an orchard full of peach trees. These were the fabled peaches of immortality (*xiantao* 仙桃 or *pantao* 蟠桃), the source of the elixir of eternal life. By the Tang dynasty, the goddess was especially associated with the "control of immortality and her power to mediate between the divine and human realms. . . . [Furthermore] she sanction[ed] all ascents to transcendence."[133]

The Queen Mother of the West was associated with Mount Tai in several ways. The consort of the goddess is sometimes referred to as the King and Sire of the East (Dong wang gong 東王公) or the King Father of the East (Dong wang fu 東王父). Liu Zenggui has shown that some Han tomb engravings equate the King Father of the East with the Lord of Mount Tai (Taishan jun 泰山君).[134] Just as the *fangshi* magicians connected Mount Tai with the mystic Penglai, both Liu Zenggui and Lü Jixiang argue that Mount Tai was closely linked with the Queen Mother of the West's home, Mount Kunlun.[135]

In addition to the garden of the peaches of immortality, another important site in the Queen Mother of the West's mystical land is the Turquoise Pond or Pool (*yaochi* 瑤池).[136] The original name of the pool in the goddess's temple at the base of Mount Tai was the same—the Turquoise Pool.[137] Cahill observes that "the Queen Mother's Turquoise Pond on Mount T'ai and her Turquoise Pond on Mount K'un-lun are equivalents in mythical geography."[138] The close association between the Queen Mother and the God of Mount Tai can also be seen in the fact that the former middle temple of the God of Mount Tai was located just to the west of the Queen Mother Pool Temple (see Appendix, under no. 2).

The names of a number of other sites on Mount Tai were derived from the belief that ascent to the mountain's peak would aid visitors in their attempts to transcend this world and reach the heavens:

Ascend to Transcendence Bridge (no. 17)
Step to Heaven Bridge (no. 22)
Cloud Stepping Bridge (no. 26)
Cloud Gate (no. 33)
Promoted to Transcendence Arch (no. 36)

In addition, sites such as Transcendents' Bridge (no. 56) and Transcendent's Shadow (no. 74), much like the poems by Li Bo, remind pilgrims that immortals dwell in Mount Tai's mystical space.

Death

As we have seen, because of its location in the east, Mount Tai has long been associated with the beginning of life. The power of granting life is also often closely related to the ending of it. Just as the *feng* and *shan* sacrifices were prayers to Heaven and Earth, so Mount Tai's association with life and Heaven was balanced with a complementary association with death, Earth, and the underworld. During the Warring States period, religious worship in the domain of Qi included sacrifices to the Eight Deities (Bashen 八神). The offerings to each deity were to take place at different mountains and hills throughout the Shandong peninsula.[139] According to Sima Qian, offerings to the Master of Earth (Dizhu 地主) had to take place atop a hill at the base of a tall mountain and were assigned to Mount Liangfu at the foot of Mount Tai.[140] Ying-shih Yü argues that this Master of Earth transformed into the Master of the Underworld (Dixiazhu 地下主). Then, "from around the end of the first century B.C. a belief gradually arose that there was a supreme ruler called Lord of Mount T'ai (*T'ai-shan fu-chün* [Taishan fujun] 泰山府君) whose capital was located . . . [at Mount] Liang-fu," who ruled over the underworld. Yü points out that this deity was originally distinct from the God of Mount Tai. Taishan fujun, he notes, was not a name but a bureaucratic title indicating that he was a governor of the area around Mount Tai, which included both that sacred peak and the much smaller Mount Liangfu.[141] Chavannes showed that by about 6 BCE people believed that Mount Tai presided over death.[142]

There was, then, a close connection between the seat of this underworld bureaucracy and the location of the site for the *shan* sacrifice to Earth. Sima Qian, describing the *feng* and *shan* sacrifices in general terms, recorded that the *shan* ritual was performed at Mount Liangfu,[143] which was where Qin Shihuangdi in 219 BCE and Han Guangwudi in 56 CE conducted these rites. For his 102 BCE performance of the *feng* and *shan* sacrifices, Han Wudi performed the *shan* ceremony at a small hill south of Mount Tai called Mount Shilü (see Fig. 22). According to Sima Qian, the emperor chose this site because his *fangshi* advisors informed him that Shilü (石閭),

which literally means "stone village gate," was "the gateway to the village of the immortals."[144] In 104 BCE, when Han Wudi performed the *shan* but not the *feng* sacrifice, he did so at Mount Haoli (no. 63). This small hill at the base of Mount Tai also became closely connected with the underworld. Ying-shih Yü notes that in the mid–first century BCE Mount Haoli "suddenly gained popularity as an abode for the dead."[145] Chavannes cited sources that connected Mount Haoli to funeral rites by 202 CE.[146] Finally, both Mount Haoli and Mount Liangfu were connected to the underworld in a song by Lu Ji 陸機 (261–303).[147]

By the middle of the second century CE, texts began to speak of the dead "returning to Mount Tai."[148] Chavannes observed that by 250 CE the term "to go to Mount Tai" was a euphemism for "to die."[149] And Zhang Hua 張華 (232–300 CE), in his *Bowuzhi* 博物志, stated that Mount Tai was in charge of people's souls and knew the lengths of their lives.[150] Thus, the deity in charge of the Chinese underworld evolved into the God of Mount Tai.

Buddhism, with its key component of reincarnation, first arrived in China during the first century CE. This Buddhist concept combined with the Chinese notion of the underworld with its entrance at Mount Tai, and the underworld or purgatory became a transitional place where a soul underwent judgment and punishment before being reborn. The soul spent seven days in each of seven separate courts headed by a king. The melding of Indian and Chinese concepts of an afterlife can be seen as early as the second and third centuries CE when some of the earliest translations of Buddhist texts into Chinese used "Mount Tai" to translate the Sanskrit term for the underworld or purgatory (*niraya* or *naraka*).[151] The entrance to purgatory, and the subsequent exit for the soul back into the world, was at the base of Mount Tai, and the personified God of Mount Tai became the judge or king in charge of the seventh court.

Between the third and seventh centuries, Chinese cultural practices further influenced this system, and three additional courts were added, for a total of ten, ruled over by the Ten Kings (*shi wang* 十王).[152] The synthesis of Indian and Chinese concepts of the afterlife was well developed by the seventh century, and the Ten

Kings were mentioned in texts as early as 664.[153] In the Chinese system, the whole process was bureaucratized. Souls appeared before the kings just as criminals appeared before a magistrate. Instead of constables, however, the kings were assisted by various demons. As necessary, souls were tortured or punished before moving on to the next court.

Almost certainly as a means of competing with Buddhism, religious Daoism adopted the concept of purgatory by the twelfth century with only minor renamings of some of the kings. In both the Buddhist and the Daoist systems of purgatory, the King of Taishan (Taishan wang 泰山王) was in charge of the pivotal seventh court (see Fig. 3). This deity was also called the God of Mount Tai (Taishan shen 泰山神) and the Great Emperor of the Eastern Sacred Peak (Dongyue dadi 東嶽大帝).[154]

With the adoption of this conception of the afterlife, Mount Haoli supplanted other nearby hills associated with the underworld and became the only entrance and exit for souls undergoing reincarnation. Mount Haoli's increased importance can be seen in the fact that during the last three performances of the *feng* and *shan* sacrifices (in 666, 725, and 1008) the *shan* ceremony was conducted at the hill immediately to its east, Mount Sheshou (no. 62). Until the 1930s, a popular temple dedicated to the Ten Kings was situated on top of Mount Haoli (no. 63).

Temples dedicated to the Ten Kings and their courts in purgatory, later usually called Eastern Sacred Peak Temples (Dongyue miao 東嶽廟), were built throughout the country by the Song dynasty.[155] In the late imperial period, one of the most popular temples in Beijing was the Dongyue miao.[156] Some of these temples divide the underworld bureaucracy into ten courts, each under the jurisdiction of one of the Ten Kings. Other temples, mirroring the complex Chinese bureaucracy, subdivided the ten courts further into seventy-two to seventy-six bureaus (*si* 司).[157] The large Dongyue miao in Beijing and two of the underworld temples at Mount Tai had separate altars for all the bureaus (see Appendix, nos. 2 and 63).[158] Real-life bureaucratic red tape and imperfection found their way into many popular tales of the afterlife featuring errors made by the underworld bureaucracy (but never by the God of Mount Tai).

Somewhere in every Eastern Sacred Peak temple were depictions of departed souls suffering tortures under the supervision of a king or judge. These depictions might take the form of scroll paintings (see Fig. 3, p. 11), wall murals, statues, or even dioramas with stuffed dummies. These images were intended to promote moral behavior and to motivate prayers for departed relatives who might be suffering torments similar to those depicted.

Another supernatural figure associated with Mount Tai as a locus for death was Taishan Shi Gandang 泰山石敢當. The legends and practices surrounding this figure were originally unconnected to Mount Tai. A Song dynasty account records the discovery of a stone in Fujian from the Tang dynasty engraved with the name "Shi Gandang." Legend has it that Shi Gandang lost his life saving an emperor from an attempted assassination. Because of his courage and loyalty, he was greatly admired. The Tang engraving dubbed him the "queller of hundreds of ghosts." People erected plaques engraved with his name in areas particularly susceptible to evil spirits, such as T-shaped intersections and dead-end streets. Shi Gandang was such a fierce opponent to evil spirits and ghosts that they fled at the sight of his name and left those who had erected the plaques unmolested. Besides being a name, the three characters *shi gan dang* can be read the "stone that dares to resist."[159]

At some point, probably because of Mount Tai's connection to the underworld, people began adding the characters for Mount Tai before Shi Gandang's name on these plaques. Plaques with the inscription "Taishan Shi Gandang," sometimes with the addition of a fearsome tiger's head at the top, have been found all over China, dating back at least to the late seventeenth century.[160] Many people read the phrase "Taishan shi gandang" as "the stone from Mount Tai that dares to resist" rather than as a name of a demon queller. As we saw above, nature worship on Mount Tai honored the mountain itself as well as rocks on its surface. Rocks taken from the mountain's slopes retained some of the mountain's powers. What better to control demons or ghosts than a piece of the mountain that guards the entrance to the underworld?

In Shandong a local legend evolved to explain the demon queller's connection with Mount Tai.

A very strong and brave woodcutter named Shi Gandang lived on Mount Tai. He was taught martial arts and magic by an old Daoist (*lao Dao* 老道). One day a goblin (*yaoguai* 妖怪) came to Wang Yuanwai's house and put his daughter into a coma. Many Daoists (*Daoshi* 道士) used charms and incantations to exorcize the demon, but to no avail. Wang Yuanwai sent out a bulletin to be posted all around the region. Wang offered half his family's wealth as a reward. In addition, if the person who saved his daughter was a young, unmarried man, he could marry the daughter. Shi Gandang saw the notice and decided to give it a try. Shi asked Wang to prepare a magic sword and a set of tight-fitting clothes, while he wrote out a charm. He pasted the charm over the door to the daughter's room. At dusk Shi put on the clothes, and grasping the sword, he went into the daughter's room. At the third watch, there was a fierce wind, and the goblin arrived. He laughingly tore down the charm and burst into the room. Shi yelled out: "What goblin dares to enter? Taishan Shi Gandang is here!" The goblin turned and fled back to his cave.

Wang gave half of his wealth to Shi. Shi and Miss Wang were married, and Shi moved into the Wang household.

The goblin was so frightened he dared not leave his cave for over a month. Eventually he ventured out again and cast a spell over someone in another village. The villagers heard of Shi Gandang and sent someone to ask him to come. Shi set off to the village. Before Shi arrived, the goblin heard of his coming and fled. The villagers were elated. But soon the goblin appeared in another village. Shi went there, scared off the goblin, but then the goblin went elsewhere. This went on for a year. Shi returned home for the New Year's. His wife asked how he was doing, and he explained. She suggested a means of avoiding all his running around. "Why doesn't every village put up an inscription with your name? When the goblin sees the plaque, it won't dare enter the village." This idea worked, and word soon spread until all villages had a stone inscription with the five characters "Taishan Shi Gandang."[161]

By learning martial arts and magic within the sacred precincts of Mount Tai, Shi Gandang gains an advantage over other Daoists, who fail to control the goblin. The God of Mount Tai's role as a judge or king in the underworld gives him control over creatures such as the goblin in the story. Thus, Shi Gandang, drawing on the God of Mount Tai's authority in the underworld, can quell the goblin.

Wilt Idema's summary of several thirteenth- and fourteenth-century dramas that include pilgrimages to Mount Tai suggests that people viewed the God of Mount Tai as a deity who resolved past wrongs through retribution and rewards. Among the traits of the deity and his assistants is the ability to see afar, similar to that Confucius experienced on this sacred site.[162] Such attributes fit well with the god's charge of judging the souls of the dead and then sending them forth again in new forms. In these dramas, the god is associated with a return to life after an unjust death. *Little Sun the Butcher* (*Xiao Sun tu* 小孫屠) features the resurrection of a strangled, filial man by an officer of the God of Mount Tai.[163] In *Little Zhang the Butcher Immolates His Child to Save His Mother* (*Xiao Zhang tu fen'er jiumu* 小張屠焚兒救母), a man pledges to offer his son "as a stick of incense" at Mount Tai if his mother recovers from a severe illness. In the course of the play, a child is indeed burned alive in an incense oven on the mountain, and the mother's health is restored. However, unbeknownst to the man, the God of Mount Tai, out of compassion for his filial piety, substituted the child of a swindler before the sacrifice. In the end the filial Butcher Zhang is reunited with all of his family, and the evil swindler is left childless.[164] The just are rewarded, the evil punished, and the God of Mount Tai sees all.

The Abandon Life Cliff (no. 57), near the top of Mount Tai, was a site for numerous filial sacrifices similar to that of Butcher Zhang. According to tradition, people believed if they sacrificed their lives by jumping off this cliff, the mountain deities would transform this act of "filial" duty into the cure of an ill relative. Given the hierarchical nature of filial duties, these sacrifices tended to be undertaken to save the lives of parents or parents-in-law. The practice became so prevalent that in 1523 the governor of Shandong ordered that a wall 300 feet long and 15 feet high be erected at the top of the cliff in order to prevent people from taking their lives. An inscription on the wall included the phrase "False sacrifice is false love." Despite the walls and warnings, however, people were leaping from this cliff as late as 1924.[165] In this practice, we can see the belief in the mountain as well as in the God of Mount Tai's jurisdiction over the length of people's lives. Also behind this practice was the belief that the underworld bureaucrats had to balance their books. The ill elder's life could be extended only through a reciprocal shortening of the life of the younger relative.

By the twelfth century, various rituals and prayers connected with the dead and the afterlife had become widespread throughout China, both geographically and within the social hierarchy. Buddhist and Daoist rites for the dead, worship of the Ten Kings, the Ghost Festival, and the accompanying performances of various genres of the Mulian story had become quite popular.[166] A specific example of this can be seen in the building of Dongyue temples to the Ten Kings and their purgatorial courts throughout the country. The popularity of rituals that sought to smooth the transition to a new life for recently departed relatives seems to have impacted the overall character of pilgrimages to Mount Tai. Although the open nature of the Tang and Song period *feng* and *shan* sacrifices contrasted with the secret ceremonies of Qin Shihuangdi and Han Wudi, they still involved only an elite audience of officials. Tang poets such as Li Bo and Du Fu emphasized private, mystical journeys. However, by the late thirteenth century, Mount Tai had become the destination for thousands of pilgrims from all social backgrounds. Indeed, an official document from 1313 complains about pilgrimages to Mount Tai in honor of the God of Mount Tai in his guise as a judge in the underworld: "Nowadays . . . even runners, wrestlers, actors and whores . . . congregate from all directions; the crowd has to be counted in the tens of thousands and the hubbub lasts for days on end."[167] It seems that the growing popularity of death rituals led many people to bring their appeals on behalf of deceased relatives closer to the underworld. And what better place to make their voices heard than the entrance to the underworld at Mount Tai?

Life

Given Mount Tai's associations with the sunrise and beginning of life, it was only logical that it became the center of a fertility cult. The focus of this cult was the Goddess of Mount Tai.

Fig. 24   The main temple to Bixia Yuanjun, the Goddess of Mount Tai, on top
of the mountain (no. 58) (photograph by the author, 1995).

The only certain date in the development of the worship of this
goddess is 1008, when a statue of a woman, supposedly from the
Han dynasty, was discovered in what became known as the Jade
Maiden Pool (Yunü chi 玉女池) on top of Mount Tai. The statue
was discovered while Song emperor Zhenzong was atop the mountain for the *feng* sacrifice. The emperor ordered that a jade replica of
the statue be placed in a shrine to be built adjacent to the pool. This
shrine was called the Bright Truth Temple (Zhaozhen guan 昭真觀,
no. 58), and it developed into the temple that became the main goal
of pilgrims during the late imperial period (see Fig. 24). Zhenzong
believed that the statue represented a goddess, and he gave her the title "Heavenly Immortal, Jade Maiden, Bixia Yuanjun" (Tianxian
Yunü Bixia Yuanjun 天仙玉女碧霞元君), later also known as the
Goddess of Mount Tai (Taishan Niangniang 泰山娘娘).[168]

Tianxian means "heavenly immortal"; *xian* 仙 is the same term
used in the cult of immortality. The title *yunü* 玉女, "jade maiden,"
is used to refer to perfected or transcendent beings. According to
Suzanne Cahill, "the jade maidens are celestial attendants, minor
goddesses who carry the Queen Mother's messages, serve the
peaches of immortality at transcendent feasts, and entertain guests
with performances. . . . They also write out charms and teachings
to transmit to humans, guard the texts of holy works, [and] witness oaths."[169]

Bixia is somewhat more complicated. The characters *bi* and *xia* connect the goddess to Mount Tai and also have associations with the Queen Mother of the West. *Bi* 碧 means "dark blue-green jade" and by extension that particular shade of green.[170] In Chinese cosmology, the east in general and the Eastern Sacred Peak specifically are associated with dawn, the beginning of life, and the color green (*qing* 青). Liu Hui argues that the connection between the colors led to the character *bi* being attached to this goddess.[171] In addition, *bi* was also a term used in Tang poetry to describe mountains and transcendence. In Li Bo's sixth poem about Mount Tai, for example, it describes mountains: "Transcendent people wander to cyan [green/*bi*] peaks."[172] The Tang poet Yu Xuanji 魚玄機 (ca. 844–ca. 868) used it to compare three beautiful women to the jade maiden servants of the Queen Mother:

> At the cyan [green/*bi*] window, they must be
>   embroidering phoenix slips.
>
> . . . .
>
> I suspect that they once acted as girl attendants
>   at the Turquoise Pond[173]

The character *xia* 霞 means "the light at dawn or dusk" or "the color of the clouds at dawn or dusk."[174] Liu Hui asserts that the combination *bixia* connects the term specifically to dawn light because green is connected with the east, the direction of the sunrise.[175] The *Hanyu dacidian* dictionary states that *bixia* is often used to describe places inhabited by gods and immortals and identifies the earliest usage of this two-character compound as a poem written by Li Bo, in which it describes a mountain.[176] *Yuanjun* 元君 is a Daoist title for female deities.[177] Generally the goddess was called Bixia Yuanjun, Bixia, or Taishan Niangniang.[178]

Beyond the discovery of the statue and the construction of a shrine in 1008, it is difficult to trace the early development of the worship of Bixia Yuanjun. Clearly these acts alone did not immediately lead to popular veneration. For example, although the thirteenth- and early fourteenth-century dramas studied by Idema contain pilgrimages to Mount Tai, the focus of the pilgrims' prayers is the God of Mount Tai. Bixia Yuanjun is not even mentioned. However, less than a hundred years later her main temple was enlarged, and by no later than 1500 she had become one of the most popular deities in northern China.[179] Evidence of her widespread appeal by the early sixteenth century is found in the implementation of a new policy by the Ming government. In 1516, the government took advantage of the numerous pilgrims paying homage to Bixia Yuanjun at her temple on top of Mount Tai and implemented a so-called incense tax (xiang shui 香税).[180] There is an interesting give-and-take in the popularity of these two mountain deities. As worship of the Goddess of Mount Tai increased, veneration of the God of Mount Tai decreased.

This shift away from the "male" toward the "female" probably began in the mid-fourteenth century. This change was manifested in the condition of temples to these two deities on the mountain. By the Northern Song period, there were three temples dedicated to the God of Mount Tai on the mountain, the so-called lower, middle, and upper temples. The lower temple, the Dai Temple, is situated in the city of Tai'an at the base of the mountain and dates at least to 56 CE (see Appendix, no. 2). The middle temple was located just to the west of the Queen Mother Pool Temple (no. 4). Although its original date of construction is unknown, it existed during the Tang dynasty.[181] The upper temple (no. 44) was situated near the mountain's summit, in front of the Tang Cliff Inscription. Its origins are also unknown, but it was repaired early in the Yuan dynasty.[182]

The middle temple to the God of Mount Tai was rededicated to Laozi around the beginning of the Ming dynasty. Nie Jianguang and Chavannes described this temple as having served as the middle temple of the God of Mount Tai from the Tang into the Yuan periods.[183] Wang Shizhen 王世贞 (1526–90), who visited the mountain in 1558 and 1559, noted that the upper temple was in such a state of disrepair that "the burning of incense and candles was not possible."[184] Seventeenth-century commentaries observe that the main Dai Temple at the base of the mountain was seldom used for prayer but was instead filled with throngs crowding the merchants' stalls and viewing entertainments such as wrestling.[185]

In contrast, the main temple to Bixia Yuanjun was expanded and additional temples added. During the reign of the first Ming emperor, Hongwu (r. 1368–98), the main temple to the goddess on top of Mount Tai was completely rebuilt and enlarged.[186] An inscription erected in the temple in 1480 commemorated repairs commissioned by the emperor. In 1495 the temple was rebuilt and expanded after a disastrous fire.[187] In 1504 the Temple for Paying Homage from Afar (no. 1, p. 2), just south of the Dai Temple, was changed from a site for preliminary worship of the God of Mount Tai into a temple to Bixia Yuanjun. Another small temple to the goddess was built on the back of the mountain during the Longqing period (1567–72; see Appendix, no. 60).[188] Paralleling the history of the worship of the God of Mount Tai, by the early seventeenth century, writers began referring to the lower, middle, and upper temples of Bixia Yuanjun. The main temple on the top of the mountain became known as the upper temple. The Numinous Palace (Lingying gong 靈應宮; no. 61), built in 1611, became the lower temple, and the Red Gate Temple (Hongmen gong 紅門宮; no. 11), built in 1626, became the middle temple.[189]

Bixia Yuanjun's aggrandizement extended beyond buildings. Kenneth Pomeranz has found that, in connection with her function as a fertility goddess, Bixia Yuanjun acquired the power to set life spans and judge the dead, roles earlier assigned to the God of Mount Tai. In addition, he has uncovered tales of worshipers of Bixia Yuanjun sacrificing their lives (or at least attempting to) as a tradeoff for a parent's recovery in a manner similar to fourteenth-century accounts of actual and fictional sacrifices to the God of Mount Tai.[190] In popular woodblock prints of pantheons from the late imperial period, Bixia Yuanjun and four assistant goddesses appear more and more regularly in conjunction with the gods of the Five Sacred Peaks (see Fig. 16).

The decline in the popularity of pilgrimages to pray to the God of Mount Tai and the simultaneous increase in pilgrimages in honor of Bixia Yuanjun can be at least partially explained by the general shift toward more accessible salvation and the increase in the popularity of female deities. In *Precious Volumes: An Introduction to Chinese Sectarian Scriptures from the Sixteenth and Seventeenth Centuries*, Daniel Overmyer remarks:

These traditions emphasized the religious possibilities available to ordinary people based in their families, all of whom are assured that they are buddhas within, children of the Mother of the universe, possessors of the internal elixir of immortality. Such folk are told that if they are faithful and pious they can be saved. . . . Thus it is that after death they can avoid purgatory and go directly to the Mother's paradise.[191]

Interestingly, this trend toward more accessible salvation bypassed the purgatory over which the God of Mount Tai presided. The followers of these traditions would probably be less inclined to make pilgrimages to worship a judge of the underworld.

Simultaneous with these changes in popular piety was a burgeoning of religious practices centered on goddesses, including Bixia Yuanjun. The most popular of these was undoubtedly Guanshiyin Pusa 观世音菩萨 (more commonly known as Guanyin 观音). Guanyin is the Chinese name for the Buddhist Bodhisattva of Compassion, Avalokiteśvara. When this deity first arrived in China from India, it was represented as male. By the late imperial period, however, Guanyin had transformed into a female deity. Another popular female deity, Mazu 妈祖, initially worshipped only along the southeast coast, gained wider appeal during the Yuan dynasty and great popularity during the Ming. Originally the miracle-performing daughter of a fisherman, Mazu was later given the title Tianhou 天后, or "Empress of Heaven."[192] The Eternal Mother is a deity found in many of the sectarian texts discussed by Overmyer.

Chün-fang Yü argues that the feminization of Guanyin coincided with the emergence of other goddesses:

The emergence of the feminine Kuan-yin must also be studied in the context of new cults of other goddesses . . . the Queen of Heaven (T'ien-hou, more familiarly known as Ma-tsu), the Goddess of Azure Cloud (Pi-hsia Yüan-chün [Bixia Yuanjun]), and later, the Eternal Mother. . . . When Neo-Confucianism was established as the official ideology functioning very much like a state religion in the Ming and Ch'ing, Kuan-yin was also completely transformed into a goddess. . . .

. . . The reason the feminine Kuan-yin and other new goddesses appeared at this particular time might be connected with the antifeminist stance of established religions, chief of which was undoubtedly Neo-Confucianism.[193]

The growth of pilgrimages and temples in honor of Bixia Yuanjun fits a general pattern of popular practice set against antifeminine, bureaucratic proscriptions.

Pilgrims had prayed to the God of Mount Tai primarily in his guise as the judge of the seventh court of purgatory. Because of his position as an official in the underworld, he was seen as austere and unforgiving and often portrayed overseeing tortures in the underworld (see Fig. 3, p. 11). In contrast, Bixia Yuanjun, like her counterparts Guanyin and Mazu and the Virgin Mary in the Christian West, was seen as compassionate and approachable (see Fig. 4, p. 13). She was especially efficacious in responding to prayers for children, particularly for male heirs.

These two mountain deities are representative of the differences between Chinese goddesses and male bureaucratic deities. Many male gods in the official pantheon were part of a celestial bureaucracy, which paralleled the strict hierarchy of the Chinese bureaucracy. The celestial pantheon began at the lowest level with the stove gods in individual households and local earth gods. Above the earth gods were city gods, and above them were regional gods. Only high officials could pray to the higher-level deities. Most people prayed to their local earth god to intervene on their behalf with higher-level deities.[194] Chinese goddesses, in contrast, were much more approachable. According to Steven Sangren, Chinese goddesses embody all the ideal traits of mothers and "cannot be conceived as less than totally responsive to the needs of their supplicants [children]."[195] He also argues that goddesses are more accessible than bureaucratic gods such as the God of Mount Tai:

While one has access to the ancestors or territorial-cult deities only as a representative of a patriline or household, one can approach female deities as an individual. Though all deities entertain requests for assistance, bureaucratic deities are expected to react as officials, moved in part by the intrinsic justice of the request but influenced as well by bribery and promises of payment for wishes granted. In contrast, female deities are moved less by concern for justice and the expectation of repayment than by a worshiper's devotion and dependence.[196]

Bixia Yuanjun fits this model well. Examples of her sympathetic interactions with worshipers are examined in detail in Chapter 1.

Another contrast between these two deities lies in the nature of their assistants. The God of Mount Tai, usually portrayed seated behind a tribunal desk, was assisted by bureaucrats (usually human) who kept records of crimes and confessions and by officers (usually demons) who performed tortures (see Fig. 3, p. 11). Bixia Yuanjun, however, was assisted by a communal group of compassionate goddesses, often portrayed watching a group of playful babies. Bixia Yuanjun was almost always accompanied by two goddesses and sometimes by four or even eight additional goddesses who specialized in various aspects of childbirth and early childhood.

Although Guanyin and Mazu were not part of the celestial bureaucracy, they were included on the list of deities who received imperial prayers. Despite imperial sponsorship of Bixia Yuanjun's cult during the Ming and Qing dynasties, she was never included on this list. Kenneth Pomeranz analyzes the possible reasons in "Power, Gender, and Pluralism in the Cult of the Goddess of Taishan." He argues that divergence from expected gender roles discouraged official canonization:

The leadership roles that the cult offered to women, the chance to participate in a religious sphere beyond the ancestral altar, and the cult's willingness to celebrate possible sources of female power besides maternity . . . were probably quite important to its appeal. Conversely, the importance of midwives, matchmakers, and other such women in the cult's leadership, the phenomenon of female pilgrimage, Bixia Yuanjun's own sexuality, and her apparent affinity for the obviously necessary but still threatening figure of the young daughter-in-law made it hard for some people to accept the cult as orthodox. . . .

But even these conflicts over gender may be seen as one particularly important manifestation of a more general problem: the cult's potential to serve as a conduit both for social groups that had important functions but no status in the Confucian order (eunuchs, yamen runners, matchmakers, and, in some sense, daughters-in-law) and for kinds of fervor, religious experience, and magical power that had no acknowledged place in orthodox religion and cosmology.[197]

These aspects of the cult of Bixia Yuanjun distinguish it from the worship of other goddesses and help to explain why it did not spread beyond northern China.

During the late imperial period, there were three main explanations or legends about the origins of Bixia Yuanjun. The different versions appealed to different segments of the society. The most prevalent story identified her as the daughter of a powerful male deity, most commonly the God of Mount Tai.[198] This lineage is found in many late imperial gazetteers, travelogues, and miscellaneous writings about Mount Tai written by male literati. Implicit in this genealogy is a hierarchy between the male, father deity and his daughter.

The second account of the origins of Bixia Yuanjun was also current among the highly educated elite. This version was a product of evidential learning, which became popular among many scholars during the late imperial period. One characteristic of this type of scholarship is the pursuit of the earliest possible source. Several scholars were not satisfied with the description of Bixia Yuanjun as the daughter of Mount Tai, because the evidence dated no further back than Song Zhenzong's discovery of the statue in 1008. This version of Bixia Yuanjun's origins traces her to an ancient story about the legendary Yellow Emperor. According to this story, the Yellow Emperor dispatched seven jade maidens to various places in the world. The scholars endorsing this interpretation argued that one of those maidens was sent to Mount Tai and later became known as Bixia Yuanjun. Proponents of this view included Gu Yanwu, one of the most famous practitioners of evidential scholarship.[199]

The third version of her origins was believed widely among the vast majority of the pilgrims. The main points are summarized in the earliest existing version, from the sixteenth century:

During the Later Han dynasty a devout man named Shi Shoudao 石守道[200] and his wife, surnamed Jin 金, gave birth to a daughter named Jade Leaf (Yuye 玉葉). At the age of three, she comprehended human relationships (renlun 人倫). At the age of seven, she always listened to Buddhist teachings and performed rituals to the Queen Mother of the West. At the age of fourteen, she went to live in the Yellow Flower Cave [see Appendix, no. 60] on Mount Tai, where she obtained perfection (xiu 修).[201]

This tale ties Bixia Yuanjun even more closely to the Queen Mother of the West. As mentioned in the section on mysticism, one of the Queen Mother's powers was to grant immortality. The name Jade Leaf is quite reminiscent of the general term for the Queen Mother's servants, the jade maidens. There is even a Tang poem that gives a jade maiden's name as Jade Flower.[202] A similar story is recorded in the seventeenth-century Precious Volume devoted to Bixia Yuanjun.[203] This legend and the corresponding site of her apotheosis on the backside of the mountain (no. 60) do not seem to have emerged until the early Ming period blossoming of her cult.

These three versions of Bixia Yuanjun's origins shed interesting light on differing views of her cult during the late imperial period. The first two versions, both endorsed by the literate elite, emphasize her relationship to a male authority figure. Implicit in those versions was the view that the goddess's power and authority ultimately derived from either the God of Mount Tai or the Yellow Emperor. The preference of elite men for these versions parallels Pomeranz's explanation for the lack of official standing for the cult.

In contrast, in the third version the goddess was originally a normal human being with no divine ancestors. This story fits the pattern of popular religion discussed above. Bixia Yuanjun was outside the bureaucratized male pantheon. Her humble origins were reminiscent of those of Mazu. This version of her origins dominated sectarian texts such as the *Lingying Taishan Niangniang baojuan* 靈應泰山娘娘實卷 (Precious volume of the divinely efficacious Goddess of Mount Tai) and was reinforced by the construction of a temple at the site of her apotheosis (see Appendix, no. 60).

Hierarchies of Sacred Spaces

Sacred spaces and pilgrimages have been theorized in various ways. Mircea Eliade distinguished sacred space as "qualitatively different" from all other space. He called the point created by the demarcation of sacred space the *axis mundi*, or the center of the world.[204] Although much of Eliade's conception of sacred space, especially his notion that it connects two worlds, is still generally accepted, recent scholarship has moved away from positing a single, monolithic view of any particular site and toward uncovering a multiplicity of meanings. For example, Edwin Bernbaum, in a book on sacred mountains, points out that "the attempt to reduce all views of sacred peaks to one underlying theme or archetype, no matter how comprehensive it may seem, actually limits the power of mountains as symbols."[205] John Eade and Michael Sallnow argue further that "what confers upon a major shrine its essential, universalistic character [is] its capacity to absorb and reflect a multiplicity of religious discourses, to be able to offer a variety of clients what each of them desires."[206] Simon Coleman and John Elsner caution, however, against going too far in the direction of multiple voices: "We do not deny that pilgrimage sites accommodate and perhaps even encourage multiple interpretations. . . . However, Eade and Sallnow's perspective runs the risk of discouraging analysis of how sacred space is orchestrated in pilgrimage sites, and how such organisation can have a considerable impact on the perspectives of pilgrims."[207] This view, that the study of pilgrimage must allow for multiple voices but place those voices within the context of the site itself, is also advanced by Bernbaum, Alan Morinis, and Chris Park.[208] This book follows a similar approach. The physical and historical background of the site is presented in Part I; Part II consists of analysis of multiple interpretations of Mount Tai, within the context of the material presented in Part I. A good example of placing pilgrimage within the context of the site itself is the evolution of a fertility cult at Mount Tai. It is unlikely that the cult of Bixia Yuanjun would have developed as much salience as it did if the site had not already had a long history as the source of life.

Navigating around the difficulties of Eliade's *axis mundi*, James Preston's essay "Spiritual Magnetism" offers a means for explaining hierarchies of pilgrimage sites. Preston defines his title term "simply as the power of a pilgrimage site to attract devotees."[209] He then delineates four factors that contribute to a particular site's spiritual magnetism: miraculous cures, apparitions of supernatural beings, sacred geography, and difficulty of access.[210] A single site's "spiritual magnetism" may derive from one factor or from a pair of them or even all four. Different sites have different levels of magnetism—a local pilgrimage site, for example, has weaker drawing power than a regional, national, or transnational site.

Mount Tai makes a good case study for Preston's model. The mountain's drawing power was based on all four of Preston's categories, and the strength of its magnetism is attested by the large numbers who traveled up its slopes. The vast majority of the pilgrims who prayed to the Goddess of Mount Tai were seeking a miraculous pregnancy for themselves, their wives, or their daughters-in-law. The difficult pilgrimage to the goddess's main temple on the summit of Mount Tai was undertaken only after every other option had been tried. A subsequent pregnancy would have been considered a miraculous cure, achieved through the intercession of Bixia Yuanjun. Apparitions of supernatural beings were perhaps less of a factor in Mount Tai's spiritual magnetism during the late imperial period. However, part of the mountain's sacred aura came from its past associations as a dwelling place of the immortals. As the second- or third-century CE bronze mirror inscription quoted above stated: "If you climb Mount Tai, you will see the immortals."[211] By "sacred geography," Preston means natural features that "inspire lofty emotions and high spiritual values."[212] His examples are the land of Israel for the Jews and wells, islands, and mountaintops for the Irish. Mount Tai, as the chief of the Five Sacred Peaks, a site for imperial legitimation rituals, the source of life, and the entrance to the underworld, ranks high on this scale of sacrality.

"Difficulty of access" is negotiable; if the journey is too arduous, the site will not attract many pilgrims. But if access is too easy, pilgrims may not feel they have earned enough merit or adequately demonstrated their devotion. The ascent of Mount Tai, if undertaken on one's own two feet, is indeed grueling. Furthermore, even though the practice does not seem to have been as common as it was at other sites, some pilgrims increased the labor of the climb by performing a kowtow every third step.[213] The mountain's proximity to major north–south transportation routes (both roads and the Grand Canal) and its position in the highly populated North China Plain meant that it, unlike many of China's sacred mountains, was relatively accessible for a large number of people. The presence of all four elements in Mount Tai's spiritual magnetism also demonstrates the adaptability of this sacred site. Different groups were probably drawn to the mountain more by one factor than by the others. For example, most of the illiterate women discussed in Part II, Chapter 1, were probably interested in the site's miraculous cures, whereas many of the literati men analyzed in Chapter 3 were attracted by the sacred geography.

On Mount Tai, the primary goal, or the spot on the mountain with the highest magnetism, changed depending on the era and the primary motivation or goal of the pilgrim. There was, however, one constant. For all pilgrims, the ultimate goal was the mountain's top. For all six categories explored above, the most important site was somewhere on the summit. In prehistoric times the top of Mount Tai was quite likely a site for worshiping the mountain itself as well as Heaven. This premise is supported by the symbol in Fig. 15. In addition, if the Wordless Stele (no. 48, Fig. 21) is a prehistoric megalith, this is further evidence of the antiquity of worship on the mountain's summit. This early activity probably involved worship of the mountain itself as a nature deity that could be petitioned in times of drought, flood, or famine and thanked during times of abundance. In addition, the mountain top, as closer to the heavens, was a logical place to converse with or appeal to sky deities.

Nature worship on Mount Tai during the late imperial period honored trees and springs. The most potent and popular ritual of nature worship, however, was viewing the sunrise. Mount Tai, the Eastern Sacred Peak, was directly connected with the sunrise, which, in turn, was associated with birth and renewal. Dawn on the mountain top focused the energies of many pilgrims to Mount Tai, especially the literati, whose poetry bears witness to their enthusiasm. One of the most common titles in late imperial collections of poems about Mount Tai is "Mount Tai Sunrise" ("Taishan richu" 泰山日出).

For pilgrimage groups honoring the Goddess of Mount Tai, however, the light that drew them to the top at dawn was incense burning in her temple (no. 58). Pilgrims vied with one another to be the first to light incense.[214] Many pilgrims climbed the mountain by lantern light at night to arrive at the top by the propitious time of dawn.

The focus for imperial ritual, beginning at the latest with Qin Shihuangdi's ascent in 219 BCE, was also the top of the mountain. For the five emperors who performed the *feng* and *shan* sacrifices at Mount Tai between 110 BCE and 1008 CE, the most potent ritual was the second, or main, *feng* ritual conducted on top of the mountain.

The hierarchy of historical sites also emphasizes Mount Tai's peak. The most revered and most popular visitor to Mount Tai was Confucius. One of the oldest and most widely known stories connecting Confucius with Mount Tai is the passage in the *Mencius* quoted above. For followers of the sage's route in the late imperial period, the goal was to stand where Confucius himself had "felt that the empire was small."[215] The specific site on the top where Confucius had stood was obviously open to debate (see, e.g., Appendix, nos. 40 and 43). However, no matter the specific site chosen, a pilgrim wishing to pay proper homage had to ascend to the mountain's summit.

For Mount Tai as a mystical site, the most potent place, again, was the summit. The implication of the statement on the Han mirror about seeing immortals was that one must climb to the top to see them and to have the opportunity to eat jade.[216] As we have seen, legends connected with Confucius demonstrated the mystical powers of the mountain. Li Bo's series of poems about Mount Tai are filled with mysticism and transcendence, and in two of the six poems, the place of transcendence is the summit:

> Proceeding with the clouds, I trust to the lasting wind[217]
>
> Touching heaven, I pluck the Calabash Gourd[218]

Although many of the sites on the mountain with names reflecting the goal of transcendence are not at the top, the names imply that these sites will further the individual in his or her actual physical ascent to the top and in achieving transcendence once this goal had been reached.

The focus of the Mount Tai fertility cult was, and still is, the Goddess of Mount Tai. The most efficacious site for prayers to this goddess is her main temple on top of Mount Tai (no. 58), where her cult began in 1008 with the discovery of a statue.

The focus for those visiting Mount Tai as a locus for death was the entrance to the underworld at the mountain's base (no. 63). The living, in the short term, could lessen a dead relative's suffering in purgatory through prayers at the temple at the entrance to the underworld at the base of Mount Tai. However, long-term support of dead ancestors required offerings generation after generation. Without a male heir, a family line would cease, and the ancestors would be deserted. This core belief system is behind the statement in the *Mencius* that the most unfilial act for a son was to not have an heir.[219] Long-term support of the ancestors depended on the continuance of the family line. Thus, the endless cycle of life and death, encapsulated in this single sacred site, connected the prayers for the dead with those for the yet unborn. Therefore, to honor their ancestors and avoid the stigma of the ultimate unfilial act, throughout the late imperial period millions of Chinese appealed for an heir to the Goddess of Mount Tai at her main temple on top of this sacred peak.

Two further examples demonstrate the priority of the summit over other sites on the mountain, by negation. At pilgrimage sites such as Mount Tai, where there were many possible places to present offerings and prayers, one might expect the largest temple to be the place with the greatest sacrality. However, on Mount Tai the largest temple is the Dai Temple at the base, probably because of a combination of economics and geography. It would have been prohibitively expensive to build such a large temple on top of the mountain. In addition, there was not enough level ground to contain such an edifice. Size alone does not dictate numinosity, however. As a seventeenth-century visitor noted, "The [Dai] Temple was cleaned and swept only twice a year when the local officials came for spring and autumn sacrifices. This was why, alas, the temple had long been in a state of disrepair."[220]

In many cults surrounding a religious figure, the site of enlightenment or apotheosis becomes a sacred space with a high level of spiritual magnetism. On Mount Tai, however, the site of Bixia Yuanjun's deification, located on the back of the mountain (no. 60), never superseded her temple on the summit as the dominant goal of pilgrims. Here again, it appears that the magnetism of the summit outweighed the site of the goddess's miraculous transformation. In addition, the temple on the summit dates to 1008, but the legends about the goddess's apotheosis probably did not develop until the Ming.

Interestingly, none of the focal points on top of the mountain is at the extreme peak. Clearly, other elements besides height contribute to making certain spaces on the mountain sacred. The main element is apparently an altar. Human alterations on Mount Tai, in addition to augmenting the natural essence of a site through careful application of *fengshui* tenets, also follow the long tradition of Chinese ritual practices. In the vast majority of acts of worship in China, prayers are made before an altar, on which sits an image or a tablet inscribed with the name of a deity or ancestor. Even if the image of a deity is not identified by a tablet, a written identification of the deity is usually found somewhere on the altar or directly on the image. Even illiterate pilgrims would name the deity in their prayers. Although it is difficult to date the origin of such practices, writing has been an important component of religious rituals since the oracle bones of the Shang dynasty (ca. 1766–1050 BCE). In order to honor and appeal to deities and ancestors, the proper rituals and offerings have to take place before an altar. The construction of the many shrines and temples on the mountain created appropriate sites for worship of the deities associated with Mount Tai. Even those who could not afford an altar in the home attempted to make at least a symbolic altar. In some instances, prayers were conducted before a woodblock print of a deity rather than before an altar. Even so, the image usually incorporated a picture of an altar.[221] On Bixia Yuanjun's birthday in 1995, I observed women pilgrims who could not afford the fee to climb to the top drawing an altar on the ground and placing their birthday cake offerings on it. They then knelt before their "altar," facing the mountaintop, and kowtowed (see Fig. 8).

Perhaps the most obvious evidence for the necessity of an altar comes from the *feng* sacrifices conducted on the mountaintop. Since the *feng* sacrifice used Mount Tai as an intermediary to send the emperor's prayers directly to Heaven, the highest peak would seem the logical choice for the altar. But although all these rituals occurred close to the summit, none took place on it, probably be-cause the sacrifice required a large earthen mound as an altar, which in turn required a larger, more protected, level site. In addition, the jade box containing the jade slips had to be buried in the altar mound. Since the peak of the mountain was bare rock, this pre-cluded its use as an altar mound.

Alan Morinis's introduction to *Sacred Journeys: The Anthropol-ogy of Pilgrimage* includes a useful typology of pilgrimage. As he notes, "A true typology of pilgrimages focuses on the pilgrims' journey and motivations, not on the destination shrines."[222] He lists six different types of pilgrimages, based on the primary moti-vation behind the pilgrimage:

Devotional pilgrimages "have as their goal encounter with, and honoring of, the shrine divinity, personage or symbol."

Instrumental pilgrimages "are undertaken to accomplish finite, worldly goals."

Normative pilgrimages occur "as a part of a ritual cycle, relating to either the life cycle or annual calendrical celebrations."

Obligatory pilgrimages are, as the name implies, required of believers. "The most famous . . . is the *hajj*, the fifth pillar of Islam that enjoins all Muslims to visit Mecca once in their lives."

Wandering pilgrimages have "no predetermined goal. The pilgrim sets out in the hope that his feet will be guided to a place that will satisfy his inner craving."

Initiatory pilgrimages "have as their purpose the transformation of the status or the state of participants."[223]

Many pilgrimage sites probably draw worshipers for only one or two of these reasons. Pilgrimages to a sacred spring or well, for ex-ample, would be almost exclusively instrumental. Chaucer's pil-grims sought the holy martyr Thomas à Becket both to honor him and to thank him for miraculous cures. Thus, they were on either a devotional or an instrumental pilgrimage.

Mount Tai, however, attracted pilgrims in four of Morinis's six categories, once again demonstrating that the mountain's wide-spread popularity resulted from its multiple identities. The two categories that do not apply to Mount Tai are obligatory and wandering. Besides Chinese Muslims who hope to undertake the *hajj* or the occasional abbot or master who sent an initiate on a spiritual quest, there have been no obligatory pilgrimages in China.[224] Similarly, all the pilgrims to Mount Tai seem to set out quite intentionally to travel there, rather than happening upon it in the course of their wanderings. Devotional pilgrimages to Mount Tai were undertaken primarily by male literati to honor Confucius and perhaps to present offerings to him in the Confucian Temple. This same group also journeyed to the mountain to honor, admire, and, in a sense, worship nature. The vast majority of pilgrimages were instrumental; people traveled to Mount Tai seeking pregnancies, good health, or good harvests. The most obvious normative pilgrimages to Mount Tai were connected with imperial legitimation rituals and the New Year's celebrations. In addition, prayers for a baby or for a recently departed relative were connected with the life cycle. Initiatory pilgrimages were undertaken by male literati who hoped to improve themselves while they were on the sacred slopes. In addition, women praying for sons were seeking a new identity as mothers, and prayers for relatives journeying through purgatory could assist those souls in reaching the status of ancestor.

Another important characteristic of sacred space is that it needs to be continually cultivated to retain its magnetism. On Mount Tai this phenomenon is particularly apparent in the three main temples to the God of Mount Tai. The middle of the three temples had sunk into disuse by the beginning of the Ming dynasty.[225] As mentioned above, Wang Shizhen in 1558 and 1559 deplored the dilapidation of the god's temple on top of the mountain.[226] In the early twentieth century, Chavannes noted that "The poverty of this edifice contrasts with the richness of the temple consecrated to the [Goddess of Mount Tai] . . . and demonstrates the point to which the antique, male divinity of Mount Tai has been eclipsed by the young goddess."[227] Commentaries from the seventeenth century note that the lower temple, the large Dai Temple, was used more often for entertainment and commerce than for prayers.[228] The incentive to maintain an edifice paralleled the popularity of its main deity. When offerings could no longer be made in a temple, its ability to draw worshipers vanished.

Morinis has also addressed the necessity for sites to be constantly renewed in order to attract worshipers:

The pilgrimage center must achieve a reputation for having a unique character and offering something available at no other place with which it competes for patronage. But there are constraints on how differentiated a shrine can be. It must remain within the known boundaries of its culture. Sacred centers accomplish this balancing of familiarity and differentiation by developing and projecting an image that is a magnification of some accepted ideals of the culture. . . . Cultural intensification of this sort is the central force in the creation, maintenance, and success of pilgrimage shrines. A center that ceases to embody an intensified version of cultural values goes into decline. New values and new representations of values spawn new centers.[229]

For Mount Tai, the new centers spawned by new values and representations were located on the mountain itself. Even though a particular site within the overall sacred space of the mountain might decline, the mountain itself still maintained its drawing power as pilgrims shifted from one focal point to another. And as noted by Morinis and by Coleman and Elsner, even though different groups within a society may have different motivations and expectations in journeying to a particular sacred site, all the groups operate "within the known boundaries of [their] culture."

The Economics of Attaining the Summit

Exact figures for the number of pilgrims during the late imperial period do not exist. However, based on various anecdotal and tax records, it seems likely that on average no fewer than 400,000 people made the journey each year.[230] Many traveled in pilgrimage or family groups, by donkey, cart, or wheelbarrow, or on foot. The system of inns and pilgrimage groups—including group package deals for entertainment, lodging, taxes, and transportation—was highly developed and efficient. In this section I examine the mechanics of the pilgrimage and the people who earned a livelihood by serving the pilgrims.

Although pilgrims traveled to Mount Tai throughout the year, the numbers varied considerably by the season. Zha Zhilong divided the year into three seasons: the first season lasted from the first lunar month through the fourth, the second from the fifth month through the eighth, and the last from the ninth through the twelfth. The first season was by far the busiest, followed by the last season.[231] The summer months, the period with the heaviest need for agricultural labor, were, not surprisingly, a time of few pilgrimages. During the spring season, the busiest days were New Year's, the first full moon of the year on the fifteenth of the first month, and Bixia Yuanjun's birthday (this date varied from region to region, but it occurred in either the third or fourth lunar month).[232]

From the middle of the Ming dynasty until the mid-twentieth century, the vast majority of pilgrims were illiterate peasant farmers and laborers who came to pray to Bixia Yuanjun at her main temple on top of Mount Tai (see Fig. 24). C. W. Mateer, writing in 1879, noted that groups of peasant pilgrims "had come as far as six or seven hundred *li* [300–350 kilometers]."[233] Dwight Baker, writing in the mid-1920s, listed more precise origins for some of the groups he encountered from outside Shandong: Baoding, Shunde, and Daming in Hebei province (known as Zhili province for most of the Qing period); Kaifeng in Henan province; Xuzhou in Jiangsu province.[234] The farthest of these places is Baoding, which is nearly 350 kilometers from Mount Tai. Of the extant stelae on the mountain, only two were erected by pilgrimage societies from outside Shandong province, both from Zhili province, about 300 kilometers north of Mount Tai.[235] Thus, Mount Tai's catchment area encompassed all of Shandong, southern Zhili, northern Jiangsu, northern Anhui, northwestern Henan, and possibly southwestern Shanxi provinces (see Fig. 25).[236] This area is probably best viewed as a series of concentric circles. The closer to the mountain, the lower the travel costs, and therefore the more people who made the pilgrimage.

The literate, elite visitors to Mount Tai originated from all over the empire. Typically, officials visited the mountain while en route to the capital or to a post. Those stationed near the mountain would almost certainly journey to the mountain during their tenure. Elite literati, including non-officials, would sometimes combine a visit to a friend in the area with an ascent up Mount Tai.

Many peasants traveled in organized associations (*hui* 會 or *she* 社), known most commonly as "incense societies" (*xianghui* 香會). Most of these groups were long-term associations and held regularly scheduled rituals and raised money to fund the pilgrimages.[237] These associations sometimes consisted of residents of a single neighborhood or village, but more often the members came from a number of adjacent villages. Since the cost of the journey was beyond the means of many potential pilgrims, especially for those who lived more than a day or two away, incense societies were an important component of the pilgrimage to Mount Tai. Many pilgrims, however, did not belong to a society, and it is difficult to determine the relative percentages. Susan Naquin, in her study of pilgrimages to a small mountain northwest of Beijing, also in honor of Bixia Yuanjun, estimates that at most 20 percent of the pilgrims belonged to societies.[238]

Certainly pilgrimage societies were not rare. Anecdotal evidence seems to support a figure somewhat higher than 20 percent. An official declaration from 1313 about pilgrimages in honor of the God of Mount Tai mentions that the pilgrims formed what Idema translates as "fraternities."[239] Chapters 68 and 69 of the seventeenth-century novel *Xingshi yinyuan zhuan* (Marriage destinies that will bring society to its senses), written under the pseudonym of Xizhousheng, are constructed around the journey of a pilgrimage society to Mount Tai.[240] Finally, Western accounts of the pilgrimage to Mount Tai imply that perhaps a majority of the pilgrims were members of these groups.[241]

The societies were a type of cooperative that used membership fees to raise the necessary capital for making the journey. Arthur Smith, a late nineteenth-century missionary in rural Shandong, left an excellent description of the organization of these societies:

The managers who have organized the society, proceed to loan this amount [from the membership fees] to some one who is willing to pay for its use not less than two or three per cent. a month. Such loans are generally for short periods. . . . When the time has expired, and principal and interest is collected, it is again loaned out, thus securing a very rapid accumulation of capital.

. . . [The] society gathers in its money at the end of three years, and those who can arrange to do so, accompany the expedition which sets out

soon after New Year. . . . The expenses at the inns, as well as those of
the carts employed, are defrayed from the common fund, but whatever
purchases each member wishes to make must be paid for with his
own money.[242]

Even though it is a satire, *Xingshi yinyuan zhuan* provides similar
descriptions of the functioning of a pilgrimage society, including
the loaning out of fees for a three-year period. It is possible that
such short-term loans made important contributions to the local
economies where the members lived.

The number of members in pilgrimage societies ranged "from a
half-dozen to fifty to even a hundred."[243] The leader or leaders of the
societies (*huishou* 會首) usually carried yellow, triangular flags, often with a red border and inscribed with the name of their society
and its place of origin.[244] The leaders would have been respected
members of the community chosen for their local standing, their
devoutness, their knowledge of Bixia Yuanjun and the rituals connected with her worship, and their experience with pilgrimages.
Some societies consisted only of men; we know of at least one that
had only women members. Most, however, contained both men
and women. Several groups of contemporary pilgrims with whom I
spoke in 1995 were led by older women whose authority stemmed
from their age, previously efficacious prayers, ritual knowledge, and
established relationship with Bixia Yuanjun.

Some pilgrimage societies donated portions of their earnings or
raised additional sums to pay for temple repairs, temple or altar
decorations, or memorial stelae. The inscriptions on these stelae
generally praise Mount Tai, the goddess Bixia Yuanjun, and, if appropriate, a particular temple. In addition, the stelae list the names
of the members of the society, beginning with the leaders. The list
is often divided by village, and sometimes the amount contributed
by each individual for the repairs or for the stele is indicated. A
large group of over twenty stelae erected by pilgrimage societies
between 1846 and 1937 is located on the west side of the pilgrimage
path just above the Red Gate Temple (no. 11; some of these stelae
can be seen in Figs. 8 and 12).

The earliest record of an organized society at Mount Tai is
found on a pair of large cast-iron water basins (*shui tong* 水桶)

dated 1101 and located in front of the main hall of the Dai Temple. Such basins were filled with water to be used in case of a fire. The donor society was from the district that included the town at the base of the mountain. The inscriptions on the basins give information about the society. Since this organization was local, its members may not have pooled funds to underwrite a pilgrimage, but, like later pilgrimage societies, the group was a religious society, the leader was called the *huishou*, and the inscriptions listed the members' names and their contributions.[245] As noted above, organized pilgrimage groups to worship the God of Mount Tai are mentioned in an official document dated 1313.[246] The earliest evidence of a pilgrimage society formed to worship the Goddess of Mount Tai comes from a stele from 1610 placed in a wall of the Myriad Transcendents Tower (no. 13) by a group from the Shandong provincial capital of Ji'nan.

Until recently, the predominant "paradigm" for examining pilgrimages was that developed by anthropologists Victor Turner and Edith Turner. Central to the Turners' conception is the notion of *communitas*, the bonds and camaraderie that form within a group of pilgrims on the road or at their destination. Specifically, they defined it as "a liminal phenomenon which combines the qualities of lowliness, sacredness, homogeneity, and comradeship. . . . The bonds of communitas are undifferentiated, [and] egalitarian."[247] As with Eliade's *axis mundi*, the universality of this concept has been questioned. As Coleman and Elsner remark, "the idea of pilgrimage as providing unproblematic access to 'communitas' has been criticised sharply by social scientists who argue that the Turners ignore the secularly inspired divisions between pilgrims."[248] Clearly a particular group at Mount Tai might exhibit some of the components of communitas, but there was apparently no bonding between groups of different social standing.

Communitas within any particular pilgrimage society would probably have been strong, given the members' common point of origin and their mutual membership in an organization that outlasted the pilgrimage. Interactions among family members traveling together in a less organized manner would have occurred along long-established lines. Whether such groups experienced communi-

tas with other groups while on the pilgrimage is a matter of specula-
tion. However, given dialect variations, interactions would have
been limited to those from the same region. The mode of transportation reflected the wealth of an association, and such differences
would have been another obstacle to intergroup communitas. All
impediments aside, however, all pilgrims who went to Mount Tai to
pray to Bixia Yuanjun had their devotion and its associated rituals in
common. Even if exchanges of conversation were not extensive, all
the pilgrims would have known that they shared common goals and
observed the same religious practices. Certain elements that the
Turners consider key for communitas, such as religious humility
and sacredness of purpose, applied to the pilgrims to Mount Tai.
Nonetheless, the hierarchy within pilgrimage societies, with their
business and spiritual leaders, or within families, prevent their being
completely "undifferentiated" and "egalitarian."

Those who did not travel to Mount Tai as part of a pilgrimage
society usually did so as members of family groups.[249] Almost no
one would have traveled by himself. Those who traveled in these
less organized groups were generally motivated by a vow. Vows to a
deity in China were of two main types: making a promise (xuyuan
許願) and fulfilling a promise (huanyuan 還願).[250] In the exchange of
a "promise," the supplicant pledged to perform a certain act if his or
her prayer were answered. Requests usually revolved around pressing life issues such as the birth of an heir, recovery from an illness,
or relief from debt or bad weather. One common promise was to
make a pilgrimage the following year. The promise might be made
by the person concerned or by someone else on their behalf. For example, a son might pledge to go on a pilgrimage if his parent recov-
ered from an illness. "Fulfillment" was the payment of a previous
pledge, perhaps made on a previous pilgrimage or at the supplicant's
home or local temple. Given the long-term planning of the more
organized pilgrimage societies, the members of these groups were
probably motivated less by the making of or the fulfillment of a
promise and more by the general benefits of gaining merit, escaping
calamities, good health, and forgiveness of sins.[251]

Fairly well-to-do pilgrims in the late imperial period, such as
those depicted in Xizhousheng's satirical novel, made the journey

to the mountain on donkeyback. More typically, however, the
men walked, and "the women and weaker members [were] placed
on donkeys or wheeled in barrows by the stronger."[252] Women
with bound feet were unlikely to make the long journey to the
mountain on foot. Again, donkeys were the more expensive option, and the wheelbarrows more common. These wheelbarrows
consisted of a rectangular platform with two handles at one end
and were also used for transporting goods to and from markets.
The single, large wheel was centered in front of the handles, in the
middle of the rectangle. The carrying space consisted of the narrow
ledges on either side of the wheel. Usually two women would sit
among or on top of the baggage, one on each side of the wheel.
The wheelbarrow was pushed from behind using the handles,
sometimes aided by another person pulling on ropes in the front.

Many of the pilgrims stayed at small inns during their journey to
the mountain. Such inns are mentioned in most of the thirteenth-
and fourteenth-century dramas discussed by Idema. The quality of
the accommodations would vary by the wealth of the society. In
addition to inns, pilgrims could also stay at small temples dedicated
to the Goddess of Mount Tai (usually called "goddess temples"
[niangniang miao 娘娘廟] or "Bixia Yuanjun Travel Palaces" [Bixia
Yuanjun xinggong 碧霞元君行宫]). These temples were located
about a day's journey apart all over Mount Tai's catchment area and
were much cheaper than inns. Baker mentions two of these temples:
one near the town of Dongping, seventy kilometers west and a little
south of Tai'an, and another in the provincial capital, Ji'nan, sixty
kilometers north of Tai'an.[253] Chavannes describes another of
these temples built in 1635 at Xiaotangshan 小堂山, fifty kilometers
northeast of Tai'an.[254] In 1995 I visited another of these temples on a
hill outside Boshan, seventy-five kilometers east of Tai'an (for the
locations of these temples, see Fig. 25).

These travel palaces, in addition to serving as hostels for traveling pilgrims, also served as local temples. Worshipers from the surrounding countryside could make the much shorter journey to
these temples to pray to the goddess at any time of the year. Furthermore, pilgrims who could not afford to join a society or soci-

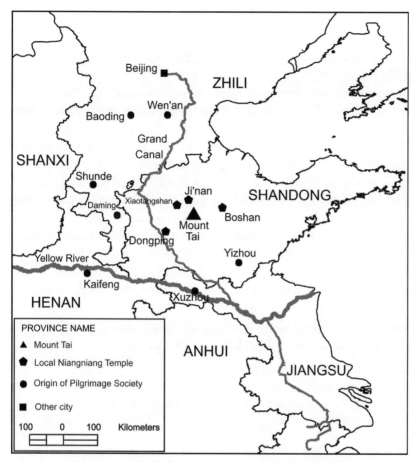

Fig. 25 Map showing pilgrimage association origins and local *Niangniang* temples, with 1820 boundaries (SOURCES: "China Historical GIS, Version: 2.0."; Baker, *T'ai Shan*, 9, 17; Chavannes, *Le T'ai Chan*, 31; Liu Yihou, "Liufang gujin"; "Chongxiu fenghuang'a Bixia Yuanjun xinggong beiji").

ety members in a year their group was not traveling to Mount Tai could make pilgrimages to these lesser temples, as the next best alternative to the main temple on top of Mount Tai.

Once pilgrims arrived at the mountain, they had several options for accommodations. The poorest would save money by climbing to the top during the night, thus avoiding having to spend a night in the more expensive inns at the base of the mountain. The phenomenon of pilgrims climbing at night created a picturesque sight of a string of lights bobbing up the mountain path—in the words of a seventeenth-century traveler—"like ten thousand bushels of glow-worms."[255]

Many pilgrims, however, spent one or two nights at the base of the mountain. Some found accommodations in combination temple/hostels located at the base of Mount Tai, just west of the city (Appendix, no. 72; and on the map in Fig. 5).[256] A stele dated 1182 states that prior to that time pilgrims had been allowed to spend the night in the large Dai Temple (no. 2) at the base of the mountain.[257] This temple does not seem to have been used for this purpose during the late imperial period. The travel palace of the Goddess of Mount Tai at the base of the mountain, however, could house only a small fraction of the pilgrims who arrived at Mount Tai. The God of War Temple (no. 66), adjacent to the pilgrimage path at the base of the mountain, also served as a native-place society for men, especially merchants, from Shanxi. Most pilgrims, however, stayed at large inns, which provided what today we would call a package tour. Zhang Dai 張岱 (1597–1684?) left this description:

Guides approach the travelers when they are only a few *li* away from the subprefectural city [Tai'an]. They lead the horses to the gate of the inn. . . . In front of the gate are a dozen stables. There are also a dozen apartments to house the prostitutes and an equal number of accommodations for the actors. I used to think that these matters were run by various people in the subprefecture; I did not know that they are managed by a [single] guide company. . . . The company sets a fixed rate for renting rooms, hiring sedan chairs, and paying mountain fees. . . . Visitors . . . are charged on the basis of three classes. . . . All visitors are met upon their arrival, entertained when they descend from the summit, and escorted when they leave.[258]

In a later account of this same visit, Zhang expressed his amazement at the efficiency of the inn where he stayed:

[Guests] came and went every day, but new arrivals never found their rooms unready; vegetarian and nonvegetarian meals never got mixed up. . . . It is simply unfathomable how the inn managed to do everything right. It is even more surprising that in the T'ai-an subprefecture there should have been five or six establishments comparable to our inn.[259]

These tour operators provided lodging, meals, stables, transportation up the mountain, payment of the government tax, and entertainment after the descent for thousands of pilgrims each day during the peak pilgrimage season.[260]

The actual ascent took two main forms. The vast majority walked, which takes four to six hours. This included many women who struggled up the mountain on bound feet. However, "besides the officials, and wealthier classes, a few of the common pilgrims, too old or infirm to walk, make the ascent in chairs."[261] These special sedan chairs, known as mountain chairs (*shanjiao* 山轎), have changed little over the past several centuries. Unlike the sedan chairs used on more level terrain, the two carriers of the mountain chairs walked side-by-side with the chair between them. The higher-end "package tours" included the cost of the sedan chair bearers, who carried people from the city all the way to the peak and back down again. Although the majority of those who walked could not afford to be carried, there was also a widely held belief that walking led to a greater accumulation of merit.[262] As mentioned above, a few pilgrims, out of a desire for greater merit or perhaps in fulfillment of a pledge, stopped every second or third step during their ascent to perform a kowtow.[263]

The chair bearers were an interesting group. This service was a monopoly of the Muslim community in Tai'an from at least the early twentieth century until the late 1930s.[264] Although this group did not worship at the temples on the mountain, they certainly benefited from the sacrality of the site. The mountain chair business still exists, but on a much smaller scale. Since pilgrims with the necessary funds can now take buses halfway up the mountain and from there take a gondola car to the top (since 1983), the market for chair rides has been drastically reduced. There are, however, still a few chair bearers who ply the pilgrimage path from the Middle Heavenly Gate (no. 23) up the steepest section of the trail to the Southern Heavenly Gate (no. 37). As in the past, the riders are the more well-to-do and, from my observations, include few if any of the rural pilgrims. The sizable Muslim community in Tai'an no longer holds a monopoly on the trade.

Another service provided by the inns in their package deals was payment of the Mount Tai incense tax required of every visitor. Pilgrims paid the incense tax to the inn where they stayed, which in turn took the tax to the Temple for Paying Homage from Afar and collected the tallies for their guests. The tax had to be paid in silver, a currency that rarely passed through the hands of peasant pilgrims. The inns, however, made money on this service, too, for they charged the pilgrims who paid them in copper a money-changing surcharge.[265]

From 1516 until 1571 there were six officials in charge of the incense tax. Two were stationed in the Temple for Paying Homage from Afar (no. 1) and another on the north side of the mountain. Their task was to collect the tax and issue tallies. An official at the Red Gate Tower (no. 11) and another at the Southern Heavenly Gate (no. 37) checked to make sure that everyone had a tally. Finally, an official stationed at the Bixia Temple on top of the mountain (no. 58) checked and then collected all the tallies. After 1571, the tally checkers at the Red Gate Tower and the Southern Heavenly Gate were eliminated, as was one of the tax collectors in the Temple for Paying Homage from Afar.[266]

From the institution of the tax in 1516 until 1580, tax collectors distinguished between Shandong residents and the residents of other provinces. Shandong residents paid five *fen* and four *li*, and nonresidents paid nine *fen* and four *li*.[267] In 1580 the tax was set at eight *fen* for everyone.[268] When Zhang Dai visited Mount Tai around 1628, the tax was twelve *fen*.[269] When the Qianlong emperor eliminated the tax in 1736, the rate was fourteen *fen*.[270]

In addition to the required tax, pilgrims were expected to shower a modest sum on each of the hundreds of beggars who made their living on Mount Tai. The organization of the beggars was quite extensive: "Year by year the beggar host comes in the first lunar month when the pilgrimage season begins. They take up their stations along the route, each at the post allotted by the beggars' guild, and there they live without stirring for the next three or four months."[271] Zhang Dai complained of them when he climbed the mountain around 1628, but he also noted the complex arrangements and not insignificant economic exchange: "As soon as I mounted the sedan chair my guide took out strings of tin pennies . . . [which] were thin as elm leaves and each of them inscribed with the characters *A-mi-t'o-fo*, were to be given to the beggars. . . . Although this type of coin circulated only among the local beggars, their total value was no less than several hundred taels of silver."[272] The pilgrims' largesse was not just a philanthropic gesture. In return for their charity, they received merit: "The pilgrims believe that anyone who climbs Tai-shan without giving something to each of them [the beggars] will not have his prayers answered when he reaches the top."[273]

Large quantities of spirit money and incense were also consumed in worshiping on Mount Tai. In the late nineteenth century Mateer counted twenty-eight shops catering to the ritual needs of pilgrims on the road between the Dai Temple and the First Heavenly Gate (no. 8).[274] Furthermore, each temple on the mountain vied for donations, either in larger amounts for special services, good works, repairs, and so on or through myriad, smaller individual outlays. These would range in scope with the means of the pilgrim, whether commoner or emperor.[275]

In addition to these mandatory expenses, many entrepreneurs supplied the incidental needs or impulses of festive pilgrims as they completed their meritorious climb. Some plied the pathway selling tea or snacks: "In the courtyards of many of them [temples], too, and on the landing outside all, were venders of tea and dough-balls and other delicacies . . . some having permanent establishments with home-made tables and sawhorse benches, most of them men who carried their stock in trade on a pole over their shoulders."[276] Additionally, it was not only at inns that entertainers found ready clients. Temple fairs held on holidays such as deities' birthdays and at New Year's were another important venue for economic exchange.[277] The fairs consisted of entertainers as well as vendors selling various wares in and around the grounds of the large Dai Temple in Tai'an:

During the continuance of the fair the front court is fitted with tea tables and stalls, &c., for the sale of various kinds of merchandize, and crowds of people are coming and going all day long. The articles sold are trinkets and toys, gold, silver, and brass jewelry and ornaments, beads and pearls, song books and play books, writing materials and fancy goods generally. There were also puppet shows. . . . There were also large numbers of fortune-tellers, sleight of hand performers, song-singers and musicians, haukers of medicines, plasters, and charms, also numerous small theatricals, many of the actors being women. Throughout the yards and courts of the temple thronged crowds of men, women and children.[278]

Pilgrims who had completed their sacred duties could relax, be entertained, and shop. Here was a chance to listen to new plays and operas. Many from small villages may have been able to buy items not available in their regular markets. Thus, the fairs connected with pilgrimage sites such as Mount Tai could be a mechanism for the spread of stories, legends, ideas, and goods. In addition, once the goal of praying to Bixia Yuanjun had been accomplished, there may have been more opportunity for different pilgrimage societies to interact (assuming their dialects were mutually intelligible) and perhaps form "communitas" bonds.

For the pilgrims themselves, these outlays were also investments. The pilgrimages were undertaken for spiritual as well as tangible needs. Both the austerities and the expense of the journey contributed to the merit the pilgrim achieved and made the deity more receptive to his or her request. Part II discusses the many spiritual, cultural, or political rewards pilgrims expected from their investment in a pilgrimage. Just to mention one key achievement for which the mountain was famous, receiving a son had very tangible social and economic consequences for the men and women involved during their lifetimes. After their death, their heirs would continue the exchange through spirit money.

Conclusion

This discussion has emphasized the multiple identities of this sacred mountain. Many of the specific sites on Mount Tai embodied more than one of those attributes. Some of the sites connected with Confucius, for example, which might at first seem to be entirely historical, were also associated with supernatural and mystical elements. Another example is the Fifth Rank Pine Tree (no. 29) connected with Qin Shihuangdi's visit. This site was certainly historical, but it was also associated with the imperial rituals performed by the emperor during his visit. In addition, the trees at this site were products of nature. As can be seen in Fig. 19, the pine trees are in close proximity to another object of nature worship, the Rock That Came Flying Down (no. 28). The pine trees were planted on a small paved terrace with a large pavilion, which became a place for climbers to rest and admire the surrounding natural scenery.

The majority of the people journeying to Mount Tai in the late imperial period approached the mountain from more than one perspective. They did not just appreciate the natural scenery or only pray for a son. The sacred site of Mount Tai, like Chinese religion in general, was multifaceted. Women who came to pray to the Goddess of Mount Tai for sons almost certainly interacted with the sacred site on other levels as well. Several of the fertility rituals derived from earlier nature worship of stones and trees. Some women participated in the ritual welcoming of the sunrise from the mountain's summit. They probably heard stories about some of the historic sites. Some also sacrificed themselves from "Abandon Life Cliff," calling upon the mountain's connections with death and the underworld. Male villagers, in addition to praying for departed ancestors at the entrance to purgatory, also supplicated Bixia Yuanjun for male heirs. Although most literati focused on the historic sites and interacted with nature as a means for self-cultivation, a few also prayed in temples to the God of Mount Tai, Bixia Yuanjun, and Confucius.

Although the visitors' interactions, motivations, and practices were multifarious throughout history, trends are visible in the mountain's general character. In pre-Qin times, the mountain, as the source of life, was the leader of the Five Sacred Peaks. It was also an important site for potent legitimating rituals. Indeed, the phrase "'going to T'ai-shan' assumed a powerful political meaning: it signified gaining possession over the empire."[279] From pre-Qin times through the early Han, the mountain was a site accessible only to a select few. Emperors announced their reception of the Mandate of Heaven, and sages such as Confucius experienced long-range sight from the mountain's heights. Both Qin Shihuangdi and Han Wudi surrounded their rites with secrecy in an attempt to maintain the exclusiveness of the site. When Han Guangwudi performed the rites in 56 CE, however, he explicitly made them far more public by performing them in front of a large group of officials.

By the first century BCE, Mount Tai was connected with the afterlife. By 250 CE the meaning of the term "going to Mount Tai" had become a euphemism for "dying."[280] As the belief that the entrance to the underworld was at Mount Tai gained popularity, especially as the mountain was absorbed into the Buddhist and Daoist concepts of purgatory, the mountain became significant for all people. By the seventh century CE, the God of Mount Tai had taken on the guise of the judge of the seventh court of purgatory, a deity who could be petitioned by anyone. Access to the mountain was still fairly restricted during the Tang and Song dynasties, limited to a select group consisting of emperors, officials, and mystic poets.

By the thirteenth century, however, large-scale pilgrimages had opened the mountain to all types of people. Subsequently, the most popular deity on the mountain, the Goddess of Mount Tai, provided supplicants with male heirs, and once again the mountain's primary focus for the majority of visitors was on life. All the beliefs, legends, and sacrality of this mountain as a locus for nature worship, imperial ritual, history, mysticism, death, and life melded together to create the context for the various groups examined in detail in Part II who ascended Mount Tai during the late imperial period.

PART II

Late Imperial
Pilgrimages

CHAPTER I

Pilgrimage as Popular Agency

Women and Men Seeking

Children and Heirs

The vast majority of visitors to Mount Tai in the late imperial period were non-elites who traveled in pilgrimage associations and family groups to pray in the main temple to Bixia Yuanjun near the mountain's summit. The majority came from poor rural areas in the pilgrimage catchment area. Most were illiterate. Some, of course, came from urban areas, and some were at least semi-literate. But for all, the primary motive was to pray for a son. As we shall see, however, although the women and men discussed in this chapter had much in common, differences in gender roles and expectations influenced their actions on the mountain and the overall identities of these members of late imperial Chinese society.

Elite Constraints on Popular Agency

The ideal Confucian social system was a pyramid-shaped hierarchy, with upright and moral leaders at the top. For the society to function correctly, every household—the blocks making up the pyramid's base—had to observe correct moral practices. One of the duties of the local-level representatives of the central government was to encourage correct mores within their jurisdictions. Prior to their first appointment, most magistrates had studied only the Confucian classics and knew little about the day-to-day work-

ings of the bureaucracy. In addition, since Ming and Qing law for-
bade serving in one's home province, the magistrates often did not
understand the local dialect or know local customs. In response,
handbooks for magistrates became quite widespread during the late
imperial period. One popular guide, written in 1694 by Huang Liuhong (黄六鴻) and reprinted numerous times throughout the Qing
dynasty, addressed a number of issues pertinent to popular pilgrimages. For example, Huang identified "correct" religious practice:

> In ancient times people worshiped only their ancestors to show that they
> remembered their origins; they did not worship anything else. People of
> subsequent generations, misled by the idea of the existence of spiritual be-
> ings, worshiped and implored blessings from myriad gods. Thus sacrificial
> ceremonies were performed in an unorthodox way. People abandoned
> the true way of worship and believed in witchcraft and incantations.[1]

Huang cited a well-known passage from the *Analects* about religion:
"Confucius said, 'Devote yourself earnestly to the duties due to
men, and respect spiritual beings but keep them at a distance. This
may be called wisdom.' "[2] In another section, Huang explicitly advised magistrates about which religious practices to encourage:
"The magistrate therefore should issue proclamations to the effect
that with the exception of the people's own ancestors and the officially sanctioned gods, such as the city god and the gods in charge
of weather-related phenomena, which influence the livelihood of
the people, they should not worship any bogus deity."[3] Huang and
other advocates of a strict social order apparently felt that people
were being lured by heterodox and superstitious beliefs.

Elite ideals were also expressed in the "household instructions"
(*jiaxun* 家訓) often included in family genealogies and quite common by the mid-Ming.[4] Although these rules were sometimes more
permissive about religious practices than more official sources such
as magistrates' handbooks, they often stressed the primacy of ancestor worship.[5] Indeed, in one set of household instructions from
1849 three of twelve short rules refer to ancestor worship:

> Repair the ancestral temple.
> Establish ritual fields.
> Preserve ancestral graves.[6]

A number of restrictions in these elite sources focused specifically on the seclusion of women. According to Huang Liuhong, for example, "Staying within the confines of their homes is the proper behavior of women with correct upbringing."[7] A refrain common in household instructions echoes this sentiment: "Maintain the dignity of the women's apartments."[8] Magistrates thus found the moral system they had studied with such great diligence for the examinations reinforced in their own lineages' rules as well as in the handbooks they read to prepare themselves for their role as representative of the government.

Literati apprehensions about women appearing in public and skepticism about popular religion found combined expression in injunctions against allowing women to visit temples, in both household instructions and magistrates' handbooks. In an article on clan rules, Hui-chen Wang Liu paraphrases two different sets of household instructions from the mid- to late nineteenth century on women visiting temples: "It is regarded as revoltingly vulgar for females to brush shoulders with strangers, and especially for them to make pilgrimages to temples."[9] The dominant attitudes leading to "prohibitions concerning wives were animated by an underlying sexual anxiety."[10] Elite men worried that by mingling with strange men, women would endanger their chastity. This fear of illicit sexual activities in temples was quite explicit in Huang's advice to county magistrates. Huang discussed what he believed women actually did in temples under the pretext of worship in two different sections of his handbook. In the section entitled "Prohibiting Indiscriminate Worshiping," Huang claimed that sometimes women "actually participated in orgies on the premises." And in "Prohibiting Women from Visiting Temples," he asserted that women "seek liaisons with dissipated youths in secret passages of monasteries."[11]

Literati fear of the potential subversive power of temples in relation to sexuality is vividly evident in an episode from the erotic novel *The Carnal Prayer Mat* (*Rou putuan* 肉蒲團) by Li Yu (李漁, ca. 1610–80). The novel was written in 1657 and reprinted in at least a dozen different editions during the eighteenth and nineteenth centuries.[12] Near the beginning of the novel, the main character, called Vesperus in the translation by Patrick Hanan, takes up residence in a temple where women pray for babies. Although it is not a *niangniang* temple, the anxieties expressed in the novel could easily be transferred to those temples as well. The rationale for Vesperus's choice of residence is explained as follows:

Why was he willing to pay such a high rent to stay at this temple? Because the Immortal Zhang was extremely efficacious and women flocked to him from far and wide to pray for sons. It was Vesperus's idea to treat the temple as an examination hall. . . . Sure enough, he found that every day brought several groups of ladies to the temple to burn incense. . . .

Vesperus rose early each morning and, dressed as smartly as the leading man in a play, paced endlessly back and forth. . . . When he saw any women approaching, he would duck out of sight behind the throne and listen while the Taoist priests communicated the women's prayers. He would watch as the women took incense sticks and knelt down, carefully observing their looks and demeanor.[13]

Throughout the novel Vesperus has numerous adulterous affairs, several with women he first observed at the temple. Since his behavior clashed with the ideal social and moral system, *The Carnal Prayer Mat*, like all Chinese erotic "novels[,] can end only with the libertine's punishment and repentance."[14] The eventual punishment of the adulterer, however, would certainly do nothing to alleviate the sexual anxieties male readers might have had about allowing their wives or daughters-in-law to visit temples.

Unscrupulous men were not the only perceived threat to women who frequented temples. Huang believed that other women, particularly those from outside literati households, were just as likely to lead wives and daughters astray, often acting as co-conspirators in illicit affairs: "Female intermediaries, such as marriage brokers, procuresses, female quacks, midwives, sorceresses, or Buddhist or Taoist nuns, often act as go-betweens for people indulging in sensual debauchery. Many innocent women from good families are enticed by these female ruffians."[15]

In addition to the dangers of sexual misconduct, many elite men sought to prevent women from visiting temples because women were often seen as the source of superstitious or heterodox practices within a family.[16] In a set of late nineteenth-century lineage rules, a patriarch worried about the possibilities of heterodoxy:

" 'There is no more degenerate custom than for wives to visit temples, burn incense, go out to the lantern festival, watch plays, or to contract sworn sister relationships and to consort with monks, nuns or shamans.' "[17] Thus, from the male literati perspective, a family's honor, prestige, and stability were endangered on two fronts if their women visited temples. Women's chastity and purity were endangered by encounters with strange men, and ritual and religious orthodoxy were at risk because women might be beguiled by false beliefs. Given the anxieties about women venturing outside their household compound or visiting local temples, pilgrimages to distant sites, from a male literati perspective, were to be avoided at all costs. On such a journey, the chance of sexual encounters and exposure to sectarian religions was far greater than during a trip across town.

The late seventeenth-century novel *Xingshi yinyuan zhuan* is a scathing criticism of what the author saw as the moral depravity of contemporary society, including pilgrimages by women. As Glen Dudbridge notes, "The author's pseudonym Scholar of the Western Chou (西周生) [Xizhousheng] . . . betray[s] an attitude of high-minded nostalgia for a society of archaic Confucian perfection, and his book presents a complex commentary on that lost utopia, making a rich use of satire by inversion."[18]

The novel contains two chapters about a group of women on a pilgrimage to Mount Tai. The wife, Xue Sujie, insists on going to Mount Tai against the wishes of her husband, Di Xichen, and her father-in-law. The pilgrimage is organized by two women who are portrayed as using a pilgrimage society to gain both economically and socially from association with the upper-class Xue Sujie. At one point, Xue Sujie's brother, Xue Rubian, in discussing his sister's plans with another character, describes the sedan chairs used on the mountain to carry wealthier pilgrims to the top: "Haven't you seen people riding in those mountain chairs? It's all right on the way up, but on the way down they sit in the chair facing backward, the women face to face with the carriers; if the woman falls backward, her feet are more or less right on the carriers' shoulders." Behind this comment is the view that a woman's feet were among, if not *the*, most erotic parts of her anatomy. A little later in the story, Xue Rubian tries to convince his sister not to join the pilgrimage: "In my view, sister, you ought not to go. Do women from good families join societies and go on pilgrimages with other folk? . . . Should someone from a respectable family go running through the streets burning incense, waving flags, and beating drums along the road to Tai'an zhou, showing their face in full view?"[19] This criticism of women abandoning all decorum and leaving their proper place of seclusion stands in marked contrast to the celebration of the feats of well-respected literati intoxicated by the grandeur of Mount Tai (see Chapter 3).

In order to see the statue of the Goddess of Mount Tai in the temple at the top of the mountain, it was necessary to stand on something. In the novel, Xue Sujie climbs on her husband's shoulders "while he grasped her two legs with his hands."[20] Here Sujie's feet are in full view. This single scene concentrates what the author was trying to express in his novel. As Dudbridge notes, "Here pilgrimage, marriage, social defiance, gentry nausea and authorial prurience all strike their boldest, most memorable attitudes."[21] The sight of Xue Sujie using her husband as a stepstool to the heights of communion with the increasingly powerful goddess is one literatus's response to the dangers of women empowering themselves on pilgrimage to Mount Tai and, by implication, the danger of empowering women within any context.

These injunctions did apparently keep elite women away from Mount Tai, or at least kept their journeys out of the written record. Many non-elite women did, however, make the pilgrimage to Mount Tai. It is difficult to determine the exact percentage of pilgrims who were women. For the pilgrimage in honor of Bixia Yuanjun at the smaller site of Miaofengshan, northwest of Beijing, Naquin believes that women made up less than 10 percent of the pilgrims in the early twentieth century.[22] Anecdotal accounts from Chinese and foreign visitors imply that well over 10 percent of the pilgrims to Mount Tai were women.[23] Kenneth Pomeranz, in his study of Bixia Yuanjun, asserts that women constituted a majority of the pilgrims to Mount Tai. Although possible, the evidence for this statement is not conclusive.[24]

The only solid evidence for the percentage of female pilgrims comes from stelae erected by pilgrimage societies. Thirty-eight pilgrimage society stelae from several sites on Mount Tai are summarized in Table 1. The stelae date from 1610 to 1937, with most from the nineteenth and early twentieth centuries. These stelae list a total of nearly 12,000 names, of which just over 3,950, or 33.3 percent, are those of women. Ten of these societies consisted only of males. All but one of the earliest sixteen associations listed women members. One stele from 1830 lists 101 members, all of whom were women. Obviously these stelae represent only a small portion of all the pilgrimage societies that visited Mount Tai and do not take into account the pilgrims who did not belong to societies. Nonetheless, in combination with the anecdotal evidence, it seems reasonable to conclude that at least one third, but possibly more, of the pilgrims to Mount Tai during the late imperial period were women.[25]

Bixia Yuanjun and Popular Agency

Non-elite men and women who prayed to Bixia Yuanjun and her companion deities seem to have been attracted to them for the same reasons that made other goddesses such as Guanyin and Mazu so popular. Part of Bixia Yuanjun's appeal was her equal treatment of all people. In this, she is like other Chinese goddesses, who, "unlike their male counterparts, do not favor the wealthy and influential over the poor, insiders over outsiders, or men over women."[26] Bixia Yuanjun was endowed with these generous and compassionate traits in popular religious texts, which were written primarily for lay religious believers. In a seventeenth-century precious volume or *baojuan*, Bixia Yuanjun is described as:

> without partisanship
> no matter whether stupid or estimable
> no matter whether male
> no matter whether female
> no matter whether poor or rich
> no matter whether nobly [born]
> no matter whether low [born]
> [Bixia Yuanjun] sees and judges all the same[27]

Table 1

Pilgrimage Society Stelae Inscription Data

	Year	Number of women	Total members	Percent women	Notes	Location on Fig. 5
1	1610	7	42	16.7%		no. 13
2	1673	235	626	37.5		no. 15
3	1721	69	128	53.9	4 leaders, 2 women	no. 60
4	1779	2	109	1.8		no. 15
5	1779	0	9	0	Wen'an county, Shuntian prefecture, Zhili	no. 15
6	1783	118	168	70.2		no. 4
7	1789	1	17	5.9	Wen'an county, Shuntian prefecture, Zhili, 1 man, his mother, 1 other man noted	no. 15
8	1825	247	616	40.1	2 leaders, 1 woman	no. 11
9	1830	101	101	100		no. 4
10	1832	99	139	71.2		no. 11
11	1844	48	290	16.6	4 leaders, all women	no. 4
12	1846	85	129	65.9		between 11 and 13
13	1846	58	101	57.4		no. 4
14	1855	124	260	47.7		between 11 and 13
15	1858	112	144	77.8		between 11 and 13
16	1869	50	100	50		between 11 and 13
17	1869	0	198	0		between 11 and 13
18	1886	0	98	0		between 11 and 13

No.	Year			%		
19	1887	10	22	45.5		no. 60
20	1888	2	32	6.3		between 11 and 13
21	1892	0	14	0		between 11 and 13
22	1893	124	1,324	9.4		no. 11
23	1899	0	32	0		between 11 and 13
24	1900	0	30	0		between 11 and 13
25	1912	110	521	21.1		between 11 and 13
26	1914	52	68	76.5		between 11 and 13
27	1915	0	36	0		between 11 and 13
28	1915	315	830	38		between 11 and 13
29	1915	26	70	37.1		between 11 and 13
30	1921	0	322	0		between 11 and 13
31	1922	192	746	25.7	10 leaders, 7 women	between 11 and 13
32	1922	58	182	31.9		between 11 and 13
33	1924	39	410	9.5	26 leaders, 22 women	no. 11
34	1924	0	135	0		between 11 and 13
35	1931	50	100	50	2 women, 1 man specially noted	between 11 and 13
36	1935	11	35	31.4		between 11 and 13
37	1937	0	22	0		between 11 and 13
38	?	1,612	3,680	43.8	no date, probably 1920s–1930s	between 11 and 13
	TOTAL	3,957	11,886	33.3%		

This was a marked difference from the mundane world as defined by laws. The punishments in the Ming and Qing legal codes varied according to the status and gender of the perpetrator and the victim. In addition, wealthy people had a distinct advantage in lawsuits. The ideal orthodox, hierarchical moral and social system placed many people in inferior positions. The lower echelons' attraction to a deity who did not focus on maintaining the social hierarchy is not surprising.

In another popular religious source, a *miaojing* or wondrous scripture dated to around 1607, Bixia Yuanjun was assigned the specific task of looking after the welfare of women:

At the end of the millennium, people followed [a course that] opposed the ancient Dao. . . . It reached the point that there were women who did not know their previous lives nor the karma which [they] were receiving in their present lives. . . . [Women] had improper desires and greed. . . . [Women] insulted their parents-in-law, deceived and disgraced their sisters-in-law. [Women] were purposely unvirtuous and they abused their children. . . . [Bixia Yuanjun] watched the multitudes who suffered from these degeneracies. [She] was ceaselessly sympathetic and compassionate in teaching enlightenment to womenkind. [She] got the masses [of women] out of torment.[28]

The difference in the type of justice meted out by the two Mount Tai deities is marked. Whereas the God of Mount Tai, as a judge in the underworld, often invoked torture, Bixia Yuanjun was sympathetic and sought to end torment through self-enlightenment.

Also popular are myths or legends about how Bixia Yuanjun came to be in charge of Mount Tai. This legend exists today in several versions, which vary only in details. A convocation of the gods realizes that Mount Tai is the only mountain without a ruling deity. They agree that this should be remedied and that the deity who can prove she or he reached the top of the mountain first will become the ruler of Mount Tai. A god proceeds to bury a wooden fish at the top of Mount Tai as his proof. Bixia Yuanjun is informed of this by a friendly old woman, who in some versions is the goddess Guanyin. The old woman tells Bixia Yuanjun to climb the mountain, dig up the wooden fish, bury one of her embroidered shoes further down, and then rebury the fish above her shoe.

When the assembly of gods views the evidence, control of Mount Tai goes to Bixia Yuanjun.[29]

Bixia Yuanjun the trickster appears even more human and therefore more approachable. Mahadev Apte has argued that joking brings the participants closer together.[30] In an article about a playful medieval French saint, Amy Remensnyder shows that the saint's joking created intimacy between herself and her believers.[31] The legends about Bixia Yuanjun similarly create personal relationships between the goddess and her followers.

Gender and Family Duties

Male prerogatives in late imperial China meant that they could freely travel outside the home, could become officials, were not affected by restrictions on the ownership of property, and were not discouraged from taking long journeys. Although many factors contributed to the favoring of men over women, one of the most influential was ancestor worship. The Chinese system of ancestor worship was connected with the concept of filial piety (*xiao* 孝). The character *xiao* symbolizes this all-encompassing concept quite succinctly. The character consists of an elder (*lao* 老) being carried or held up by a child (*zi* 子). Filial piety was a reciprocal, albeit hierarchical, relationship. Parents brought their children into the world and protected them and supported them in their childhood. In return, children, particularly sons, were to respect and obey their parents and support them in their old age. Ancestor worship was similarly reciprocal and hierarchical. The dead relied on their descendants to provide them with the correct offerings at appropriate times throughout every year and to care for their graves. In return, dead ancestors satisfied with the respect shown by their descendants aided living family members. "A person worships his ancestors because he is obligated to do so as an heir or descendant. . . . But neglect of worship is the most common reason given for misfortunes attributed to the agency of the ancestors."[32]

Ancestor worship was patrilineal in its organization. Male ancestors were worshiped by male descendants. Without a male heir, the entire line of ancestors would be left unattended. A set of family instructions from the early twentieth century presents an interesting formulation of the eternal patriline: "What Buddhists refer to as previous lives and the lives to come stems from their theory of rebirth and transmigration of souls. I think what has happened before yesterday—the father and the ancestors—are really the previous lives, and that what will happen after today—the sons and the grandsons—are really the lives to come."[33] Thus, "in the Chinese family system, parents' foremost obligation was rearing a male heir to carry on the descent line. This imperative introduced a decided preference for sons into reproductive decisions, especially among ordinary commoners with limited means."[34] Indeed, according to Mencius, the most unfilial act of all was not having an heir.[35] Thus, although being a man brought with it many privileges, it meant a sometimes all-encompassing obligation to produce a son. Indeed, "if a Chinese died before his father, the father beat the coffin— symbolically punishing the son for unfilially having abandoned his duties of caring for his parents in this world and the next."[36]

The importance of sons can be seen in household instructions. As Furth notes, they "were focused on sons, who were imagined as physically adult, sexually developed, capable of work, and, above all, likely to marry. The patriarchs addressed these sons personally, whereas their wives were spoken of in the third person, as outsiders and dependents to be managed by others." Furthermore, "Like the descent line itself, the instructions ideally formed part of a chain of transmission along a continuum that transcended mortality." Both the emphasis on male family members and the linkage between the past and the future can be seen in an excerpt from Huo Tao's (1487– 1540) "Report to the Ancestors' Temple": May our Ancestors above confirm this law and we descendants below keep it. Send down wealth and blessings, giving us health and long life. Bring us sons and grandsons and a good reputation in future generations. Protect this house: let it not be cut short, but grant it prosperity."[37]

The actions of male pilgrims on Mount Tai demonstrate the importance they placed on fulfilling their familial duties. Because they saw themselves as situated between their ancestors and their descendants—the past and the future, death and life—they focused on both the God of Mount Tai and Bixia Yuanjun. To the God of

Mount Tai, they made offerings to expedite deceased relatives' journeys through purgatory, and to Bixia Yuanjun, they prayed for heirs, to project their families into the future.

The offerings and prayers on behalf of the dead took place at the entrance to purgatory at the base of the mountain, in the temples on Mount Haoli (Fig. 5, no. 63). When Chavannes visited the site in 1907, he observed "a veritable forest of funeral stelae" erected in the compounds of these temples. Most of these stelae were erected jointly by members of one or more communities, joined together in a religious association, to honor deceased ancestors. Many of the stelae identify the area as the "site where one makes offerings to relatives of the three previous generations."[38] Unfortunately, this "forest" was subsequently harvested for its stone, and a detailed content analysis is not possible. However, Chavannes reproduced what he described as two representative examples.

Ancestral stele dating from 1903:

Shandong, Ji'nan prefecture, Changshan county, eastern circuit, association of the communities of Five Mile Bridge and Dao Village. Tablet (*wei* 位) for relatives of the three previous generations.[39]

Ancestral stele dating from 1906:

Shandong, Ji'nan prefecture, Changshan county, southern circuit, Meng Family Dike village residents sacrifice with respect at the place where reside [the souls] of their ancestors.[40]

Although these short inscriptions do not explicitly state which members of these communities erected them, since all ancestors belonged to male lines of descent, it was quite likely that men were the predominant worshipers at Mount Haoli. The first inscription cited above in particular uses language found in other contexts of male ancestor worship. The term *wei* (位), for example, was also used for ancestral tablets placed on altars within the household or in lineage halls. And men, not women, were the expected performers of major rituals honoring ancestors and their soul tablets.

In *Xingshi yinyuan zhuan*, the pilgrimage society stops at the temples on Mount Haoli.[41] Although the details of this particular episode are excessive and highly moralizing, it is significant that the author chose to highlight the husband's activities on behalf of his ancestors at this site for intercession. The main focus of chapters 68 and 69 is the corruption of the two female pilgrimage society leaders and the dangers of allowing women to go on pilgrimage to Bixia Yuanjun's main temple. By the end of chapter 69, the author has certainly accomplished this, and he could easily have ended the episode without a visit to Mount Haoli. Despite the author's highly satirical and exaggerated style, he was apparently familiar with pilgrimages to the mountain, as is attested in his descriptions of the pilgrimage society and the package tour supplied by the inn. Therefore he must have found the men's practices at the temples on Mount Haoli disturbing enough to warrant his attention. Since he had already amply criticized female religious practices in his descriptions of the pilgrimage to Bixia Yuanjun's main temple, his intent seems to have been to chastise another group in this scene. The character the author highlights in this section is Di Xichen, the husband of Xue Sujie, and the object of his censure is the irrational behavior of a son who mistakes the moneymaking efforts of the priests as filial duty.

Male pilgrims prayed for sons in the context of continuing their family line, but their journeys reveal additional aspects of their identities. Some focused on the God of Mount Tai as a judge in the underworld, hoping that he would intercede with the bureaucracy in purgatory on behalf of recently departed relatives. Literati accounts also suggest that lower-class men made the pilgrimage primarily to escort female family members, who were the real pilgrims. Some went to assist women, such as a son Mary Mullikin saw in the 1920s or 1930s carrying his mother both up and down the mountain.[42] Paul Bergen, writing in 1888, observed that "sometimes whole families make the journey, in which case the women and weaker members are placed on donkeys or wheeled in barrows by the stronger."[43] Hampden DuBose observed "aged matrons, supported by their grandsons" around 1885.[44] Others may have been prompted, as the weak husband in *Xingshi yinyuan zhuan* was, by a desire to protect or control their wives' public conduct and interactions with strange men and to prevent unsanctioned female reconstructions of identity. Men may also have been motivated by the strong mother-son bond, as suggested in the examples above.

Thus male pilgrims, no matter which motivation dominated, were at least partially acting out of familial duty.

Men and women were particularly attracted by the goddess's efficacy in granting miraculous pregnancies. Not surprisingly, this was the main reason that women were drawn to the goddess. Thus, the men and women in pilgrimage societies or familial groups journeying to Mount Tai alike seem to have shared the goal of an heir. Men, however, would not have interacted with goddesses in the same manner as women; nor was their motivation the same. Although both genders prayed for baby boys, the women concentrated on sons as a means of strengthening their position in the family in the present and during their old age, whereas the men sought heirs to project their family indefinitely into the future.

In seeking a baby boy, both the husband and the wife sought the identity of being a parent. Both groups were apparently upholding the principle of filial piety by praying for baby boys. Yet even this underlying principle of Chinese society was open to differing interpretations and desires, particularly for those individuals seeking to create the specific identity of father or mother. Men sought male heirs as a means of continuing their family, to provide for their ancestors and for themselves once they became ancestors. As Margery Wolf puts it, "A man defines his family as a large group that includes the dead, the not-yet-born, and the living members of his household."[45] Women, however, sought sons in order to gain benefits during their lifetimes. Women and their sons formed what Wolf calls a "uterine family."[46] In addition to bringing them status in their husband's family, sons provided women security and happiness.[47]

Hsiung Ping-chen, in an article on the relationships between mothers and their sons in late imperial times, reaches similar conclusions:

A mother often harbored quite different goals in wanting to assist and to push her boy for success than the father. For, in the traditional social hierarchy . . . a woman could hardly acquire any public acclaim for herself. The personal ambitions she entertained, and the social recognition she cherished, she had to achieve through men, and her son was the most promising candidate for realizing her wishes. . . .

A mother felt she was entitled to her son's permanent primary allegiance. . . . Many a mother, accordingly, frequently reminded her sons exactly what was expected of them. . . .

In pressing her sons to work harder, the mother made it clear that on their performances lay . . . the single hope of vindication for their dedicated and suffering mother.[48]

A son, as the member of late imperial society most likely to have a chance at mobility and advancement, was an important channel of authority for the one who had his "permanent and primary allegiance."

Emily Martin, in "Gender and Ideological Differences in Representations of Life and Death," makes a similar case for differences in how Chinese men and women relate to death, birth, and marriage. She maintains that male ideology celebrated social links and sought eternal status. In contrast, female ideology focused on biological reproduction and cyclical change.[49] An obvious focal point for men was preservation of the family line. For women, a focus on the uterine family emphasized both social and biological connections and brought female and male (in the mother-son bond) together.

The different expectations that men and women of the late imperial period had at the birth of a baby boy is concretely demonstrated by several passages in the seventeenth-century *baojuan* about Bixia Yuanjun.[50] In this text, a childless, pious couple is chosen to publish and disseminate the religious text. The couple is introduced in chapter 10, and reappear throughout the remainder of the text. In their prayers, the wife always requests "a son" or "a child," whereas the husband usually requests a "descendant." Listed below are the examples of these prayers from the precious volume. References to the wife (*furen* 夫人), née Dong (*Dong shi*):

1. asks Mother [Bixia Yuanjun] begging for a child (*zi* 子)
2. there is [a woman] née Dong
   told her husband
      "be at ease, don't be troubled
      [only] request of Niangniang
      to come to [our] family altar
      [and] give [us] a son (*ernan* 兒男)"

3. "only request that I [become]
    a birth mother (*shengshen mu* 生身母)"
4. kneels before Venerable Mother, requesting a son (*ernan*).
5. does not request [things to] eat, does not request [things to] wear, only asks Venerable Mother for no calamities, also asks for a child (*zi*).
6. Tells Holy Mother
    "give to me one son (*yige erlang* 一箇兒郎)."
7. Niangniang's supernatural powers will send [her] one small son (*yige xiao ertong* 一個小兒童).[51]

References to the husband, usually referred to as the Elder (*zhang-zhe* 長者):

1. The Elder contemplates the past [and] considers the future. For people in the [current] generation, severing one's descendants (*houdai* 後代) [is like] cutting down a tree [and leaving] no shade.
2. begs for descendants (*houdai*).
3. The Elder, [because he has] no children tells Niangniang
    "[I] want to obtain descendants (*houdai*)"
4. Venerable Mother's supernatural powers will send [him] descendants (*houdai*).[52]

Thus the woman focuses on her biological connection with her child, whereas the husband looks at the future son's social position within his family line. Although on two occasions the husband requests a son,[53] the wife never requests descendants.

A pilgrimage society stele provides additional support for the argument that men in Chinese society tend to emphasize social relations and eternal position through their patriline. All 98 members of the society that erected stele number 18 in Table 1 (dated 1886) were men. Interestingly, among the things the text of the stele lists as requests made of the goddess Bixia Yuanjun are "heirs" (*si* 嗣) rather than sons or children.

Female Networking

Women pilgrims to Mount Tai and other sacred sites contravened China's orthodox moral and social system, which emphasized the importance of secluding women. Segregation, of course, ran contrary to pilgrimage. Female identity was the product of both the overall system, including literati proscriptions, and actual practice. The literati tried to keep women away from temples, where, unsupervised, they might "seek liaisons with dissipated youths in secret passages of monasteries."[54] Yet, close attention to female pilgrims to Mount Tai shows that such proscriptions miss a key point: namely, the oral pilgrimage tradition and practice of women omitted men through the formation of sisterhoods, playful trickery, Bixia Yuanjun's special relationship with women, the transmission of oral traditions, and efficacious practice attained through matrilineally imagined relationships. Thus, female ritual authority on Mount Tai went beyond re-creating that keystone of the patrilineal system, a male heir. A woman might find herself being identified as—or forced to respond to literati characterization as—the provider of an heir for her husband's patriline, a dutiful daughter or daughter-in-law, a suspicious sectarian leader, a domineering wife, or a ruffian. The same women, within their pilgrimage groups, households, and communities, may have gained ritual authority as leaders of pilgrimage groups, successful pilgrims, mothers, grandmothers, or ritual experts based on identities within a communal, gender-exclusive, efficacious, practice-based meritocracy.

Before Bixia Yuanjun was assigned to look after women, one of the depravities to which women had been reduced was that they "did not understand themselves."[55] Subsequently, Bixia Yuanjun's "compassionate light shone everywhere, even every dark and small place . . . and she enlightened creatures according to the great ultimate."[56] Although any religious leader or deity might teach enlightenment, there are parallels to the help Bixia Yuanjun specifically offered women. She can be seen as someone, like a mother or grandmother, from whom women seek instruction and understanding about who and what they are.

For centuries, women have been going on pilgrimage to Mount Tai to pray for sons, the protection of newborns, cure of illnesses, health, and wealth. Women went there to discuss their problems with Bixia Yuanjun or, as women in Shandong call her, *lao nainai* 老奶奶, "*old* grandma," a designation only used for Bixia Yuanjun. Indeed, contemporary women pilgrims say they *gen lao nainai tanyitan* 跟老奶奶談一談, "are having a chat with old grandma."

Although they pray more formally as well, they speak to and of
Bixia Yuanjun in homely or familial terms. Contemporary women
pilgrims emphasize the importance of praying sincerely and from
the heart. In addition, several women I interviewed stressed the importance of explaining your situation and requests to the goddess.

Nainai 奶奶 is an informal term equivalent to "gran" or
"grandma." Although references to some of Bixia Yuanjun's assistant goddesses occasionally contain the term *nainai*, they are usually given the title *niangniang* 娘娘, "mother" or "woman." As a
title for a goddess, *niangniang* has been variously translated as "our
mother," "goddess," and "mother goddess." Among the goddesses
connected with Mount Tai, the term *nainai* was usually reserved
for Bixia Yuanjun. At least in Shandong and possibly elsewhere in
northern China, in reference to deities, the term *lao nainai* has
been used only for Bixia Yuanjun. To refer to a goddess as *nainai*
places her generationally before and above a *niangniang*. Given the
cultural reverence toward older people, to address a goddess as *nainai* rather than *niangniang* is to grant her more respect and place
her in a higher position. A personal and informal term, *lao nainai*
contrasts with the formal, written term for a grandmother, *zumu*
祖母. This term, which would have been employed in male literati
writings, translates literally as "ancestor mother" or "ancestral
mother" and would refer only to a paternal grandmother.

Several factors contribute to the popular appellation of *lao nainai* for Bixia Yuanjun. First, as mentioned above, it is a title of respect and reverence. In addition, since Bixia Yuanjun is almost always accompanied by other goddesses (usually with the title
niangniang), it is a means of setting her above her assistants and
acknowledging her higher status. Also, the name suggests an intimate, familial relationship rather than a larger-scale official hierarchy. Finally, a fertility goddess who is, at least figuratively, a
grandmother is more efficacious than one who is a mother, since
her children have also demonstrated their fertility.

Women's journeys to Mount Tai were motivated in part by a
desire to chat with this understanding and compassionate grand-
motherly figure and in part by a sense of duty. Pilgrimage could
fulfill a promise for past benefits, for example, the recovery of a

sick relative. Also, by praying for an heir, a woman was fulfilling a duty to her husband's family and their ancestors, as well as to her natal family, which would not want to bear the shame of having married out a barren woman.

While on pilgrimage, women enjoyed a degree of freedom from some of the restrictions of daily life, and they could chat with *lao nainai*, who was especially responsive to requests for male heirs. In late imperial China, a woman's position and authority within her marital family increased dramatically once she gave birth to a boy. Indeed, some anthropologists who have done recent fieldwork in Shandong believe that a woman does not become a full member of her husband's family until she gives birth, or in some cases until she gives birth to a son.[57] Margery Wolf makes a similar observation based on her fieldwork in Taiwan and the People's Republic of China: "Only with birth of her first son does [a woman] acquire a relationship that gives her identity and status that cannot be severed. She has begun her *own* family."[58] Furthermore, many women viewed their sons as the means for social and economic advancement as well as providers in their old age.[59] Thus, women's pilgrimages, in addition to allowing them physical mobility, gave them authority through rituals asking for a male baby.

To create an atmosphere congenial to female networking and intimate mother-son relationships, the Goddess of Mount Tai is almost always accompanied by two or more assistant goddesses as well as votive baby boys. On Mount Tai, Bixia Yuanjun appears alone only in small shrines such as those shown in Figs. 12 and 13 (pp. 24 and 25). In all the halls and temples on Mount Tai as well as temples to the goddess elsewhere, Bixia Yuanjun is accompanied by at least two assistants. The assistant to Bixia Yuanjun's left, the position of honor, on Mount Tai and in most other temples is the Goddess of Eyesight, Yanguang Niangniang 眼光娘娘. The other assistant, on Bixia Yuanjun's right, on Mount Tai is always the Goddess of Conception, Songzi niangniang 送子娘娘; elsewhere it is sometimes the Goddess of Descendants, Zisun Niangniang 子孫娘娘. Larger groupings include a total of five, seven, or nine goddesses—odd numbers are considered luckier than even ones. A single temple or shrine, woodblock print, or religious text never included more than eight assistants along with Bixia Yuanjun, for a total of nine goddesses; however, three was most common. The groupings of five, seven, or nine always included the three main goddesses; the additional goddesses, however, were not fixed but often included the Goddess of Smallpox, Douzhen Niangniang 痘疹娘娘. For a list of all the assistant goddesses, derived from a variety of sources, see Table 2. In addition, some texts and temples also associated Bixia Yuanjun and some of her assistants with the Queen Mother of the West.[60]

The three main goddesses were usually portrayed with specific iconographic traits. Bixia Yuanjun wore a crown or headdress with three phoenixes, one facing forward and the others to the right and to the left. The phoenix was a symbol of the empress and the female gender. In her hands she held a *hu* 笏 or a *gui* 圭 tablet, a symbol of authority (see Fig. 4, p. 13). On this tablet there was usually an outline of the Big Dipper (Beidou 北斗), consisting of lines connecting seven stars; this outline was sometimes reduced to three stars connected by two lines.[61]

The Goddess of Eyesight also wore a phoenix headdress or crown. Her distinctive iconography is the eye she holds in her hands (see Fig. 26). The Goddess of Eyesight was the only one of Bixia Yuanjun's assistants whose link to pregnancy or childhood is not readily apparent. Since this goddess was Bixia Yuanjun's most honored assistant, the connection is worth exploring. Mount Tai was associated with the beginning of the day and hence the origin of light. There may have been an association between the source of light and good eyesight. Furthermore, tales such as Confucius seeing a horse from the top of Mount Tai show that people may have associated this sacred space with excellent vision. One further link may be the correlations of the Five Phases. As noted above, Mount Tai is associated with the wood phase or element, as are the eyes (*mu* 目 or *yan* 眼), and, thus by extension, with the east and thus Mount Tai.[62] Two springs on the mountain were believed to cure eye ailments. Shrines to the Goddess of Eyesight were built at these springs (see Appendix, nos. 67 and 68). Special offerings to the Goddess of Eyesight were embroidered pairs of eyes, which were hung from her statue.

Table 2

The Goddess of Mount Tai and Her Assistant Goddesses

English translation of title(s)	Romanized title(s)	Chinese title(s)	Duties
Goddess of Mount Tai Bixia Yuanjun Heavenly Immortal, Jade Maiden Holy Mother Old Grandma	Taishan Niangniang Bixia Yuanjun Tianxian Yunü Shengmu Lao Nainai	泰山娘娘 碧霞元君 天仙玉女 聖母 老奶奶	Prayed to for general well-being and for sons
Goddess of Eyesight	Yanguang Niangniang	眼光娘娘	Cures eye illnesses
Goddess of Conception	Songzi Niangniang Songsheng Niangniang	送子娘娘 送生娘娘	Prayed to for conception
Goddess of Descendants (Goddess of Children and Grandchildren)	Zisun Niangniang	子孫娘娘	Prayed to for conception
Goddess Who Determines Time of Birth	Zhusheng Niangniang	注生娘娘	Prayed to for auspicious birthdate
Goddess Who Hastens Birth (Midwife Goddess)	Cuisheng Niangniang	催生娘娘	Prayed to during difficult deliveries
Goddess of Nursing	Naimu Niangniang Ruyin Niangniang Rumu Niangniang	奶母娘娘 乳飲娘娘 乳母娘娘	Prayed to for sufficient milk

Goddess of Smallpox	Douzhen Niangniang Tianhua Niangniang Banzhen Niangniang	痘疹娘娘 天花娘娘 瘢疹娘娘	Beseeched to give a child a light case, or cure a serious case
Goddess of Scarlet Fever	Banzhen Niangniang	瘢疹娘娘	Beseeched to give a child a light case, or cure a serious case*
Goddess of Guidance	Yinmeng Niangniang Yinmu Niangniang	引蒙娘娘 引母娘娘	Protects children from wandering into danger†
Goddess of Healthy Upbringing	Peigu Niangniang Peiyang Niangniang	培姑娘娘 培養娘娘	Guarantor of nourishment or protector of girls‡

* The Chinese name of this goddess is the same as one alternative name of the Goddess of Smallpox. It can only be translated as the Goddess of Scarlet Fever when one of the other goddesses in a given list is given one of the other titles for the Goddess of Smallpox (Douzhen niangniang or Tianhua niangniang).

† Lowe (The Adventures of Wu, 1: 18) described the role of this goddess as guiding the soul into the correct body.

‡ Anne Goodrich (Peking Paper Gods, 107, 119) explains that this goddess looked after girls by, among other things, helping them to be good looking and to find good husbands. In addition, she states that an image of this goddess was usually placed inside a bride's sedan chair.

SOURCES: Images at the beginning of the precious volume about Bixia Yuanjun (Baojuan, 1: 1–5); Goodrich print collection 1931, Columbia University, C. V. Starr East Asian Library; woodblock prints donated to the Field Museum of Natural History in Chicago by Mrs. Eva W. Dunlap in January 1924 (acquisition numbers 27410 to 27453); Anne Goodrich, Peking Paper Gods; Lowe, The Adventures of Wu, 1: 18–19; Lü, Taishan niangniang xinyang, 37–45; Werner, Dictionary of Chinese Mythology, 46, 300, 354, 505, 512, 513; and Zhao Xinggen, Zhongguo baishen quanshu, 348–49.

Fig. 26   The Goddess of Eyesight. Detail of a colored painting
from the late Qing dynasty, in the Tai'an Municipal Museum
(photograph by the author, 1995).

Bixia Yuanjun's other main assistant, the Goddess of Conception,
or sometimes the Goddess of Descendants, also wore the phoenix
headdress. In her hands, instead of a tablet or an eye, she held at
least one baby boy (see Fig. 27). Her altar was usually covered with
small votive babies, which women used in rituals connected with
prayers for conception. This goddess presided over the key first
step in the successful bestowing of children, and hence prayers to
her preceded those to the other goddesses connected with children.
Modern pilgrims stated that in praying to Bixia Yuanjun and the

Fig. 27   The Goddess of Conception. Detail of a colored painting
from the late Qing dynasty, in the Tai'an Municipal Museum
(photograph by the author, 1995).

Goddess of Conception for a child at Mount Tai, they emphasize
rituals associated with conception and prevention of miscarriage.

It may seem strange to find the Goddess of Smallpox in a group
of goddesses connected with conception and childbirth. In China,
however, smallpox was closely connected to birth:

In the Ming and Qing eras, smallpox was almost universal in China and
struck in early childhood. . . . Recovery from smallpox cleansed the child

of the remnants of pollution inherited from the gestational state and allowed it to slough off the last bodily tie with the mother. Emerging finally from the polluted life-threatening disorders of infancy and early childhood, it passed from nature into culture and could be seen as now having a chance of living to grow up.[63]

Thus, smallpox deities were thought to play a crucial role in determining whether a child survived the series of potentially fatal hardships from conception through independence from the mother.[64]

The widespread popularity of Bixia Yuanjun and her assistant goddesses throughout northern China can be seen in woodblock prints. Despite the lack of official, government recognition, Bixia Yuanjun and her assistant goddesses appear in many popular woodblock prints, including a number of prints of pantheons (see Fig. 16, p. 34).[65] Prints of deities were either burned as an offering to the deity portrayed or placed somewhere within a household (the picture was usually changed annually at the New Year) and worshiped in the same manner as a figure of a deity at an altar.[66] The prints destined to be burned were usually less intricately carved, printed only with black outlines on cheaper paper, and colored only cursorily. These prints were quite inexpensive and within the means of even the very poor.[67] In addition to burning these prints, poorer people may also have used these cheaper prints as altar prints. Many of the woodblock prints designed to be burned were part of a set of 100 deities (*bai fen* 百分), which were offered during the New Year's festivities.[68] In Northern China these popular sets included Bixia Yuanjun and many of her assistants.[69]

The most important ritual in praying to the Goddess of Mount Tai and her community of goddesses is called "tying a baby doll" (*shuan wawa* 拴娃娃).[70] In its most basic form, this ritual involves burning incense and praying to Bixia Yuanjun for a baby. The supplicant ties a length of red string or yarn around the neck of a baby doll. This act ritually secures a baby's spirit within the womb of the woman who ties the string. Usually the doll, with the string still tied around its neck, is left on the altar in the temple or shrine. Another contemporary practice involves placing a sanctified piece of red cloth on the bed of the couple trying to conceive. After burning incense and praying for a baby in the main temple to Bixia Yuanjun on top of Mount Tai, the individual purchases a piece of red cloth blessed by the monks. The belief is that the cloth will pass on some of the goddess's powers and lead to conception.

The most complex contemporary ritual combines these two simpler rituals. The woman desiring a baby wraps the doll very tightly in a red cloth. After placing the doll on the altar, she has a chat with *lao nainai* and tells her that she wants a little baby boy. Next she burns incense and kowtows three times. Then she removes the doll from the altar, carries it home carefully, and places it either on or immediately next to the bed. One informant emphasized the importance of wrapping the doll tightly to ensure against miscarriage or premature birth.[71] It is noteworthy that most information on this ritual is passed from woman to woman. Although the monks in the main Bixia Temple on top of the mountain explained the two simpler rituals to me, they made no mention of this more complex one.

H. Y. Lowe's semi-autobiographical, detailed description of folk customs in Beijing from the 1910s to the 1930s contains a similar description of this ceremony. Lowe's book describes various folk customs by tracing events in the Wu family. The "tying a baby doll" ceremony occurs when Old Mrs. Wu takes her daughter-in-law to pray for a baby boy:

Old Mrs. Wu certainly did her best to obtain for her only son, Kwang Tsung, a male child as she had done her part beautifully in the periodical burning of incense in the courtyard and with the saying of silent prayers to the Goddess of Children (called in Chinese, Tse Sun Niang Niang [子孫娘娘] which literally means the Goddess of Sons and Grandsons!). Moreover, it was she who was responsible for young Mrs. Wu's special pilgrimage to the Tung Yueh Miao (東嶽廟), the Temple of the Sacred Eastern Mountain,[72] to perform the "baby tying ceremony." . . .

The "baby tying ceremony" was simple. After lighting bundles of incense . . . and inserting them in the big burner provided for the purpose, young Mrs. Wu, in a manner described to her in detail by her neighborhood women friends, selected from among the numerous images of babies in the Hall of the Goddess of Sons and Grandsons, her favourite and tied a piece of red thread around its neck, while silently praying that the image come home with her to be born as her son.[73]

Lowe's description of the ceremony attests to its continuity. The ceremony has remained essentially unchanged over the past sixty years. In this earlier account, it is also women, not monks, who teach one another how to perform the ritual. Old Mrs. Wu and the younger Mrs. Wu's female friends give advice about the best way to choose the doll and perform the prayers. What the women do in choosing a favorite doll—creating an individual bond based on the doll's engaging qualities—may reflect the differences in the self-creation of an identity and the interdependence of hierarchically arranged but mutable groups that women sought in going to "have a chat with old grandma." For Margery Wolf, writing specifically about the key distinctions between the male and the female self in China, "the female self is constructed and reconstructed from relationships that require constant renewal," and it is for this reason that "relationships are the *source* of their identity, [so] women nurture and value them in their own right, rather than for their symbolic implications."[74]

A late Qing woodblock print titled "Dajie shuan wawa" 大姐拴娃娃, or "Oldest Sister Ties a Baby Doll," illustrates the ceremony (see Fig. 28).[75] This print was a New Year's decoration from the printing center of Yangliuqing, near Tianjin, and dates from the Guangxu period (1875–1908). In the late imperial period, as well as in contemporary China, New Year's prints are put up each year (often by women) as colorful household decorations. Although the master printers and block carvers were men, much of the coloring of the New Year prints was done by women.[76] This print is especially useful since it includes text in addition to the picture. This is a high-quality woodblock print, which would have been put up in someone's home probably as an altar to the goddesses, not burned as an offering. It is quite likely that at least one person within the type of household that would have purchased a print such as this would have been literate enough to read the text on the print. However, the picture itself provides the same information as the text, and literacy would not have been mandatory for understanding the ritual portrayed.

The picture represents the interior of a temple to Bixia Yuanjun and two of her assistants, the sort of shrine or temple often called a *niangniang*, or goddess, temple. The print depicts four women visiting a *niangniang* temple to pray for babies. The goddess at the center altar is Bixia Yuanjun. The goddess on her right is not identified, but is one of the associate goddesses responsible for childbirth, probably the Goddess of Descendants. On the left is the Goddess of Conception. The arrangement of the dolls on the altars, some of them performing acrobatics, strongly resembles photos of *niangniang* altars in the Eastern Sacred Peak Temple in Beijing from the late 1920s.[77] Each of the four women is described in the text and labeled in the picture. Oldest sister Zhao is selecting a doll from the right-hand altar. Second younger sister Qian is playing with one of the dolls at the far right end of the center altar. Third woman Sun is kneeling before the main altar table, just to the left of the incense burner on the floor. Fourth sister-in-law Li is reaching to tie a piece of red yarn around one of the dolls in the arms of the Goddess of Conception (left altar). The figure to the right of the central altar table, ringing the bronze bowl, is a Daoist nun. The other two figures on the rug, both wearing black vests, are servants of one or more of the women visiting the temple. The servant closest to the bottom of the print is holding a bundle of incense.

The text at the top of the print reads:

Oldest sister Zhao is just 18. She has been out of the women's quarters [been married] for 3 years, without conceiving. With a single-hearted focus, she desires to go to the *niangniang* temple and plead before *Niangniang* for a baby. She enters the temple gate. After praying, she takes out a piece of red yarn. From atop the altar table [she takes a doll and] ties [the yarn] fast.

Second younger sister Qian smiles broadly, for tomorrow is the eighteenth of the fourth month.[78] In her heart, she thinks of going to the temple. Inside the *niangniang* temple she will tie [a string around] a baby doll. She performs her toilette and does her makeup very carefully. She dons a silk taffeta garment over [a lower layer of] silk netting. As she walks, she sways like a willow in the wind. Within the group of married women, she is the most beautiful. She ties [a string around] an excellent baby doll. She dangles a toy to amuse him.

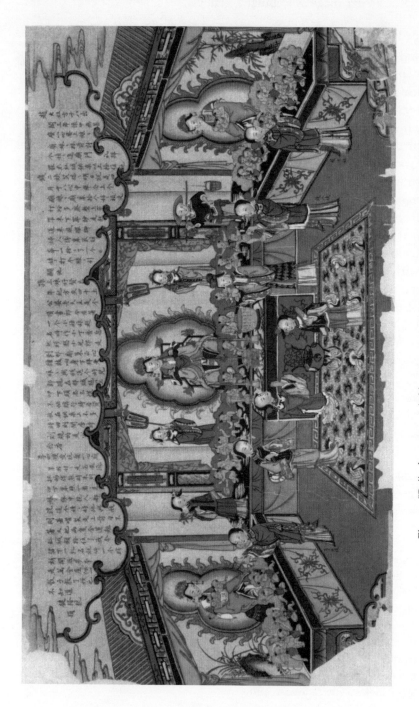

Fig. 28 "Dajie shuan wawa" (Oldest sister ties a baby doll). Woodblock print. Qing, Guangxu period (SOURCE: Wang Shucun, *Yangliuqing nianhua*, pl. 64).

Third woman Sun is very good and virtuous. Her age is just over 40. Her father-in-law and mother-in-law are old. Her husband is a scholar. They all only can look upon a small girl. The name picked for her is Little Lilac. Suddenly [third woman Sun] longs for a son. She walks to the temple. With a true heart, [she listens to] the sounding of the bell and drum. She bows and prays to *lao niangniang*: "Send me a good son." Kneeling on top of the woolen rug, she kowtows. Without recklessness and unhurriedly, before leaving, she places incense money on top of the altar table. Not long afterwards, she returns to the women's quarters. From time to time, with heartfelt [devotion], she burns incense.

Fourth sister-in-law Li loves to play. Single-mindedly, she desires to tie [a string around] a baby doll in the temple. When she moves, it is like the blowing wind, the movement is extremely graceful. When she arrives, she looks all around inside [the temple]. She sees [the baby doll] *niangniang* holds to her bosom. Everyone says that baby is good. "He pursed [his] lips and laughed at me." She goes in front but can't reach. [Not until she] stands on the tips of [her] golden lilies [bound feet] is she able to tie the red yarn. "I now leave a milk-name, and call you a naughty [boy]. My family is one of infinite wealth. Maybe you will lose it all with the dice? I don't know." Inscribed by the Jianlong Printing House [Yangliuqing, Tianjin][79]

In addition to being a colorful New Year's decoration, the print demonstrates how to pray for a baby through both the text and the picture. Here, as in the more recent examples of the ceremony, although men may have had a hand in the composition and production of this print, women are the represented teachers. Purchasers of the print (often women) learn about the ceremony from the actions of the four women, assisted by the Daoist nun. In contemporary China and in Lowe's account, as mentioned above, women are the ones who most frequently pass on the knowledge related to praying to Bixia Yuanjun.

The text and print instruct worshipers who desire a child in the four basic components of the ritual. First, upon entering the temple, look around for a good doll (oldest sister Zhao and second younger sister Qian are doing this in the picture). Second, with a true heart bow in time with the beating of the bell and drum and pray to *lao niangniang*, and continue praying while you kneel and perform a kowtow (third woman Sun in the picture). Third, tie a piece of red yarn or string around the neck of the doll you have chosen, symbolically making it your baby (fourth sister-in-law Li in the picture). Fourth, burn incense (in the print there is an incense burner, and one of the maids is holding a bundle of incense). According to the text, third woman Sun takes the incense home to burn, and the incense the maid at the bottom of the print is holding is probably for that purpose.

The discussion of third woman Sun's situation is the only one that mentions other family members. She, along with her husband and her in-laws, is desirous of a son. Zhao, we are told, is married and Li's family is rich, but there are no references to other family members. What comes across in the text is that these women are acting independently. None of them, not even Sun, are sent to the temple by their husbands. This temple and its associated ritual are solidly in the domain of women.

Another aspect of these women's visit to the temple, which comes across in both the picture and the text, is their enjoyment of the process. There is none of the austerity and formality that might accompany a visit to the God of Mount Tai in his guise as a judge in purgatory. The women look forward to their visit and enjoy themselves while there. Two of them are quite playful. In the text, second younger sister Qian dangles a toy in front of the doll she has chosen. In the picture, we see her playing with the doll's feet. According to the text, "Fourth sister-in-law Li loves to play." In the text, she and her chosen doll tease each other. The baby laughs at her, and she muses that he may gamble away the family wealth. In the picture, Li, a red string in her hands, reaches toward a doll, which in turn extends a hand toward her.

To judge from repeated elements in the text, two components of the ritual are seemingly more important than the rest. First, one must approach the entire process, especially the prayers, sincerely and truthfully. Second, each woman must tie a red string around a doll, symbolically making it her baby. One element not found in these instructions is a fixed prayer that everyone must recite. Rather, each woman individually discusses her situation with the goddess. She "has a chat with old grandma." Women pilgrims one hundred years later have the same attitude. The third woman straightforwardly asks *lao niangniang* to "send me a good son," and the fourth woman wonders about the possibility of her future son becoming a gambler.

This print proves that the ritual of tying a baby doll dates at least to the late nineteenth century. Almost certainly the appearance of the ritual in reproduction implies that the ritual was well developed and widespread. It is not unreasonable to hypothesize that the ritual was practiced in the early nineteenth or even in the eighteenth century. Although I have not been able to find an earlier reference to this ritual, dolls were presented as offerings in the main temple to Bixia Yuanjun on top of Mount Tai at least as early as 1740. Among the items that survived the calamitous fire of that year are eight silver dolls (*wa* 娃).[80]

"Oldest Sister Ties a Baby Doll" contrasts sharply with texts written by males, which sought to keep women out of temples. In the print, not only are women encouraged to visit the temple, but they do so without male escorts. All the figures in the print are women: the four pilgrims, the three goddesses, the nun, and the two servants. There is no hint of the illicit encounters men feared. They are visiting the *niangniang* temple, and nothing else.

Present-day female pilgrims control their ritual space in ways similar to the women depicted in "Oldest Sister Ties a Baby Doll." In addition to burning incense and spirit money, women offer food and clothing, especially embroidered shoes for bound feet, to Bixia Yuanjun or the Goddess of Conception. Although, as we saw in the legends about how Bixia Yuanjun came to control Mount Tai, shoes had special connotations for her, offerings of shoes in connection with prayers for children are not limited to this goddess.[81] Eberhard explains that the reason behind this offering is "child" and "shoe" have the same pronunciation in south China.[82] Both 鞋 (shoe) and 孩 (child) are pronounced *hai* in the Shanghai dialect[83] and *hai* in Cantonese.[84] In northern dialects, however, the word for shoe is pronounced *xié* (鞋) and that for child *hai* (孩). The reason for offering shoes for children in northern China may thus be a pun borrowed from southern dialects.

In many cultures, including China, preparing food and making clothing are areas over which women have control, power, and authority. In *Holy Feast and Holy Fast*, Caroline Walker Bynum argues, "To prepare food is to control food. Moreover, food is not merely *a* resource that women control; it is *the* resource that women control."[85] In China, at least, women were also the ones who sewed for the family and therefore exerted some control over clothing in addition to food. Their gifts and offerings are made with their own hands. They are highly personal. In addition, women are the ones who pass on the traditions about praying to "old grandma." To judge from my observations in 1995 and 2000, there is little contact between the monks in Bixia Yuanjun's main temple and the worshipers. Most supplicants who wanted to know how to burn incense and spirit money asked the women who were selling it, not the monks. The focal point of the pilgrimage today is the incense oven just below the main temple to Bixia Yuanjun near the top of Mount Tai. This is where prayers accompany the smoke of the burning offerings to the goddess, but the monks visited the oven only at the end of the day to empty the offering box. Women incense sellers and other female pilgrims are the ones who most often offer advice about offerings. Women were also the preservers of ritual in the ceremony described in Lowe's book about Beijing in the 1910s–1930s. Today women continue to carry on and pass along the oral tradition, in contrast to the literate tradition, long dominated by men.

Another ritual or custom associated with prayer for babies on Mount Tai is the placing of small stones or pebbles in the crook of tree branches or on top of other stones or stelae (see Fig. 8, p. 20). This practice is based on spoken Chinese, which, because of the many homophones, is rich in puns. Pilgrims to Mount Tai that I encountered in 1994 and 1995 explained that the act of placing the stone, *yazi* (*ya* 壓 or *ya* 押, both of which mean "to press down"; *zi* 子 is shortened from *shizi* 石子, "pebble"), is a homophone for a word meaning "child"—*yazi* 犽子. So, someone placing a stone (again, the majority who do so are women) express a wish for a child through this pun. Other references suggest a different second character for the pun. This version is dependent on local dialect or pronunciation. In Shandong the retroflex syllables *zhi, chi, shi* are pronounced *zi, ci, si*. This version of the pun involves the word *yazhi* (壓枝 or 押枝), "press down the branches," pronounced *yazi* in Shandong.[86] The "pressing the branches" pun was probably the original, and the original practice of placing stones in the crooks of branches eventually spread to placing them on top of other rocks. This version of the pun is further substantiated by the fact that the most common trees on Mount Tai, pines and cypress, have long been associated with fertility rituals in China, as have stones.[87]

This association of cypress with children is also found in another Mount Tai ritual, again, based on a pun in the local dialect. Women pick a cypress twig (*baizhi* 柏枝, pronounced *baizi* in Shandong) and stick it in their hair. This is a pun for one hundred (many) children (*baizi* 百子). In addition to being a convenient homophone for "one hundred," cypress, as an evergreen, is also a symbol for youth.

The "tying a baby doll" ritual, like the placing of stones, now encompasses other forms beyond its initial meaning. On Mount Tai the tying of a red string as a fertility ritual has spread to other objects. Contemporary pilgrims often alter the Chinese phrase for the ritual from *shuan wawa* to *shuanzi*. *Shuanzi* is also the local pronunciation of *shuanzhi* (拴枝), "tying a branch." This pronunciation is a pun meaning to "tie a child" (*shuanzi* 拴子), the implication, just as in the "tying a baby doll" ceremony, being that by tying the string a woman will attach a baby's spirit to her. Therefore many trees and bushes that bear the pebbles of the *yazi* ritual also have pieces of red string tied to their boughs. The *shuanzi* ritual has further altered to include tying red string to objects in temples, such as incense burners, which have become numinous because of their location.

Although the female ritual authority associated with Mount Tai may at first seem ephemeral, it extended far beyond one ceremony or one pilgrimage. In many rituals, women played at most minor roles. They were excluded from all official rituals since they could not become officials. Although they did participate to a degree in family rituals, it was the patriline that was worshiped, and the husband's family that was the focus. In the rituals associated with the Mount Tai goddesses, however, women were the primary or sole actors. These rituals focused on prayers for male heirs, the core of the Chinese patriarchal family system and of Chinese society as a whole. Thus, they cannot be seen as insignificant or minor.

The authority gained by praying for and giving birth to a son extended beyond a woman's performance of a ritual or a pilgrimage to the mountain. A woman's efficaciousness in rituals and prayers could establish her authority in her community. Oral interviews with several groups of contemporary pilgrims in 1995 revealed that they were led by older women whose authority stemmed from their age, previously efficacious prayers, ritual knowledge, and established relationship with Bixia Yuanjun. In a village in rural Shandong in 1995, I discussed the correlation between ritual practices and female community with Kimberley Falk, a colleague conducting anthropological fieldwork in the village. We concluded that women in the village did indeed retain authority beyond their visits to Mount Tai, particularly in the areas of birth and recovery from illnesses. The leadership role of women in pilgrimage societies is not just a phenomenon of the late twentieth century. Several of the stelae erected by pilgrimage societies on Mount Tai list women among the leaders of societies made up of men and women. For one group that was 71 percent women, all four leaders were women.[88]

In many regions of China, including Shandong, a bride would return to her natal home for a visit on a specific day shortly after the wedding. In addition, in many regions natal home visits are part of the New Year's festivities for women. Since most marriages took place between families in the same small market area, it was possible for women to visit their natal homes at other times of the year throughout their married lives. The natal family is called the *niangjia*, "the mother's house." Frequent visits and stays longer than a couple of days were and are quite common. There are even examples of women continuing to reside in their *niangjia* for several years after marriage and in some cases after the birth of children.[89] These practices, like pilgrimages by women, go against written customs. According to the literati-endorsed orthodox social rules, married women were to live permanently in their husband's household. There is a strong parallel between women's pilgrimage to Mount Tai, with an emphasis on sincere chatting and pleasure in women's society, and visiting their natal families. The customs of women visiting their *niangjia*, like those of women visiting Bixia Yuanjun temples, "are easily overlooked—they are not readily presented formally and they are distinctly asymmetrical with the standard patrilineal forms. They are nonhierarchical and relatively egalitarian."[90] Women in Shandong and other areas where visits to natal families were common extended their area of interactions and agency beyond the male ideal of the enclosed women's quarters, to include their *niangjia*, both maternal and spiritual.

The use of affinal kinship as a metaphor in religion is also seen in the worship of Mazu, another compassionate goddess, in Taiwan:

It is significant that the kinship metaphor used in describing the related phenomena of pilgrimages . . . and temple branching . . . is affinal rather than agnatic. The deity images present in branch temples are similar to brides who return on a customary visit to their natal homes (*lao-niang-chia* [*lao niangjia*]). During annual pilgrimages these images are taken from branch temples . . . and returned to home temples where they are passed over the incense burners and ritually rejuvenated. An agnatic metaphor, such as the branches of a lineage, would imply a hierarchical, corporate relationship among temples; but branch temples are organizationally independent of the older temples. Consequently, the strong affective relations between women and their natal homes provide a better analogy for the relations between temples.[91]

A similar relationship can be seen between the Bixia Temple on top of Mount Tai and the local temples in the Mount Tai catchment area (the travel palaces in particular; see Part I, "Economics of Attaining the Summit"). Although there was an obvious hierarchy between the goddess Bixia Yuanjun and the women who prayed to her, the relationship was quite personal and intimate. Therefore, as for Mazu temples, a hierarchical, agnatic metaphor would be wholly inappropriate to describe the relationship between female worshipers and Bixia Yuanjun.

An even more direct connection between Bixia Yuanjun and women visiting their natal families is found in an early twentieth-century anthropological work on Shandong. Georg Stenz, who did his fieldwork primarily in southern Shandong, noted that young wives visiting their natal families at New Year's had to choose the day of their journey carefully, for the Goddess of Mount Tai would protect them only on certain days.[92]

Mothers also visited their married daughters.[93] This, too, has parallels with the worship of Bixia Yuanjun. For health, financial, and other reasons, many women could not and cannot make an annual pilgrimage to Mount Tai. In areas without a Bixia Yuanjun temple nearby, women could set up shrines in their homes for worship on the goddess's birthday. In contemporary Shandong, such home shrines include some sort of image of Bixia Yuanjun—a photograph of the statue in the main temple, a cloth scroll of the goddess, even a drawing of the goddess cut from a box of Mount Tai brand liquor—and a holder for burning incense.[94] In the late imperial period, women could have used woodblock prints of the goddess in their home shrines. So, although the women could not always visit *lao nainai* at her own home, they could invite her into theirs.

Some of those who make the journey to Mount Tai have to be creative in their use of ritual space. The most efficacious site on Mount Tai is the incense oven just below the main temple to Bixia Yuanjun on top of the mountain. This is because all prayers and requests are sent up to Chinese deities with the smoke of the incense and spirit money burned by the offerer. In 1995, the cost of the mandatory mountain ticket (30 *yuan*) was beyond the means of many pilgrims, and the incense oven just above the Red Gate (Fig. 5, no. 11), the highest point where one could burn incense before having to buy a ticket, became the focal point of the pilgrimage for the majority of pilgrims (see Fig. 29). As noted in Part I, several women created their own ritual space beside the trail by placing their food offerings above a line they had scratched in the ground, and then performing their prayers and kowtows while facing the top of the mountain (see Fig. 8, p. 20).[95] The women's flexibility in adapting to the environment allowed them to circumvent the restrictions placed on them by the male authorities in charge of the mountain tickets.

Fig. 29   Pilgrims burning offerings to Bixia Yuanjun on her birthday, just above the Red Gate (no. 11) near the bottom of the mountain. This was a new focus of pilgrimage in the mid-1990s because many people could not afford the ticket that would allow them to climb to the main temple to Bixia Yuanjun on top of the mountain (photograph by the author, 1995).

Conclusion

Women formed communities with one another in transmitting knowledge of *lao nainai* and her assistant goddesses and the various rituals associated with their worship. These communities were reflected in the communal grouping of the goddesses and in

the legends about Bixia Yuanjun, who gained control of Mount Tai
with the assistance of another, older woman. Her token, and thus
the symbol of her power, was an embroidered shoe. This quintessentially feminine item was a product of skilled female handiwork.
In the context of the parallel between women visiting their *niangjia* and going on pilgrimage to worship Bixia Yuanjun, the women
in "Oldest Sister Ties a Baby Doll" were not dressing up to impress
men, as male literati sources might imply, but to look their best for
a visit "home." The women looked forward to visits to the *niangniang* temple with anticipation and excitement, just as they might a
visit home. They thoroughly enjoyed their visits. They teased the
babies and chatted with the communal group of goddesses—
mothers and grandmother. They told *lao nainai* their wishes and
fears. Her patient listening and attitude projected love, caring, and
confidence.

Although women leaving their homes to go on a pilgrimage
seems to fit the Turners' model of pilgrimage as a liminal experience, the parallel between the pilgrimage and visiting one's *niangjia* diminishes the degree of liminality. Certainly a pilgrimage was a
departure from everyday life, and the travel probably took most
non-elite women and men beyond their routine boundaries. As the
discussion of visits to *niangjia* shows, however, the regular travels
of women in late imperial China reduces the uniqueness of the
journey to Mount Tai. Just as Caroline Walker Bynum has found
for medieval European women, there is no evidence among female
pilgrims to Mount Tai of the inversion expected under the Turners' model.[96] Instead, women on pilgrimages to Bixia Yuanjun and
her assistants acted in ways not much outside the bounds of their
everyday lives, which included trips to other villages to visit with
women.

The actions of men and women on Mount Tai reveal a contrast
between oral and literate culture in China. The women focused on
oral prayers, which they learned through conversations with other,
usually older, women. The woodblock print, although it does contain some text, was still predominantly a New Year's decoration,
and it instructed via the picture as much as it did through the text.
This contrast between oral and literate cultures can be seen all over

the mountain. Mount Tai is covered with male literati poems and accounts of their visits. Highly literate wordplays (see Chapter 3) differ considerably from the oral and aural puns practiced by women described above. Puns, whose significance resides in wish fulfillment through use of practical tokens, also altered the character of the sacred spaces. Although each individual trace was ephemeral, communally they left their mark on the mountain through generations of placing stones, tying red ribbons, and snapping branches.

Most individuals and groups have multiple identities, with one identity taking precedence over another as context dictates. It is certainly not uncommon to find contradictions within individuals or groups. Thus, although most non-elite women's pilgrimages emphasized oral traditions and puns, stelae evidence suggests that some women pilgrimage group leaders were interested in leaving written records. Although the *niangjia* visits and Bixia Yuanjun pilgrimages indicate mobility, celebratory reunions outside the patriline, and female networking, Judd makes a case that although women visiting their natal families "may well enjoy these visits, they are also a fulfillment of duty." In addition, Judd explains, "minimally, these are visits to see relatives and especially parents, but the visits may also keep economic ties active. In some cases the married-out daughter contributes labor to her *niangjia*."[97] The labor contribution would likely include food preparation, mending, and sewing. This also strongly parallels the relationship between women and Bixia Yuanjun. Women's offerings to the goddess often include food or clothing items they made themselves.

By far the dominant identity for an illiterate male pilgrim to Mount Tai in the late imperial period was as a member of a family, which required that he both produce an heir and honor his ancestors. He therefore prayed to the Goddess of Mount Tai for an heir and paid his respects to his ancestors at the entrance to purgatory. Most of these men, however, had another identity as parts of uterine families. This identity, as loving sons of compassionate mothers, may help to explain the contradiction between the precept that women should not go on pilgrimage and the fact that many did so. Men likely found that their obligation to the male side of the family to produce an heir or their duty as filial sons to escort or send a female relative on pilgrimage overrode the proscriptions against female pilgrimage. Additionally, as Emily Martin notes, men saw childbirth as being within the women's sphere, and therefore women had to participate actively in prayers for pregnancy. Many men, particularly those with close ties to their mothers, may have been drawn to the goddess of Mount Tai for her maternal aspects. Unlike male gods who adhered to bureaucratic rules or were susceptible to bribery, her compassion toward sincere believers made her more approachable to men of lower social standing and lesser economic means. This in turn may have made it easier for men to countenance women's pilgrimages to pray to her, for acceptance might be in keeping with the exceptional quality of her influence, with its emphasis on sincerity rather than previous actions and pity rather than retribution.

Although male pilgrims did at times allow their identity as loving sons to surface on pilgrimages to Mount Tai, their primary identity as preservers of the male line did seem to take precedence. A stele erected primarily by a man and his mother in 1789, in the Mother of the Big Dipper Temple (no. 15),[98] attests to mother-son bonds and Bixia Yuanjun's compassion, as well as men's drive to extend themselves into the future:

Devout believer (*xinshi* 信士) Liu Yihou and his mother, neé Gao, of Wen'an county, Shuntian prefecture [Zhili], donate money and materials to help advance the grandeur of the Goddess of Mount Tai. After meritorious achievements on the summit, we erect this stele here at the Mother of the Big Dipper Temple, as a record of our reverence at this time. Exalted Mount Tai, master of the boundaries of [the state of] Lu, Heavenly Immortal's (*Tianxian* 天仙) seat for protecting, [site from where] Holy Mother (*Shengmu* 聖母) presides over distant places, personal dwelling place of Bixia, known as Yuanjun. Intelligent, true, and straight [in distinguishing between] the fortunate and virtuous, [versus] the misfortunate and immoral, she is a numinous official (*ling guan* 靈官), protector of the Law (*hu fa* 護法), primordial woman (*yuan nü* 元女) who pities and exhorts. She bestows merit on the world and, through virtue, aids the living. With sincere hearts we pray on the summit for prolific sons and prolific grandsons. From there [the summit] to the Mount Tai lower temple,[99] the winding path is long. In between is the hermitage and vegetation presided over by the Mother of the Big Dipper Temple. [The goddess] will provide for many children, her fortunate protection [extends] to the myriad people. The pilgrimage society members offered prayers to the Completely Perfected (*mi zhen* 彌眞).[100] Our requests have already been fulfilled, thus this inscribed text. May the vertical inscription on [the cap of] this stele, "be honored for all generations" (*liufang gujin* 流芳古今), instill merit, instill virtue, and never be destroyed. Erected by the devout believer Liu Yihou, his mother, neé Gao, and Zhang Zhudun on New Year's Day, first month, fifty-fourth year of Qianlong [January 26, 1789]. [followed by names of an additional fourteen men][101]

The relationship between Liu Yihou and his mother was emphasized at both the beginning and the end of the stele. The mother-son bond was obviously important for these two. It was also at least tacitly respected by the other members of the association who inscribed their names to the stele. Although the nature of most of the sources makes it difficult to assess relationships among male pilgrims, it seems likely that at least the element of comradeship contained in the Turners' term *communitas* existed.[102]

The compassion often associated with mothers is seen in several of the descriptions of Bixia Yuanjun. She "protects," "pities," "aids," provides children, and rewards those with "sincere hearts." In addition, however, she has taken on some of the attributes of the God of Mount Tai. She is a "numinous" and just official, who appropriately rewards the upright while exhorting the immoral.[103]

Although "prolific sons and prolific grandsons" seems to echo the language associated with the woman in the *baojuan* text, the request for sons, not heirs, emphasizes descendants or heirs. The appeal actually projects at least three generations into the future by asking for grandsons who will reproduce. The woman in the *baojuan* never overtly requests many children and, on two occasions, asks for just one son. A uterine family requires only one son, whereas continuation of a family is most assured through generations of many men. Furthermore, the phrase "be honored for all generations" calls upon the mountain to extend all the association members' families infinitely into the future.

Literati injunctions aside, countless women made the pilgrimage to Bixia Yuanjun's temple near the peak of Mount Tai during the late imperial period. Some popular sources such as the woodblock print even encouraged women to visit temples to Bixia Yuanjun. The discrepancy between the male literati ideal of women remaining secluded in their quarters and the reality that multitudes of them actually journeyed to Mount Tai suggests that the social and moral system either was being circumvented or was operating at a different level. The system was much more flexible in practice than in its ideal written form. Since the Chinese social and moral system was and is a *hierarchical* set of rules, regulations, restrictions, and principles, a higher principle can apparently overrule lesser injunctions. In the context of women visiting Mount Tai, the paramount concern that weakened restrictions against such travel was filial piety. In China, filial piety extends beyond respect and obedience to one's living elders. Ancestor worship was an integral part of Chinese culture. Anyone who did not have an heir to continue the family line, in addition to having no one to take care of his generation's funerals and present offerings after their deaths, also deprived all ancestors of the rituals due them—hence Mencius' comment. Since women were visiting Mount Tai in order to pray for an heir, they were upholding this keystone of the moral and social system.

There is also another parallel with women's visits to their *niangjia*. Just as women visiting their natal families seemed to go against the patriarchal system of exclusive residence in the husband's house, women going on pilgrimage clashed with literati ideals of female seclusion. Some of Ellen Judd's conclusions about *niangjia* visits are applicable here as well:

The customary practices [of women visiting their *niangjia*] address dimensions of women's social relationships in a model that is not attentive to them. It could be effectively argued both that this relationally reinforces the official model and that it undermines it. These customary practices reinforce the model in structuring the active role of women, who are indispensable to it, in modes—such as respect and care for aging parents—that do not challenge the model and may actually stabilize or strengthen elements of it. Simultaneously, they legitimate an active role for women and enable women to make some choices in a field of competing demands.[104]

Women's pilgrimages to Mount Tai reinforced the social and moral system because they were praying to continue their husband's family line. Simultaneously they were also experiencing mobility, a sisterhood relationship with other women, and ritual authority both on the mountain and at home. These activities of illiterate women during the late imperial period greatly expand our understanding of the gender system beyond elite precepts.

Although many men apparently accepted that filial piety overruled restrictions against female pilgrimage, grudging male permission does not present a complete image of how Chinese society functioned when conflicts arose. It does not account for the active role that women did and still do take during their pilgrimages and in their lives in general. These findings are quite similar to Dorothy Ko's conclusions about elite, literate women in the seventeenth century: "By implicating women as actors maneuvering to further their perceived interest from within the system, I see them as architects of concrete gender relations, the building blocks from which the overarching gender system was constructed. Instead of outright resistance or silencing, I describe processes of contestation and negotiation."[105] In historical sources such as the woodblock print as well as in contemporary pilgrimages, women controlled rituals and space. Many women were able to leave their homes and experience the mobility and sisterhood of pilgrimage. Some, as attested by stele inscriptions, acted as leaders of pilgrimage groups consisting of both women and men. In addition to the heightened spiritual atmosphere, interaction, and mobility women experience on pilgrimage to Mount Tai, their pilgrimage preparations present opportunities for establishing influence and authority within their home communities. The potential for them to enhance their esteem and bond to *lao nainai* continue into their home and community life. This is especially true if they are perceived as successfully intervening in health, good fortune, or the production of male heirs as a result of their piety.

CHAPTER 2

Pilgrimage as Legitimation

Manchu Emperors in

Chinese Sacred Space

During the late imperial period, two Manchu emperors visited Mount Tai. Xuanye 玄曄, the Kangxi emperor (r. 1662–1722), visited Mount Tai in 1684, 1689, and 1703. On the first and last occasions, the emperor ascended to the peak of Mount Tai. In 1689, he performed rituals at the base of the mountain but did not climb to the summit. Xuanye's grandson, Hongli 弘曆, the Qianlong emperor (r. 1736–95, d. 1799), made the journey nine times, in 1748, 1751, 1757, 1762, 1771, 1776, 1780, 1784, and 1790, climbing to the top six times (in 1748, 1757, 1762, 1771, 1776, and 1790).[1] In interacting with Mount Tai, these two emperors used the mountain to further personal as well as dynastic goals. In addition, the emperors expressed their Manchu and personal identities in their relationships with this sacred peak.[2]

Many actions of these emperors support the view that the Manchu rulers adopted Chinese conceptions of proper rulership in order to legitimate their rule in the eyes of the Han Chinese elite. Other acts, however, did not conform closely to Chinese precedent. The Kangxi emperor orchestrated his behavior on Mount Tai with Manchu as well as Han Chinese audiences in mind. Although on many levels the Qing emperors took on the mantle of the Son of Heaven as the rulers of China proper,[3] they were, especially during the seventeenth and eighteenth centuries, non-Chinese rulers of an empire that included non-Chinese peoples. Until recently, much scholarship on the Qing dynasty asserted that the Manchus were successful because they adopted Chinese ways and culture, because they became "sinicized." However, "new scholarship suggests just the opposite: the key to Qing success, at least in terms of empire-building, lay in its ability to use its cultural links with the non-Han peoples of Inner Asia and to differentiate the administration of the non-Han regions from the administration of the former Ming provinces."[4] Similarly, Mark Elliot, in a study of Manchu identity, declares "I believe that the Qing dynastic enterprise depended both on Manchu ability to adapt to Chinese political traditions *and* on their ability to maintain a separate identity."[5]

Ning Chia, in a study of the rituals overseen by the bureaucratic institution created by the Manchus to rule the areas outside the former Ming territories, concludes: "The cultural sources for the imperial political power of the Chinese empire were expanded to include both agricultural and nomadic heritages, and the image of the emperor to be both the Chinese Son of Heaven and the Inner Asian great ruler."[6] The Qianlong emperor, in particular, saw himself as a universal ruler and overtly portrayed himself as the ruler of five peoples: the Manchus, Mongols, Tibetans, Uighurs, and Chinese.[7] He also portrayed himself in different ways to the different peoples in the empire. David Farquhar has shown, for example, that Tibetans and Mongols saw the early Qing emperors as reincarnations of the bodhisattva Mañjuśrī.[8] Rawski argues that the "Qing rulers patronized Confucianism for the Han Chinese, shamanism for the northeastern peoples (the Manchus), and Tibetan Buddhism for the Mongols and Tibetans. The rulers also supported Islam, the religion of the Turkic-speaking Muslims of Central Asia [the Uighurs]."[9]

However, even within the context of fulfilling their role as the Son of Heaven—a Han Chinese identity—for their rule over China proper, the Manchu emperors found ways to express their own cultural heritage. A prime example of Manchu manipulation of a Chinese tradition was the Qianlong emperor's compilation of an enormous collection of literature known as the Four Treasuries (*Siku quanshu* 四庫全書). On the surface, this was a highly orthodox undertaking. Compiling in one collection all the treasures of Chinese writing particularly suited current trends in eighteenth-century scholarship. However, the Qianlong emperor also manipulated this project as a means to censor anti-Manchu literature and to propagate a constructed Manchu history and cultural identity.[10]

Analysis of the interactions between these Manchu emperors and Mount Tai adds to our understanding of the multifaceted nature of Qing rulership. Even on Mount Tai, they manifested their Manchu identity. Their rejection of major Han imperial precedents, the remapping of Mount Tai into Manchu territory, and the Qianlong emperor's addition of the mountain and its cultural treasures to his personal collection demonstrated their confidence in reshaping this quintessentially Chinese sacred site. The actions of these two emperors on the mountain also reveal important differences in their personal styles of rulership as well as changes in imperial behavior because of the consolidation of Manchu authority.

Earlier Imperial Precedents

The actions of these two Qing emperors on Mount Tai were shaped by many factors, not the least of which were the precedents set by past emperors. The God of Mount Tai was the only deity on the mountain who received state sacrifices, and from antiquity through the Ming all official prayers offered at the mountain were either addressed to the God of Mount Tai directly or to be passed along by him to Heaven (as in the *feng* sacrifice). Tang and Song debates over the necessity of performing these sacrifices still held resonance in the late imperial period. In order to put the Qing emperors' rejection of the *feng* and *shan* sacrifices in context, this section begins by summarizing Howard Wechsler's study of early Tang ritual and Suzanne Cahill's article on Song Zhenzong's performance of the sacrifices.

The second Tang emperor, Tang Taizong (r. 627–49), made detailed plans for conducting the sacrifices. Although he scheduled the sacrifices on three occasions, he never actually followed through. The question he posed to those urging him to do so was: Was not a highly respected emperor such as Han Wendi, who had

not performed the rites, a better ruler to imitate than the much re-
viled Qin Shihuangdi, who had? Moreover, Tang Taizong continued, Heaven was honored in the annual sacrifices at the altar in the
southern suburbs of the capital and did not need to be honored on
Mount Tai as well.[11]

An exchange between Tang Taizong and one of his high officials,
Wei Zheng 魏徵, resulted in a list of prerequisites for the sacrifices:
"general domestic peace; the submission of China's border neigh-
bors; the appearance of auspicious omens; abundant harvests; generally favorable economic conditions; and a demonstration of both
the personal merit and virtue of the ruler. Wechsler notes that this
demanding list combined with the rarity of the performances made
a decision to conduct the sacrifices an act loaded with "the possible
implication of hubris." Indeed, at least one Qing dynasty scholar
praised Tang Taizong "for not having been seduced . . . by the
grandeur of the ceremonies."[12]

Although Tang Taizong was eventually convinced by his advisors that he was worthy enough to perform the sacrifices, factors
beyond his personal control caused him to cancel them. In 632,
poor economic conditions were responsible for the cancellation; in
642, an inauspicious comet; and in 648, military campaigns, costly
construction projects already under way, and flooding.[13] Probably
the main rationale for the Qing emperors' rejection of the sacrifices can be found in a comment of Wei Zheng: "[The success of]
rulers lies in their virtue, not in [their performance of] the Feng
and Shan."[14]

Tang Gaozong's (r. 650–83) many military victories in the 660s
and a healthy economy were seen as justifications for his performance of the rites in 666. Tang Gaozong has often been portrayed
as a weak ruler because of the dominance of his wife, Empress Wu,
who defied the traditional role of the empress by taking an active
part in her husband's running of the country. In addition, she convinced her husband, over ardent protests by court officials, that she
be allowed to conduct secondary rituals connected with the *shan*
sacrifice of 666.[15] Empress Wu has been traditionally denigrated as
one of the worst women in Chinese history because she eventually
founded her own dynasty, displacing one of her sons, the only

woman in Chinese history to assume the title "Son of Heaven."
Tang Gaozong's reign, because of his connection with Empress
Wu, was subsequently seen as tainted, and this fact consequently
made him a dubious model for later debates about the *feng* and
shan sacrifices.

The other Tang emperor to perform the sacrifices, Tang Xuanzong (r. 713–55), although he is often held up as a great romantic
figure, is also a controversial ruler. Tang Xuanzong's infatuation
with his concubine Yang Guifei 楊貴妃 (d. 755) has been traditionally viewed as a major cause of the An Lushan rebellion in 755.
This rebellion is in turn often seen as the beginning of the decline
of the Tang dynasty. In addition, Tang Xuanzong, who performed
the *feng* and *shan* sacrifices after a religious text fell from Heaven to
the base of Mount Tai, has been portrayed in Chinese sources as
susceptible to religious forgeries.[16]

Song Zhenzong (r. 998–1022) was a devout Daoist and surrounded himself with religious advisors. In the first lunar month of
1008, a "heavenly text" (*tianshu* 天書) fell to earth in the capital.
Because of this auspicious event, the emperor's religious advisors
convinced him to perform the *feng* and *shan* ceremonies at Mount
Tai. As if to reinforce this decision, on the sixth day of the sixth
lunar month, another "heavenly text" fell to earth at the base of
Mount Tai. The emperor arrived at Mount Tai to perform the
ceremonies in the tenth lunar month. During this time, there were
numerous auspicious signs, including five-colored clouds, yellow
light from the moon, and a crown or halo on top of the sun.[17]

Although many scholars and official historians subsequently
characterized Song Zhenzong as extremely gullible and credulous,
Cahill demonstrates that his acceptance of the heavenly text was a
reasonable reaction for a devout Song dynasty Daoist.[18] Many of
the attacks on the emperor can be seen as infighting among court
factions. However, some of the remonstrances of an important official, Sun Ji 孫籍, who opposed the sacrifices, apparently influenced how this emperor's performance of the *feng* and *shan* sacrifices was viewed by the Qing dynasty emperors. In 1008, China
was in imminent danger of military attack from, or even conquest
by, the Khitan Liao dynasty, which had inflicted a severe defeat on

Song troops in 1004. Sun argued that the emperor, like Han Wudi and Tang Xuanzong, was making the mistake of following his religious advisors instead of knowledgeable and competent officials. In addition, Sun also "pointed out that no Sung emperor had ever performed the *feng* and *shan*, though the issue had often been discussed, because none felt his prestige and virtue to be of sufficiently high order. The preconditions for the performance of the two greatest of all sacrifices have not yet under Sung come into existence. By performing them, the emperor had betrayed his sacred trust."[19]

No Ming emperors visited Mount Tai. Instead, they sent special envoys to offer prayers on their behalf. In addition to regularly scheduled annual, autumn sacrifices in honor of the god, there are references to thirty-nine other official prayers offered during the Ming dynasty. The vast majority of these prayers, twenty-six, appealed to the god as a nature deity, asking for relief from droughts, floods, earthquakes, and other natural disasters. Another six prayers addressed the god in his role as intermediary with Heaven, announcing the Ming dynasty's receipt of the Mandate of Heaven or the ascension of a particular emperor. Four prayers, all early in the dynasty, between 1395 and 1407, appealed to the god for assistance in military pursuits. The other three prayers, all offered during the reign of the Jiajing emperor (r. 1522–66), appealed to the god as the source of life. In 1532 the emperor's emissary appealed to the god for an imperial heir. In 1538 thanks were offered for the successful delivery of a son. In 1561, in honor of the emperor's birthday, the envoy delivered a prayer thanking the god for long life.[20]

Zhu Yuanzhang 朱元璋, the founder of the Ming dynasty, did not send an official to Mount Tai to announce the new dynasty until 1377, nine years after the founding of the dynasty. In the prayer, the emperor explained that the delay was due to continued unrest within the country. Here we can see some of the same rationales used in past dynasties for not performing the *feng* and *shan* sacrifices. Likewise, the emperor also justified sending an envoy rather than personally offering his announcement on the grounds that the continuing need to safeguard the country prevented him from traveling to Mount Tai.[21]

The question of performing the *feng* and *shan* sacrifices was raised during the reign of the Yongle emperor (r. 1403–24). According to Zha Zhilong, an official in the Court of Imperial Sacrifices, in an effort to curry favor, requested that the emperor perform the *feng* sacrifice at Mount Tai. The emperor, however, denounced the suggestion.[22] At some point between 1501 and 1504, during the reign of the Hongzhi emperor (r. 1488–1505), several high-ranking officials convinced the emperor to abandon his plans for an expensive performance of Daoist rituals on top of Mount Tai.[23]

In addition to the official state-endorsed prayers to the God of Mount Tai, members of the Ming imperial family also offered unofficial prayers to Bixia Yuanjun as well as support for her main temple on top of the mountain. In 1532, when the Jiajing emperor sent an official emissary to pray to the God of Mount Tai for an heir, his mother, the empress dowager, sent someone to the mountain to offer a prayer to Bixia Yuanjun for an imperial son.[24]

In 1585 the Wanli emperor (r. 1573–1620) ordered a major remodeling and repair of the main Bixia temple. He also commissioned a bronze statue of the goddess and the so-called Bronze Pavilion (Tong ting 銅亭) to house the statue.[25] This pavilion is also known as the Golden Palace (Jin que 金闕), a Daoist term for a residence of immortals.[26] The Bronze Pavilion and the statue were placed in the middle of the main courtyard of the temple.[27] All these commissions were undertaken in hopes that these pious acts would elicit the goddess's compassion and help in curing the failing eyesight of the emperor's mother.[28]

The Wanli emperor commissioned another pious act on behalf of his mother in a different temple. A statue of the Empress Dowager Xiaoding 孝定 in the guise of the Nine Lotus Bodhisattva (Jiulian pusa 九蓮菩薩) was placed in a hall in the Heavenly Text Temple (Fig. 5, no. 73). The empress dowager was a devout Buddhist and felt a close affinity with the Nine Lotus Bodhisattva, a manifestation of Guanyin in many sectarian scriptures.[29] During the Chongzhen emperor's reign (1628–44), a statue of his mother, Empress Dowager Xiaochun 孝純, as the Bodhisattva of Wisdom (Zhishang pusa 智上菩薩) was placed in another room in the Heavenly Text Temple.[30] In 1611, a younger sister of the Wanli emperor, the Princess Ruian (Ruian changgongzhu 瑞安長公主), commissioned a printing of a religious text about Bixia Yuanjun.[31] During the Longqing period (1567–72), a member of the imperial family, Zhu Muyi 朱睦㮹, commissioned the building of a small temple to Bixia Yuanjun on the back side of Mount Tai (no. 60).[32]

Dynastic Legitimation: The Kangxi Emperor and Dual Identity

The Manchu Qing dynasty officially replaced the Ming dynasty in 1644. The Manchu hold on the Mandate of Heaven, however, was by no means assured by the ritual act of ascending the throne in Beijing. Ming loyalists and rebelling generals kept Manchu control of China in doubt until 1681. The final holdout of Ming loyalists on Taiwan was not crushed until 1683. In the following year, 1684, the Kangxi emperor undertook his first southern tour, traveling from Beijing to Zhejiang province. One of the main purposes of this tour was to legitimate the Manchus' claim to the Mandate of Heaven in the eyes of the Chinese: "Throughout his tour Kangxi made every effort to play the role of a traditional Confucian monarch. . . . [Furthermore,] the various functions and ritual ceremonies which Kangxi enacted as well as his very presence among the populace served to confirm his legitimacy and demonstrated his intention to rule his Chinese subjects as a Chinese-style monarch."[33] In addition, this and other tours gave the emperor the opportunity to assess the competence of local officials, survey the state of river conservancy projects, and evaluate the lives of the people.[34]

Indeed, such imperial tours of inspection fit well into Han Chinese literati views of good governance. Wechsler, in his study of Tang imperial rituals, points out that "on tours of inspection, emperors who lived in relative political isolation could gauge firsthand the quality of local government and popular sentiments toward the dynasty. By personally visiting outlying areas they demonstrated a tender, Confucian concern for the masses. Inquiring into government, they might ameliorate the most intolerable of local economic or social ills."[35]

This first southern tour was more than an opportunity for the Kangxi emperor to portray himself as an ideal Chinese ruler and to inspect his realm and people. It was also a victory tour. The Manchus' grasp of China was now firm, and a southern tour was a natural means both to celebrate and to demonstrate the submission of China to these mounted northern warriors. The emperor's physical presence in the territories through which he traveled demonstrated his rule over those lands and people. In essence, he took physical possession of this now thoroughly conquered and subjugated territory.

His various performances certainly had ample audiences of Han Chinese literati. In 1684, in addition to Manchu clansmen and imperial guards, the emperor was accompanied by "about ninety men drawn from among the grand secretaries, Hanlin academicians, Board presidents, department directors, censors, [literary] doctors, diarists, all these in turn being accompanied by the necessary secretaries and clerks. The total must have been one thousand persons."[36] In addition, the audiences for the emperor's tour were increased by residents and officials of the areas through which he passed:

Statutes of 1675 had laid down that whenever the Emperor traveled through an area, all officials living within one hundred *li* must come and welcome him. . . . These statutes were enforced in 1684 by officials from the Court of State Ceremonial, who rode out ahead of the cortege ordering all officials within a hundred *li* to assemble the local elite (*hsiang-shen*) and scholar-commoners (*shih-min*) in their area to kneel and greet the Emperor on his arrival and departure.[37]

As they knelt before the emperor, these officials and members of the local elite were also reminded of the fact that the Son of Heaven was a foreign ruler. On the penalty of death, all of them wore their hair in the Manchu style—a shaved forehead with a queue in the back. The officials also wore Manchu-style ceremonial robes:

Official formal clothing consisted of the *chaofu* or court robe which preserved some of the features of original Manchu costume from preconquest times. . . .
. . . The curved overlapping right front was a shape derived from an animal skin, and fastened with loops and toggles, again nomadic in origin.

The long fitted sleeves . . . [are] thought to have developed so that the wearer could bend his arm more easily while hunting. The sleeves ended in horse-hoof cuffs, originally intended to protect the hands when the wearer was riding in bad weather.[38]

A further reminder of the nomadic, nonagricultural heritage of this ruler and his bodyguards was displayed throughout these tours in their excellent horsemanship. When the officials caught sight of the emperor, it was quite likely that they would have seen him on horseback. In addition, on at least one occasion during the southern tour of 1684, the emperor had Manchu bannermen put on a display of their horsemanship. The emperor and his entourage also occasionally stayed overnight in Manchu-style tents.[39]

Given the Kangxi emperor's goal of asserting and legitimizing his rulership over China, it was quite logical that on the 1684 tour he would ascend China's most ritually potent mountain—Mount Tai. Just by including it on the itinerary of his first southern imperial inspection tour, the Kangxi emperor associated himself with his famous predecessors who had ascended the mountain. His act of visiting an important site both demonstrated his knowledge of Chinese culture and history and showed that this territory was now part of a Manchu empire.

The "Chart of Mount Tai," now held in the Number One Historical Archives in Beijing, extended the Kangxi emperor's symbolic possession of Mount Tai beyond the duration of his visits (see Fig. 30). Although the chart has not been dated by the Number One Archives, references on the map itself support a date of around 1684, the time of the Kangxi emperor's first visit to the mountain.[40] This chart is an excellent example of a political map that signified the possession of the territory portrayed.[41] The Manchus had taken military possession of Mount Tai in 1644, when they overthrew the Ming dynasty. The Kangxi emperor, however, took physical and personal possession of the mountain when he climbed it, on foot, in 1684. During the Qing dynasty, the "Chart of Mount Tai" was stored in the Imperial Household Department within the Forbidden City. Thus, even when the emperor was no longer on the mountain, he was still in personal possession of the

Fig. 30 Detail of "Taishan ditu" (Chart of Mount Tai). Ca. 1684;
held in the Number One Historical Archives in Beijing.

mountain in the form of this map. That this was a political map
rather than a scenic painting is underscored by its portrayal of administrative details. The map neatly records the physical details of
the mountain and the names of eighty-one important sites, including the official offices in the city at the mountain's base, without
picturing a single person or animal.

The Kangxi emperor asserted Manchu possession of Mount Tai
in a much more compelling manner by documenting that the

mountain's roots lay in his own homeland. In an essay entitled
"Mount Tai's Mountain Veins Originate in the Changbai Mountains," the Kangxi emperor utilized the principles of Han Chinese
geomancy or *fengshui* and the Han Chinese system of evidential
learning[42] to support his claim that Mount Tai had direct connections with the region of his lineage's origins. The Changbai Mountains separate the Korean peninsula from Manchuria. According to
the foundation myths of the Kangxi emperor's lineage, the Aisin
Gioro, their first ancestor came from the Changbai Mountains.[43]
Although this essay is not dated in any of the collections in which
it appears, it probably was composed around the time of the emperor's first two visits to Mount Tai.[44] Some of the places referred
to in the text are labeled in Fig. 2 (p. 8).

> Mount Tai's Mountain Veins Originate in the Changbai Mountains
> ("Taishan shanmai zi Changbaishan lai" 泰山山脈自長白山來)

In ancient as well as present times, [we hear] discussion of the mountain
veins (*shanmai* 山脈) of the Nine Districts [Inner China], but only Mount
Hua [the Western Sacred Peak] is said to be the tiger and Mount Tai the
dragon. Geomancers also merely say that Mount Tai specially stands in
the east, spreading left and right to [provide] shelter for protection. Without studying the roots of Mount Tai's dragon, how can we know the
places where the veins issue forth? I [the emperor], through careful investigation of the terrain, deeply studying geographic connections, and dis-
patching people in ships to survey the sea, know that in fact Mount Tai's
dragon arises in the Changbai Mountains.

The Changbai Mountains stretch continuously south from Mount
Wula.[45] In all parts of the [Changbai] Mountains, hundreds of springs run
quickly down, forming the origins of three great rivers, the Songhua, the
Yalu, and the Tumen. Their [the Changbai Mountains'] southern foothills divide into two stems. One stem points to the southwest. . . . The
other stem goes west and then north . . . where it again splits into two
branches. The northern branch goes to Shengjing,[46] where it forms the
Tianzhu and Longye mountains, and then bends to the west. . . . The
western branch enters Xingjingmen and becomes Kaiyun Mountain. It
[then] zigzags to the south, continuously rising and lowering, [forming]
range upon range of mountains, extending to Iron Mountain at the port
of Lüshun [Port Arthur] in Jinzhou, it then [appears] as Longji [island],
sometimes it is hidden [beneath the sea], sometimes it is visible. Huang-

cheng, Tuoji, and other islands [in the Gulf of Bohai] are all places where it is visible. Within the sea the dragon is hidden, [but] in Dengzhou in Shandong it rises up [out of the sea], resulting in Mount Fu and Mount Danyai. It travels more than 800 *li* to the southwest, resulting in Mount Tai, [rising] loftily into the sky, coiled and crouching, the chief of the Five Sacred Peaks.

Although the ancients did not reach [the conclusions] of this essay, the topography truly proves them. If there are those who doubt that the strength of a mountain can be continuous even through the realm of the sea, or that a mountain's form and essence (*xingqi* 形氣) can be compared to and called a dragon, they have no basis [for their doubts]. Ban Gu[47] states that "form (*xing*) and essence (*qi*) have heads and tails." Now, *fengshui* masters[, when referring to dragons,] use [the terms] "pass through straits" (*guo xia* 過峽) and "water realm" (*jie shui* 界水). The Gulf of Bohai, then, is Mount Tai's large "pass through straits" [place]. Wei Xiao, of the Song dynasty, states in his *Explanation of Geography* (*Dili shuo* 地理説) that "[dragons] can be attached to rivers or enter the sea." Thus, that the Changbai Mountains' dragon enters the sea and becomes Mount Tai is assuredly so. Mount Tai's positioning is further evidence, it faces southwest with its back to the northeast. . . . Therefore [our] reasoning is clear and intelligible.[48]

According to the emperor's carefully laid out proofs, this sacred mountain's dragon veins, like its emperor, originated in the Changbai Mountains and spanned a vast geographic area stretching all the way to the center of Shandong province. The emperor proudly points out that he personally arrived at this conclusion through careful investigation of both the physical terrain and past literature. Using the evidential techniques popular among many scholars of the time and demonstrating an awareness of the cartographic fervor of some of his Jesuit advisors, the Kangxi emperor claimed a level of illumination that "ancients did not reach."[49] The emperor's personal industriousness and penetrating mind along with the elemental potency of Mount Tai and the Changbai mountains were reciprocal proofs unto themselves. The emperor subtly shifted the subject of the essay from Mount Tai to the Changbai Mountains. He began his essay, perhaps with a Han literati audience in mind, with his desire to understand "Mount Tai's dragon." By the end of his essay, after his detailed tracing of the "dragon's veins" to his homeland, however, he had adroitly transferred his audience's attention to the "Changbai Mountains' dragon," which "becomes Mount Tai." He framed a narrative of sacred space familiar to officials and literati, with its own history of associations and significances, within the newly emerging Manchu historiography. The implied parallel with his lineage's history was almost certainly a primary goal of this essay. The Aisin Gioro lineage originated in the Changbai Mountains and the leader of that clan, the Kangxi emperor, now controlled and possessed China, represented in the essay by the sacred Mount Tai.

Many actions undertaken by the Kangxi emperor on Mount Tai were much less overt in their assertion of Manchu dominance. Indeed, much of his behavior wholeheartedly endorsed and adopted the practices of an ideal ruler as theorized in the Classics, including the *Analects* and the *Mencius*. Imperial actions, however, often go beyond mere stereotypes. Wu Hung, in an analysis of Qing portrait painting, notes that "the notion of 'stereotype' . . . overlooks the dialectical relationship between convention and invention. True, a dominant model in literary and artistic production is essentially conservative, but deliberate variations on an existing model also serve to measure creativity."[50] In this article Wu shows how a series of paintings of twelve beautiful Chinese women, commissioned by Yinzhen 胤禛, the future Yongzheng emperor, while he was still a prince, demonstrate a Manchu "desire to exercise power over a defeated culture and nation."[51] In another article, Wu discusses the hidden meaning behind the many portraits of the Yongzheng and Qianlong emperors in costume or masquerade. One painting portrays the Yongzheng emperor and his young son Hongli, the future Qianlong emperor, dressed in the garb of ancient Confucian scholars: "Here these two Manchu rulers have themselves become representatives of Chinese culture; their virtues are manifested through traditional Chinese symbols, most notably bamboo and pines. The emperors' disguise, therefore, legitimates their possession and appropriation of the Chinese cultural tradition by denying, however artificially, their image as outsiders who came to own this tradition through seizure."[52] Although Wu Hung's articles focus on the Yongzheng and Qianlong emperors, his analysis of the image of Manchus' possessing and appropriating Chinese culture applies equally to the Kangxi emperor. Indeed, given the precarious nature of the empire during the early part of the Kangxi emperor's reign, one could argue that demonstrating Manchu mastery of Chinese culture was even more important for him than for his descendants.

When we examine the Kangxi emperor's often conscious endorsement of accepted Chinese rituals and actions on Mount Tai, it is also important to place this Manchu ruler in the historical setting of seventeenth-century perceptions of late Ming failings. Frederic Wakeman portrays the early seventeenth century as a time when "the social fabric of the empire began to unravel . . . the poor and starving went to the cities . . . [and] public services collapsed." He notes further that "the peasant rebellions of the late Ming were generated by a combination of repeated famines during the 1630's and '40's, and widespread government disintegration."[53] Supporters of the Qing in the seventeenth and eighteenth centuries looked back on the late Ming as a period when the pervasive obsession of the scholar-elite class with objects undermined the society. According to Craig Clunas:

[The] effeteness and unfitness of the Ming elite . . . in fact became an important plank of Qing state ideology; as in an extension of the venerable 'Mandate of Heaven' theory of state decline, it was argued that not just the Ming ruling house but the entire Han Chinese ruling class had lost the legitimate mandate through factionalism, internal dissension and an unseemly degree of attention to selfish aesthetic gratification at the expense of practical affairs.[54]

The Kangxi emperor's records of his trips to Mount Tai, which emphasize inspection, good governance, and concern for the poor, suggest a sharp antipathy to such effete self-gratification.

The performance of rituals was an extremely important aspect of rulership in China. An official record of the Kangxi emperor's first visit to Mount Tai in 1684 shows him dutifully fulfilling this role:

The 10th day, *renyin* [1684.11.16]. The emperor arrived in Tai'an county. At noon, he began ascending Mount Dai. The emperor rode on a horse through the Red Gate and traveled for a little over a *li*. He then traveled by foot up stone stairways, traveling for [another] 40 *li*. In the afternoon, the emperor climbed to the top. He performed rituals (*xingli* 行禮) in the Tianxian Hall of the Zhaozhen Temple.[55] He climbed again, several hundred paces to the northeast to the Dongyue Temple and performed rituals (*xingli*). He climbed again, a bit over one hundred paces to the northwest and performed rituals (*xingli*) at the Jade Emperor Temple. . . .

The 11th day, *guimao*. . . . Early on this day, the emperor led the accompanying officials in performing rituals (*xingli*) in the Tianxian Hall. . . . At the *chen* hour [7–9 A.M.], the emperor walked about on Dai's peak and then descended. The day approached noon. . . . The emperor went to the Dongyue Temple in the imperial carriage and personally sacrificed (*si* 祀) to the God of Mount Tai in the Junji Hall.[56]

In these selections, the emperor engaged in appropriate imperial ritual acts at the three main temples on top of Mount Tai as well as at the large temple at its base. In addition, the emperor's ascending "by foot" was an important, highly visible, acknowledgment of his respect and reverence for this sacred peak. The statements that the emperor "led the accompanying officials" and "personally prayed" can be seen as examples of the emperor demonstrating to the Han literati that he knew how to lead performances of their rituals. At the same time, his assertion of power and authority over the Han officials would have appealed to the Manchu elite in his party. Reverence for Mount Tai astutely balanced this control with respect for a sacred space potent to most groups of Han Chinese.

One way in which the Kangxi emperor went beyond the stereotyped behavior of a correct monarch was his choice of the temple where he first, and most frequently, prayed. When the emperor reached the summit of the mountain, the first temple he entered was the main temple to Bixia Yuanjun. The next morning, the only temple he entered on the mountain's peak was this same temple. Traditionally Mount Tai was famous for imperial rituals because of the *feng* and *shan* sacrifices, which used the God of Mount Tai as a messenger between the emperor and Heaven. Thus, traditionally, the primary recipient of imperial worship was the God of Mount Tai, not Bixia Yuanjun. What motivated the Kangxi emperor to give primacy to this goddess? Possibly he chose to reflect the popular preference for this compassionate deity and thus appeal to the majority, the illiterate northern Han population. This trickster deity, who protected sincere believers, may have particularly appealed to this emperor, who also sought to protect commoners from abuses. Perhaps he wanted to emphasize her role as a fertility goddess and her close affiliation with the concept of filial piety and continuing family lines. Indeed, he may even have prayed to her to continue his own dynastic line beyond the length of previous foreign-ruled Chinese regimes. He may also have been emphasizing his rejection of a suggestion that he perform the *feng* and *shan* sacrifices, since in those ceremonies emperors presented their offerings to the God of Mount Tai.

An important visual source for the Kangxi emperor's visits to Mount Tai is a series of handscrolls he commissioned to celebrate his southern tour in 1689. This imperial patronage of the arts co-opted a Chinese medium and directed literati energies into a Manchu historiography project. Nonetheless, these scrolls paint the Kangxi emperor in classical Chinese terms. This visual endorsement of him as an ideal ruler in the established style also allowed an adaptation of the Kangxi emperor to suit a literati vision. For, as Wen Fong notes, "In the political arena, archaism as an artistic imperative found a correlative in political reform, both artistic and political reform being driven by the same impulse and inspired by the vision of an archaic, mythic purity. . . . Thus, painting was very much bound to the vicissitudes of Chinese civilization, and painting in late imperial China remained the voice of a Chinese sensibility."[57] Imperial sponsorship of the arts, in addition to being an important patronage for artists, also demonstrated an emperor's cultivated, aesthetic taste. The potential for being criticized for imitating the effete, aesthetically and introspectively directed late Ming literati was minimized by the circumscribed audience of these imperial handscrolls. They were made by and for a very limited, prestigious audience. If they circulated beyond the artists and the Kangxi emperor, they would still likely announce only to the high literati, future emperors, or court historians the impeccable performance of the second Qing emperor within the ritually potent, traditional heartland of the Middle Kingdom.

The Kangxi emperor's endorsement of the painter Wang Hui 王翬 (1632–1717) as the main artist for the project would certainly have served to demonstrate his artistic knowledge since Wang "was probably the most renown[ed] artist of the day."[58] Wang and a number of assistants officially began work on the *Pictures of the Southern Tour* (*Nanxun tu* 南巡圖), a series of twelve large hand-scrolls, around 1691 and completed the commission by 1698. Each scroll recorded a separate section of the journey. This commission offered the Kangxi emperor "the opportunity to present himself in harmony with the most revered traditions of scholarly painting."[59] Perhaps more important, "As conquerors of a different ethnic and cultural background than their Chinese subjects, the Manchu sovereigns used paintings to support their claim to be legitimate rulers of China."[60] As Wu Hung has demonstrated, there were underlying messages in many of the paintings commissioned by the Kangxi emperor's immediate successors; the *Pictures of the Southern Tour* also contain important political messages about Manchu rule.

The third scroll in the series covers a section of the journey in Shandong province. It begins in Ji'nan, the provincial capital, heads south to Mount Tai, and from there continues further south to the town of Mengyin, for a total of 200 kilometers. This third scroll, held at the Metropolitan Museum of Art, measures 67.8 cm wide by 1,393 cm long. The figure of the emperor appears only once in each scroll. In the third scroll, he appears near the beginning astride a horse on top of the city wall of Ji'nan.[61] Like the traditional Son of Heaven, he is under an imperial umbrella, but emphasizing his Manchu identity, he chose to appear on a horse rather than seated or standing. The central subject of the third scroll is not the imperial image; instead the scroll "culminates in the scene of majestic Mt. Tai where officials are making preparations for the arrival of the emperor."[62] As the scroll is unrolled (from right to left), some members of the imperial retinue enter from the right and arrive at Ji'nan. The emperor on his horse on the city wall looks south toward Mount Tai. Further to the left, a continuous line of officials on horseback precede the emperor and the main body of his procession, going ahead to prepare for his

Fig. 31   Detail from painting of the Kangxi emperor's southern tour in 1689; section showing the altar at the base of Mount Tai. Wang Hui and assistants, 1691–98. Third handscroll
from the series *Pictures of the Southern Tour* (The Metropolitan Museum of Art, Purchase,
The Dillon Fund Gift, 1979 [1979.5]; reprinted by permission).

arrival. The horsemen wend their way along twisting mountain
roads, through increasingly tall peaks, to arrive at Mount Tai (see
Fig. 31).

The eyes of the viewer, drawn continually from right to left by
the forerunners on horseback, naturally stop at the section with
Mount Tai, the only place in the scroll where the horsemen come
to a halt. Here, two higher-ranking officials with peacock feathers
in their hats have dismounted at the mountain's base and are wait-
ing for the emperor to arrive. They stand just below a temporary
altar set up at the base of the mountain, where the emperor will
perform the prescribed ceremonies (see Fig. 31; the two officials'
horses are being held by grooms off to the right). These two members of the emperor's retinue are joined by other figures, probably
the local officials, members of the local elite, and scholar-
commoners ordered to gather to welcome the emperor. The figures in the long robes gathered around the temporary altar are

most likely Daoist monks from various temples on the mountain. Further along in the scroll, to the left of Mount Tai, the procession of forerunners continues the progression, but now through decreasingly tall hills, arriving at the town of Mengyin, with the hills disappearing beyond (to the left of) the town.

Although Mount Tai is the key visual subject in the third scroll as a whole, in the section portraying the mountain the focus is further concentrated on the altar where the emperor will conduct the rituals. In this aspect, the painting accurately captures the tone of the official accounts of the Kangxi emperor's 1689 visit. On that visit he did not climb the mountain; instead, "the emperor arrived at the base of Mount Tai, faced Mount Tai, and led all the civil and military officials in performing rituals (*xingli* 行禮). The emperor then entered Tai'an County City through the north gate. He went to the Junji Hall in the Dongyue Temple, where he led all the civil and military officials in performing rituals (*xingli*)."[63] This visual focus on the site for the performance of imperial ceremonies at Mount Tai is also reflected and reinforced in the scroll's title: "The Third Scroll: From Ji'nan Prefecture Through Tai'an Department, with Performance of Ceremonies at Mount Tai."

The imperial rituals conducted at the mountain were also the subject of the colophon at the beginning of the third scroll:

The third scroll. We respectfully painted the arrival of the emperor in Ji'nan, where he climbed and inspected the city walls. All the populace together raised hands to their foreheads [in salutation]. They rejoiced to look upon the imperial countenance. Thereupon, the imperial retinue wound its way along mountain roads to Tai'an department. The emperor specially led all the officials in the retinue in completing rituals (*zhili* 致禮) at Mount Tai. At that time the sacred peak's spirit was efficacious and auspicious. Peaks and ridges towered aloft, clouds and trees soared gracefully. The elders of Tai'an sang and danced, filling the road.[64]

This emphasis on ritual clearly placed this Manchu ruler in the long history of Chinese emperors who followed the important Confucian precept of conducting rites and sacrifices correctly. To paraphrase Wu Hung, here we see the Kangxi emperor in the guise of a Confucian scholar who "legitimates [his] possession and appropriation of the Chinese cultural tradition" and demonstrates his "authority to rule China."[65] Indeed, Wen Fong, in a discussion of the third scroll, emphasizes that "the landscape resonates with symbolic overtones as the peaks, rising to a crescendo, express the favor of heaven bestowed upon the Manchu Son of Heaven."[66]

The twelve handscrolls of the *Pictures of the Southern Tour*, like the "Chart of Mount Tai" held in the Number One Archive, are examples of the concept that possession of a map or a painted representation of territory connotes real authority and control over the actual land.[67] If the Yongzheng emperor's possession of paintings of Chinese women could symbolize southern China and his desire to control and rule China, the Kangxi emperor's paintings of his southern tour can be read as an even more blatant extension of Manchu control over the former Ming territories.[68] While the emperor was journeying in the south, he gained actual possession of the land through his presence; the paintings representing his 1689 tour continued this connection even when he was physically removed far to the north.

Even though the intended audience for this handscroll would never have included peasants, the emperor's significance to the people was depicted by portraying commoners looking up to the emperor on top of the city wall in Ji'nan. As was the emperor's prerogative, he is facing south, and all his subjects are facing north, as was customary. The enthusiastic welcoming given the emperor by the crowd at Ji'nan and the dancing and singing of the Tai'an elders mentioned in the colophon represent spontaneous expressions of the people's approval of the Kangxi emperor's rulership. Such public endorsements of Chinese rulers were traditionally seen as signs of an upright and just ruler. These widely held beliefs were expressed in the writings of many Confucian philosophers and can be seen in these two excerpts from the teachings of Mencius:

7A.13: Mencius said: ". . . Under a true king . . . the people feel magnificent and at ease with themselves."

7B.14: Mencius said, "[In a state] the people are the most important, . . . Therefore to gain [the hearts of] the peasantry is the way to become an emperor."[69]

Popularity among the people was seen as a sign of Heaven's approval. Wang Hui's sentiments, as expressed in his colophon, were also reflected in an official record of the Kangxi emperor's 1684 visit: "As [the emperor] passed [up the mountain], there were cries of 'Long live the emperor!' "[70] It was important to the Kangxi emperor that records of his southern tour show that he had been well received not only by Han literati but also by the equally crucial mass audience.

A closely related concept was the belief that auspicious events occurred during the reigns of just and upright emperors as signs of Heaven's approval. The storm that forced Qin Shihuangdi to take refuge was subsequently interpreted as a sign of Heaven's disapproval. In contrast, auspicious events such as those connected with the pilgrimage of Song Zhenzong in 1008 were seen as positive signs and approval of his reign. An official account directly connected the Kangxi emperor's visit in 1684 with the auspicious reign of the emperor Han Wudi:

According to accounts in the *Hanshu*, [when the emperor Han] Wudi ascended Mount Tai, there were no wind and rain storms. Historical writings mark this as an auspicious event. Now, our emperor is examining all regions and inspecting the famous mountains. When he climbed up and down [Mount Tai], the sky was clear and the weather was calm along all four frontiers. The myriad deities were numinous and favorable.[71]

So, while the cheering crowds substantiated the Kangxi emperor's rule from below, auspicious phenomena from above demonstrated Heaven's endorsement.

Another traditional means of assessing the performance of individual emperors was the belief that a monarch's ability to rule was reflected in the state of public-works projects such as flood control, granaries, and temple repairs. While on top of Mount Tai in 1684, the Kangxi emperor ordered that "the Mount Tai incense tax for this year should not be sent to the relevant boards; [instead] use it for the assembled workmen's pay and have them reverently repair all the temples on top of the mountain."[72] These auspicious signs and projects again distinguish this Manchu emperor from his late Ming, Han predecessors.

While on Mount Tai, the Kangxi emperor took the opportunity to impress on the Chinese literati his mastery of the skills of a scholar:

The emperor wrote in the imperial hand the four large characters "Earth's myriad beings bring virtue into harmony" (*kunyuan xie de* 坤元 叶德) for a plaque to be hung in the hall. The emperor returned to the Imperial Travel Palace and wrote in the imperial hand the four large characters "Illumines all Heaven and Earth" (*puzhao qiankun* 普照乾坤) and the two large characters "Cloud Peak" (*yun feng* 雲峰), which were shown to the attendant officials. The bold brush strokes were powerful and vigorous. The resultant writing [exhibited] an orderly spirit. The countenance [of the characters] was luminous and bright. The separate perfections of paper and ink were like the vastness of Heaven and Earth and as splendid as the Milky Way. . . . None of the calligraphy of emperors and kings passed down from antiquity reaches this level.[73]

Exaggerations of his skill aside, the Kangxi emperor demonstrated to the officials in his retinue his skill in choosing appropriate phrases and transferring them to paper. This official diary entry suggests the Kangxi emperor's "orderly spirit" wielded cosmic influence in the sphere of Chinese letters akin to Mount Tai's control over the "vastness of Heaven and Earth."

In addition to keeping the country in good order and being compassionate and upright, emperors were expected to be accomplished in various literary arts such as calligraphy, poetry, composition of appropriate phrases for commemorative plaques, and naming sites or temples. Among these skills, calligraphy was probably the most important:

Calligraphy, the ancient art of the written word, was for the Chinese an art of paradigm, perceived as a means of expressing the dynamic forces of the natural world. . . . Known as the trace of the brush, a calligraphic work represents the brush as an extension of the calligrapher's body and physical movement. . . .
   . . . Concerned with both the present and a long past, calligraphy is at once the most rigorously convention-bound and the most fiercely individualistic of the graphic arts. In executing the written character, the artist is not only a practitioner but a historian and critic as well . . . reaching an understanding of such critical concepts as substance and ornament, tradition and self, orthodoxy and rebellion, archaism and renewal.[74]

The Kangxi emperor certainly understood the importance and significance of calligraphy in Chinese culture:

For the Kangxi emperor, whose rule was supreme over both Chinese and Manchu populations, exemplary brush writing was a means to demonstrate mastery of Chinese literati culture. . . .

. . . [Furthermore, he] knew that presentation of his calligraphy was a way to honor and create a bond with officials whom he wanted to court as loyal supporters.[75]

All the emperors who climbed Mount Tai left some permanent evidence of their visits for posterity. In addition to the plaque described above, the Kangxi emperor also issued orders for the disposition of the other two samples of imperial calligraphy and construction of a small pavilion:

Having taken and moistened my brush, the completed calligraphy of the four characters "Illumines all Heaven and Earth" can be placed on a plaque in a pavilion to be built at the Place Where Confucius Saw the World Was Small [no. 43]. The other calligraphy of the two characters "Cloud Peak" can be carved into the stone [adjacent] to the [Tang] Cliff Inscription on the top of the mountain.[76]

Although the pavilion and plaque no longer exist, the Kangxi emperor's calligraphy "Cloud Peak" (*yun feng* 雲峰) can still be seen (see Fig. 7, p. 19). The carving of the emperor's composition, in his own calligraphy, into the face of Mount Tai was another way of possessing the mountain—marking it as part of his dominion.

The Kangxi emperor's composition on top of the mountain offers further insight into the emperor's view of himself and his conception of rulership. The terseness of the phrase "Illumines all Heaven and Earth" makes the subject quite ambiguous. Like much classical Chinese, the interpretation depends on context. In this instance, the site forms the context. Since the emperor composed and wrote the phrase on Mount Tai, the mountain itself is a likely subject; the phrase would then be read "[Mount Tai] illumines all Heaven and Earth." Since the Kangxi emperor ordered that this example of his calligraphy "be placed on a plaque in a pavilion to be built at the Place Where Confucius Saw the World Was Small," another likely subject is Confucius. This interpretation was adopted by P. A. Tschepe in the early twentieth century and endorsed by Dwight Baker in the mid-1920s.[77] This reading results in the phrase "[Confucius] illumines all Heaven and Earth." A third possible subject is the author: "[I] illumine all Heaven and Earth." The Kangxi emperor was probably well aware of the ambiguity of this phrase, and he may even have consciously desired to conflate himself with Mount Tai and Confucius. Given the content and implications of his essay on Mount Tai's dragon veins, the Kangxi emperor—the possessor and ruler of China and the Son of Heaven—may well have seen himself as the equal of this sacred mountain or as a sage like Confucius. The emperor's view of himself as able to illuminate the entire universe is further supported by a passage from the official diary entry for the first day he spent on top of Mount Tai in 1684. In reference to the emperor's calligraphy, the diary recorded that "placards bearing the imperial ink illuminate this famous mountain."[78]

Another aspect of the third scroll of *Pictures of the Southern Tour* supports the explanation of the Kangxi emperor's promotion of himself as a source of illumination. The Kangxi emperor's position in the third scroll is an important statement about his rule over China and over Mount Tai. The emperor certainly had a say in what is portrayed in each of the scrolls and would surely have paid special attention to his own representation.[79] As mentioned above, in the third scroll, he appears on top of the Ji'nan city wall, facing south. To the south of the emperor, members of the imperial retinue, local officials and notables, and monks await his arrival at the temporary altar at the base of Mount Tai. In a sense, Mount Tai itself, a symbol of China, also awaits the emperor's arrival.

Two events during the emperor's visit to Mount Tai in 1684 provide additional support for the view that the Kangxi emperor sought to set himself apart from and above his Chinese subjects and to distance himself from past Chinese rulers and scholars. As he did in his essay on the dragon veins, in these two instances he again actively constructed an image of the Manchus as not just militarily but culturally superior.

The first situation involved a suggestion regarding Abandon Life Cliff (no. 57). Ming officials, in the hope of discouraging suicides at this location, changed the name to Love Life Cliff, erected a wall, and posted an interdiction against suicide.[80] On the 1684 tour, after spending the night on the mountain, the emperor had risen early, watched the sunrise, and performed rituals in the main Bixia Temple.

[Later] an attending official mentioned the Abandon Life Cliff and asked if the emperor wished to go and see it. The emperor replied: "The ignorant people have no understanding; they are misled by ignorant and preposterous words, such as abandoning one's life is filial. They do not understand that bodies, including hairs and skin, are received by us from our fathers and mothers, and one dare not destroy or damage them.[81] This is why Zengzi was so extremely careful.[82] Moreover, parents love their children and are anxious when they are ill. If children have already killed themselves, they cannot care for their parents; this [act of suicide] is not filial. This and other places like it do exist; the upright and proper must give clear instructions to prohibit such acts. Make sure that the commoners do not err through [the practice of improper] customs. What would be the purpose of seeing such a place?!"[83]

In 1670, at the age of sixteen, the young Kangxi emperor had issued what is known as the *Sacred Edict*. The edict, which consists of sixteen short maxims, became "widely recognized as the most concise and authoritative statement of Confucian ideology."[84] Two of these maxims are particularly important for understanding the emperor's reaction:

1. Esteem most highly filial piety and brotherly submission, in order to give due importance to the social relations.

7. Extirpate strange principles, in order to exalt the correct doctrine.[85]

The Kangxi emperor's concise summary of his interpretation of Confucianism itself exemplified his standing as a Chinese scholar and reinforced his position as the Son of Heaven.

The suggestion that the author of the *Sacred Edict* would want to visit such a site gave the Kangxi emperor an opportunity to lecture the assembled officials on several essential components of Confucianism. This reprimand could almost be taken as an explanatory lecture on the first and seventh maxims of the *Sacred Edict*. He praises filial piety but denounces superstitious and incorrect acts, such as suicide, as utterly stupid and unfilial. In this exchange, we come face to face with a ruler with strong beliefs. More important, we see this Manchu ruler showing Chinese officials how to apply the tenets of Confucianism, which all of them had memorized to pass their examinations, to a practical situation.[86]

The Kangxi emperor also claimed and demonstrated his cultural superiority in the position he took on the *feng* and *shan* sacrifices. If the Kangxi emperor's sole purpose in going to Mount Tai had been to legitimate his reign by co-opting Chinese tradition, then surely performing the ancient *feng* and *shan* rituals, an act that proclaimed the success of the dynasty, would seem to have been the ideal format. However, neither the Kangxi emperor nor the Qianlong emperor performed these ancient ceremonies.

Sometime between late 1683 and the emperor's departure on his southern tour in November 1684, an official named Cao He 曹禾 (ca. 1638–99) memorialized the throne suggesting that the emperor take advantage of the beginning of a new sixty-year cycle (in 1684) and proclaim a new reign title and perform the *feng* and *shan* sacrifices at Mount Tai.[87] Not only did the Kangxi emperor reject this rather sycophantic proposition, but he also took the opportunity to sing the praises of his own reign while attacking as excessive previous performances of the *feng* and *shan* sacrifices. The emperor's basic argument was that the competent and compassionate day-to-day execution of his duties was what counted, not some archaic and self-serving ritual. Furthermore, the implication that an emperor who performed the *feng* and *shan* sacrifices had fulfilled all his duties to the people and to Heaven contradicted the Kangxi emperor's philosophy of rulership. As emperor, he asserted, he had to attend directly to all aspects of the empire on a daily basis. If he failed to oversee the maintenance, for example, of flood-control projects, then many might suffer. Governing was an ongoing process, and success could never be declared at any particular moment. Any emperor who made such a claim, he argued, was guilty of empty boasting.

A number of factors and precedents contributed to the Kangxi emperor's rejection of Cao He's suggestion. Given the importance of evidential scholarship in the late seventeenth century, the fact that *feng* and *shan* sacrifices are not mentioned in the Classics carried great weight in questioning their validity. Wechsler, in his analysis of the Tang dynasty performances of the rituals, notes that the lack of any pre-Qin reference "suggests that the sacrifices were not originally part of Confucian legitimation theory."[88] In addition, all but one of the emperors known to have performed these sacrifices had some sort of character flaw. Qin Shihuangdi was viewed as a burner of books, executor of scholars, and follower of superstitious advisors. Han Wudi was also criticized for his reliance on magicians in his pursuit of immortality. Tang Gaozong was chastised for being under the domination of Empress Wu. Tang Xuanzong's passionate love affair with Yang Guifei was seen as the beginning of the decline of the Tang dynasty. Song Zhenzong was seen as having been susceptible to improper religious advice and as being at least partially to blame for the series of military defeats that eventually led to the humiliating retreat of the Song court to the south in 1127. Only Han Guangwudi was morally unsuspect. Thus, by and large, these Han Chinese emperors were probably not the sort of rulers the Kangxi emperor wanted to cite as precedents for his own reign and dynasty. Since their flaws revealed their susceptibility to the blandishments of their advisors, the Kangxi emperor's rejection of Cao He's advice distinguished him even more forcefully as an active ruler.

The official diary of the emperor's actions on November 17, 1684 (the same day he chastised the official who suggested he visit the Abandon Life Cliff), records the Kangxi emperor's listing of his many positive attributes and the auspicious signs present during his tour:

On that day the emperor ordered the Grand Secretary Mingzhu, saying "I [the emperor] am extremely diligent morning and night, I industriously seek to govern [the country]. In a peaceful place deep within the palace, I remembered the people with deep feeling. An auspicious time for conducting an inspection tour was chosen, in order that I could investigate the unknown sufferings of the people.

This trip to various destinations and the climbing of Mount Tai and going to its sacred and historical places, is like witnessing the past. To glance at this group of mountains, to come to look at the Nine Regions, truly is to be in full possession of the places of scenic beauty below Heaven and to investigate Nature's wonders."[89]

For the emperor, the tour of inspection was yet another concrete example of how, on a daily basis, he actively pursued good governance. Here the Kangxi emperor skillfully presented himself as both a cosmic overlord of the sacred geography and a diligent, sympathetic protector of the people.

Further on in the entry for the same day, the emperor's compassion is said to elicit auspicious reactions from the populace:

On this imperial inspection to various destinations, the emperor clearly inquired among the people. The commoners' sufferings are completely understood. Taxes and compulsory labor services have been remitted, sympathy given to the aged and respected, and pity to the poverty stricken. . . . White-haired elders and young children have looked forward to this inspection tour. As the imperial carriage passes through the land, cries of welcome fill the streets.[90]

The emperor seems to be asking, "With such overt acknowledgment of the benevolence of my reign, what need do I have of secret, hidden rites?"

The Kangxi emperor's condemnation of the *feng* and *shan* sacrifices was quite direct. The conclusion of the official diary entry for that same day reads:

The emperor's mind has great breadth, having enumerated and examined all of the records, he criticized the literature on the *feng* and *shan*. . . .

Previous climbers of the Sacred Peak Dai achieved merit through orderly sacrifices (*si* 祀). Examination of the ancient rites has been the method followed for many generations. [However, the new] placards bearing the imperial ink illuminate this famous mountain; offered on Dai's peak, they also will last forever. People can see that those jade covers and the gold seals[91] [of the *feng* and *shan* rituals] only propagated brags and boasts. Why did those seventy-two [ancient] rulers follow that path?! So, we know that the emperor's level of conduct surpasses that of the hundred kings. Chroniclers will manage the documents; there is only inexhaustible praise![92]

This sentiment was reiterated in the concluding lines of a poem composed by the emperor entitled "Climbing Dai":

I desire, with close officials, to venerate true government;
there is no longer any need for gold seals and jade covers.[93]

These two sources express the Kangxi emperor's belief that the
feng and *shan* sacrifices were superstitious practices, or, in the
words of his *Sacred Edict*, did not "exalt the correct doctrine."

The Kangxi emperor's attitude toward the *feng* and *shan* sacrifices was vehemently upheld by his grandson, the Qianlong emperor. In 1770, the Qianlong emperor composed a stele inscription
commemorating a renovation of the Dai Temple at the foot of the
mountain. Referring to Cao He's memorial urging the Kangxi emperor to perform the *feng* and *shan* sacrifices, the Qianlong emperor wrote: "[The Kangxi] emperor ordered the Nine Chief Ministers to deliberate [on the issue], and they condemned [the
suggestion to perform the *feng* and *shan* sacrifices]. This is a truly
perfect ruling! This is a truly perfect sentiment!"[94] Although the official diary and Kangxi emperor's poem suggest a blanket condemnation of the sacrifices, the gist of the Qianlong emperor's argument is that the sacrifices may have been valid rituals in antiquity,
but by the time of the Tang dynasty they had become tainted. To
practice them now would be to stoop to superstitious practices.
The Qianlong emperor had made this point earlier in a poem written in 1748:

Climbing the *Feng* Terrace
(Deng feng tai 登封臺)

[The time of] the Yellow Emperor is distant indeed, it is
    not possible to know;
if the seventy-two rulers all [employed] a single precedent.
The esteemed ancient methods of the gold seals, jade covers;
brocade ropes and stone box of the *feng* ceremonies
    were secret.
I have come to the mountain's peak and searched out
    ancient traces;
trusting only what I can fix my eyes on, I aspire to the
    "Cloud" strokes.
. . . .
From Yao and Shun down to the present;
there has been no [ruler who] can report the day he
    completed [the Mandate].[95]

The Qianlong emperor echoes his grandfather's sentiments about the impossibility of ever fulfilling the Mandate of Heaven, because governance was an ongoing process. To emphasize his disdain for past performers of the *feng* and *shan* sacrifices, the Qianlong emperor had this poem engraved on a stele erected on the Ancient *Feng* Sacrifice Terrace on top of the mountain (no. 50). According to tradition, this was the site where Qin Shihuangdi and Han Wudi had performed the *feng* sacrifice.[96] The allusion to "'Cloud' strokes" (*yun bi* 雲筆) refers to the two characters "Cloud Peak" (*yun feng* 雲峰), written by the Kangxi emperor in 1684 and engraved onto a cliff-face at the top of the mountain. Thus, the only historic traces seen by the Qianlong emperor that he deemed worth aspiring to were those left by his grandfather.

It would be unreasonable to read ulterior political motives and messages into all the emperor's actions on Mount Tai. Sometimes a less imperial side of his personality is visible. Much like any literati visitor, he is capable of enjoying the sights. In a collection of writings about his southern tour, the Kangxi emperor wrote:

On the eleventh [*sic*—should be tenth] day, arrived at Mount Tai. The stone path was extremely steep. Unhurriedly climbed on foot. Ascended 40 *li* to the Imperial Tent Cliff, [where] a waterfall cascaded. The Fifth Rank pine is withered but still in the cliff-side. Perhaps later people will also continue to [re]plant it. Entered the Southern Heavenly Gate. Touched the Qin period Wordless Stele.[97]

Here we see the emperor appreciating the scenery and literally touching the past as he communes both with nature and with history.

The emperor also participated in the ceremony common to all visitors to the mountain: "Spent the night on top of Mount Tai. . . . The next day climbed to the Sun Viewing Peak to watch the sun rise."[98] Although these more personal accounts do not appear in the official records, they also added to his aura as a cultured and sophisticated ruler. The literati who saw him during his ascent could identify with these actions since they were the typical activities of elite visitors. Despite the carefree tone of these passages, the emperor's physical contact with this important historical, cultural, and religious site created a direct connection between this foreign ruler and China's culture, past rulers, and present elite.

Personal Legitimation: The Qianlong Emperor and Collecting as Identity

By the time Hongli came to the throne, Manchu rule was firmly established. Although the Qianlong emperor devoted considerable effort to preserving Manchu culture and creating a Manchu history, conditions within the empire no longer required that the emperor actively legitimate Manchu rule.[99] Instead, the Qianlong emperor concentrated much of his energy on guaranteeing a prominent position for himself in the annals of history. He sought to portray himself to his contemporaries, and, perhaps more important, to posterity, as the best universal monarch ever.

The Qianlong emperor's interactions with Mount Tai built on those of his grandfather. However, in pursuit of his desire to project his omnipotence into the future, the Qianlong emperor far outperformed his grandfather, at least in quantity. The Qianlong emperor visited Mount Tai nine times. Hongli's mother, the Empress Dowager Xiaosheng 孝聖, accompanied him on the first seven of his visits to the mountain (every visit until her death in 1777). The Qianlong emperor also wrote many more poems about the mountain and left more inscriptions on the mountain than did the Kangxi emperor.[100] Thus, many of the Qianlong emperor's actions on Mount Tai can be interpreted as expressions of his own style of rulership, as distinct from that of his grandfather. In addition, although the Qianlong emperor, like his grandfather, performed official state rituals at Mount Tai, the increased political stability of the empire allowed him to express his Tibetan Buddhist piety openly.

Portraits of the Qianlong emperor in various guises demonstrate his conception of himself as a universal ruler. One painting of the emperor, *One or Two?*, depicts the emperor in the guise of a Confucian scholar surrounded by many Chinese artifacts. Hanging just behind the emperor is another portrait of him. Wu Hung notes that the emperor's inscription and signature on the composition tell us much about his conception of himself:

Qianlong explains this composition in his inscription:

> One or two?—
> My two faces never come together yet are never separate.
> One can be Confucian, one can be Mohist.
> Why should I worry or even think?

At least three versions of this painting exist and all bear this poem, but Qianlong signed each version with a different name. One of his signatures refers to himself as Narayana, a Buddhist deity with three faces.[101]

The statement about this one ruler representing all rulers is also exemplified in the variety of personae in which the emperor posed for portraits: Manchu warrior, Confucian scholar, Chinese emperor, Daoist priest, Bodhisattva, and caring father.[102]

Hongli's first act in relation to Mount Tai, although it does not bear directly on the analysis of his interactions with the mountain, probably had a large impact on the poorest visitors to the mountain. On January 6, 1736, he issued an edict rescinding the incense tax. His motivations for ending the tax can be seen in excerpts from the edict:

If people cannot pay the tax, then they will not be able to promise to climb the mountain and enter the temple. . . . I [the emperor] believe that the common people should be able to offer incense to beseech the deities and that their wishes must be heard. It is not necessary to take in these tax monies. Thenceforth, the funds of this incense tax are to be forever abolished and rescinded. If pilgrims have the desire to bestow incense money, they must be able to pursue every desire. They will not need to calculate in the amount [of the tax]; also they will not have to abandon their promises [to give money] to be collected and kept by this mountain's Daoist priests. [The priests will] use this capital to cover the costs of repairing shrines, temples, and the mountain path. [Since this regulation will] prevent [the monies] from passing through the hands of officials, then there will not be even the slightest illegal profits. Make this forever known as the regulation.[103]

Hongli's decree ended a burdensome tax that prevented many from making the pilgrimage to the main Bixia temple. If the edict had coincided with a visit to Mount Tai, the emperor's motivations would be more apparent. If the process for ending the tax had begun under his father, Hongli's edict would almost certainly have mentioned this. Perhaps the edict came in response to a memorial sent by an official from Shandong. In addition, it was common for a new emperor to issue various clemencies and tax reductions shortly after ascending the throne, although these were usually one-time or short-term declarations. It is possible that Hongli took the Kangxi emperor's temporary redistribution of the tax during his 1684 visit to Mount Tai as a precedent. Whatever his motivations were, the result was that more people could afford to make the pilgrimage. Thus, Hongli's act can be seen as one of compassion and piety.

Although Mount Tai attracted believers from all of China's major socio-religious traditions, the God of Mount Tai and Bixia Yuanjun were Daoist deities. The large Dai Temple at the mountain's base was the primary location for both the Kangxi and the Qianlong emperors' performance of the state-sanctioned sacrifices at Mount Tai. Although the God of Mount Tai was included in the officially recognized Chinese pantheon, Bixia Yuanjun was not and never received state sacrifices.[104] The accepted methods and precedents for performing all state rituals were recorded in the *Qinding da Qing huidian shili* 欽定大清會典事例 (Collected statutes of the Great Qing with precedents).

State sacrificial rituals were categorized as great, middle, and miscellaneous (*dasi* 大祀, *zhongsi* 中祀, *qunsi* 群祀). The great sacrifices were restricted to key agricultural deities and the imperial ancestors.[105] Because of his different roles, sacrifices to the God of Mount Tai fell into two of these categories. The god received middle-level sacrifices in his role as the leader of the Five Sacred Peaks and the source of all life. These sacrifices were conducted at the base of the mountain in the Dai Temple.[106] In his guise as a judge in the underworld, the god received miscellaneous-level sacrifices. These official sacrifices were conducted in the Eastern Sacred Peak Temple in Beijing.[107] In official records, the terms *ji* 祭 and *si* 祀, translated in this work as "sacrifice," were used only of state-sanctioned rituals. Thus, the official accounts of the two Qing emperors' visits to Mount Tai refer to only the official sacrifices to the God of Mount Tai in the Dai Temple as *ji* or *si*. All other rituals conducted by the Kangxi emperor, such as those in the Bixia

Temple, are described by the generic term "performed rituals," or *xingli* 行禮.

There was, however, a significant shift in the language to describe the Qianlong emperor's observances. Instead of the generic "performed rituals," the emperor "offered incense," or *nianxiang* 拈香.[108] *Nianxiang* refers to the act of holding a few sticks of incense in the hands and offering them to a particular deity, often Buddhist. Both the Qianlong and the Kangxi emperors were devout believers in Tibetan Buddhism.[109] However, the Kangxi emperor's need to consolidate and legitimate Manchu control over China precluded him from overtly performing Buddhist rituals on this quintessentially Chinese sacred site. One of the Kangxi emperor's key audiences on Mount Tai was Han Chinese literati. In order to maintain control of China proper, the Manchus needed the cooperation of a sizable portion of the Han literati. Kai-wing Chow, in a study of ritual in late imperial China, argues that during the early Qing dynasty Han Chinese literati emphasized Confucian rituals as a means not only of resisting Buddhism and expressing a Chinese identity but also of defying Manchu authority.[110] It would have been politically disadvantageous for the Kangxi emperor to perform Buddhist rituals at a site Han Chinese literati strongly identified with their culture and history.

By the time of the Qianlong emperor's reign, the empire was much more stable, and the government no longer needed to recruit scholars from among those who had served the Ming or whose fathers had. Besides official records that refer to the Qianlong emperor "offering incense," some of the gifts the emperor bestowed on the Dai Temple also demonstrate the change in the political climate since the time of his grandfather.

Several of the Qianlong emperor's gifts to the main temple at the base of Mount Tai expressed his own religious beliefs as well as those of many of the conquest elite. In 1764 the emperor bestowed a set of five altar vessels on the Dai Temple. These vessels bear the Eight Auspicious Symbols of Buddhism.[111] In addition, these ritual vessels are quite similar to several sets on Buddhist altars in the Forbidden City.[112] Other Buddhist items given by the Qianlong emperor and by his mother to the Dai Temple included several sets of the Eight Auspicious Symbols, a gold Dharma Wheel, a number of porcelain "pure water ewers," ritual bowls, and several sets of the Seven Royal Treasures.[113]

Several of these items are more specifically Tibetan Buddhist. For example, two ritual bowls (one of lacquer, the other of porcelain) have a shape typical of Tibetan bowls.[114] Moreover, each bowl is decorated with the stylized Sanskrit characters often found on Tibetan Buddhist ritual objects. The decorations at the base of each bowl are probably the representations of human skulls found on many Tibetan Buddhist items. One of the sets of figures consists of eight deities bearing the Eight Auspicious Symbols above their heads, floating on clouds.[115] The faces of the deities were strongly influenced by Tibetan art. With these gifts, the Qianlong emperor was expressing his own personal faith and piety. In addition, because he gave these gifts only to the site where Chinese official rituals were conducted, he may have been making a political statement about the power and authority of the Manchu elite.

One feature of Mount Tai is impossible to ignore—the enormous inscription the Qianlong emperor ordered to be engraved on the south face of Mount Tai. As the name implies, the Inscription of 100,000 Feet (*Wanzhang bei* 萬丈碑, Fig. 5, p. 16, no. 31; see also Fig. 23, p. 57) is quite large, if not quite up to this hyperbole. The inscription is a rectangle twenty meters tall by nine meters wide; each character measures one meter square.[116] The text consists of a poem written by the emperor during his 1748 ascent. The outline of the inscription is visible from the foot of the mountain, and even from several kilometers away on a clear day.

This enormous inscription reflects the Qianlong emperor's attitude toward Chinese art. His connoisseurship built on Chinese conceptions of collecting. "From the earliest times, Chinese rulers regarded the possession of ancient writings and pictures as evidence of the authority bestowed upon them to rule. The history of imperial art collections . . . reflects a deep faith in cultural tradition, the belief that only those with a clear vision of the past can uphold civilization's future."[117] An emperor—the mediator between Heaven and Earth—who devoted much time and energy to collecting in the present positioned himself as a crucial link between the past and the future.

The sixteenth and seventeenth centuries were also a period of obsessive collecting among the literati.[118] During this period, "objects became associated with certain qualities and historical figures. . . . By loving a particular object, the devotee was striving to claim allegiance to that quality or to emulate that figure. . . . It was again an easy leap to attribute these virtues to the object itself."[119] Furthermore, a mania for a particular type of object endowed the collector himself with the characteristics of that class of objects.[120] Positioning themselves between the past and the future, imperial collectors, in imitation of these literati, could associate themselves with and possess the various moral qualities of the items in their collection. Unlike literati collectors, however, the early Qing emperor-collectors—especially the Qianlong emperor—had the imperial authority and purse at their disposal.

Given the tradition of associating possession of the cultural past with the authority to rule, as well as this late Ming practice of literati collecting and the early Manchu rulers' desire to control China, it is not surprising, to quote Jan Stuart, that they "used collecting and connoisseurship to broadcast their power. . . . Kangxi, Yongzheng, and Qianlong equated possessing art with both the idea of being personally cultured and the notion of being the overlords of Chinese culture." By possessing ancient works of art such as paintings and bronzes, "Qianlong reinforced that he was the rightful legatee of ancient tradition."[121] The Qianlong emperor took imperial art collecting to an unprecedented level. For example, by 1745 the paintings in the official catalog of his collection alone numbered over 1,700.[122] Indeed, much of the current collections of both the National Palace Museum in Taibei and the Palace Museum in Beijing once belonged to the Qianlong emperor. As Harold Kahn notes, "The Qianlong emperor understood as well as any who came before him that monumentalism was essentially a political aesthetic. It did not need to please, only to inspire and command—respect, fear, loyalty, belief. It was public but not popular art, meant to reaffirm hegemonic sovereignty, omnicompetence, imperial legitimacy and the natural, harmonious order of things."[123]

Mere possession of art was not sufficient in and of itself to demonstrate imperial authority over the culture the works represented. Each work had to be marked to prove ownership and to express power by stamping it with a seal. "In Chinese civilization seals were symbols used to indicate ownership, to authenticate documents, and to establish political or religious authority."[124] The imprinting of marks on objects in the imperial collection reached a peak during the Qianlong emperor's reign: "He spent much of his energy as an aesthete writing inscriptions and implanting his more than one hundred state and personal seals all over the masterworks in his collection."[125] The emperor did not limit his marking to paintings alone, he also engraved his writings and names on ancient ceramic, jade, and wood objects.[126]

Not surprisingly, many modern art collectors and art historians are dismayed by what they deem the defacing of art treasures by the Qianlong emperor because of his mania for inscribing poems and stamping his seals. Harold Kahn, however, has convincingly argued that the exercise had

extra-esthetic function[s]. . . . It was not so much the royal prerogative as the royal duty to remain at the head of the arts even if, in the process, the art was destroyed. The paintings, after all, were the private possessions of the throne; the imperial script and seals were the possessions of the realm. Their appearance was an assertion not only of artistic sensibility (however warped) but of dynastic grandeur.[127]

An important component of the Qianlong emperor's collecting was his development of a particular style of connoisseurship. Kohara Hironobu traces the development of this style and shows that "the emperor and his staff came to consider the painters of the past as signs or ciphers only. They valued the subject of a painting more than the painting itself. Similarly, they considered the colophons on a painting to be more informative than the painting itself." Kohara argues that this "over-reliance on texts and documents" was a major source of weakness in the emperor's connoisseurship.[128] Like the emperor's ardent employment of his seals, the Qianlong emperor's style of connoisseurship also had political implications. By mandating a connoisseurship that emphasized colophons, the emperor heightened the value of the inscriptions he added to the

paintings and other artifacts in his collection. The poems he wrote
on them and his seals not only marked the works as his possessions
but also increased the value of the work. The fact that a work bore
his seal, calligraphy, or words could become more important than
the original work itself.[129] Here we see a manifestation of the obsessive collecting that was particularly prevalent in the late Ming.
Judith Zeitlin argues that the obsessive collector's acts of possessing
were "not the self loving the *other*, but the self loving the *self*."[130] A
line from Harold Kahn succinctly captures the Qianlong em-
peror's tendency to leave his mark on the works in his collection.
The reference is to the emperor's propensity for commissioning
portraits of himself: "Perhaps the most egocentric aspect of the
emperor's lust for collection was the collecting of himself."[131]

Two ceramic pieces incised with compositions by the Qianlong
emperor, discussed by Jan Stuart in her article about dilettantism as
statecraft, demonstrate the endurance of the Qianlong emperor's
personal style of connoisseurship. What interests Stuart about
these pieces is not that one is a thirteenth-century Jun ware bowl
or that the other is a twelfth-century Cizhou-type ceramic pillow,
but the inscriptions carved into their glazes. Stuart uses these and
other works to show that the Qianlong emperor used aesthetic appreciation as a means of expressing political power.[132] Although
Stuart is probably not approaching these works in the manner that
the Qianlong emperor may have hoped, in a sense his style of connoisseurship was successful, for these works are important because
of what the emperor's alterations tell us about his style, method of
rulership, and perpetuation of his aura of imperial authority.

The Qianlong emperor's incision of his poem on the face of
Mount Tai echoes his placing of a colophon and impression of his
seal on a work of art in his collection. If we consider Mount Tai a
work of art in his collection, then the inscription, viewed from a
distance (see Fig. 23, p. 57), is like the imperial seal on a painting.
This seal literally proclaims the emperor's possession of this sacred
peak. Just as his possession of art demonstrated his possession of
culture, the Qianlong emperor's assertion of his authority over and
possession of Mount Tai—an extremely important religious, cultural, and historical site—demonstrated the emperor's control and

authority over China's past, present, and future (for this seal carved into stone was meant to last for eternity). In addition, as Zeitlin has shown for late Ming literati collectors, the possession of an object endowed the object's owner with particular virtues. Thus the emperor associated himself with the powers of this sacred site, especially its power as the source of life.

The Inscription of 100,000 Feet is also an imperial colophon chiseled into the face of a real landscape, rather than painted onto an artistic depiction. This massive inscription, within the context of the Qianlong emperor's conception of connoisseurship, exposed visitors to the grandeur of this Manchu emperor. By inscribing Mount Tai, the Qianlong emperor not only added his own name to the short list of past emperors who had also made the journey up its sacred slope but openly declared his superiority to them. The sheer size of the area of the inscription (nine meters wide by twenty high) is nearly twice as large as the previously largest inscription, the emperor Tang Xuanzong's Cliff Inscription (5.3 meters wide by 13.3 meters high; see Fig. 7, p. 19). In addition, the Qianlong emperor's inscription is the only imperial relic on Mount Tai that can be seen from the foot of the mountain. The position of the inscription, facing south, also reinforces its imperial nature, since it was the imperial prerogative to face south.

The text of the poem gives additional insight into this ruler's views on statecraft:

Sun Facing Cave
(Chaoyang dong 朝陽洞)

The high peak embraces a deep ravine
dawn's light first shines here.
Thus the name "Sun Facing"
most famous mountains have a place with such a name.
This place is the opening in the cloud gate
there are several *mu* of level ground.
The resulting structure of this tranquil place
opens a window on the clear, beautiful [scenery].[133]
Passing up through this impassable mountain, joyfully
　　reach this level place
rest before continuing further.

Engaging in the study of enlightenment merely
   through scenery
cannot exhaust or guard against the tendency to
   wait for things to come one's way.[134]

The use of quotations from Du Fu and Han Feizi demonstrated the emperor's command of Chinese literature. The final line is even more important, however, for understanding his conception of himself. He argued against seeking enlightenment or complete understanding through the pursuit of only one activity. Here we can see the emperor's conception of himself as a universal ruler who rules over many peoples and myriad traditions. In an article about the costume portraits or masquerades of the Yongzheng and Qianlong emperors, Wu Hung argues that these types of portraits "demonstrate the emperor's uncontrollable desire to dominate any existing tradition, whether it be Confucian, Daoist or Buddhist."[135]

Another less imposing inscription by the Qianlong emperor further demonstrates his style of connoisseurship. Here the emperor's "colophon" is attached to a sample of calligraphy rather than the entire mountain. The calligraphy in question consisted of the two characters "Cloud Peak" written by the Kangxi emperor in 1684 and inscribed on the cliff face just to the west of the Tang Cliff Inscription. On his 1748 ascent up Mount Tai, the Qianlong emperor composed a poem in honor of these two characters, which, along with several other poems, he then ordered inscribed just below his grandfather's calligraphy (see Fig. 7, p. 19). The Qianlong emperor's poem "Climbing the *Feng* Terrace" cited above also honors these two characters.

Here again the Qianlong emperor did not feel that a work of art was complete, or completely part of his collection, until he had added a colophon or an impression of one of his many seals. The arrogance of this act is quite apparent if we consider the amount of respect the Qianlong emperor showed his grandfather. For example, in 1795 the Qianlong emperor resigned the throne to one of his sons so that his reign would not last longer than that of his grandfather. Although on the surface this was a highly filial act, it also served to heighten the prestige of the Qianlong emperor—there were almost no precedents in Chinese history for imperial retirements.

In the poem "Reverent Eulogy to the Imperial Ancestor's Cliff Inscription of the Two Large Characters 'Cloud Peak,'" the Qianlong emperor honored his grandfather's choice of actions on Mount Tai:

> Dragon pearls, the twin kernels of the carved
>   [characters] "Cloud Peak"
> Occupy the towering high myriad sceneries.
> They do not resemble the thousand-plus characters
>   of the Cliff Inscription
> Originally only used to boast of the *feng* sacrifice
>   on the Eastern [Peak].[136]

The first line of the poem praises the calligraphy of the Kangxi emperor's inscription. The poem then compares the Kangxi emperor's inscription to the Tang Cliff Inscription, which recounts Tang Xuanzong's performance of the *feng* sacrifice in 726, to the latter's disadvantage. The Kangxi and the Qianlong emperors did not perform the *feng* and *shan* sacrifices because they believed the rites had become superstitious practices. In addition, the Kangxi emperor felt that the Tang inscriptions' claims of perfection were mere "brags and boasts,"[137] a sentiment echoed in his grandson's poem.

Although the Qianlong emperor praised his grandfather's calligraphy and his decision not to conduct the *feng* and *shan* sacrifices, he also took advantage of the imperial prerogative to add his own inscription to a work in his "collection." As emperor, everything under Heaven belonged to him. By inscribing his own poem, the Qianlong emperor also asserted his own power and authority. His modifications and additions asserted control over the things in his collection and his feelings of being secure in his inheritance from his grandfather. However, these assertive actions relative to the Kangxi emperor's legacies pale in comparison with the Qianlong emperor's audacity relative to earlier Han Chinese emperors, who had invested the *feng* and *shan* with the full weight of legitimation. The "Inscription of 100,000 Feet" dwarfed Tang Xuanzong's eulogy. When the jade tablets containing Song Zhenzong's address to Heaven from the *feng* sacrifice of 1008 were discovered in 1482, the Ming emperor ordered that the tablets be reburied on the mountain's summit.[138] When the same tablets were rediscovered in 1747, however, the Qianlong emperor incorporated them into his collection.[139]

An order by the Qianlong emperor during his last visit to Mount Tai further suggests that the Manchu emperors may have associated the goddess Bixia Yuanjun's efficacy in providing male heirs with the continuation of the Qing imperial line. After climbing the mountain in 1790, the Qianlong emperor "ordered all the imperial sons . . . to perform reverent rituals (*zhanli* 瞻禮) in the Bixia Temple."[140] This is the only reference to the imperial princes in any of the records pertaining to the Qianlong emperor's visits to Mount Tai. This order demonstrates the emperor's belief that an appeal to the Goddess of Mount Tai to continue the imperial line would be efficacious. In invoking Bixia Yuanjun to continue their lineage, the Kangxi and Qianlong emperors were overlapping with the vast majority of the Han Chinese visitors to the mountain. Ironically, even as the two emperors made a conscious break with a major, elite Han tradition in rejecting the *feng* and *shan* sacrifices, they drew closer to non-elite Han Chinese pilgrims.

The Kangxi emperor used the stage of Mount Tai to address multiple audiences in multiple periods. He appealed to the majority of Han Chinese as well as the Han and Manchu elites for recognition of his political legitimacy. For the multitudes of Han Chinese who journeyed to the mountain to pray to Bixia Yuanjun, he, too, demonstrated his devotion to this efficacious deity by praying in her main temple and redirecting the proceeds of the incense tax to the repair of the temples they patronized. He led Han Chinese officials in those established rituals of theirs that he chose to reaffirm and refrained from performing Buddhist rituals that might have antagonized or alienated them. For the Manchu portion of his audience, he tied Mount Tai, and the entirety of Chinese territory that it represented, to the Changbai Mountains. Through his southern tours, he also demonstrated Manchu control of that territory. In denouncing previous emperors' major rituals of validation of their dynasties and themselves, he projected Manchu superiority back in time. His actions, writings, and inscriptions created precedents for his own posterity as well as for the Han Chinese members of the empire. The Qianlong emperor, less concerned with and less dependent on dominating and consolidating various audiences, shifted the emphasis from multiple, subordinate audiences to himself as main performer and audience. Although both emperors were concerned with legitimating their identities and with preserving them into the future, the Kangxi emperor's actions gestured toward strengthening and perpetuating the Qing dynasty, whereas the Qianlong emperor's accented his own reign and personality. Their actions, unlike those of most who prayed to the Goddess of Mount Tai, were not humble or egalitarian or based on sincere entreaties. Instead, these two emperors were intent on transforming not themselves but sacred space itself.

CHAPTER 3

Pilgrimage as Literature

Reading Oneself into the Past and

Writing Oneself into the Future

Literati interactions with Mount Tai reveal much about the motivations, identities, and self-conceptions of these elite males. Their interest in history dominated their writings about the mountain and their building projects. This engagement with the past was reinforced by, and in turn helped to drive, a burgeoning publishing industry. As leisure travel increased dramatically during the late imperial period, so did the demand for historical works on popular destinations. In addition, literati also focused on self-cultivation. On Mount Tai, this most often manifested itself in contemplative retreats into the natural landscape. Literati writings on this pursuit make it clear that their approach to self-rectification was syncretic and drew on both the writings of Confucius and the practices of Daoist mystics. What characterizes all their writings about the mountain, especially those engraved onto its surfaces, is a compelling drive to write themselves into a literary lineage—a chain of scholars that begins with Confucius and extends, without end, into the future.

Literati approached Mount Tai with multiple identities. They were historians, disciples of Confucius, admirers of Li Bo, builders, poets, and good administrators. However, all their writings, whether expressing a single identity or multiple ones, were intended to project a positive image of themselves to future genera-

tions of scholars. A poem by Ye Fen 葉份, a minor Ming official
who received his *jinshi* degree in 1523, is an excellent example of the
varied ways in which one literatus might approach Mount Tai.[1]

Mount Tai Chant
(Taishan yin 泰山吟)

Mount Dai, leader of myriad peaks,
great guardian, protector beacon of the East.
Lofty alp presiding over [the Gulf of] Bohai,
soaring alp controlling the [Yellow] River and
    the Yi[2] streams.
Numinous place where one returns to the grotto
    abode (*dong fu* 洞府),[3]
auspicious site (*fu di* 福地)[4] where one is enlightened
    in the venerable temple.
How can Shilü[5] reveal the secret haze?
or the turquoise fragrance (*yao fen* 瑤芬) shut out
    the withering and drooping [of everyday life]?
While inspecting, Yu made burnt offerings on a
    sacrificial mound,
[King Cheng of] Zhou made an imperial tour to the
    Ming Tang altar [at Mount Tai] to acknowledge the
    overthrow [of the Shang dynasty].[6]
Distant, alas, are the seventy rulers,[7]
[they are now only] meaningless names handed down
    in documents.
For Emperor Qin there was no numinous atmosphere,
Han Wu[di] did not obtain immortal skills.
[Now only] the enfeoffed pine is elegant in the midst
    of the slope,
and the planted cypress are abundant on the southern edge.
I came at the time of the spring moon,
repeating crags open into misty clouds.
I step through the Heavenly Gate into boundlessness,
the twisting path passes through windings and curvings.
I had a sincere audience with Bixia [Yuan]jun,
a cold rinse in the Jade Maiden Pool.
I ponder the intent of the jade slips,
while facing the cliff inscription and touching the carvings.[8]
Flowing and resting clouds appear like weavings,

or as spirits roaming astride hornless dragons.
In the morning I climb the Sun Viewing Peak,
the sunrise is supported on a mulberry branch.
My breath transforms into mist,
below in the world occur wind and thunder.
I overlook endlessly vast *qi* 氣,
how could I be able to distinguish tiny Ying?[9]
I distantly think of riding a yellow crane,
throughout Heaven and Earth, accompanying it
   wherever it goes.

Ye begins as a poet praising the mountain's lofty position of prominence over an area stretching from the Yellow River to the Gulf of Bohai. Next, he dwells on the mystical aspects of the mountain, evoking Daoist terms for places where immortals dwell and where the adept might reach a higher level of existence, even though Ye humbly questions his own abilities to break through the barriers of this world. The mystic gives way to the historian, who recounts the actions of distant sage-rulers and laments their passing. Of Qin Shihuangdi and Han Wudi's unsuccessful attempts to reach immortality, he notes that the only immortal aspects of their visits are the Fifth Rank Pine Tree and the Han cypresses. Next, like Li Bo, he climbs above the clouds. There he joins the many pilgrims praying to the Goddess of Mount Tai and purifying themselves in her pool. Once again he becomes the historian, analyzing Tang Xuanzong's relics and his performance of the *feng* and *shan* sacrifices. Once more a mystic, he is renewed in the morning as he witnesses the sunrise. His breath merges with the mists emanating from the mountain's hidden caverns. Like Confucius, he finds the world below vast indeed. Yet, unwilling to compare himself to the sage, he remarks that his sight lacks the necessary penetrating power. Like many of his predecessors, he discovers that his desire to soar freely over the world lies just outside his grasp. Ye's different identities evoke different layers of the mountain's complex past. In addition, Ye's poem projects his erudition into the future and enables later readers to admire his understanding of the history connected with this famous site and his subtle allusions to other writings and visitors. Yet his humility in not claiming to be as farsighted as Confucius or to be able to ride the yellow crane saved him from ridicule by future generations, who might have seen such images as overstepping his position in the literary lineage.

An important aspect of identity is how we define ourselves in terms of our differences from others. Like many elite groups around the world and throughout history, the literati of late imperial China often focused on their education as a primary means of separating themselves from the rest of society. They also attached great importance to connecting with history. For literati, the history of Mount Tai stretched back to the legendary times of the sage-rulers Yao and Shun. Those who traveled to Mount Tai during the late imperial period approached the mountain within the context of all the history and culture set out in Part I. Literati placed themselves in a continuum stretching from the past into the future by means of the skill and tool that set them apart from the rest of society: literacy. They linked themselves to the past through both reading and writing. They both read and wrote travelogues, stele texts, inscriptions, poetry, and gazetteers. In some instances these men intentionally altered the mountain not just as a means of honoring nature but also as a way of separating themselves from the other visitors to Mount Tai. Any inscriptions or labels automatically separated them from the illiterate majority.

One wordplay carved into the mountain in 1899 by Liu Tinggui 劉廷桂 is especially illustrative of messages that separated the literati from the illiterate. Carved in a rock are the two characters 虫 and 二. This inscription is a visual pun based on the internal components of the two Chinese characters 風 (wind) and 月 (moon), and thus, in marked contrast to the oral puns discussed in Chapter 1, inaccessible to the illiterate. By writing the characters for wind and moon without their borders (*wubian* 無邊), Liu was implying the four-character phrase *feng yue wubian* 風月無邊 and commenting on Mount Tai's natural beauty—"limitless natural beauty."[10]

As we have seen in the preceding chapters, peasants and emperors approached Mount Tai with a variety of motivations and expectations. The same was true of the highly diverse group that I am labeling "literati." Thus, for example, an official's position dictated that he interact with the mountain as a representative of the state; a wealthy scholar on a leisure trip around the empire was free of these restraints; indeed, he might have been considered to be usurping official prerogatives had he performed certain rites. Or, for example, although the vast majority of literati apparently did not pray to the Goddess of Mount Tai, there were a few who did. Moreover, a single individual, like Ye Fen, could interact with the mountain on more than one level. To judge from writings about the mountain, most literati consciously thought about historical events as they viewed sites such as the Fifth Rank Pine Tree or the Tang Cliff Inscription, enjoyed the natural scenery, and perhaps sought self-improvement.

This multiplicity of approaches to this multivalanced site is reflected in poems written by literati in the late imperial period. Table 3 categorizes 1,190 poems about Mount Tai written by Ming and Qing period literati. Since any such categorization is subjective, I use these data not to make a statistical argument but to demonstrate broad trends and themes. First, the poems fall into several overarching categories; different authors emphasized the aspect or aspects of the mountain that held the most meaning for themselves. The first category may require an explanation. Poems with multiple themes are, for the most part, longer than four lines. No one theme dominates, and typically these poems contain references to natural sites or phenomena as well as to historical sites or events; in addition, some make religious allusions.

Table 3
Ming and Qing Period Poems About Mount Tai by General Topic

Topic	Ming (336 poets)	Qing (161 poets)	Total (497 poets)
Multiple themes	389 (55.7%)	128 (26.1%)	517 (43.4%)
Nature	131 (18.7%)	208 (42.4%)	339 (28.5%)
History	91 (13.0%)	92 (18.7%)	183 (15.4%)
Religion	88 (12.6%)	63 (12.8%)	151 (12.7%)
TOTAL	699 (100%)	491 (100%)	1,190 (100%)

SOURCES: Liu Xiuchi, *Taishan daquan*, 1143–311; SDS, 497–500; and Ma Mingchu, *Taishan li-dai shi xuan*, 96, 138, 145.

Experiencing History

The late imperial increases in both the number of literati travelers to Mount Tai and the number of inscriptions, poems, travelogues, and gazetteers they composed were part of a general trend that began in the sixteenth century. As commercialization, and the economy in general, expanded during the Ming and Qing dynasties, the population exploded, more than doubling from the late fourteenth to the early seventeenth centuries.[11] A proportional expansion in the wealthier, literate classes was not, however, matched by a concomitant rise in the number of official government posts, the traditional route for social advancement. Thus, "as the literati grew in number far beyond the capacity of the bureaucracy to accommodate them, alternate life-styles arose that sought fulfillment outside of official careers."[12] Traveling, writing, and publishing were some of the activities pursued by the literati.[13] The increase in the numbers of travelers was not due to demographics alone. In order to travel to famous sites such as Mount Tai, literati needed to know how to get there. The publication of route books and specialized gazetteers devoted to specific sites facilitated such travel. As Timothy Brook notes, "The proliferation of route books in the Ming-Qing period reinforces the suspicion that not only were greater numbers of travelers in need of guides but the route network on which they were traveling was becoming more complex."[14] Brook also points out that inns along these routes, a support industry integral to increased travel, became more common during the sixteenth century.[15] Although the greatest impetus for the improvement of routes and the publication of guides to them was increased commercial activity, literati travelers also benefited. Consequently, the growth in travel literature followed the general "expansion of woodblock printing into a large-scale industry in the sixteenth century."[16]

The most concrete examples of the literati treating Mount Tai as an important historical site can be found in travelogues (*youji* 遊記) and gazetteers (*difang zhi* 地方志) about the mountain. Travelogues were firsthand accounts of the author's journey, usually only a few pages in length; gazetteers, or local histories, were longer compilations, usually devoted to administrative regions. Both genres benefited from increased travel and the expansion of the publishing industry. The style of most of these works fits into the conceptual framework of the philosophical system dominant during the last part of the late imperial period, evidential learning.[17] A number of such gazetteers about the administrative area around Mount Tai were compiled, most of which are listed below:

Hong Zhi 弘治, *Tai'anzhou zhi* 泰安州志 (Gazetteer of Tai'an subprefecture), 1488.

Ren Honglie 任弘烈, *Tai'anzhou zhi* 泰安州志 (Gazetteer of Tai'an subprefecture), 1603.

Zhang Yingfang 張迎芳, *Tai'anzhou zhi* 泰安州志 (Gazetteer of Tai'an department), 1723.

Cheng Zhilong 程志隆, *Tai'anxian zhi* 泰安縣志 (Gazetteer of Tai'an county), 1760.

Yan Xishen 顏希深, *Tai'anfu zhi* 泰安府志 (Gazetteer of Tai'an prefecture), 1760.

Huang Qian 黃鈐, *Tai'anxian zhi* 泰安縣志 (Gazetteer of Tai'an county), 1782.

Xu Zonggan 徐宗幹, *Tai'anxian zhi* 泰安縣志 (Gazetteer of Tai'an county), 1828.

Local gazetteers such as these catalogued geographic features, provided a history of the region and biographies of distinguished residents, described famous sites, and discussed the local economy. Some of these gazetteers include information about Mount Tai, but most concentrate on other aspects of the local area and refer readers to gazetteers specifically about the mountain.

In the sixteenth century a specialized subgenre, which Brook calls "topographical gazetteers," developed; among them are works devoted to specific mountains.[18] There are five multiple-chapter (*juan* 卷) and several single-chapter "topographical gazetteers" on Mount Tai. These sources discuss the history of various sites on the mountain, reprint a selection of past writings on Mount Tai, and give biographies of famous visitors. Listed below are all five of the longer works and three of the better-known shorter ones:

Wang Ziqing 汪子卿, *Taishan zhi* 泰山志 (Gazetteer of Mount Tai), 4 *juan*, 1555.

Zha Zhilong 查志隆, *Dai shi* 岱史 (A history of Dai [Mount Tai]), 18 *juan*, 1587.

Xiao Xiezhong 蕭協中, *Taishan xiaoshi* 泰山小史 (Short history of Mount Tai), 1 *juan*, ca. 1640.

Kong Zhenxuan 孔貞瑄, *Taishan jisheng* 泰山紀勝 (Record of the beautiful scenery of Mount Tai), 1 *juan* (26 leaves), 1673.

Nie Jianguang 聶劍光 (Nie Wen 聶鈫), *Taishan daoli ji* 泰山道里記 (An itinerary of Mount Tai), 1 *juan* (91 leaves), 1763.

Song Enren 宋恩仁, *Taishan shuji* 泰山述記 (Records of Mount Tai), 12 *juan*, 1790.

Tang Zhongmian 唐仲冕, *Dai Lan* 岱覽 (An overview of Dai [Mount Tai]), 33 *juan*, 1793.

Jin Qi 金棨, *Taishan zhi* 泰山志 (Gazetteer of Mount Tai), 20 *juan*, 1801.

The authors of three of these works represent a good cross-section of the types of literati who wrote about and visited Mount Tai. Nie Jianguang was a native of Tai'an. He was a member of a local elite family that was wealthy enough to allow one of its members to devote himself to writing. He never obtained a degree through the examination system and never held an official post. Based on the number of reprint editions and his work's current availability in libraries, *An Itinerary of Mount Tai* was probably the most popular text about the mountain from the late eighteenth century up to the early twentieth century. Its small size, in comparison to works like those by Tang and Jin, made it a more convenient reference for travelers. Tang Zhongmian (1753–1827) did receive the coveted highest degree, the *jinshi*. Like many other degree holders during the late imperial period, however, his accomplishments did not gain him an official post. Instead, when his father was assigned to an official post in Shandong, Tang followed and soon established himself as director of the Mount Tai Academy in Tai'an (Taishan shuyuan 泰山書院). During his tenure at this non-governmental position, he wrote *An Overview of Dai*. Jin Qi represents the ideal of literati attainment—an official with literary accomplishments. Jin, like Tang, held the coveted *jinshi* degree, but unlike Tang he obtained official office. Jin became prefect of Tai'an prefecture in 1794. He began working on the gazetteer the next year and completed it in 1798; printing began in 1801.[19]

The influence of evidential learning on writings about Mount Tai is demonstrated in the prefaces to the two longest mountain gazetteers. Both reveal a concern that there be a "complete" record of all texts, events, and history related to the mountain. Ruan Yuan 阮元 (1764–1849), then Shandong provincial director of education, wrote a preface to Jin Qi's *Gazetteer of Mount Tai* in 1801. Ruan began by lamenting the previous lack of a complete record of Mount Tai and cited Nie's *Itinerary of Mount Tai* as an example of a work that was incomplete and too short. He added that because of the importance of Mount Tai, it was imperative that there be a complete record, with accounts of the seventy-two performers of the *feng* and *shan* sacrifices, records of inscriptions, and Qing imperial writings.[20] Hong Liangji 洪亮吉 (1746–1809), in an 1807 preface to Tang Zhongmian's *An Overview of Dai*, made many of the same points as Ruan. Hong also noted that there were no "complete" records about Mount Tai (neither preface mentions the existence of the other supposedly thorough survey of the mountain; Jin does occasionally quote from Tang, however). Hong evokes Mount Tai's 3,000-year history as evidence that a work like Tang's was needed, and he praises Tang for preserving this history for the future.[21] By emphasizing completeness and history, these literati created something of a historical genealogy of Mount Tai that ensured their own inclusion.

Evidential scholarship and the increasing popularity of travel literature also had an impact on poetry written about Mount Tai. Many poems with multiple themes can be seen as condensed guides or histories of the mountain. Ye Fen's poem at the beginning of the chapter is an excellent example of this genre of "gazetteer-style" poems.

Writing on and about the mountain emphasized previous visitors and the histories of buildings and sites. Even poetry in praise of the natural beauty of Mount Tai participated in a tradition that could not be ignored by educated late imperial literati. Mount Tai was imbued with history. Literati visitors were walking in the footsteps of many famous leaders: the Yellow Emperor, the sage-rulers Yao and Shun, Han Wudi, Han Guangwudi, Tang Gaozong, Tang Xuanzong, Song Zhenzong, and later the Kangxi and Qianlong emperors of the Qing dynasty. They could look on the same scenery as famous poets such as Du Fu and Li Bo. However, the most important historical visitor to Mount Tai, from the perspective of literati, was the sage himself, Confucius. Mount Tai, like the sage's home at Qufu, became a site to visit and perform rites in honor of Confucius and his contributions to Chinese thought and culture.

Consequently, late imperial literati raised a number of edifices in honor of Confucius on Mount Tai. At the base of the mountain was the arch marking the Point Where Confucius Began His Ascent (no. 9; erected in 1560). On top were the Viewing Wu Peak (no. 39) and an arch marking the Place Where the Sage Saw Wu (no. 41; erected in 1757), both of which commemorated Confucius' amazing vision. The Pavilion of Heaven and Earth (no. 43; built in 1684) supposedly marked the point from which Confucius saw that the world was small. The largest edifice in honor of Confucius, the Confucian Temple on top of the mountain (no. 40), was constructed in 1583 or 1584. These arches, pavilions, and the temple reminded visitors of Confucius' ascent and honored the sage's wisdom and farsightedness (both literal and figurative). They also challenged visitors to test their own vision.

Self-Cultivation

At first glance, the differences between literati visitors to Mount Tai and pilgrims journeying to worship Bixia Yuanjun seem to far outweigh their similarities. Literati who wrote travelogues about their journeys to Mount Tai rarely, and then usually only fleetingly, mentioned the multitudes of illiterate pilgrims ascending the mountain to pray to Bixia. Two exceptions are the travel accounts by Wang Shizhen and Zhang Dai.[22] However, even these two obviously had no great interest in, and certainly little interaction with, the peasant pilgrims. In general, literati appear more interested in pursuing secular rather than sacred goals. Their focus on history might make them seem more like tourists than pilgrims.

However, just because most of these men were not praying before altars in temples does not mean that their journeys were devoid of the spiritual. The danger of applying distinctions such as "pilgrim" versus "tourist" is that they may be quite alien to the culture being studied, if not misleading. The Western propensity to create a strict dichotomy between the sacred and the secular grew out of the Enlightenment and flourished in the first hundred years of the social sciences. Chinese literati of the late imperial period, many of whom practiced evidential scholarship, might, like many Enlightenment thinkers, seem to have focused more on empirical, book research and therefore to have been reluctant to engage in mystical or faith-based activities. Such dichotomies, however, can hinder research on many premodern societies, and recent scholarship has begun to challenge the sacred/secular divide.[23]

In the previous section of this chapter, on the literati fascination with history, I intentionally referred to these men as "visitors" making journeys or traveling to the mountain and avoided using the term "pilgrims" to describe them. If all literati actions could be included under the rubric of historical appreciation, then perhaps the tourist/pilgrim distinction would be appropriate. However, literati in the late imperial period did not limit themselves to viewing historic sites. A quick glance at Table 3 demonstrates this point quite readily. A significant number of poems deal with natural, mystical, or religious sites or events. In addition, the largest category comprises poems that address at least one additional theme besides history.

The general principles of Neo-Confucianism that dominated literati thinking during the late imperial period were a synthesis of earlier Confucian, Daoist, and Buddhist thinking. The Confucian idea of self-cultivation was mirrored in the key Daoist concept of the individual's integration with nature. According to Richard Strassberg, "The Confucius of *The Analects* . . . found positive value in limited excursions into Nature to discover scenes of moral symbols that would illuminate the ideal qualities of the Noble Man. . . . This view of the self reading its perfected image in the landscape is a basic assumption that underlies not only Confucian but also later lyrical modes of travel writing."[24] Stories of Confucius' all-encompassing gaze from atop Mount Tai meshed well with this worldview.

Not unlike the young German romantics of the *Bildungsroman* tradition, many Chinese literati were searching for themselves in the natural setting of Mount Tai. They admired nature, often to the point of worship. They performed good deeds, such as planting trees and restoring temples. In all these actions, they sought self-cultivation and moral rectification. Therefore, literati visits to Mount Tai in the late imperial period correspond to two definitions of pilgrimage, devised by Victor Turner and Alan Morinis. In their ascents up Mount Tai, these men sought to have "direct experience of the sacred, invisible, or supernatural order . . . in the immaterial aspect of inward transformation of spirit or personality"[25] or to find "a place or a state [of mind that they] . . . believe[d] to embody a valued ideal."[26] Thus, literati who emphasized self-cultivation in their visits to Mount Tai were indeed pilgrims on spiritual journeys.

Although both Confucianism and Daoism encouraged interaction with nature, Daoist meanderings did not have the same concrete goals as did Confucian travels:

In contrast to travel as a purposeful activity whose ultimate goal was the restoration of moral and political order, the *Chuang-tzu* [*Zhuangzi*] presents travel as liberation from the unnatural constraints of society, a spiritualized venturing forth into the unrestricted realm of authentic being (*tzu-jan*) [the natural] much like the self-generated movement of the *Tao*. If the purpose of the Confucian itinerary can be summed up in the ideals of self-cultivation and ruling the world, the phrase "free and easy wandering" (*hsiao-yao yu*) . . . became the bywords of all who, following the *Chuang-tzu*, sought escape from the strife of the dynastic scene.[27]

Although the rationales underlying Confucian and Daoist travels in nature were quite distinct in the original sources, by late imperial times, if not earlier, it was rare to find an individual whose motivations did not owe much to both systems, as well as other ideas. We can see this hybridization in Brook's assessment of late Ming attitudes toward retreats into nature:

[The literati] placed a high aesthetic value on the appreciation of beautiful scenery and historical sites. . . . This quest for eminent sites in the late

Ming was animated by a veneration of refuge and retreat. What the gentry sought were places set apart from the bustle of everyday life, places that could be symbols to them of their ideal of separation from all that corrupted moral perfection . . . the symbol of the mountain served explicitly to identify these men and their institutions with the convention of separation from mundane concerns.[28]

The desire to retreat to mountain tops for separation, purification, and escape from moral and physical corruption led to travel. Travel, in turn, led to a focus on the journey itself and its rigors as a part of the process of separation and personal growth, as Pei-yi Wu notes:

By the sixteenth century the journey metaphor had become a commonplace in the Neo-Confucian discourse on *hsüeh* [*xue* 學], one of the key notions of Confucianism. The term is usually translated as "to learn" or "to study." . . . It can also mean "to emulate" or "to imitate," as in "imitation of the sages." . . . For many Neo-Confucians in the late sixteenth and seventeenth centuries the endeavor or the regimen of striving as denoted by *hsüeh* took on a more subjective turn as it became increasingly strenuous and exigent.[29]

Although both Brook's and Wu's studies focus on the sixteenth and seventeenth centuries, the idea of traveling in nature and especially to a mountain as a means for self-fulfillment remained valid for literati interactions with Mount Tai throughout the eighteenth and nineteenth centuries, and for some even into the early twentieth century.

On Mount Tai the idea of imitating the sages in order to transform oneself was particularly associated with Confucius. The belief that this sage had transforming powers is reflected in the name chosen for a pavilion erected during the Ming dynasty on the future site of the Confucian Temple (no. 40). This pavilion was called the "Passed by and Transformed Pavilion" (Guohua ting 過化亭).[30] The name implies not only that Confucius transformed every place and everyone he passed but also that through imitation (*xue*) of Confucius the visitor or pilgrim, too, might be transformed.

The conception of travel to a mountain as a personal journey involving interactions with the landscape can be seen in some of the maps printed with travelogues. A good example is Zhu Yun-jing's (朱雲燥) 1752 *A Record of Daizong* (Mount Tai). The ascent up the mountain is portrayed in a series of seventeen maps. In most of the maps, two small figures progress up the mountain. Others have just one figure; a few have none. The reader or viewer seems to follow the author and a companion on their journey. At least as portrayed in these maps, the two take the travails of their travel seriously, for they ascend on foot, rather than in mountain chairs. Although thousands of pilgrims, as well as beggars, entertainers, chairbearers, and vendors, crowded the central path up the mountain, Zhu depicted the mountain as a vast natural space, devoid of people. He and his fellow adventurer are dwarfed by the grandeur of the scenery. Dressed humbly, they open themselves to the transforming powers of nature. Like many literati, Zhu endorsed the belief that travel, such as that to the peak of Mount Tai, was a valid, if not essential, form of self-cultivation and moral rectification.

A stele from 1797 about the planting of cypress trees on Mount Tai provides a window into the mind-set of literati toward this sacred mountain and their motivations for altering its space. The author of this stele was Jin Qi, who also compiled the *Mount Tai Gazetteer* of 1801. Jin was the local prefect when he composed this inscription about tree planting. He explained how the idea for planting trees originated with preparations for a visit from the Shandong provincial judge, Kang Jitian 康基田, in 1796:

At this time [Jin] Qi [ordered that] 1,000 branches from cypress trees [growing beside] tombs be placed along the sides of the mountain trail. His Honor [Kang] saw this and joyfully said, "All this cultivates and protects the mountain's numinosity (*ling* 靈). Cannot this be done everywhere?" Following this, [Kang] contributed some of his salary to initiate an increase of 10,000 seedlings. Zhang Tingmu, the Tai'an district commandant, was ordered to supervise the workmen. In the spring of *dingsi* [1797], [after] performing rituals to honor Mount Tai along the lower twists of the Huan River, . . . more than 20,000 trees were planted.[31]

What began most likely as a gesture to make the judge's visit more pleasant resulted in a project to "cultivate and protect the mountain's numinosity." Officials were in charge of looking after the

welfare not only of the people but also of the land within the area
of their jurisdiction. Kang, not stopping at mere beautification, at-
tended to Mount Tai's spiritual welfare. Drawing on the sacred
space of the mountain as a source of life, Kang participated in the
renewal of life, the transformation of others, good adjudication,
and the promotion of good government and proper behavior:

Commencing from this point, all people, men and women, from all quarters will come here as guests, look up at the towering appearance, and
admire the verdant atmosphere. . . . Moreover, famous mountains soar
and large rivers run crystal clear and in great profusion; they transform people [bestowing upon them] the abilities of heroes, and they
transform things [bestowing upon them] the usefulness of the pillars of
the state. . . . His Honor [Kang] uses the planting and nurturing of these
trees as a metaphor for the meaning of *shuren* 樹人.[32]

The trees planted on the mountain do more than just augment the
mountain itself, they also help to uplift and nurture the people as
well. *Shuren* refers to the cultivation or fostering of human talent.
The term was extremely apt in this context, because *shu* means
"tree." The trees increased the mountain's numinosity, which in
turn allowed visitors to the mountain to focus their gaze beyond the
lush greenery into their own minds, where they would extend the
cultivation to themselves. Thus, we find in this project a concrete
example of the attitude toward nature expressed by Confucius.

Other natural phenomena admired during visits were old trees
or ones with odd shapes. In the Dai Temple at the foot of the
mountain were the Han cypresses and the Tang Acacia. One wall
of the Temple of the God of War (no. 66) near the beginning of
the pilgrimage path is built around the branches of a cypress tree.
A label on the outside wall, visible as one ascended the path, reads
"Number one Han cypress." Just below the Myriad Transcendents
Tower (no. 13) are the Three Righteous Cypresses (*san yi bai*
三義柏). Opposite the entrance to the Mother of the Big Dipper
Temple (no. 15) is the Reposing Dragon Acacia. A long trunk-like
branch stretches along the ground creating the image of a dragon.
Jin Qi's mountain gazetteer includes images of eight cypresses in
the Dai Temple and one of the Tang Acacia (see Fig. 20, p. 38).[33]

Another stele by a literati-official illustrates a slightly different twist on the idea of nature as a source of moral rectification. This stele was erected in 1886 to commemorate the repairing of the Temple for Paying Homage from Afar (no. 1). The author, Wu Shikai, then county magistrate of Tai'an, expounded on the virtues of making repairs to temples: "[With their work] on expanding [the temple's] bearing and their trust in the spirits, scholars and people courteously pray regarding litigations and judgments. [There is] nothing [for which meritorious repairs] will not turn the face and clean the heart. . . . And I hope that those who look after the land [through meritorious repairs] will perfect their virtue (*xiu de* 修德)."[34] Here people take a more active role in their pursuit of moral rectification through cultivation rather than conservation of the space. Although the space benefited from the work, the stated goal was directed more at benefiting individuals.

Pavilions not connected with temples served as places of reflection and meditation. Many literati contemplated nature from these pavilions, expressing their thoughts and moods in poetry. The rectifying characteristics expected from this sort of contemplation of nature are apparent in the name of one pavilion, the Cleansing the Heart Pavilion (Xi xin ting 洗心亭; see Appendix, no. 37). This pavilion was built in 1797 by Jin Qi, on top of the mountain.[35] One of the most popular pavilions among literati was the Sun Viewing Pavilion (no. 53), built during the Ming on the Sun Viewing Peak. Watching the sunrise was an important component of literati itineraries, indeed an almost mandatory event when climbing mountains in China and elsewhere in East Asia. As we have seen, the event was especially apt on Mount Tai, and literati who went to Mount Tai for the natural surroundings usually performed this ritual of welcoming the sun. Yao Nai's 姚鼐 (1732–1815) 1774 account of the sunrise is just one example of literati reverence for this natural phenomena:

at the fifth watch I sat with Ziying in the Sun Watching Pavilion, awaiting the sun rise. . . . To the east of the pavilion, below our feet, all was clouds. Gradually, tens of white, mountain-like peaks appeared among the clouds. All the way up to the heavens there was a strip of surprising color, which changed in an instant into five colors. Above the sun it was vermillion, almost cinnabar (*dan* 丹), below was a rosy glow.[36]

Cinnabar, or red mercury, was a common ingredient in immortality pills, and seems to echo back to the transcendent poetry of Li Bo. Not surprisingly, literati could react quite differently to the scenery on the mountain. Yao's somewhat passive observation of the natural beauties on the mountain contrasts with an earlier visitor's unbridled appreciation.

The famous literatus Wang Shizhen, probably "the most important man of letters of the sixteenth century,"[37] wrote an account of his visit to Mount Tai in 1576. Wang was a powerful and influential high-level official, but, as Ann Waltner shows, he was strongly attracted to Daoist mysticism. In this excerpt from his travelogue, the scenery caused him to break free from social constraints:

I was so inspired by the sight [of the waterfall] that I became uninhibited. Standing barefoot in the rapid stream next to boulders, I ordered wine and emptied large cups of it in quick succession. My loud singing shook the leaves of the trees overhead. All my companions cheered me on: some harmonized with me while others came down and drank the wine that was being brought to me.[38]

Drinking wine while admiring the scenery seems to have been a common pastime. Although wine may not have been the cause of their boisterousness, Kong Zhenxuan painted a similarly colorful account of three friends' ascent of Mount Tai in 1673: "We took along wine and cakes for a two-day journey. . . . We were as one in our contentedness. We gave voice to our thoughts through parables; then we wrote poems and songs in accordance with the rules of rhyme on the themes of particular sights."[39]

Aside from drinking and singing bouts, literati were inspired by Mount Tai's natural setting to transcend mundane life in another way as well. We can see this in the names of a number of arches erected over the Pilgrimage Path. In the gorge of the last steep ascent was the Promoted to Transcendence Arch (no. 36), and just beyond the Southern Heavenly Gate (no. 37) was an arch erected during the Ming with the inscription "Within ascendance." The names of these two arches evoked Mount Tai's connection with a higher, more perfect world.

The journey from the mundane world to this higher level was fraught with much struggle and transformation:

An old Chinese legend had it that fish from all rivers and seas assemble under a certain cascade in the Yellow River. Those who succeeded in leaping above the cascade and thus passing through *Lung-men* (Dragon Gate) would be transformed into dragons while those who failed would have their foreheads branded and their gills exposed. . . . The legend . . . reached back to the archetypal motives of test, challenge, or ordeal that abound in any quest story. . . .

Related to the figure of Lung-men is the *kuan* [*guan*], literally a "pass" or fortified checkpoint with gates and walls. A *kuan* is usually so strategically located that a traveler cannot easily go around it. . . . The successful negotiation of a *kuan* guarded by hostile forces often occurs as one of the most memorable episodes in the life of a Chinese hero. . . . In the vocabulary of spiritual journey Lung-men and *kuan* are cognates. . . . Both are spatial figures reminiscent of the rites of passage, rituals of initiation, ordeals, or tests of personal worth; the challenge is fraught with perils but also promises great advances. . . . To the religious Taoists a sequential system of *kuan* is more or less symbolically located in every human body, and to achieve immortality one must follow an elaborate program of penetrating each. . . . This topographical term also abounds in Ch'an Buddhist discourse, with the *wu-men-kuan* (gateless pass) one of the most famous Ch'an paradoxes.[40]

Wu Hung explains that gates symbolically divide space into an interior and exterior. They create a boundary that can be crossed. Furthermore, a series of gates links "broken spaces into a continuum."[41] This analysis of the mystical symbolism of gates and passes is an excellent primer for reading the literati landscape on Mount Tai. The Pilgrimage Path up Mount Tai passes through a series of gates erected by literati, mostly during the late imperial period.

As the literatus passed through each gate, he crossed another boundary in his search for himself at the top of this sacred peak. Just north of the city, he passed through the Daizong Arch (no. 3, built in 1563), whose title invokes the ancient name for the mountain. Next the first of three heavenly gates (no. 8, erected during the Ming), reminded him that he was on the correct route to heights that approach Heaven. The arch marking the Point Where Confucius Began His Ascent (no. 9; 1560) alerted the pilgrim that he was walking in the footsteps of the sage. Just above, the Heavenly Stairs Arch (no. 10; 1563) put him on notice that his goal lay at the end of an arduous climb. (Ironically, the arduous nature of the journey would have been largely symbolic since most literati were carried up in mountain chairs.) He then passed through the base of the Myriad Transcendents Tower (no. 13; 1620). At the Ascend to Transcendence Bridge (no. 17), the pilgrim passed safely over the Center Stream.

As he ascended closer to the summit, he was repeatedly reminded of his otherworldly or transcendent goal, the difficulties of his journey, and the history and natural beauty of the mountain:

Cypress Cave (no. 18)
Ascent to Immortality Tower (no. 20, Jiajing period [1522–1566])
(Arch of the) Ridge Where the Horses Turn Back (no. 21)
Step to Heaven Bridge (no. 22)
Second Heavenly Gate (no. 23)
Cloud Stepping Bridge (no. 26)
Esplanade of the Imperial Tent (no. 27)
Rock That Came Flying Down (no. 28, 1603)
Fifth Rank Pine Tree and the Fifth Rank Pine Tree Arch (no. 29)
Inscription of 100,000 Feet (no. 31, 1748)
Opposing Pines Pavilion (no. 32)

At Cloud Gate (no. 33), the pilgrim began the steepest, most difficult part of the ascent (see Fig. 14, p. 26, and Fig. 23, p. 57). Looking up, he would have seen the Southern Heavenly Gate standing like a fortress (guan 關) in the crook of a pass (guan 關). The combination of the military and geographical meanings of the term were reinforced by the fact that just behind this "fortress" in the pass was a temple to the God of War (Guandi 關帝). Before the pilgrim could pass through the final heavenly gate, he, like the legendary fish seeking to reach "dragondom," had to progress through the Dragon Gate Arch (no. 34). The symbolic language of all the other sites was strengthened by this overt reference to that quest tale.

Between the Dragon Gate Arch and the Southern Heavenly Gate was the Promoted to Transcendence Arch (no. 36). Following in Li Bo's footsteps, a Qing dynasty traveler, Yu Shu 余恕, wrote a poem about this arch and the transforming nature of the summit of Mount Tai:

> Peerless like climbing the mountain on the two
>   feet of a monk,
> One thousand stories and ten thousand steps go
>   to the lofty peak.
> I already know that the source of the transcendents' road
>   is not far,
> but do not believe that I can also ascend the Heavenly flight.
> The wild wind off the ridge startles like a tiger in ambush,
> white mist in the clouds rises and flies like the [giant]
>   Peng [bird].
> Suspended on the cliff I do not dare decline the toils,
> a night in the Cinnabar Hut [passes as quickly as the
>   light in] a shallow lamp.[42]

"Cinnabar Hut" was an allusion to the residence of the immortals. Although Yu Shu strained to reach the lands of immortality, they remained beyond his grasp. Nonetheless, he demonstrated his willingness to strive to reach the next level of challenge.

Joining a Literary Lineage

Literati attempted to obtain immortality and contact with future generations primarily through their own writings. Visitors to Mount Tai sought to use their poems, travelogues, gazetteers, and inscriptions to associate themselves with past scholars and to project something of themselves into the future. Every arch, every pavilion, every temple on the mountain bears the name of every literatus involved in its construction. Their knowledge of history told them how ephemeral even the monuments on Mount Tai could be without preservation and reconstruction in later generations. Their contributions were reinforced by acknowledgments in gazetteers and travelogues and on stelae of their participation in building projects. In their writings, they often placed their actions within a historical framework through references to past notables who had visited the site or engaged in earlier construction and repairs. In 1858, the prefect of Tai'an, Lai Xiu 來秀,[43] repaired the Pavilion for Paying Homage from Afar: "Before, during the Song and Tang dynasties it was called Yaocanmen. . . . In the previous Ming dynasty, because its scale was too narrow, public funds were used to restore and enlarge [the pavilion]. . . . Separation of the temples began in Qianlong 33 [1768], under the provincial governor, the Honorable Fu Ming'an."[44] The next repairer of this same temple also listed his predecessors, which now included Lai Xiu:

In the Ming a statue of Yuanjun was respectfully made and placed within the temple. . . . In our dynasty, during the Qianlong reign, the provincial governor, the Honorable Fu began repairing the temple. One hundred years later, the [Tai'an] prefect, the Honorable Lai [Xiu], recommenced repairs in Xianfeng *dingsi* [1857]. . . . In the spring of Guangxu *jiashen* [1884], [Wu] Shikai, when asked in this year to take up my post [as Tai'an county magistrate], humbly accepted. [The prefect], the Honorable Jin [had already] transmitted the request to the next level [of the bureaucracy] to provide funds for repairing the building in front of the Dai Temple. Also anxious about this pavilion's gradual dilapidation, in a previous order Prefect Tao[45] once contributed 50,000 *qian* and personally collected the money for the craftsmen who completed the repairs.[46]

These rosters of names, carefully repeated and honored again, reassured donors that they could avoid erasure or supplantation. This practice reinforces a key concept from the first passage of the *Classic of Filial Piety*: "We develop our own personality and practice the Way so as to perpetuate our name for future generations, and to give glory to our parents. This is the end of filiality."[47]

Merely engraving a few words on a stone or cliff face was no guarantee of future respect. In fact, an improperly executed inscription could doom the author or sponsor to perpetual ridicule and scorn. This was especially true of those who had the impropriety to efface a previous inscription with their own text. Precisely because they had failed to respect the code of remembrance and had disrupted the literary lineage, they were vilified in perpetuity. During the Ming dynasty, one Zhai Tao 翟濤 engraved three large characters over Song Zhenzong's inscription, the Song Cliff Inscription. Zhai's characters "obliterated thirty or forty characters from each column" of the emperor's inscription.[48] Both Zhai's characters and his ignominy survive today; recent gazetteers and commentaries still censure his act.[49]

Another individual, also from the Ming dynasty, Lin Tun 林焞, suffered a similar fate after engraving four large characters over a Tang-period inscription.[50] Unlike Zhai, whose misdeed was merely recorded, Lin received the full force of Zhang Dai's extremely acerbic brush. The four characters Lin carved into the cliff were *zhong* 忠, *xiao* 孝, *lian* 廉, *jie* 節 (the cardinal Confucian virtues of loyalty, filiality, honesty, and integrity). Zhang Dai sarcastically remarked, "These four characters are within his mind, but he did such evil!"[51]

Zhang Dai did not limit his attacks to those whose work defaced that of others. He also ridiculed the content of inscriptions:

But the beggars were only one of two abominations; the other was the visitors' disgusting practice of inscribing on rocks as well as on the tablets they erected such trite phrases as "Venerated by ten thousand generations" or "The redolence continuing for an eternity." The beggars exploited Mount T'ai for money while the visitors exploited Mount T'ai for fame. The land of Mount T'ai, once pure, was now everywhere desecrated by these two groups.[52]

His sarcasm is further evidenced in his comment that the best inscription on Mount Tai is that on the Wordless Stele (no. 48).[53] Having one's name or words preserved for future generations was insufficient. The inscription had to demonstrate a high degree of literary merit or moral rectitude. To garner a positive image in the future, a late imperial author needed to treat past members of the literary lineage with "loyalty, filiality, honesty, and integrity."

The records of actions undertaken by officials reveal not only the duties they performed but also, perhaps, those they felt would impress future generations. Official duties included prayers on behalf of the people as well as the maintenance of temples. Although an individual might pray for a sick parent, many stele inscriptions contain references to an official petitioning on behalf of all the people under his jurisdiction: "Honorable Kang of Taiyuan undertook the orders of the Son of Heaven to inspect Shandong and

Liaodong to find out whether the government was not flourishing or all was successful. In the 3rd month of *bingchen* [1796], the judge fasted and then climbed the mountain in order to pray for blessings for the people."[54] After performing the necessary official rituals, he prayed for the well-being of the general populace and thus fulfilled his patriarchal role toward the people.

Well-maintained buildings and temples were considered a sign of an able and upright official. A handbook for magistrates popular throughout most of the Qing dynasty stated that magistrates should take steps to ensure that temples were "kept in repair and sacrifices offered at proper intervals."[55] The following stele inscription shows an official at work:

[Since the last repairs,] wind and rain have broken [the roof] and encroached, rats and small birds have pierced through [the walls] and made holes, gradually the red [color of the walls] has faded and decayed, [now] later we must make up for these defects. . . . Work began in the second month of *yiyou* [1885] and was completed in the second month of the next year, *bingxu* [1886]. . . . From the main building down to the main door, [workers] corrected deficiencies and straightened slants, painters refreshed wall murals and smoothed over that which was peeling. The statues inside and the stone beasts and ornamental pillars outside were set in order, nothing is not bright and decorated; cinnabar walls and joists were redecorated, all looks different.[56]

This stele text gives the impression that the ravages were natural and that good management compensates for the natural extremes of Mount Tai.

Naming a site with an appropriate historical or poetic reference was seen as an important skill of a learned man. A well-chosen name not only evoked visions harmonious with the site but also demonstrated the namer's knowledge of history and literature. A famous example of naming as a test of education is found in Baoyu's labeling of the sites in the family garden in chapter 17 of Cao Xueqin's famous eighteenth-century novel *Dream of the Red Chamber*. This importance placed on naming can be traced to the idea of the "rectification of names" (*zhengming* 正名) in the *Analects*: "Confucius said, '. . . If names are not rectified, then language will not be in accord with truth. If language is not in accord with truth, then things cannot be accomplished.'"[57]

For these reasons, the naming of sites at places such as Mount Tai was subjected to a high level of scrutiny. Just as Baoyu's father scoffed at many of the names chosen by his son, so other literati, like Zhang Dai, criticized names of sites on the mountain. A good example of an error in naming is found in an inscription carved into the Arch of Fifth Rank Pine Tree. According to Nie Jianguang and Jin Qi, at some point between the late Ming and 1763, there were actually five pine trees at this site. Someone mistakenly thought that the phrase "wu dafu" meant "five officials" (i.e., the five trees) rather than the "fifth-rank official" and thereby incorrectly inscribed the stone at the top of the arch.[58] Here Nie and Jin were ridiculing the ignorance of the engraver, for such a mistake could result only from not knowing the site's connection with Qin Shihuangdi.

Another instance of improper naming is associated with a tree not far up the mountain from Fifth Rank Pine Tree. Just above the Sun Facing Cave (no. 30) is an inscription marking the former site of the Local Scholars Pine (chu shi song 處士松). Here "local scholars" refers to the Confucian scholars and erudites (rusheng boshi 儒生博士) from Qi and Lu, the two states bordering Mount Tai, whose advice Qin Shihuangdi chose to ignore. The tree that formerly stood at this site was given this name during the Ming dynasty as a means of honoring those Confucian scholars and "shaming" (xiu 羞) Qin Shihuangdi.[59] This name won praise from later literati such as Xiao Xiezhong and Nie Jianguang. However, an inscription carved in 1562 gave the Local Scholars Pine another name, the Solitary Dafu (duli dafu 獨立大夫).[60] Dafu was a reference to the title Qin Shihuangdi gave to the tree under which he took refuge from the storm. This name, although with less subtlety, makes the same allusions as the other name. However, it was sharply criticized by Nie Jianguang. Since Qin Shihuangdi had enfeoffed the Fifth Rank Pine Tree to spite his Confucian advisors, who, Nie asked rhetorically and acerbically, could ennoble this tree as the Solitary Dafu?[61]

The literati consensus about the appropriate name for a site is reflected in gazetteers and travelogues, as well as on maps. Maps could be carved on stelae, and rubbings made of them. Maps were also included in gazetteers and sometimes in travelogues. Unlike longer sources, however, maps did not have space to discuss history or give multiple names for a single site. Therefore, a map was the product of the maker's editing. He chose what he believed were the most important sites to be labeled and what he felt were the best or most appropriate names for those sites.

The title of a work and its contents were also meaningful editorial decisions important to the image one wished to project. A particular selection or title could determine which future literary lineage would admire the work. Perhaps the most obvious example can be found in writings about the Fifth Rank Pine Tree. Apparently no one saw anything to gain from praising the "book burner" at a site where Heaven had punished him. Thus when writing about this site, all authors make their condemnation of Qin Shihuangdi quite clear. In a similar vein, those who wrote about the Local Scholars Pine not only demonstrated their disdain for the emperor but also associated themselves with scholars who spoke out against despotic rulers. Indeed, the pine tree was especially apt for such an association, because pines symbolized steadfastness and self-discipline.[62]

An example of editorial self-selection is found in Kong Zhenxuan's short gazetteer, *Record of the Beautiful Scenery of Mount Tai* (1673). Kong was a native of Qufu and a member of the clan that claimed descent from Confucius.[63] He therefore positioned his writings to conform with what he perceived to be the correct interpretation of Confucius' works. Kong Zhenxuan's gazetteer, even in its title, emphasized the enjoyment of natural settings over the spiritual. The gazetteer listed only a few temples, the most obvious exclusion being the goal of the vast majority of pilgrims, the Bixia Temple on top of the mountain. Even when he mentioned a temple, Kong generally discussed the beautiful scenery or points of historical interest. For example, his comments on the Queen Mother Pool Temple point out the depth of the spring. Although he noted in passing that people pray to the Eastern Sacred Peak

and to Bixia Yuanjun in the Dai Temple, he chose to emphasize
the halls in which imperial sacrifices took place and the Han Cypresses, and the Tang Acacia on the grounds of this temple. His
preface, quoted above, reflects his title and the overall tone of the
body of the work:

We took along wine and cakes for a two-day journey. From the time we
entered the landscape, we paid close attention to everything. The clouds
were dense, the dirt [of everyday life] far away. We were as one in our
contentedness. We gave voice to our thoughts through parables; then we
wrote poems and songs in accordance with the rules of rhyme on the
themes of particular sights.[64]

Other examples of attempts to associate oneself with a particular
lineage can be found in poetry. Literati interested in evidential
learning, for example, might choose to write a long poem invoking
ancient texts and early visitors. Those more inclined toward mystical experiences might echo lines or titles from Li Bo or Du Fu. For
example, a number of late imperial poems appropriate the title of
Du Fu's famous poem about Mount Tai, "Gazing on the Sacred
Peak" ("Wang yue" 望嶽).

More complex positioning for future audiences can be found in
conflicts over two sites on the mountain. A little north and above
the Mother of the Big Dipper Temple a trail branches off the Pilgrimage Path to the east and leads to the Stone Sūtra Vale (no. 16).
The vale consists of a large expanse of fairly smooth bedrock at a
slight incline. During the Northern Qi dynasty (550–77), someone
carved a portion of the text of the Buddhist Diamond Sūtra (Jin-
gang jing 金剛經) into the face of the bedrock. Not only did the act
of carving a Buddhist text on a Daoist mountain express the calligrapher's faith, but it also challenged the notion that Mount Tai was
Daoist and Confucian sacred space. Even though late imperial literati may not have shared the carver's Buddhist faith, they did admire his calligraphy, which was reproduced in many calligraphy
books as a model for emulation.

Around 1550 an unknown scholar, to express his opposition to
the presence of a Buddhist sūtra on this sacred mountain, attempted to reinscribe this sacred space by carving a passage from

Fig. 32 "Classics Rectify" inscription in the Stone Sūtra Vale (no. 16). To the left of the two large vertical characters is a passage from the *Mencius*. These are engraved perpendicular to the inscription of the Diamond Sūtra (part of a character from that inscription can be seen on the horizontal rock surface in the lower right) (photograph by the author, 1995).

one of the Confucian Four Books, the *Great Learning*, onto a rock just above the *Diamond Sūtra*.[65] This inscription was destroyed during the reign of the Kangxi emperor.[66]

In 1578, Censor-in-Chief Li Bangzhen 李邦珍 inscribed another text in opposition to the *Diamond Sūtra*. On the vertical face of a rock projecting into and above the center of the Buddhist text, Li inscribed two large characters meaning "the norm rectifies" or "the Classics rectify" (*jing zheng* 經正; see Fig. 32). Li's inscription begins with the passage from the *Mencius* from which the phrase is taken:

Meng Ke [Mencius] said: "The superior man seeks simply to bring back the [true] standards (*jing* 經); with these standards rectified (*jing zheng* 經正), the common people become roused [against incorrect teachings]." *Jing* 經 also means "classic." Now we use the Sagely Classics (*shengjing* 聖經)[67] to bring back the [true] standards. Therefore we say: "Classics rectify."[68]

Li's inscription stated by placement and size that the ancient *Confucian* classics rectify, whereas the Daoism practiced on the mountain and the Buddhism of this "false classic"[69] had no redeeming value. There were literate Daoist priests and Buddhist monks resident on Mount Tai throughout the late imperial period. They, too, wrote about the mountain, and no doubt positioned that writing to fit their own particular interpretations of this sacred mountain—interpretations that probably differed significantly from those of most of the elite men discussed in this chapter. Unfortunately most of the records that could be used to pursue even a cursory analysis of such writings no longer exist. The few biographies of Daoists or Buddhists found in the gazetteers are far too short to allow meaningful analysis. The most obvious evidence of support for religious institutions on the mountain can be found in the stelae commemorating the restorations of temples. However, as shown in selections from such stelae quoted above, many of these repairs were undertaken as part of an official's duties and were not necessarily a reflection of personal belief or piety. There are, however, at least two inscriptions on the mountain that express the engraver's personal faith. Both inscriptions consist of the single character *fo* 佛, the Buddha or Buddhism, carved into natural stone. Both are adjacent to the central Pilgrimage Path, one just above the Myriad Transcendents Tower (no. 13, see Fig. 6, p. 18), and the other in the upper stretches of the Happy Three Li (no. 25).

The conflicts played out on the mountain were sometimes within and not just between adherents of different faiths. The Confucian Temple on top of the mountain (no. 40), for example, was the site of contentions among admirers of Confucius. The first temple to Confucius on the mountain was built in 1583 or 1584. It consisted of "a wall with one gate around three buildings. . . . The main building contained an image of Confucius; in the two side buildings were [images of Confucius' disciples] Yan, Zeng, Si, and Mencius."[70] When Zha Zhilong visited the temple in 1586, however, he found that "only the bronze statue in the Kongzi Yai [Temple to Confucius] remains, and it is half destroyed; as for [the images of] Yan, Zeng, and Mencius, nothing can be seen." Zha ordered that the shrine be repaired and new statues installed.[71]

The men who destroyed the statues were almost certainly scholars who considered themselves followers of Confucius (*rusheng* 儒生). In 1530, after an extremely contentious debate, the emperor adopted a series of major reforms in the worship of Confucius and his disciples. All existing images in Confucian temples were to be destroyed and replaced with wooden spirit tablets.[72] The contentions around this issue still existed in 1586, when Zha, then an official, insisted on reinstalling the statues in the temple despite the 1530 regulations. In order to protect these new statues from dissenting Confucianists, Zha ordered two Daoist priests (*daoshi* 道士) to take up residence in the temple.[73]

Conclusion

Much of the naming, inscribing, mapping, and building on Mount Tai was undertaken by literati of the late imperial period. They desired to draw nearer to their history and forge links with past heroes. However, they were interested in much more than historical sites. They connected to nature through poetry recitation and composition. They built pavilions and arches as markers for the discovery and cultivation of themselves. The gap that separated them from ordinary "pilgrims" was not their apparent lack of religious devotion; rather, their spiritual devotion was focused more on literate than on oral culture, more on Mount Tai and Confucius than on Bixia Yuanjun. They wrote themselves into long lineages of perfected persons through travelogues and inscriptions. They substituted the writing brush and chisel for incense smoke.

An excellent example of a literatus's multifaceted interaction with the sacred space of Mount Tai is found in Zhang Pengge's 張鵬翮 (1649–1725) poem "Han Cypress" (1710). This poem was inscribed on a stone beside one of the Han dynasty cypress trees in the Dai Temple:

> The ancient cypress has leaned toward the green range[74]
>   for a thousand years,
> on the Taiping Summit[75] one feels the vastness of heaven.
> Clear skies, like the time when white cranes came dancing,
> beyond the clouds one obtains a carefree, calm regard.[76]

The poem in honor of a tree can be taken as an example of literati admiration for and worship of nature. The poem's title reiterates and perpetuates the tree's name. This particular tree was believed to have been planted during the Han dynasty by Han Wudi. The poem was written because of the tree's antiquity, but perhaps also because of its imperial connections. "Green" in the first line is the character *bi* 碧 discussed in the sections on mysticism and life in Part I. This was an obvious attempt by the author to link his poem to the highly regarded poetry of the Tang period, in which this color was a favorite for describing mountains. Ever since Song Zhenzong included the character *bi* in his title for the Goddess of Mount Tai, however, any use of that character in reference to Mount Tai, at least obliquely, referred to the goddess. The second line is a reference to Confucius' finding the world small. Zhang's experience of the vastness of Heaven simply inverts the image from the *Mencius*. The third line refers to an event alleged to have occurred in 680. According to legend, a flock of cranes dove into a spring at the base of the mountain, which accordingly became known as the White Cranes Spring (no. 64) and subsequently had the sweetest water on the mountain. Despite the deaths of the cranes, this episode was seen as propitious.[77] Zhang's intent here was not so much to refer to a specific event, but to declare the auspiciousness of his own time and compare the clear skies of his age to those present during a highly propitious event. In the context of Mount Tai's history, a reference to "clear skies" was an overt contrast to the storm encountered by Qin Shihuangdi. Indeed, this same image was invoked in the official record of the first ascent by a Qing emperor in 1684: "Now, our emperor is examining all regions and inspecting the famous mountains. When he climbed up and down [Mount Tai], the sky was clear and the weather was calm along all four frontiers. The myriad deities were numinous and favorable."[78]

The Kangxi emperor was still on the throne when Zhang wrote his poem. It seems likely that Zhang's reference to "clear skies" was meant as praise of the emperor's rule.[79] The tone of the last line of Zhang's poem is reminiscent of the escape from everyday life expressed on the Han dynasty mirror and in Li Bo's poetry. All three celebrate divinity, epic cloudscapes, and a sublime perspective. Thus, this single poem evokes Mount Tai as a locus for nature worship, imperial ritual, history, and mysticism. In addition,

Zhang's use of the character *bi* may also refer obliquely to the life-giving powers associated with the mountain.

Just as it was for the women pilgrims to Mount Tai, Turner's model of pilgrimage is only partially useful in understanding late imperial literati pilgrimages. Many activities undertaken by literati on Mount Tai were not distinct from or liminal in comparison to more everyday activities. Literati enjoyed nature, wrote and recited poetry, engaged in the naming of sites, and enjoyed the camaraderie of their male friends within their own gardens as well as on the mountain. The liminality of their journeys is a matter of degree. The sacred space of Mount Tai allowed a greater departure from the mundane and a closer self-inspection. The traces of Confucius, Li Bo, and others on the mountain allowed literati to approach the dragon gate, closer to the immortals. They were indeed pilgrims who sought "direct experience of the sacred, invisible, or supernatural order . . . in the immaterial aspect of inward transformation of spirit or personality."[80]

Literati often commented on the camaraderie they enjoyed with their traveling companions, which corresponds quite closely to Turner's concept of communitas. As Kong Zhenxuan put it, "We were as one in our contentedness."[81] Ties to other scholars, however, transcended short-term communitas ties with friends. Ming and Qing literati from all over the empire were bound together by literacy, a shared knowledge of the Classics, history, and poetry. This relationship among literati on Mount Tai comes closer, perhaps, to the links found by Benedict Anderson among imperial bureaucrats.[82] However, this model, too, falls short of explaining the extended community of late imperial Chinese literati.[83] These literati were extremely conscious of both the past and the future. They sought to include themselves in an immortal lineage of literati. By inscribing the sacred space of Mount Tai with their own words, they affiliated themselves with those who had come before them and sought to guarantee that they would be remembered and admired by future generations of likeminded men.

 Conclusion

By the late imperial period, Mount Tai's religious, historical, and political associations, in addition to creating a focus of attention at Mount Tai, offered rich resources for appropriation and adaptation. Oral and written narratives combined with artifacts to form overlapping layers of elements so varied and copious that selective re-emphasis, elision, and modification were as much required as expedient. The past was a deeply resonant source for people heavily invested in filial piety. The creativity with which each disparate group entered itself into the oral, written, and physical records of Mount Tai and inscribed its sacrality into its own imagined or recorded lineage stemmed both from the society's common adherence to filiality and from the myriad associations that had grown up around this sacred peak. Thus, within the social diversity, one also finds unity. Despite different motivations, goals, and identities, despite contentions and conflicts, all those who journeyed to Mount Tai during the late imperial period shared a core set of beliefs and practices that tied them together into one larger society. Some of these can be inferred from the evidence presented above about the interactions of various groups with Mount Tai; namely, a reverence for: filial piety, hierarchy, lineage, nature, writing, and ritual.

Mount Tai's role as a source of life and death gave it vast drawing power. All who went there envisioned the mountain as a place

with the power to conceive, sustain, prolong, reincarnate, or ter-
minate existence. Each group, according to its mentalities, stressed
a different type of life, site of worship, form of ritual, and object of
desire. By developing a close relationship with the goddess and offering food and clothing, women sought Bixia Yuanjun's help in
producing sons. They prayed for sons in order to improve their
position in their husband's family and to provide for their own
well-being in their old age. Illiterate men sought to honor their deceased ancestors both by placing memorial tablets at the entrance
to purgatory and by praying on the top of the mountain to Bixia
Yuanjun to continue their family lines. Although sons meant different things to women and men, a basic conception of the importance of filial piety was at the root of their desires. For the literati,
filiality at Mount Tai was the tie that bound them into a seamless
lineage of past, present, and future scholars. For the Kangxi and
Qianlong emperors, the mountain was a site that had the power to
conserve their imperial lineage and dynasty yet not compromise
their Manchu identity.

Another shared characteristic of the groups visiting Mount Tai
was the belief in hierarchy. The Kangxi and Qianlong emperors
were vested in their positions of power and prestige as the Son of
Heaven. The Kangxi emperor also crafted his writings about and
actions on the mountain in such a way as to place Manchus and
himself hierarchically above Han Chinese. He did not stoop to
performing rituals that were "mere brags and boasts." He, not the
ancients, discovered Mount Tai's dragon veins. The Qianlong emperor sought to be the apical collector. His collections were larger,
his seals more numerous, his colophons more copious, and his inscriptions more imposing than those of previous Han emperors
and his grandfather. Male literati viewed their skill of literacy as
placing them above the rest of society. They also perceived hierarchies within their own group. It was important to write oneself
into the correct lineage. One needed to praise and condemn past
figures appropriately. A literatus's integrity, knowledge, and skills
as a writer elevated him to a position of respect in the eyes of later
scholars. Even in pilgrimage societies, groups that might appear to

have been fairly egalitarian, hierarchy was important. Although Bixia Yuanjun treated all equally, late imperial Chinese society, like most societies, distinguished between leaders and the led. Even the all-women societies had leaders. Their families, too, were built around hierarchies. Although crises, such as smallpox or a difficult labor, could temporarily bring a lower-level goddess into prominence, there was also a broadly defined, rigid hierarchy within the community of goddesses.

The importance of hierarchy for these groups is one reason why Turner's concept of communitas has only limited usefulness for studying Chinese pilgrimages. Hierarchical differentiation precluded fellowship among the various segments of the society. No universal communitas was possible. The motivations and expectations of emperors, literati, and peasants did not overlap enough for them to bond with one another. In addition, even within each group hierarchies prevented Turner's egalitarian bonds. When Wang Shizhen wrote that in his drunken ecstasy "all my companions cheered me on: some harmonized with me," he made it clear that he was the person carrying the tune and paying for the wine the others were drinking (see Chapter 3, p. 210).

Lineage propagation was a major focus for all the groups making pilgrimages to the mountain. The Kangxi and Qianlong emperors were intent on their descendants' continuing to fill the position of Son of Heaven and on incorporating Mount Tai's dragon and its physical monumentalism into their Manchu background as part of their heirs' patrimony. Literati were intent on writing themselves into a literary lineage that extended from the incisive vision of Confucius through the mystical aesthetics of Li Bo to themselves and their successors. Peasant men focused on their patriline, both backward through ancestors and forward through heirs. Women strove to create uterine families and tie them into their *niangjia*, centered around a potent and compassionate grandmother, Bixia Yuanjun.

The concepts of liminality and communitas are even more irrelevant to two emperors intent on transforming not themselves but sacred spaces. As we saw in Chapter 3, many of the literati's

activities on Mount Tai were not distinct from or liminal in comparison to their everyday activities. Accounts of families traveling
together and the forests of stelae at the temple to the God of
Mount Tai suggest that far from a liminal or temporarily inverted
experience, the pilgrimage of an illiterate male was often an extension of his filial behavior as a member of a patriline or a member
of a uterine family. Here, I believe, Turner's concept of liminality
can further explain men's mixed identities on the mountain. The
liminal space of Mount Tai may have allowed them to give greater
voice to their uterine family identity.

Perhaps a concept of equal or greater importance than liminality
is vision. Groups sought the summit for the literal and spiritual vision it afforded, a vision that was a key emphasis of worshipers of
the God and Goddess of Mount Tai and of Confucius. Confucius'
range and profundity of vision on the mountain drew the highest
levels of literate society, including emperors. The Goddess of Eyesight drew many others, mostly but not all from the illiterate
masses. The Wanli Emperor commissioned repairs at the main
Bixia Temple to benefit his mother's eyesight.

For all these groups, the sacrality of Mount Tai originated in its
natural form. Many pilgrims sought the healing properties of the
mountain's natural springs and used its rocks and cypress boughs
as parts of ritual puns. Literati sought the transforming powers of
nature. For the Kangxi emperor, Mount Tai was the head of a vast
underground dragon that connected his homeland with the heart
of the territory he had recently conquered completely. He an-
chored his nomadic past to this solid, stationary sacred peak, tying
himself to a Chinese past but also securing a future for himself and
his lineage, both as the Son of Heaven and as a Manchu. For the
Qianlong emperor, the mountain was a beautiful, natural landscape to be stamped with his seal and included in his collection.

Although writing was the defining characteristic of the literati,
its importance was widely accepted. Writing and reading set the
literati off from the rest of the society and gave them a place in the
scholarly lineage. Literacy allowed the Qing emperors to read, en-
dorse, refute, and create precedents. Reading and writing Chinese

helped them fulfill the role of the Son of Heaven. Reading and writing Manchu helped to maintain their identity and to separate them from the Han Chinese. Writing in Chinese society was also important for the illiterate. Writing added significance and power to objects, even when the viewer found it unintelligible. Woodblock prints as well as statues of deities on altars, for example, bore the written name of the deity. If the deity were not correctly named, then the supplicant's prayer might not reach its destination.

Although each group conducted different rituals, the correct performance of rituals was imperative if the petitioners were to receive what they desired and not bring retribution on themselves or their heirs. Men and women praying to Bixia Yuanjun had to pray before altars with her image; they had to burn incense, and they had to pray sincerely. In addition, women who desired a baby had to perform specific rituals such as tying a string around the neck of a doll. The Kangxi and Qianlong emperors paid close attention to which rituals they conducted and how they performed them. It was important for both rulers that they *not* perform the *feng* and *shan* sacrifices. For political expediency, the Kangxi emperor chose not to perform Buddhist rituals; the changing political atmosphere allowed the Qianlong emperor to perform them as a means of expressing his personal identity. For literati the correct performance of ritual was extremely important. Throughout the centuries, there were intense debates about the validity and appropriateness of performing the *feng* and *shan* sacrifices. The carving of Confucian texts adjacent to a Buddhist sūtra on a Daoist mountain points to the belief that some rituals were more correct than others. In addition, conflicts centered on the Confucian Temple on the top of the mountain manifested the intense debate within late imperial intellectual circles about the correct way to perform rituals in honor of Confucius.

Much recent scholarship in cultural history has concentrated on groups outside dominant power structures. Although this work is often exemplary in its scholarship and adds essential information to our historical knowledge, as William Sewell notes, "It is important to remember that much cultural practice is concentrated in and around powerful institutional nodes. . . . Studies of culture need to pay at least as much attention to such sites of concentrated cultural practice as to the dispersed sites of resistance that currently predominate in the literature."[1] Mount Tai pilgrimage lends itself to an examination of a broad spectrum of Chinese society. This work differs from other studies of Mount Tai not only by not focusing just on the elite but also by not excluding them. This balance and the ability to study an "institutional node" and subordinate groups at the same time is largely a product of the characteristics of the site itself. Mount Tai is one of the most famous mountains in China. It lies within the ritually potent, traditional heartland of the Middle Kingdom, adjacent to the major land and canal routes connecting the capital to the north with the economically and culturally rich Jiangnan area to the south. It is far less isolated than most of China's sacred mountains. Thus it drew members of the elite to its slopes. However, since it was neither the seat of imperial or even provincial power nor a site with a major monastic institution, it was also a place somewhat removed from the centers of power and thus one where historians can also examine the lower echelons of Chinese society.

It is also important to realize that "subordinated groups must to some degree orient their local systems of meaning to those recognized as dominant; the act of contesting dominant meanings itself implies a recognition of their centrality."[2] The best example of this in my study is found in the female pilgrims to Mount Tai. In their pilgrimages, they could experience the agency and authority denied them in the orthodox rules of behavior. Yet, they still operated within the larger social context and could not ignore all its structures. Despite male literati proscriptions, countless women made the pilgrimage to Mount Tai during the late imperial period. Thus, the system was much more flexible in practice than in its ideal written form. Women's visits were constructed in terms of the uterine family and the *niangjia* as a journey to "talk with old grandmother." Because women visited Mount Tai to pray for sons, they were upholding the important concept of filial piety by providing heirs. Even as historians acknowledge that subordinate

groups frequently worked within the system, it is important to realize that both the actors and the system regularly operated with
more flexibility than is often assumed.

It is not just in the elements that unified late imperial Chinese
society, as represented in pilgrimage to Mount Tai, that this study
suggests overlaps across the groups of pilgrims. Some of the characteristics that distinguished groups in general terms also reveal
commonalities. Even the communal groups of women and goddesses displayed hierarchies and at times an emphasis on justice and
judgment, rather than working outside the system. Although the
literati emphasized literacy, especially correct moral and aesthetic
interpretations, women passed on ritual practice through oral puns
and stories of Bixia Yuanjun's trickery. Nonetheless, writing was a
revered and crucial element in the offerings, altars, paper money,
and pilgrimage society stelae, as were carefully crafted prayers (albeit they were judged more in terms of sincerity and clarity of requests than for their historical allusions). On the other hand, recitation and repetition of key poems and singing were also parts of
the literati's interaction with Mount Tai. Certain groups, such as
monks, nuns, Muslim chairbearers, innkeepers, actors, and wrestlers, as well as officials with a chance to skim the incense tax, prof-
ited from the pilgrims. Yet these travelers also expected a return on
their investment in the form of sons to support them in their old
age, good crops, better health, higher official position and recognition, or greater control over conquered territories.

The Kangxi emperor's essay in which he wrote Mount Tai into
the Manchu empire is one of the distinctive visions of Mount Tai
from the late imperial period. Throughout the twentieth century,
and now into the twenty-first, Mount Tai continues to be used as a
symbol for all of China. Both the Republican and the Communist
regimes have tried to secularize and appropriate this sacred site for
their own ends. Much of this has involved using the mountain as a
symbol of nationalism, a topic outside the scope of this work.[3]

Beginning in 1928, the Republican government sought to convert the sacred space of Mount Tai into a secular and revolutionary
space. At this time, the government was attempting to reduce the

influence of what it deemed the "superstitious" influences of religion by confiscating temple lands and conducting antisuperstition
campaigns.[4] In 1928 the Daizong Arch (see Fig. 10, p. 22) at the base
of the mountain was painted Republican blue and adorned with an
image of Sun Yatsen as well as some of his texts.[5] Mary Mullikin
states most of the arches on the pilgrimage trail as well as temple
doorways were painted blue.[6] A photo in her article shows the
Southern Heavenly Gate (see Fig. 14, p. 26) covered with Republican political slogans, such as Sun Yatsen's "Three People's Principles" and "The public owns, the public rules, the public enjoys."[7]
Both the Republican and the Communist governments have used
the sacred space of Mount Tai as a place to honor heroes in an attempt to make the mountain into revolutionary space.[8] A book of
revolutionary songs published in 1958, for example, uses Mount Tai
as a symbol for the new China. The title of the book and of the
first song is *Mount Tai's Territory, Who Dares Move It.*[9] The cover
shows Mount Tai as a soldier shaking a fist at an American ship in
the Taiwan Strait. In the picture and the words of the song, Mount
Tai stands for all of China and for the towering strength of the
united Chinese people. A highly potent use of Mount Tai as a
symbol of China can be found in the sacred space of Mao Zedong's
mausoleum in Beijing. Mao's body lies directly on a large piece of
polished black stone from Mount Tai.[10]

For much of its existence, the Chinese Communist Party sought
to sever the Chinese people from their past traditions, because they
were deemed "feudal" and oppressive, a philosophy that often resulted in the destruction of temples, homes, gardens, and other
buildings connected with historical sites. In 1965 the government
forced all the monks and nuns residing on Mount Tai to leave the
temples and re-enter secular life. At the same time the government
also severely restricted all pilgrimages. With Deng Xiaoping's
launching of the Four Modernizations, however, came a relaxation
of restrictions. People were able to once again visit local temples
and pilgrimage sites. In 1985 monks and nuns were allowed to return to the temples on the mountain. With the market reforms and
the suppression of the 1989 Tiananmen protesters, many Chinese

lost their faith in communism. Subsequently, the party turned to actively promoting traditional cultural practices and history as a means of encouraging national identity and national pride, as well as appropriating past regimes. Although much of the recent restoration of temples and historic sites can be viewed as a bid for both foreign and domestic tourist monies, these sites are also being promoted because of their importance to Chinese history and their ability to reflect and reproduce Chinese traits and characteristics. A recent work titled *Mount Tai: Symbol of the Chinese Spirit* quotes the famous author Guo Moruo 郭沫若 (1892–1978): "Mount Tai is part of the epitome of Chinese history and culture."[11]

In 1987 the United Nations Educational, Scientific, and Cultural Organization (UNESCO) named Mount Tai a "World Heritage" site. In obtaining this endorsement and in advertising its significance, the government has been conspicuously silent about Mount Tai's religious role, noting only that "Mount Tai possesses outstanding universal significance and value in the natural sciences, aesthetics and historic culture."[12] Nonetheless, the government, motivated by tourism and historical relevance, has restored many of the temples, shrines, pavilions, and the Pilgrimage Path itself.

Much on the mountain has changed. The entrance to purgatory is no longer visited, a gondola traverses the distance between the Middle and Southern Heavenly Gates, and vaccines have rendered the Goddess of Smallpox obsolete. However, those who climb Mount Tai's slopes today, like their late imperial counterparts, do so for a variety of reasons and motivations. Although there are no longer any emperors, political leaders still inscribe the stones of Mount Tai. In 1991, Li Peng, then prime minister, wrote: "Protect this world heritage site, protect the Eastern Sacred Peak Mount Tai."[13] Besides referring to its UNESCO status, he emphasized the natural and historic aspects of the mountain.

The busiest day of the year is now May Day, when thousands swarm over the mountain admiring the scenery, reading the inscriptions, and even reciting the poems of Du Fu and Li Bo, much like the literati of the late imperial period. Pilgrims, including organized groups, still pray to Bixia Yuanjun. Two tombs of local

Communist Party members at the base of the mountain (nos. 79, 82), an attempt to create a revolutionary space on this sacred site, were recently reappropriated by local worshipers. During the spring pilgrimage season in 1995, both tombs were covered with cypress twigs, a borrowing from the fertility ritual. During my visit in the summer of 2000, the largest pilgrimage group was from Taiwan, a further sign of the growing ties across the strait. Yet despite all these changes, Bixia Yuanjun's temple on top of the mountain still attracts numerous believers whose prayers rise with the smoke of their offerings.

Appendix

APPENDIX

Gazetteer of the Main
Sites on Mount Tai

This Appendix provides descriptions and histories of the more important temples, pavilions, and natural formations that were, and in many cases still are, on the itineraries of pilgrims to this holy mountain. It is unlikely that any single pilgrim or visitor was interested in or comprehended the historical or cultural significance of all the sites described here. As we have seen, different sectors of Chinese society approached the mountain with different goals and expectations, which conditioned where they directed their feet and their gaze. The main body of this Appendix follows the central route of ascent beginning from the large temple in the city of Tai'an and proceeding up to the summit. The sites discussed at the end of the Appendix are located in the immediate environs of Tai'an and either would have been visited after the descent or were places the pilgrims stayed.

The heading for each item listed below (with the exception of the city of Tai'an) begins with a number; these correspond to the numbers marked on Fig. 5 (p. 16). An English translation of the name is followed by the Chinese name first in transliterated form and then in Chinese characters. The number in parentheses is that assigned to the site in Chavannes's 1910 study of Mount Tai.[1] Chavannes visited the mountain in 1897 and 1907; all references to what he saw refer to those dates. Information on current conditions, unless otherwise noted, is drawn from my visits in 1994, 1995, and 2000.

THE CITY OF TAI'AN 泰安

The earliest recorded name for the settlement at Mount Tai's base is Village of the Sacred Peak Dai (Daiyue zhen 岱嶽鎮). This settlement probably came into existence in order to support the temple at the base of the mountain and to house and feed those who came to worship. During the Warring States period (481–221 BCE), the closest town of notable size to Mount Tai, Bo 博, was about 15 kilometers to the southeast of present-day Tai'an. During the Han dynasties (202 BCE–220 CE), Mount Tai was located in the mid-level administrative region known as Mount Tai commandery (Taishan jun 泰山郡). The capital of the commandery was at the town of Fenggao 奉高, about 25 kilometers east of Tai'an. During the Han, the town of Bo was the administrative center of a county (*xian* 縣), the lowest level of the Han administration and just below the commandery. During the Northern and Southern Dynasties (317–589 CE), the capital of the commandery was relocated to Bo. During the Northern Wei (386–534), Bo was renamed Boping 博平. The name was changed to Bocheng 博城 during the Sui dynasty (589–618). During the Tang (618–907), the city of Bocheng was reduced to a county-level administrative seat.[2]

In 666, in honor of his performance of the *feng* and *shan* sacrifices at Mount Tai, Tang Gaozong adopted a new reign name, Qianfeng 乾封, that reflected the auspiciousness of the occasion; *feng* refers to the sacrifices to heaven (*qian*). Tang Gaozong also renamed Bocheng Qianfeng. In 972, the administrative seat of the county was relocated to the Village of the Sacred Peak Dai. This village, now called Qianfeng, was located on the same site Tai'an occupied during the late imperial period and where the Dai Temple is located today.[3]

When Song Zhenzong visited Mount Tai to perform the sacrifices in 1008, he, too, renamed the town at the mountain's base as a means of commemoration. Since Song Zhenzong decided to perform the sacrifices because a magical book had fallen from the heavens at Mount Tai, he renamed the town Fengfu 奉符. *Fu* means "auspicious omen," and *feng* "to receive." He also ordered that Fengfu be a new town to be built just to the southeast of the old one. The previous site was then renamed the Old City (*jiucheng* 舊城). During the Jin dynasty (1115–1234), the name of the town was changed to Tai'an, and the city was moved back to its previous site, where it has remained to the present day. In addition, during the Jin, Tai'an became the seat of the larger, surrounding administrative jurisdiction, Tai'an zhou 州, or prefecture. This status continued throughout the Yuan dynasty (1279–1368). During the Ming and early Qing dynasties Tai'an was the seat of two levels of territorial administration—the larger *zhou* (subprefecture during the Ming and department during the Qing) and the smaller *xian* or county. In 1735 the administrative status of Tai'an was raised from *zhou* (department) to *fu* 府 (prefecture). From 1735 until the end of the dynasty in 1911, the city of Tai'an remained the seat of both the *fu* and the smaller *xian*.[4]

During the Ming dynasty a stone wall, a little over 3.5 kilometers in length with a gate on each side, was built around the city.[5] The city wall, which no longer exists, was probably torn down in the 1950s. The southern gate was off-center, so that it aligned with the large Dai Temple (see Fig. 5, p. 16). The Dai Temple itself was aligned with the opening of a valley between two arms of the mountain that reach out toward the city and temple. The main Pilgrimage Path proceeds up this valley. According to Chinese geomancy, a south-facing space between two arms of a mountain was an extremely auspicious spot for a temple, city, or tomb.

I. TEMPLE FOR PAYING HOMAGE FROM AFAR,

YAOCANTING 遙參亭 (CHAVANNES NO. 219)

According to an inscription inside the temple: "Yaocanting was originally connected to the Dai Temple (no. 2). Earlier, during the Song and Tang dynasties it was called Yaocanmen [Gate for Paying Homage from Afar]. All who had matters [to conduct] at the Sacred Peak had to first look up with reverence and pray here before entering the actual main door of the Dai Temple."[6] In 1504, this open pavilion was converted from a place of preliminary worship to Mount Tai to an enclosed space to worship the Goddess of Mount Tai. The main building within this enlarged temple complex continues to house the Ming-period bronze statues of the Goddess of Mount Tai flanked by her two main assistants, the Goddess of Eyesight and the Goddess of Conception. In front of the temple is a stone arch dating from 1770. Immediately south of the arch is a stone-lined pool, which was built in 1880. The water for this pool comes from the spring-fed pool in the Queen Mother Pool Temple (no. 4) as a means to heighten the alignment of this temple and the Dai Temple with which it was associated. Most contemporary pilgrims bypass this temple and the large Dai Temple just to the north.[7]

2. DAI TEMPLE, DAI MIAO 岱廟
(CHAVANNES NO. 218)

This large temple was dedicated to the God of Mount Tai (Taishan shen 泰山神, Dongyue dadi 東嶽大帝). It was the lower of the so-called three temples to the god. The middle temple was located just to the west of the Queen Mother Pool Temple (no. 4), and the upper temple was on top of the mountain (no. 44). Dai is an old name for Mount Tai found in ancient texts such as the *Book of History*. The earliest mention of a temple at the base of the mountain occurs in Ma Dibo's account of his visit in 56 CE. Ma noted that there were many large cypress trees in the temple purported to have been planted by Han Wudi. Although Ma's account does not prove that a temple existed during the time of Wudi's reign, it does seem reasonable to assume that the temple was not new, nor the trees young, in 56 CE. Two cypress trees in one of the courtyards of the temple today are called the "Han Cypresses." In one of the western courtyards is a locust tree (now dead) called the "Tang Acacia" (*Tang huai* 唐槐) (see Fig. 20, p. 38). All the temple courtyards and walls are adorned with inscriptions and flowing calligraphy written during the last thousand years.

Previously the temple was called Sacred Peak Temple (Yue miao 嶽廟). The present temple location and general outline probably date from not much earlier than the Northern Song dynasty. The temple complex is surrounded by a wall almost four meters high with a circumference of 1.5 kilometers. Before the old city walls were taken down, the temple occupied much of the northwest quadrant of the city. A stone arch standing between the Temple for Paying Homage from Afar (no. 1) and the main gate to the Dai Temple was erected in 1672. The central north-south axis of this temple also passes through the center of the Temple for Paying Homage from Afar as well as the two arches just to the south of each of these temples. This axis is aligned with the opening of a valley at the base of the mountain.

When Song Zhenzong visited Mount Tai in 1008 CE, he commissioned a building within the temple in honor of the "Heavenly Text." The oldest stele in the temple, from 1009, commemorates the construction of this Heavenly Bestowal Hall (Tiankuang dian 天贶殿). Although the stele still exists, the building probably no longer resembles the original Song structure. Because of numerous fires and remodelings, most of the halls and shrines in the temple today date from the Ming and Qing dynasties. The current Heavenly Bestowal Hall is the largest building in the complex and contains the statue of the God of Mount Tai. The current statue was dedicated in 1984; the previous statue was destroyed in 1966 during the Cultural Revolution. This is the third largest temple or palace building in China today. The largest is in the Forbidden City in Beijing; the second largest is the Confucian Temple in nearby Qufu.

The west, north, and east walls on the inside of the Heavenly Bestowal Hall are covered with a fresco painting. The painting measures 3.3 meters tall by 62 meters long. On one level, the fresco represents a tour of inspection by the God of Mount Tai. The content is divided into two distinct parts: the god departing on his tour of inspection and the god returning. At another level, however, the painting depicts Song Zhenzong's visit to Mount Tai in 1008 to perform the *feng* and *shan* sacrifices. Until quite recently, the fresco was believed to be the original painting dating from the Song dynasty. However, Mi Yunchang, in his introduction to a book on the temple, refutes any such possibility. Mi points to the numerous fires and rebuildings of the hall as making any such preservation impossible. Mi also notes that Qing period painting styles are apparent throughout the fresco. Furthermore, there are sacrificial vessels depicted of a style not used during the Song. Mi concludes that although the fresco conserves some older styles, the current painting dates from the early Qing dynasty.[8]

Small alcoves around the edges of the central courtyard used to contain depictions of the seventy-five tribunals of the courts of purgatory with departed souls undergoing tortures. Most of the images were no longer extant when Chavannes visited. They were completely gone when Baker visited in the 1920s.[9]

3. DAIZONG ARCH, DAIZONG FANG 岱宗坊 (CHAVANNES NO. 115)

This large, three-arch stone gate is aligned on the same north-south axis as the Dai Temple and the valley at the base of the mountain (see Fig. 10, p. 22). The arch was first erected in 1563.[10] This was probably the site at which the Kangxi emperor led rituals in honor of Mount Tai in 1689.

4. QUEEN MOTHER POOL TEMPLE, WANGMUCHI MIAO 王母池廟 (CHAVANNES NO. 99)

Just to the east of the Pilgrimage Path is this temple to the goddess Wangmu, Queen Mother of the West (Xiwangmu 西王母). The temple was built on a slope facing south. Immediately inside the gate is a stone-lined pool fed by a spring. A reference to this pool in a Tang inscription attests to the antiquity of this temple. The original name of the pool in the temple was Turquoise Pond (Yaochi 瑤池).[11] For further discussion of the Queen Mother of the West and this temple, see the "Life" section in Part I. This is the only temple on Mount Tai that currently has resident Daoist nuns.

The walls enclosing the compound of this temple today include not only the original Queen Mother Pool Temple but also the adjacent God of Medicine Temple (Yaowang miao 藥王廟, Chavannes no. 98). This enlarged temple contains three shrine halls. The main hall, the Wangmu Palace (Wangmu gong 王母宮), is situated above and north of the pool. This hall houses a statue of Wangmu, flanked by two assistants. A second shrine, situated in the former God of Medicine Temple, is called Big Dipper Hall (located in the western part of the Queen Mother Pool Temple). This hall now contains statues of three goddesses: in the center is the Mother of the Big Dipper (Doulao Yuanjun 斗姥元君), on her left (to the east) is Guanyin, and to the west is Bixia Yuanjun. This statue of Bixia Yuanjun, a gift of the Wanli emperor of the Ming dynasty, was originally placed in a bronze pavilion in the main Bixia temple on top of the mountain (no. 58); it was later moved to the Numinous Palace (no. 61).[12] A third shrine building, the Lüzu Tower (Lüzu lou 呂祖樓, Chavannes no. 100), lies above and to the north of the Wangmu Palace. Lüzu, or Lü Dongbin 呂洞賓, was one of the Eight Immortals.

The so-called Middle Temple to the God of Mount Tai (Dong-yue zhong miao 東嶽中廟) used to lie between the Queen Mother Pool Temple and the Pilgrimage Path. The date of its original construction is unknown, but during the Tang dynasty it was called the Daiyue guan 岱嶽觀. According to Chavannes, the middle temple was active from the Tang through Yuan dynasties. When Chavannes visited, the temple grounds had been converted into a temple in honor of Laozi.[13]

5. LÜZU'S CAVE, LÜZU DONG 呂祖洞

(CHAVANNES NO. 103)

Legend has it that when Lü Dongbin lived on Mount Tai during the Tang dynasty, he resided in this cave, across a small stream to the east of the Wangmu Pool Temple.

6. STREAM BEND WHERE THERE IS A HORNLESS

DRAGON, QIU ZAI WAN 虯在灣 (CHAVANNES NO. 101)

This bend in the stream is located just north of Lüzu's Cave (no. 5). For a discussion of a miraculous story about this hornless dragon, see the "Mysticism" section in Part I.

7. TRANSCENDENT HORNLESS DRAGON CAVE, QIUXIAN DONG 虬仙洞 (CHAVANNES NO. 106)

This cave is just north of Lüzu's Cave (no. 5). For a discussion of a miraculous story about this hornless dragon, see the "Mysticism" section in Part I. In between the Transcendent Hornless Dragon Cave and the Queen Mother Pool Temple is another twist in the stream, which is called Little Penglai (Xiao Penglai 小蓬萊), a reference to the fabled land of the immortals.[14]

8. FIRST HEAVENLY GATE, YITIANMEN 一天門 (CHAVANNES NO. 94)

Back on the main Pilgrimage Path, this arch was erected in the Ming dynasty by Vice Commissioner Long Guang 龍光. It was repaired by Governor Li Shude 李樹德 in 1717. Nie states that it marks the beginning of the Pilgrimage Path (*pandao* 盤道). It is the first of three heavenly gates (see nos. 23 and 37 below for the other two).[15]

9. POINT WHERE CONFUCIUS BEGAN HIS ASCENT (ARCH), KONGZI DENGLIN CHU (FANG) 孔子登臨處 (坊) (CHAVANNES NO. 93)

Erected in 1560 by Zhu Heng 朱衡, governor of Shandong, Hu Zhi 胡植, a superintendent of the Grand Canal, and Liu Cunyi 劉存義, a Shandong investigating censor. The phrase across the top of the arch, which gives it its name, refers to the passage in the *Mencius* about Confucius' ascent of Mount Tai. A vertical couplet refers to Confucius' sage-king character and to emperors coming to Mount Tai to pray. According to Nie, Confucius rested or lodged here during his visit. Nie also notes that the arch reminds passersby of the passage from *Mencius* and the story in the *Liezi* about Confucius meeting the happy Daoist hermit. Many believe that this is the "eastern hill" mentioned in the *Mencius*, from which Confucius "felt that Lu was small."[16]

10. HEAVENLY STAIRS ARCH, TIANJIE FANG 天階坊
(LISTED UNDER NO. 92 IN CHAVANNES)

Erected in 1563 by Gao Yingfang 高應芳, a regional inspector. This arch, the other two arches just below (nos. 8 and 9), as well as the Red Gate (no. 11), are all aligned on the same axis, which corresponds fairly closely to the axis set by the Dai Temple (no. 2) and the Daizong Arch (no. 3) below. Above the Red Gate, however, the Pilgrimage Path must weave around too many rock outcroppings and hills to allow further alignment along this axis.[17]

11. RED GATE, HONGMEN 紅門
(CHAVANNES NOS. 89–92)

This large gate stands in the middle of the Pilgrimage Path. Its name comes from the red color of a rock outcropping above it, to the west, which resembles a door (*Hongmen shi* 紅門石). The gate was part of a larger complex that included the Red Gate Temple (Hongmen gong 紅門宮), Flying Cloud Tower (Feiyun ge 飛雲閣), and Buddha Hall (Fo dian 佛殿). The Red Gate Temple was the so-called middle Bixia Yuanjun Temple. The upper temple is on top of Mount Tai (no. 58); the lower temple (no. 61) used to be near Mount Sheshou, southwest of the Tai'an city wall. The Red Gate Temple was first built in 1626. The main hall of the temple, on the north side of the courtyard, used to contain statues of Bixia Yuanjun and her two main assistants, the Goddess of Eyesight and the Goddess of Conception. These statues were probably destroyed during the Cultural Revolution. Today, on the north side are two statues: to the west is a Ming dynasty bronze statue of the Nine Lotus Bodhisattva (Jiulian pusa 九蓮菩薩) and to the east is a modern statue of Bixia Yuanjun. Against the east and west walls are two bronze statues of lesser Buddhist deities, now performing the role of attendants or door guards. The statues of the Nine Lotus Bodhisattva and the two lesser Buddhist deities were originally in the Numinous Palace (no. 61).[18] The statue of the Nine Lotus Bodhisattva was commissioned in honor of the Wanli emperor's mother (see Chapter 2). The shrine building on the west side of the temple courtyard now contains a modern statue of Guanyin holding a crying baby.

The Flying Cloud Tower, also known as the Guanyin Tower (Guanyin ge 觀音閣), was the name for the shrine building on top of the gate over the Pilgrimage Path. It originally contained a statue of Guanyin; it now contains modern statues, including one of Guandi, the god of war.

Across the pilgrimage path from the Red Gate Temple was the Buddha Hall, also known as the Maitreya or Laughing Buddha Court (Mile yuan 彌勒院). This site had previously been a place for imperial retinues to change out of their ceremonial robes in preparation for the steep climb ahead. In 1994 and 1995, it was being used as a museum.[19] In 2000, however, it had been restored to its original use as a temple.

12. SMALL SHRINE TO BIXIA YUANJUN

(NOT IN CHAVANNES)

This small shrine and incense oven was just north of the Red Gate on the west side of the pilgrimage path (see Fig. 12, p. 24). The shrine contained a small statue of Bixia Yuanjun. It did not have an official name in Chinese. In 1995 this was an important point of worship for pilgrims coming to pray to Bixia Yuanjun. By 2000 the shrine had been torn down to accommodate an expansion and restoration of the Red Gate Temple (no. 11). Just north of this site is a small "forest" of about thirty pilgrimage society stelae (see Fig. 8, p. 20).

13. MYRIAD TRANSCENDENTS TOWER, WANXIAN

LOU 萬仙樓 (CHAVANNES NO. 86)

This tower, like the Red Gate, was built over the Pilgrimage Path. It was constructed in 1620. The main deity worshiped in the shrine on top of the tower originally was Wangmu; other deities included Bixia Yuanjun. When Chavannes visited, however, the statues on the main altar of the shrine were of Bixia Yuanjun and her two main assistants.[20] The current arrangement apparently follows the original design. The position of honor is held by a statue of Wangmu. Other statues are of Bixia Yuanjun, her two main assistants, and Laozi.

14. REVOLUTIONARY MARTYRS' MEMORIAL STELE,
GEMING LIESHI JINIAN BEI 革命烈士紀念碑
(NOT IN CHAVANNES)

This monument is probably best described as an obelisk rather than a stele. It commemorates the 708 people who died during the liberation of Tai'an from the Nationalists. The monument was begun in 1946 but was later destroyed by the Guomindang and then rebuilt in 1953.[21] It stands between the Pilgrimage Path and the small Center Stream (Zhong xi 中溪), which flows down this valley. Across the stream from the Martyrs' Memorial is a spring whose water is thought to be particularly good for making tea and is often collected by area residents.

15. MOTHER OF THE BIG DIPPER TEMPLE,
DOUMU GONG 斗母宮 (CHAVANNES NO. 85)

An earlier temple built on this site was called Dragon Spring Monastery (Longquan guan 龍泉觀), after a nearby spring. The current building design and name date from 1542. The temple consists of three connecting courtyards. The main gate is on the west side of the center courtyard. The building on the north side of this central court originally contained the main shrine to the Mother of the Big Dipper (Doumu). This statue had 24 arms on each side, and her head was surmounted by a double crown of additional tiny heads. Forty smaller idols, representing deities of various stars, flanked the Mother of the Big Dipper on both sides. The eastern hall off the central court used to contain statues of the three Bodhisattvas Guanyin, Wenshu 文殊 (Sanskrit Mañjuśrī), and Puxian 普賢 (Sanskrit Samantabhadra). These statues, however, were destroyed in 1966. The main shrine building in the northern court used to contain a statue of Guanyin in the position of honor with Bixia Yuanjun and her two main assistants in other places in the hall. The southern court was primarily devoted to a teahouse but also contained a statue of the Maitreya Buddha. A stone-lined pool, using water from the Dragon Spring, called the Natural Pool (Tianran chi 天然池) was built in the southern court during the Guangxu period (1875–1908). The original statues of the Mother of the Big Dipper and Maitreya were destroyed during the Cultural Revolution.[22]

The northern shrine in the central court now contains a bronze statue of the Bodhisattva of Wisdom (Zhishang pusa 智上菩薩). This statue, commissioned in honor of the Ming Chongzhen emperor's mother, was moved here from the Numinous Palace (no. 61), when that temple was destroyed around 1972. In 1994 and 1995, the statue was labeled as Guanyin and was also called so by the resident Buddhist nun. To all intents and purposes, since the people praying to the statue appealed to it as Guanyin, it had become a statue of Guanyin. In 2000, however, the statue was labeled the Bodhisattva Dizang 地藏.[23] To the east of the large statue is a smaller image of the Goddess of Conception. On a small altar on the east wall is a statue of Bixia Yuanjun. The only trace of the Mother of the Big Dipper is a photocopy of a photo of a statue of her, placed on the altar to Bixia Yuanjun. In the northern building of the north court, the position of honor is held by a bronze statue of Bixia Yuanjun, flanked by her two main assistants. On the west wall is a small clay statue of Guanyin. None of the buildings in the southern court now contain statues.

This temple was originally a Daoist nunnery. According to Chavannes, Daoist nuns were in residence up to 1906. However, several Chinese sources, including a recent Mount Tai gazetteer, assert that early in the Kangxi reign Buddhist nuns took up residence. Whether they were Daoist or Buddhist nuns is unclear, but in 1906 they were expelled from the temple. Most sources do not explain the cause of the expulsion. However, current oral tradition holds that a local official expelled them for running a brothel in the temple. Some time in the 1910s or early 1920s, Buddhist nuns took up residence in the temple.[24] In 1994 and 1995, this was the only temple on Mount Tai with a resident Buddhist nun. In 2000, however, she was no longer in residence and had not been replaced.

16. STONE SUTRA VALE, VARIOUSLY SHIJING YU 石經峪 OR JINGSHI YU 經石峪 (CHAVANNES NO. 77)

A little to the north and above the Mother of the Big Dipper Temple (no. 15) is a path branching off the main Pilgrimage Path to the east leading to the Stone Sūtra Vale. The vale consists of a large expanse of fairly smooth bedrock at a slight incline. During the Northern Qi dynasty (550–77) someone carved the text of the Buddhist *Diamond Sūtra* (*Jin'gang jing* 金剛經) into the face of the bedrock. The name of this calligrapher and Buddhist devotee is uncertain, and different texts give different names, but the period of the inscription seems to be universally accepted. Each character of the inscription measures 50 centimeters square. The famous reformer and scholar Kang Youwei 康有爲 (1858–1927) described it as the best example of the *bangshu* 榜書 calligraphic style. The inscription originally consisted of around 2,700 characters out of the whole text of about 5,100 characters. Primarily because of water erosion, today only 1,067 characters remain. The characters from the inscription have been reproduced in many calligraphy books as models for emulation.[25]

Around 1550 an unknown Confucian scholar inscribed a passage from one of the Confucian Four Books, the *Great Learning*, onto a rock just above the *Diamond Sūtra*. This inscription was destroyed during the reign of the Kangxi emperor.[26]

In 1578, Censor-in-Chief Li Bangzhen 李邦珍 inscribed another pro-Confucian inscription next to the *Diamond Sūtra*. On the vertical face of a rock projecting into and above the center of the Buddhist text, Li inscribed two large characters meaning "the Classics rectify" (*jing zheng* 經正) and a passage from the *Mencius* (see Fig. 32, p. 220).[27] For analysis of this text, see Chapter 3. A post-1949 graffiti on a rock at this same site adds another competing philosophy. In rather crude characters, someone carved the phrase "Long live Chairman Mao."

Just to the west of the inscription is the High Mountains, Flowing Streams Pavilion (Gaoshan liushui ting 高山流水亭). It was built by a high-ranking official in 1572 as a place to admire the scenery.[28]

17. ASCEND TO TRANSCENDENCE BRIDGE, DENG XIAN QIAO 登仙橋 (CHAVANNES UNDER NO. 75)

This bridge, just north of the trail to the Stone Sūtra Vale, takes the Pilgrimage Path from the west to the east side of the Center Stream.

18. CYPRESS CAVE, BAI DONG 柏洞 (NOT IN CHAVANNES)

Just after crossing the Ascend to Transcendence Bridge (no. 17), the path enters a stretch shaded by large cypress trees planted on both sides of the path. The tree branches leaning over from both sides create the effect of a tunnel. This name was carved into a rock to the east of the trail, just north of the bridge, in 1899.[29]

19. SUN YAT-SEN MEMORIAL STELE, VARIOUSLY ZONGLI FENG'AN JINIAN BEI 總理奉安紀念碑 OR SUN ZHONGSHAN XIANSHENG JINIAN BEI 孫中山先生紀念碑 (NOT IN CHAVANNES)

This obelisk was erected in 1929 in honor of Sun Yat-sen. It was put up shortly after Sun's body passed through Tai'an en route from Beijing to Nanjing.[30]

20. HEAVENLY PITCHER TOWER, HUTIAN GE 壺天閣 (CHAVANNES NO. 74)

This tower, like the Red Gate (no. 11) and the Myriad Transcendents Tower (no. 13), is built over the Pilgrimage Path. A tower was first built on this site during the reign of the Ming Jiajing emperor (r. 1522–66). The original name was Ascent to Immortality Tower (Shengxian ge 昇仙閣). It was repaired and renamed Heavenly Pitcher Tower in 1747. The name comes from the belief that the land of the immortals consists of many mountains in the shape of pitchers. A less literal translation of the name might be Land of the Immortals Tower. Some people say that the hill behind the tower resembles one of those where the immortals dwell. One line of a couplet on either side of the door in this gate describes this as the halfway point up the mountain. Just north of the tower is the Hall of the Goddess (Yuanjun dian 元君殿, Chavannes no. 73). When Chavannes visited, this hall held statues of Bixia Yuanjun and four of her assistants.[31] Presently it contains statues of Bixia Yuanjun and her two main assistants.

21. (ARCH OF THE) RIDGE WHERE THE HORSES TURN BACK, HUIMA LING (FANG) 廻馬嶺 (坊) (CHAVANNES NO. 71)

A stone arch identifies this spot as the point beyond which horses can climb no further (see Fig. 9, p. 21). The ascent from here to the Second Heavenly Gate (no. 23) is quite steep and winding. An inscription of unknown date along this stretch of the path refers to the route as "precipitous peaks and twisting paths."[32]

22. STEP TO HEAVEN BRIDGE, BUTIAN QIAO 步天橋 (NOT IN CHAVANNES)

Here the path crosses back over to the west side of the Center Stream.

23. SECOND (OR MIDDLE) HEAVENLY GATE, VARIOUSLY ERTIAN MEN 二天門 OR ZHONGTIAN MEN 中天門 (CHAVANNES NO. 66)

Although the Heavenly Pitcher Tower (no. 20) is closer to the exact halfway mark, this arch is the more popularly accepted midpoint between the First Heavenly Gate (no. 8) and the Southern Heavenly Gate (no. 37). It is here that climbers can get their first glimpse of the Southern Heavenly Gate since passing through the Daizong Arch (no. 3) far below. One can also see what a formidable ascent remains. Just beyond this arch the western path meets the main, central path. It is now possible to take buses to the Middle Heavenly Gate and then ride a gondola to the top (passengers disembark to the west of the Southern Heavenly Gate). The gondola began operating in 1983. It was closed in 2000 for a complete renovation. There is a second gondola, also accessible by bus, which ascends the northwest side of the mountain.

24. BENEVOLENCE PAVILION, CI EN TING 慈恩庭 (NOT IN CHAVANNES)

This pavilion was built in 1988 by a Taiwanese man whose prayers for a son had been answered.

25. HAPPY THREE LI, KUAIHUO SANLI 快活三里 (CHAVANNES NO. 60)

This name refers to a short stretch of path that is fairly level.

26. CLOUD STEPPING BRIDGE, YUNBU QIAO 雲步橋 (NOT IN CHAVANNES)

Here the Pilgrimage Path passes over the Western Yellow Stream (Huang xi he 黄西河).

27. ESPLANADE OF THE IMPERIAL TENT, YU ZHANG PING 御帳坪 (CHAVANNES NO. 55)

According to tradition, when Song Zhenzong climbed Mount Tai, he stopped and rested at this point. Several holes in the bedrock are purported to be where tent poles were placed. Baker states that the emperor's tent was not placed at a better spot higher up because that would have been too close to the place where the infamous Qin Shihuangdi took refuge from the storm (no. 29).[33]

28. ROCK THAT CAME FLYING DOWN, FEILAI
SHI 飛來石 (CHAVANNES NO. 54)

This rock fell from the cliff above, landing here in 1603. Chavannes notes that the phrase "came flying down" (*feilai*) implies a miraculous origin.[34] Indeed, a small cave-like space at the base of the south side of this large boulder bears the stains of many years of smoke from incense and paper money burned here. When the rock first fell, it landed just to the east of the Pilgrimage Path. In the early 1980s, the path was re-routed so that the stone now lies just to its west. In April 1995, someone had placed a small altar to the God of Caves and Rocks (Dongfu shi shen 洞府石神) beside the rock (see Fig. 19, p. 37).

29. FIFTH RANK PINE TREE, WUDAFU
SONG 五大夫松 (CHAVANNES NO. 53)

This is the site where Qin Shihuangdi supposedly took shelter from the wind and rain in 219 BCE. In thanks to the tree for the shelter and to spite the learned Confucian scholars, the emperor enfeoffed the tree as a *wudafu*, or noble of the fifth rank. Over the centuries, as one pine tree died, another was planted. Two of the trees now growing at this site were planted during the reign of the Yongzheng emperor (1723–35).[35] The site consists of a small terrace with a pavilion and is a popular place to rest before the final ascent. On the path between the Rock That Came Flying Down (no. 28) and the Fifth Rank Pine Tree is another arch, the Fifth Rank Pine Tree Arch (see Fig. 19, p. 37).

30. SUN FACING CAVE, CHAOYANG
DONG 朝陽洞 (CHAVANNES NO. 50)

A former name for this small cave was Cloud Facing Cave (Yunyang dong 雲陽洞). Baker notes that this name reflects the belief that "this and the other caves of T'ai Shan have from time immemorial been . . . the dwelling places of the rain-giving clouds and mists which the farmer prays for."[36]

At least as early as the mid-seventeenth century, the use of the cave shifted from a site for rain worship to that of a shrine for Bixia Yuanjun. By the time Xiao Xiezhong wrote his *Short History of Mount Tai* around 1640, an image of Bixia Yuanjun had been carved into the back wall of the cave.[37] Outside the cave to the west, there used to be a small goddess hall. This cave and the scenery nearby were the inspirations for the Qianlong emperor's poem (no. 31).

Just above the cave is an inscription marking the former site of another pine tree, the Local Scholars Pine (*chushi song* 處士松), also known as the Solitary Dafu (*duli dafu* 獨立大夫). This tree was given these two names during the Ming dynasty as a means of honoring scholars and simultaneously shaming Qin Shihuangdi's enfeoffment of the Fifth Rank Pine Tree. Ironically, the tree blew down in a storm in 1603.[38] For more on this tree, see Chapter 3.

31. INSCRIPTION OF 100,000 FEET, WANZHANG BEI 萬丈碑 (CHAVANNES NO. 51)

This is a large inscription on the face of the mountain above the Esplanade of the Imperial Tent. As the name implies, the inscription is quite large, although not quite the size the name implies. Another name is the Qing Dynasty Cliff Inscription (Qing moyai 清摩崖). The inscription is a rectangle twenty meters tall by nine meters wide; each character measures one meter square.[39] This inscription is the Qianlong emperor's most ostentatious addition to the sites on Mount Tai. The text consists of a poem written by the emperor during his 1748 ascent (for the text of the poem, see the "Personal Legitimation" section of Chapter 2). The rectangle of the inscription can be seen from the foot of the mountain, and on a clear day even from south of the city of Tai'an (see Fig. 23, p. 57).

32. OPPOSING PINES PAVILION, DUISONG
TING 對松亭 (NOT IN CHAVANNES)

This pavilion faces Opposing Pines Mountain (Chavannes no. 46). The name refers to the many pine trees growing on both sides of the narrow gorge through which the Pilgrimage Path ascends at this point. An adjacent arch over the path was named Opposing Pines Arch. This pavilion was a popular place to admire the scenery and listen to the wind soughing through the pines. The Qianlong emperor praised this spot as the most beautiful on the entire mountain.[40]

33. CLOUD GATE, YUN MEN 雲門
(NOT IN CHAVANNES)

There was never an actual gate here; instead the name refers to the two sides of the narrow gorge. The name alludes to the idea that as you climb the mountain, you pass through the clouds and end up at the gate into heaven. This marks the start of the final stage of the climb to the Southern Heavenly Gate (no. 37). In the one kilometer from the Cloud Gate to the Southern Heavenly Gate, 1,630 steps make a vertical ascent of 400 meters. Ma Dibo, in his 56 CE account of his ascent, referred to a point, probably near here, called the Celestial Pass (Tian guan 天關).[41]

34. DRAGON GATE ARCH, LONGMEN
FANG 龍門坊 (CHAVANNES NO. 42)

The narrow valley here was called the Dragon Gorge (Long yu 龍峪). This spot is considered the entrance into the dragon and was therefore also called the Dragon's Mouth (Long kou 龍口). The extremely difficult ascent makes the metaphor of climbing up a Dragon's throat quite apt. There used to be a small shrine to the Dragon King at this point. Ironically, this shrine to the water god was washed away in one of the many floods that rush down this narrow, rocky chasm. The section of the stairs from the Cloud

Gate up to the Dragon's Mouth is considered to be the first of three sets of "Eighteen Twistings." Since the beginning of the last ascent is slightly less steep than the rest, it is called the "Gradual Eighteen Twistings" (Man shiba pan 慢十八盤).[42]

35. STAR OF LONGEVITY SHRINE, SHOUXING TING 壽星亭 (CHAVANNES NO. 41)

This small shrine, adjacent to the Promoted to Transcendence Arch (no. 36), was originally a shrine to the Star of Longevity. It now contains a small statue of Bixia Yuanjun (see Fig. 13, p. 25).

36. PROMOTED TO TRANSCENDENCE ARCH, SHENGXIAN FANG 昇仙坊 (CHAVANNES NO. 40)

Like many of the names on Mount Tai, this again refers to the idea that at the mountain's peak one can transcend into Heaven. From the Dragon Gate Arch (no. 34) to this point is called the "Not Gradual, Not Intense Eighteen Twistings" (Buman bujin shiba pan 不慢不緊十八盤). Above this arch is the most difficult stretch of the climb up Mount Tai, the "Intense Eighteen Twistings" (Jin shiba pan 緊十八盤). In this section of the path, a rough trail diverged off to the east, leading directly to the main Bixia Temple (no. 58). This route at one time was a popular alternative for pilgrims coming to pray to Bixia Yuanjun.[43] In 1995, only a few devout worshipers, mostly older women, took this much rougher route. In 2000, stone stairs had been installed from this point directly to the Bixia Temple.

37. SOUTHERN HEAVENLY GATE, NANTIAN MEN 南天門 (CHAVANNES NO. 3)

This gate is actually a tower and, like several other similar structures on the mountain, was built over the Pilgrimage Path. Another name for it is the Third Heavenly Gate, in reference to the First Heavenly Gate at the base of the mountain (no. 8) and the Second or Middle Heavenly Gate about halfway up (no. 23).

The image of this gate sitting at the top of the gorge is quite well known and has become a symbolic representation of Mount Tai (see Fig. 14, p. 26, and Fig. 23, p. 57). Just north of the gate, facing each other on opposite sides of the path, are two small shrines. The two bronze statues in these shrines date from the Wanli period (1573–1619). The new *Mount Tai Gazetteer* notes that the statues are of female deities but does not specify which ones. In 1995, pilgrims prayed to both as Bixia Yuanjun. Immediately north of these two shrines is a building that was once a shrine to Guandi, the God of War. This temple now houses a bronze statue of the God of Mount Tai.[44]

At this point the Pilgrimage Path turns to the east. It passes through an arch, originally put up during the Ming dynasty, bearing the inscription "within ascendence" (*sheng zhong* 升中). This arch was destroyed near the end of the Qing dynasty. A new arch bearing the inscription "Heavenly Street" (*tianjie* 天街) was built on the same spot in 1986. The term Heavenly Street applies to this east-west section of the path between the Southern Heavenly Gate and the main Bixia Temple (no. 58). North of this arch is the site of the former Imperial Residence (Yuzuo 御座, Chavannes no. 9). This building was constructed as a temporary lodging for the Kangxi emperor while he was on top of the mountain in 1684. It was rebuilt in 1747 in preparation for the Qianlong emperor's visit in 1748. Just to the east of the emperor's lodge was a pavilion built by Jin Qi, the prefect of Tai'an, in 1797. As the name implies, the Cleansing the Heart Pavilion (Xixin ting 洗心亭) was a site for experiencing the transformative powers of nature.[45] Currently, on the site of this former imperial building and continuing along the northern side of the Heavenly Street are a number of small buildings housing hostels, restaurants, and souvenir shops.

38. WHITE CLOUD CAVE, BAIYUN DONG 白雲洞 (CHAVANNES NO. 45)

This cave, like the Sun Facing Cave (no. 30), was traditionally associated with the mountain's powers as a rain deity. A passage from the Gong Yang commentary on the *Spring and Autumn An-*

nals describes this cave as the place where clouds "come forth bounding against rocks, and they muster together in less time than of the bending of a finger or the turning of a hand. In less than two mornings they cover with rain the whole of the Empire."[46]

On a smooth rock face inside the cave there is a faint ink print of a deity flanked by two attendants. The deity seems to be seated on a lotus flower, and is therefore probably Buddhist. Since this image is not mentioned in any of the historical or modern guides, it is probably of recent origin.

39. VIEWING WU PEAK, VARIOUSLY WUGUAN FENG 吳觀峰 OR WANGWU FENG 望吳峰 (CHAVANNES NO. 13)

Legend has it that Confucius and his disciple Yan Yuan were standing on top of this peak when Confucius espied the horse tied to the gate of the capital city of Wu. The peak has had this name since at least 56 CE.[47]

40. CONFUCIAN TEMPLE, KONGZI MIAO 孔子廟 (CHAVANNES NO. 30)

Some sources refer to the hill behind this temple as "Confucius' Cliff" (Kongzi yai 孔子崖); this is the origin for another name for the temple (Confucius' Cliff Temple, Kongzi yai miao). A building honoring Confucius' ascent up Mount Tai came quite late in the history of monuments on the mountain. A small shrine was first built on this site during the Ming dynasty. It was called the "Passed by and Transformed Pavilion" (Guohua ting 過化亭).[48] The name implies that Confucius transformed everyone and everything he passed. This was only a pavilion, however, and not a place of worship with altars, tablets, or images.

The first temple to Confucius, designed as a place to worship him, was first conceived during the Jiajing period (1522–66) but was not built until 1583 or 1584. The temple consisted of three small buildings containing images of Confucius, some of his disciples, and Mencius.[49] For more on this temple, see the "Joining a Literary

Lineage" section in Chapter 3. After 1949, the temple and figures steadily declined, and apparently the only original image now surviving is a stone engraving of Confucius.[50] In 1994 and 1995 the temple was undergoing restoration. By 2000 the restoration was complete.

41. PLACE WHERE THE SAGE SAW WU, VARIOUSLY WANGWU SHENGJI 望吳聖跡 OR WANGWU FANG 望吳坊 (CHAVANNES NO. 31)

This arch is at the base of the stairs leading up to the Confucian Temple (no. 40). Like the Viewing Wu Peak (no. 39), it commemorates Confucius' farsightedness. It was erected by Li Shude, governor of Shandong. It was gone when Chavannes visited. A new arch was put up in 1984.[51]

42. BIG DIPPER TERRACE, BEIDOU TAI 北斗台 (CHAVANNES NO. 32)

This structure is a large masonry cube built during the Wanli period. The cube is transected by two passageways, running east–west and north–south, through its base. A staircase leads to the top platform. Chavannes describes two pillars on the platform, which represented Mount Tai and the Big Dipper, "who are like assistants, one on the earth, the other in the sky, to the supreme divinity." The platform fell into ruins during the Republican period but was rebuilt in 1984.[52]

43. PAVILION OF HEAVEN AND EARTH, QIANKUN TING 乾坤亭 (CHAVANNES NO. 20)

A small temple was built on this site in the Ming dynasty. When the Kangxi emperor climbed Mount Tai in 1684, he composed a plaque and ordered the pavilion to be rebuilt. This plaque written by the Kangxi emperor gave the pavilion its name: "Illumines all Heaven and Earth" (*puzhao qiankun* 普照乾坤). Inside the pavilion another inscription read: "Place where Confucius saw the world was small" (*Kongzi xiao tianxia chu* 孔子小天下處). Behind the pavilion, in 1837 Yan Jizu 顏繼祖 engraved a stele with the same phrase "Place where Confucius saw the world was small." The pavilion was almost completely gone when Chavannes visited. Today no trace of it remains.[53]

44. EASTERN SACRED PEAK TEMPLE, DONGYUE MIAO 東嶽廟 (CHAVANNES NO. 37)

The foundation stones are all that remain of this uppermost of the three temples to the God of Mount Tai. The original date of construction is unknown, but it was repaired during the Yuan dynasty.[54] Baker believes that it flourished during the Tang dynasty and the early part of the Northern Song.[55] From the beginning of the Ming dynasty, the cult and temple to the God of Mount Tai slowly declined as worship of Bixia Yuanjun increased. When Baker saw the temple in the early 1920s, he described it as "one of the most insignificant temples of the group on the peak."[56] Earlier, Chavannes noted that "the poverty of this edifice contrasts with the richness of the temple consecrated to the [Goddess of Mount Tai] . . . and demonstrates the extent to which the antique, male divinity of Mount Tai has been eclipsed by the young goddess."[57] The temple underwent periodic restorations up until the Xianfeng period (1851–61).[58]

45. TANG CLIFF INSCRIPTION, TANG MOYAI BEI 唐摩崖碑 (CHAVANNES NO. 38)

This is a large inscription on a cliff face immediately behind the site of the Eastern Sacred Peak Temple (see Fig. 7, p. 19). The text of the inscription, entitled "Eulogy Commemorating Mount Tai" ("Ji Taishan ming" 紀泰山銘), is a text written by Tang Xuanzong recounting the *feng* ceremony he performed in 726. The inscription measures 13.3 meters tall by 5.7 meters wide. The inscribed surfaces of the characters were originally colored gold. The characters were regilded in 1959 and again in 1982.[59]

Song Zhenzong wrote a text in 1008 recounting his receipt of the Heavenly Text, thanking Heaven for its beneficence, and describing his performance of the *feng* and *shan* sacrifices, which he had engraved onto a cliff face immediately to the east of the Tang inscription. This Song Cliff Inscription was less impressive than its Tang predecessor and subsequently suffered the ignominy of having a later inscription carved across its face. The text in this inscription was the same as that on a large stele erected by Song Zhenzong to the south of the Tai'an city wall (see no. 71).[60]

Just to the west of the Tang inscription are the two large characters Cloud Peak (*Yun feng* 雲峰), written in the Kangxi emperor's hand in 1684. Below these two characters, the Qianlong emperor inscribed several poems written in 1748.

46. GREEN EMPEROR TEMPLE, QINGDI GONG 青帝宮 (CHAVANNES NO. 34)

The Green Emperor was one of five legendary emperors associated with the five phases or elements. The color green (*qing*) was associated with the east, and therefore the Green Emperor was in ancient times associated with Mount Tai, the Eastern Sacred Peak. Emperors visiting the mountain in 595 and 1008 offered prayers to the Green Emperor, and the Qianlong emperor offered incense at this temple in 1748. Baker noted that this temple had "been allowed to fall into serious neglect during recent times." Today nothing of this temple remains.[61]

47. JADE EMPEROR SUMMIT (TEMPLE), YUHUANG DING 玉皇頂 (CHAVANNES NO. 18)

The Jade Emperor is the supreme deity in the Daoist pantheon. This temple was built in 1483 around the highest point on Mount Tai. In the center of the courtyard, a stone balustrade surrounds the mountain's highest point. The roof tiles are made of iron in order to resist the wind. The main hall contains a statue of the Jade Emperor. Nie Jianguang states, and my own observations of contemporary visitors confirm, that visitors climbed (and climb) to the peak because it is the highest point, not because of this temple.[62]

48. WORDLESS STELE, WUZI BEI
無字碑 (CHAVANNES NO. 19)

This large, dressed stone stands just below the Jade Emperor Summit (no. 47). It is over 5 meters in height and is 1.25 meters wide on each side at its base (see Fig. 21, p. 39). Tradition has it that this was the stele erected by Qin Shihuangdi in honor of his ascent in 219 BCE. Many authors during the Qing dynasty, however, associated the stele with the more benign emperor, Han Wudi. Jiang Fengrong, however, argues that the Wordless Stele formed part of the ritual space for Qin Shihuangdi's *feng* sacrifices. According to Jiang, the so-called "Wordless Stele" demarcated the northern edge of the platform where Qin Shihuangdi performed the ceremony in 219 BCE. He argues that the stone was a marker known as a *shique* 石闕. Contrary to these various arguments, however, it is quite likely that this is a megalith dating from prehistoric times.[63]

49. FATHER-IN-LAW PEAK, ZHANGREN
FENG 丈人峰 (CHAVANNES NO. 16)

The name Taishan has taken on the meaning of "father-in-law," or *zhangren* (丈人). This derives from a historical tale from the Tang dynasty recorded by Duan Chengshi 段成式 in the late eighth century CE:

When Emperor Xuanzong celebrated the *feng* and *shan* ceremonies in 725, Zhang Yue had the title of the commissioner of the sacrifices. His son-in-law, Zheng Yi, at that time was a minor functionary of the ninth level. After the *feng* and *shan* ceremonies were completed, Zheng Yi found himself promoted to the fifth rank through the recommendations of his father-in-law, Zhang Yue. It happened that the emperor became aware of this brusque promotion and demanded an explanation. Zhang Yue replied: "It is due to the power of Taishan."[64]

50. ANCIENT FENG SACRIFICE TERRACE, GU DENG FENG TAI 古登封臺 (NOT NUMBERED IN CHAVANNES)

This is a small terrace on top of the mountain, between the Tang Cliff Inscription (no. 45) and the Jade Emperor Peak (no. 47). According to tradition, this was the site where Qin Shihuangdi and Han Wudi performed the *feng* sacrifice. Erected on top of the terrace is a stele inscribed with a poem written by the Qianlong emperor in 1748 (see pp. 179–180).[65]

51. ROCK THAT SEARCHES OUT THE SEA, TANHAI SHI 探海石 (CHAVANNES NO. 21)

This natural rock formation resembles an enormous finger pointing northeast toward the Gulf of Bohai.

52. SUN VIEWING PEAK, RIGUAN FENG 日觀峰 (CHAVANNES NO. 23)

This peak on the east end of Mount Tai's summit has long been the site where visitors watch the sunrise.

53. SUN VIEWING PAVILION, RIGUAN TING 日觀亭 (CHAVANNES NO. 22)

Sometime in the early Ming dynasty, the Sunlight Viewing Pavilion (Rizhaoguan ting 日照觀亭) was built on the Sun Viewing Peak (no. 52). During the Jiajing period (1522–66), the pavilion was renamed the Sea Viewing Pavilion (Haiguan ting 海觀亭), but a horizontal plaque placed on the pavilion read Sun Viewing Pavilion.[66]

54. SONG FENG SACRIFICIAL TERRACE, SONG FENG

TAI 宋封台 (NOT NUMBERED IN CHAVANNES)

This was the site of the raised altar on which Song Zhenzong performed the *feng* sacrifice in 1008. It was here that the tablets from this ceremony were uncovered and then reburied in 1482. They were uncovered again in 1747 and placed in the Qianlong emperor's personal collection.[67]

55. MOON VIEWING PEAK, YUEGUAN

FENG 月觀峰 (CHAVANNES NO. 7)

Located on the west side of the summit of Mount Tai, it balances Sun Viewing Peak (no. 52) on the east side of the summit.

56. TRANSCENDENTS' BRIDGE, XIANREN

QIAO 仙人橋 (CHAVANNES NO. 28)

This natural rock formation, consisting of a series of boulders, looks like a bridge built over a small chasm on the south side of the mountain's summit.

57. LOVE LIFE CLIFF, AISHEN YAI 愛身崖

(CHAVANNES NO. 27)

The former name of this site, Abandon Life Cliff (Sheshen yai 舍身崖), derives from a tradition that developed in association with this cliff. People came to believe that if a parent or parent-in-law were ill, then by jumping off the cliff and sacrificing one's life, one could persuade the deities to transfer the merit accrued by this "filial" act to the ill parent and restore him or her to health. In 1523 the governor of Shandong, He Qiming 何起鳴, ordered a wall three hundred feet long and fifteen feet high to be erected along the top of the cliff in order to prevent people from taking their lives. An inscription included the phrase "false sacrifice is false love." He Qiming, also in hopes of eliminating the suicides, renamed the site

"Love Life Cliff." In 1717 this wall was restored by the prefect Zhang Qifeng 張奇逢. In the face of this wall were four large stones bearing the statement "It is forbidden to commit suicide" (*jinzhi sheshen* 禁止捨身). Despite the walls and warnings, however, people continued to take their lives by leaping from this cliff as late as 1924.[68]

58. BIXIA PALACE, BIXIA GONG 碧霞宮, OR BIXIA TEMPLE, BIXIA CI 碧霞祠 (CHAVANNES NO. 35)

This is the so-called upper temple to the Goddess of Mount Tai (see Fig. 24, p. 71). The middle temple is the Red Gate Temple (no. 11); the lower temple (no. 61) used to be near Mount Sheshou, just south of the Tai'an city wall. This upper temple is the main temple in the cult of the Goddess of Mount Tai, Bixia Yuanjun. Adjacent to the temple is the Jade Woman Pool (Yunü chi 玉女池), which was where the stone statue of a woman was found in 1008. Song Zhenzong had a jade replica made of the statue and placed in a newly built shrine adjacent to the pool, which was called the Bright Truth Shrine (Zhaozhen ci 昭真祠). It was renamed Bright Truth Temple (Zhaozhen guan 昭真觀) during the Jin dynasty. During the reign of the first Ming emperor (1368–98), the temple was completely rebuilt, enlarged, and renamed the Numinous Palace (Lingying gong 靈應宮). During the reign of the Chenghua emperor (1465–87), the name was lengthened to Bixia Numinous Palace (Bixia lingying gong). An inscription dated 1480 commemorates extensive repairs commissioned by the emperor. Throughout the late imperial period, the temple underwent numerous additional repairs, including more major reconstructions in 1480, after a fire in 1495, in 1585, in 1608, shortly after a disastrous fire in 1740, and in 1770. From the Qing dynasty to the present this temple has most commonly been known by the abbreviated name Bixia Palace (Bixia gong), or Bixia Temple (Bixia ci).[69]

This is by far the largest temple on top of the mountain. The main courtyard of the temple is entered from the south. The main hall, on the north side of the courtyard, houses the main statue of the goddess. This was considered to be the holiest of all of the statues of Bixia Yuanjun. All the statues of the goddess for sale in 1994, 1995, and 2000, as well as statues recently placed in shrines on the mountain, were modeled after this statue. The main hall also contains statues of the two most important assistant goddesses: to the east is the Goddess of Eyesight, and to the west the Goddess of Conception. The hall on the eastern side of the main courtyard is also a shrine to the Goddess of Eyesight, and the hall on the western side a shrine to the Goddess of Conception.

From at least the early seventeenth century through at least the mid-1920s, the main hall was closed off with latticework doors. Pilgrims threw offerings through the latticework into the hall, trying to get them as close to the statue as possible. Although today pilgrims are still not allowed to enter the main hall, the doors are kept open, and the practice of throwing offerings into the hall no longer exists.

In 1585 the Wanli emperor ordered a major restoration of the temple. For these repairs, he commissioned a bronze statue of the goddess and the so-called Bronze Pavilion (Tong ting 銅亭) to house the statue.[70] This pavilion was also known as the Golden Palace (Jin que 金闕), a Daoist term for a residence of immortals.[71] The Bronze Pavilion and the statue were placed in the middle of the main courtyard of the temple. At some point after the disastrous fire in 1740, however, both were moved temporarily to the Temple for Paying Homage from Afar (no. 1) and then to the Numinous Palace south of the city of Tai'an (no. 61).[72] Around 1972, when that temple was mostly in ruins, the Bronze Pavilion was moved to the Dai Temple (no. 2), and the statue was placed in the Queen Mother Pool Temple (no. 4). A more standard brick pavilion with a new statue was subsequently erected in place of the Bronze Pavilion in the Bixia Palace, probably during the major repairs of 1770.

To the south of the temple compound, down a long flight of stairs, is the temple's incense oven. This was where pilgrims burned their large offerings to the goddess. Now, in order to avoid a disastrous fire, it is the only place in the temple where pilgrims can burn incense or spirit money.

The Daoist monks who resided in the temple were forced to leave in 1965. In 1985 the government allowed Daoist monks and nuns to return to the temple. In the early 1990s the nuns relocated to the Queen Mother Pool Temple (no. 4). In 1995 the abbot of the Bixia Temple was a monk who had been expelled from the temple in 1965. This is now the only temple on the mountain with resident Daoist monks. The monks belong to the Dragon Gate Branch (Longmen pai 龍門派) of the Complete Perfection School (Quanzhen jiao 全真教) of Daoism. Some of the monks were trained at the Baiyun guan (白雲觀) in Beijing.

59. SLEEPING CHAMBER PALACE, QIN GONG 寢宮 (CHAVANNES NO. 33)

This temple, located behind and to the north of the main Bixia temple (no. 58), was also known as the Rear Yuanjun Palace (Hou Yuanjun gong 後元君宮). The main hall of the temple contained an "ordinary statue of the goddess." The main point of interest in this temple, however, was the statue of Bixia in the eastern hall. During most of the year, this statue rested on a wooden bed behind curtains. However, during the rainy season, in order to prevent her clothing from deteriorating from the damp, the goddess was "asked to get up" (qing ta qilai 請他起來). The statue was taken off the bed and placed in a sitting position outside the curtains. Chavannes describes the attire of this statue as "resembling more a peasant in her Sunday best than a great lady."[73] In 1995 the temple had been replaced by a hotel, but a niche in the lobby held a modern statue of the reclining goddess.

60. REAR STONE WALL, HOU SHI WU 後石塢 (CHAVANNES NO. 26)

This name refers to a cliff on the back, or north, side of the mountain, where there are several sites important to the cult of Bixia Yuanjun. The trail descending to the cliff can be reached from paths leading down from behind the Jade Emperor Peak (no. 47) or from behind the shrine to the God of War adjacent to the Southern Heavenly Gate (no. 37). From the point where these two paths meet to just above the Rear Stone Cliff, there is now a chairlift for those who cannot walk.

According to one version of the origin myth for Bixia Yuanjun, a cave in this cliff called the Yellow Flower Cave (Huanghua dong 黄花洞) was the site of the Jade Woman's perfection or translation (*xiuzhen* 修真) into the goddess.[74] Forming an interesting contrast to this legend of the girl's translation is the tomb of the goddess near the cave. Probably the best way to account for these apparently contradictory sites would be to say that the goddess's body remained behind when she achieved perfection. A stele in front of the tomb states that it was repaired in 1735.

An adjacent grave mound is unmarked, but some legends identify it as the tomb of the white gibbon (*bai yuan* 白猿). According to these legends, a white monkey or gibbon brought a peach of immortality to the Jade Woman while she was meditating in the Yellow Flower Cave, thus aiding in her apotheosis.[75]

Near the cave and tombs there is also a small temple to Bixia Yuanjun. This temple was built during the Longqing period (1567–72) by a member of the Ming imperial family, Zhu Muyi 朱睦㮮.[76]

61. NUMINOUS PALACE, LINGYING GONG
靈應宮 (CHAVANNES NO. 166)

This was the so-called lower of the three main temples to Bixia Yuanjun at Mount Tai. The middle temple was the Red Gate Temple (no. 11), and the upper temple was the main temple on top of the mountain (no. 58). This lower temple was built in 1611. In addition to a statue of Bixia Yuanjun that Chavannes called a "colossus," this temple also housed several Ming bronze statues that had originally been placed in other temples. The Bronze Pavilion and the statue of the goddess it housed, both commissioned by the Wanli emperor, were moved here from the main or upper Bixia temple after the disastrous fire in that temple in 1740. The Bodhisattva statues of the two Ming empresses originally in the Heavenly Text Temple (no. 73) were also moved to this temple around 1860. By 1972 this temple was mostly in ruins, and the various statues and the Bronze Pavilion were moved to other temples (see nos. 2, 4, 11, 15).[77]

62. MOUNT SHESHOU, SHESHOU SHAN
社首山 (CHAVANNES NO. 173)

This small hill to the southwest of the city was the site for a number of the *shan* sacrifices. According to legend, King Cheng of the Zhou dynasty performed the *shan* sacrifice here. It is known for certain that Tang Gaozong in 666, Tang Xuanzong in 725, and Song Zhenzong in 1008 performed the *shan* sacrifice at Mount Sheshou. In 1931 the tablets from the *shan* ceremonies of both Tang Xuanzong's ceremony of 725 and Song Zhenzong's ceremony of 1008 were discovered during the process of repairing a shrine on Mount Sheshou. These two sets of the *shan* ceremony jade tablets are now held in the National Palace Museum in Taibei.[78]

63. MOUNT HAOLI, HAOLI SHAN 蒿里山
(CHAVANNES NO. 172)

This hill is immediately to the west of Mount Sheshou (no. 63). Another name for the hill is Mount Gaoli (Gaoli shan 高里山). Although it is difficult to distinguish where one hill ends and the other begins, these two hills have long been recognized as distinct. Han Wudi performed the *shan* sacrifice here in 104 BCE. This hill, however, was more important in the history and culture surrounding Mount Tai for later developments. Chavannes shows that Mount Haoli was connected with funeral rites by 202 CE. After religious Daoism adopted the Buddhist concept of purgatory, Mount Haoli came to be viewed as the entrance to the underworld. It was believed that after death all souls returned to Mount Tai, specifically to Mount Haoli (see the "Death" section in Part I).[79]

Because this hill was seen as the entrance to purgatory, a number of temples related to the afterlife were built on its slopes. These include a hall devoted to Yanluo 閻羅, one to Dizang, one to the Ten Kings of the ten courts of purgatory (Shiwang dian 十王殿), and another hall housing the 75 subdivisions of the ten courts.[80] Although it is not clear when these halls were first built, they were repaired in 1284. In the courts between these halls there once stood a veritable forest of stelae erected in the honor of deceased ancestors whose souls had returned to Mount Haoli. The hall of the 75 subcourts of purgatory is described in chapter 69 of the seventeenth-century novel *Xingshi yinyuan zhuan*. Beginning in the 1930s, all these halls and stelae were destroyed, and the materials reused.[81] Today there is virtually no trace of this once-important site.

64. WHITE CRANES SPRING, BAIHE QUAN 白鶴泉 (CHAVANNES NO. 109)

According to legend, in 680 a flock of cranes dove into a spring that once existed on this site, killing themselves. Subsequently this spring was reputed to have the sweetest water on the mountain. Just to the west of the site of this former spring was a temple to the Jade Emperor, the Jade Emperor Tower (Yuhuang ge 玉皇閣, Chavannes no. 110). Within this temple was a shrine containing the mummified body of a former monk (a so-called flesh body, or *roushen* 肉身). This monk lived from 1610 to 1703, the last sixty years at this temple. His skin had been preserved through application of many layers of lacquer. In the 1920s devout pilgrims paid to view this religious relic.[82]

   Just to the west of the Jade Emperor Tower was a temple to the God of the Big Dipper (Beidou dian 北斗殿, Chavannes no. 111). Just south of this temple was a travel palace built for the Qianlong emperor in 1770 (*xinggong* 行宮, Chavannes no. 112). The emperor stayed there during all his subsequent trips to the mountain.

   In 1994 all that remained of these temples were two arches, one marking the onetime entrance to the Jade Emperor Tower and the other the site of the White Cranes Spring.

65. TEMPLE OF THE UNDERWORLD, FENGDU MIAO 豐都廟 (CHAVANNES NO. 116)

This temple was dedicated to the Ten Kings of the underworld. By 1925 this temple had ceased to serve its original purpose and had become "a workhouse for the T'ai Shan beggars."[83] Nothing remained of this temple in 1994.

66. GOD OF WAR TEMPLE, GUANDI MIAO 關帝廟 (CHAVANNES NO. 95)

The God of War was an extremely popular deity in the Chinese pantheon. This temple was located immediately adjacent to the Pilgrimage Path just below the First Heavenly Gate (no. 8). Guandi had no particular connection with Mount Tai, and this temple had no special significance within the cult to the God of War. However, this temple, like many other temples to Guandi throughout China, served as a hostel and native-place society for travelers—especially merchants—from Shanxi province. Before being apotheosized as Guandi, the man Guan Yu was a native of Shanxi. Although the temple still exists, it is not open to the public.

67. GODDESS OF EYESIGHT EASTERN HALL, DONG YANGUANG DIAN 東眼光殿 (CHAVANNES NO. 105)

This small shrine dedicated to the Goddess of Eyesight was built on the top of Tiger Hill above Lüzu's Cave (no. 5) in 1730. It balances the shrine to the same goddess built on top of a hill to the west (no. 68). The pavilion was built next to a spring. People with eye ailments would wash their eyes in the spring, which was believed to have healing properties. The pavilion no longer exists.[84]

68. GODDESS OF EYESIGHT WESTERN HALL, XI YANGUANG DIAN 西眼光殿 (CHAVANNES NO. 200)

This small shrine dedicated to the Goddess of Eyesight was built on the top of Gold Hill, probably during the Ming dynasty. It balances the shrine to the same goddess built on top of the hill to the east (no. 67). Near the pavilion was a spring believed to have healing properties for the eyes. The pavilion no longer exists.[85]

69. TANG PRELIMINARY FENG SACRIFICIAL ALTAR, TANG FENG SI TAN 唐封祀壇 (CHAVANNES NO. 139)

This mound, to the southeast of Tai'an, was the site of the pre-liminary *feng* ceremony conducted by Tang Gaozong in 666. Cha-vannes noted that the mound no longer existed when he visited in 1897.[86]

70. SONG PRELIMINARY FENG SACRIFICIAL ALTAR, SONG FENG SI TAN 宋封祀壇 (CHAVANNES NO. 138)

This mound, also southeast of Tai'an, was the site of the prelimi-nary *feng* ceremony conducted by Song Zhenzong in 1008. There was a stele at this site commemorating the event. The mound was leveled in 1969, and the stele was re-erected in the Dai Temple in 1972.[87]

71. GREAT NORTHWARD FACING STELE TAI YIN BEI 太陰碑 (CHAVANNES NO. 143)

This stele, located just to the south of the Tai'an city wall, was made up of several stones and measured 8 meters long at the base and 2.9 meters tall. The stele was destroyed in 1951. The text com-memorated Song Zhenzong's receipt of the Heavenly Text in 1008 and thanked Heaven for its beneficence. The text in this stele was the same as that in the Song Cliff Inscription on the top of the mountain (see under no. 45).[88]

72. GODDESS TEMPLE, NIANGNIANG MIAO 娘娘廟 (CHAVANNES NO. 187)

This temple was also known as the Bixia Yuanjun Travel Palace (Bixia Yuanjun xinggong 碧霞元君行宮). It was located at the base of the mountain, to the west of the city. In addition to being a small temple to Bixia Yuanjun and her two main assistants, it also served as a hostel for visiting pilgrims. Temples like this were scattered all over Mount Tai's catchment area, usually about a day's journey apart.[89]

73. HEAVENLY TEXT TEMPLE, TIANSHU GUAN 天書觀 (CHAVANNES NO. 177)

Song Zhenzong ordered the construction of this temple near the site where the Heavenly Text fell to earth in 1008 as a commemoration of that event. The temple was built around a spring known as the Sweet or Wine Spring (Liquan 醴泉), which purportedly began to flow either just prior to or while the emperor was visiting the mountain in 1008. During the Zhengde period (1506–21), the temple became a shrine to Bixia Yuanjun. During the Wanli emperor's reign (1573–1619), a statue of the emperor's mother, Empress Dowager Xiaoding 孝定, portrayed as the Nine Lotus Boddhisatva (Jiulian pusa 九蓮菩薩) was placed in a hall in the temple. During the Chongzhen emperor's reign (1628–44), a statue of that emperor's mother, Empress Dowager Xiaochun 孝純, as the Bodhisattva of Wisdom (Zhishang pusa 智上菩薩) was placed in another room in the temple. These two statues of the Ming empresses were moved to the Numinous Palace (no. 61) during the Xianfeng period (1851–61). The statue of the Bodhisattva Jiulian is now in the Red Gate Temple (no. 11). The statue of the Bodhisattva of Wisdom is in the Mother of the Big Dipper Temple (no. 15). In 1903 the Heavenly Text Temple became a local school. It no longer exists.[90]

74. TRANSCENDENT'S SHADOW, XIANREN YING 仙人影 (CHAVANNES NO. 216)

This "shadow" is a natural occurring formation resembling the outline of a person. It is located at the opening of the western ravine on the south side of Mount Tai. A trail up this ravine is known as the Western Path (Xilu 西路) up the mountain. This western route joins up with the Central or Eastern Path just above the Second or Middle Heavenly Gate (no. 23). The Western Path was far less traveled during the late imperial period than the Central Path. Although there were a few shrines along this route, they were seldom used by pilgrims and were probably mostly visited by locals. Most who ventured up this path would have climbed to the mountain's peak via the Central Path; they would have ascended the Western Path only partway, their primary goal being admiration of the scenery. There were quite a few poems written about the scenery along the lower half of this path. Today this ravine contains a paved road that allows visitors to ride in buses up to the Middle Heavenly Gate, from which they can take a gondola to the top. Just as in the past, those who choose to walk along this route tend to follow it for the scenery rather than use it as a route to reach the top of the mountain.

75. WESTERN STREAM STONE PAVILION XIXI

SHITING 西溪石亭 (NOT IN CHAVANNES)

This small pavilion is situated on the Western Path above the stream near the Black Dragon Pool (see Fig. 11, p. 23). It was built during the Daoguang period (1821–50).[91]

76. UNIVERSAL LIGHT TEMPLE, PUZHAO

SI 普照寺 (CHAVANNES NO. 201)

This is the largest Buddhist temple on Mount Tai. It purports to date from the Tang dynasty, but the earliest evidence for its existence comes from records of repairs conducted between 1161 and 1190. It is situated in a beautiful and isolated spot between the Central and Western paths. It has been the residence of a number of famous monks throughout the centuries. Because of its isolated location, it never attracted large numbers of pilgrims. From 1932 to 1935, the warlord Feng Yuxiang 馮玉祥 (1882–1948) took up residence in the temple. Today much of the temple is devoted to a museum in his honor. In 1995 this was the only temple on Mount Tai with a resident Buddhist monk.[92]

77. REVOLUTIONARY MARTYRS' TEMPLE,
GEMING LIESHI CI 革命烈士祠
(NOT IN CHAVANNES)

Feng Yuxiang, a populist and anti-Japanese warlord, resided in the Universal Light Temple (no. 76) from 1932 to 1935. He was indirectly involved in one of the early uprisings against the Qing dynasty in 1911. He and a group of friends harbored revolutionary ideas. He planned to join several of them in a revolt in December 1911 in the city of Luanzhou. Luanzhou (now known as Luanxian), 200 kilometers east of Beijing, was a key stop on the Beijing–Mukden rail line. Feng was arrested just prior to the outbreak of the revolt in Luanzhou. Several of his closest friends were killed in the uprising, and the revolting troops were defeated by those loyal to the Qing. In honor of his friends and their soldiers, he built this memorial hall in the style of a Chinese temple in 1933. The compound is surrounded by a wall and contains a series of buildings. The northernmost building contains a tablet in the style of a spirit tablet.[93]

78. MEMORIAL STELE TO THE REVOLUTIONARY
MARTYRS OF THE 1911 LUANZHOU (REVOLT),
XINHAI LUANZHOU GEMING LIESHI JINIAN BEI
辛亥灤州革命烈士紀念碑 (NOT IN CHAVANNES)

Feng Yuxiang also erected this obelisk-like memorial in honor of his fallen friends and their soldiers in 1933 (see no. 77), south of the Universal Light Temple (no. 76) nearer the base of the mountain.[94]

79. TOMB OF FAN MINGSHU, FAN MINGSHU
MU 范明樞墓 (NOT IN CHAVANNES)

Fan Mingshu was born near Mount Tai in 1866 and died in 1947. He studied in Japan. When he returned, he worked in the field of education. He was active in the May Fourth movement. He was given a number of assignments within the Communist party in the 1930s and 1940s. He became a member of the party in 1946. His body was reburied in this tomb in 1950.[95] A couplet on the tomb states:

> Elder Revolutionary who will be remembered forever
> Eternally the people's teacher.

80. TOMB OF FENG YUXIANG, FENG YUXIANG MU 馮玉祥墓 (NOT IN CHAVANNES)

Because Feng Yuxiang had lived at Mount Tai from 1932 to 1935, when he died in 1948 it was decided to build his tomb at the base of the mountain. This tomb was built for him in 1952, and his body was placed in it in 1953.[96]

81. BRIDGE FOR THE MASSES, DAZHONG QIAO 大眾橋 (NOT IN CHAVANNES)

Feng Yuxiang built this bridge in honor of the people of Tai'an in 1935.

82. TOMB OF QIU HUANWEN QIU HUANWEN MU 求煥文墓 (NOT IN CHAVANNES)

Qiu Huanwen was a native of Shandong. He became a member of the Communist party in 1931. His tomb and stele, much more modest in scale than those of Feng Yuxiang or Fan Mingshu (nos. 79, 80), was built in 1961 above Lüzu's Cave (no. 5).[97]

Reference
Matter

Notes

Introduction

1. "Late imperial" is a somewhat fluid term. Broadly, it often refers to the entire period of the last two imperial dynasties: 1368–1911 (Ming, 1368–1644, and Qing, 1644–1911). More typically, however, it is described as beginning in the middle of the Ming dynasty around 1550 and ending in 1911. For the study of cultural phenomena, the term has been extended past the end of the Qing dynasty up to around 1920 (see Johnson et al., "Preface," x). The period used in this book, from roughly 1500 to 1920, is more appropriate for this study because, for the vast majority of Chinese who journeyed to Mount Tai, political changes such as the Ming-Qing transition or the end of the dynastic system and the beginning of the Republican era (1911–49) did not have an impact on their basic belief systems and thus on their motivations for traveling to the mountain (the Manchu imperial visits to Mount Tai are an obvious exception). Furthermore, the sixteenth century demarcates a significant shift in the deity who enjoyed the most popularity on Mount Tai. During the Yuan (1279–1368) and early Ming dynasties, worship of the God of Mount Tai, in the guise of a judge in the underworld, was the primary motivation for popular pilgrimage to the mountain (see Idema, "The Pilgrimage to Taishan"; Pei-yi Wu "An Ambivalent Pilgrim," 76; and Naquin, *Peking*, 241). By 1516, pilgrimages focused on the compassionate Goddess of Mount Tai had reached such a level that the Ming government took advantage of the situation to impose a pilgrimage or incense tax on those visiting her main temple on top of the mountain (see Sawada, *Chūgoku no minkan shinkō*,

303). In addition, the sixteenth century also witnessed a burgeoning of various types of printed sources; among the most important for the study of sites like Mount Tai are popular religious texts known as "precious volumes" or "precious scrolls" (*baojuan* 寶卷) (see Overmyer, *Precious Volumes*, ix); popular woodblock prints (*nianhua* 年畫) (see Wang Shucun, *Yangliuqing nianhua*, 1–2; and Po and Johnson, *Domesticated Deities*, 10); travelogues (*youji* 遊記) (see Pei-yi Wu, "An Ambivalent Pilgrim"; and Strassberg, *Inscribed Landscapes*, 56); topographical gazetteers such as mountain gazetteers (*shanzhi* 山志) (see Brook, *Geographical Sources*, 52); and route books (see Brook, *Geographical Sources*, 5). The second half of the sixteenth century also saw a marked increase in the erection and repair of edifices on Mount Tai. Significant changes in how people approached the mountain occurred at the end of the late imperial period as well. Both the Republican and the Communist government sought to convert Mount Tai into secular and revolutionary space. Although many people continue to ascend the mountain to pray to the Goddess of Mount Tai, the new revolutionary layers on this cultural site add dimensions, nationalism in particular, beyond the scope of this study. I address twentieth-century appropriations of the mountain in my "Signifying Mount Tai: Modern Meanings of an Ancient Site."

2. Watson, "Standardizing the Gods," 294–95.

3. Naquin and Yü, "Introduction: Pilgrimage in China," 9.

4. Rawski, "Presidential Address: Reenvisioning the Qing," 831.

5. Many sites on the mountain, as well as temple records, were destroyed either intentionally or incidentally during Nationalist and warlord "antisuperstition" campaigns, the Japanese occupation during the Pacific War, the subsequent civil war, or the Cultural Revolution.

6. Primarily descriptive works include Mateer, "T'ai San"; Bergen, "A Visit to T'ai Shan"; Tschepe, *Der T'ai Schan*; Moule, "T'ai Shan"; Ayscough, "Shrines of History"; and Mullikin, "Tai Shan." Baker, *T'ai Shan*, borrows heavily from Chavannes.

7. Kroll, "Verses from on High"; Idema, "The Pilgrimage to Taishan"; Dudbridge, "A Pilgrimage in Seventeenth-Century Fiction"; idem, "Women Pilgrims to T'ai Shan"; and Pei-yi Wu, "An Ambivalent Pilgrim."

8. Sawada, *Chūgoku no minkan shinkō*, 278–330; Pomeranz, "Power, Gender, and Pluralism"; Naquin, "The Peking Pilgrimage to Miao-Feng Shan"; and Shiau, "The Cult of Mount T'ai in the Ming."

9. Liu Hui, *Taishan zong jiao yanjiu*.

10. Shandongsheng difangshizhi bianzuan weiyuanhui, *Taishan zhi* (hereafter cited as SDS); Liu Xiuchi, *Taishan daquan*.

11. Bonnell and Hunt, "Introduction," 26.

12. Sewell, "The Concept(s) of Culture," 47.

13. Rawski, "A Historian's Approach to Chinese Death Ritual," 28.

14. Turner, *Dramas, Fields, and Metaphors*; idem, *Process, Performance and Pilgrimage*; idem, *The Ritual Process*; and Turner and Turner, *Image and Pilgrimage in Christian Culture*.

15. Coleman and Elsner, *Pilgrimage*, 212.

16. Preston, "Spiritual Magnetism," 32.

17. Natalie Davis, "From 'Popular Religion' to Religious Cultures."

18. Sewell, "The Concept(s) of Culture," 52–54.

19. Naquin, *Peking: Temples and City Life*, xxx.

20. Biernacki, "Method and Metaphor after the New Cultural History," 82.

21. Marcus, *Ethnography Through Thick and Thin*, 62.

22. Johnson, "Communication, Class, and Consciousness in Late Imperial China," 72.

Part I

1. The descriptions and categorizations of the various buildings in this section are drawn from observations during trips to Mount Tai in 1994, 1995, and 2000, reinforced by general information contained in a number of gazetteers.

2. Hanyu dacidian bianji weiyuanhui, *Hanyu dacidian*, 2: 363. Hereafter cited as *Hanyu dacidian*.

3. The Confucian Temple on top of the mountain met the first and second characteristics, but initially it had no resident caretaker (see Part II, Chapter 3).

4. Wang Jun and Wang Feng, *Tai'an & Mt. Tai*, 90.

5. Han Dezhou, *Mount Taishan*, 7.

6. Sima, *Shi ji, j.* 28, pp. 1366–67.

7. Ma Dibo, "Fengshan yiji," 11: 3167.

8. Wang Jun and Wang Feng, *Tai'an & Mt. Tai*, 29.

9. See Xiao, *Taishan xiaoshi*, 6; Nie, *Taishan daoli ji*, 9; and SDS, 295–97.

10. See, e.g., Bernbaum, *Sacred Mountains of the World*, 214; and Park, *Sacred Worlds*, 247.

11. See Kleeman, "Mountain Deities in China," 226; Naquin and Yü, "Introduction: Pilgrimage in China," 11–14; Mou and Zhang, *Zhongguo zongjiao tongshi*, 1: 8; Zhan, *Shenling yu jisi*, 66–74; and Liu Hui, *Taishan zongjiao yanjiu*, 2–8.

12. Lewis, "The *feng* and *shan* Sacrifices of Emperor Wu of the Han," 56.

13. *Mao shi*, 377 (魯頌: "閟宮"; Mao no. 300).

14. Big (*da* 大), great (*tai* 太), and utmost point (*ji* 极) (*Hanyu dacidian*, 5: 1026).

15. Ma Dibo, "Fengshan yiji," 11: 3167; trans. Strassberg, *Inscribed Landscapes*, 61.

16. Liu Hui, *Taishan zongjiao yanjiu*, 12–14; and Liu Xiuchi, *Taishan daquan*, 575–76.

17. See Mou and Zhang, *Zhongguo zongjiao tongshi*, 1: 6; and references in Liu Hui, *Taishan zongjiao yanjiu*, 3–4.

18. Liu Hui, *Taishan zongjiao yanjiu*, 4–5, 59; Liu Zenggui, "Tiantang yu diyu," 194, also glosses over the middle element and sees the symbol as a sign of early sun worship on Mount Tai.

19. Munakata, *Sacred Mountains in Chinese Art*, 4.

20. SDS, 438; see SDS, 430–38, for the dates of previous messengers and Chavannes, *Le T'ai Chan*, 279–300, for the texts of some of the prayers.

21. Baker, *T'ai Shan*, 68; see also Ying, *Fengsu tongyi*, *j.* 10, p. 69. Two caves in particular are associated with this belief: Sun-Facing Cave (no. 30) and White Cloud Cave (no. 38).

22. See Chavannes, *Le T'ai Chan*, 279–300; and SDS, 432–35. In addition to its physical isolation, another potentially influential aspect of Mount Tai's geographic characteristics was its proximity to major fault lines. The mountain lies on what geologists call a "craton," a relatively stable formation. However, a major fault lies only 150 kilometers to the east of the mountain, and other lesser ones are closer (see Dong Shenbao, "Metamorphic and Tectonic Domains of China,"467–68). The mountain's proximity to Heaven might have made it a focus for appeals of protection. Its relative stability compared to nearby fault zones may have given added impetus to early admiration and worship of this sacred peak. Official governmental records list prayers addressed to the anthropomorphized mountain deity for protection from earthquakes in 1485 (see Chavannes, *Le T'ai Chan*, 285; and SDS, 434). It is possible that similar prayers were made in earlier periods.

23. Edward Schafer, in order to suit the exigencies of translating medieval poetry, created the neologism "marchmount" for *yue* (*Pacing the Void*, 6). Although other scholars of poetry and literature have chosen to follow Schafer's lead, I prefer the clarity of "Sacred Peak." By making the term a proper noun, I feel that I avoid Pei-yi Wu's argument that this translation is too vague (Pei-yi Wu, "An Ambivalent Pilgrim," 85*n*). Both forms of the character *yue* (嶽/岳) were used in ancient times. See Hanyu dazidian bianji

weiyuanhui, *Hanyu dazidian*, 323, 338 (hereafter cited as *Hanyu dazidian*). See also Kleeman, "Mountain Deities in China," 226–27.

24. Kleeman, "Mountain Deities in China," 228.

25. *Shang shu* (Book of history), 99–100 (舜典). Shun 舜 is held up as an ideal leader because, according to legend, he passed over his own son as heir to hand over the throne to the more qualified Yu. Shun is supposed to have lived around 2250 BCE.

26. Kleeman, "Mountain Deities in China," 237.

27. See Zhan, *Shenling yu jisi*, 69–70; and Munakata, *Sacred Mountains in Chinese Art*, 4n4.

28. See Kleeman, "Mountain Deities in China," 226–27, for a summary of this debate.

29. See Sima, *Shi ji, j.* 28, p. 1355–56; and Ying, *Fengsu tongyi, j.* 10, p. 69.

30. De Bary et al., *Sources of Chinese Tradition*, 1: 199; Zhongguo daojiao xiehui and Suzhou daojiao xiehui, *Daojiao da cidian*, 215, 221.

31. See Ying, *Fengsu tongyi, j.* 10, p. 69.

32. Ibid.

33. *Hanyu dazidian*, 323.

34. Cited in Zha, *Dai shi, j.* 3, p. 29.

35. *Shang shu*, 99 (舜典).

36. *Zhou yi*, 15–16 (上經).

37. Richard Smith, *Fortune-Tellers and Philosophers*, 140–44; Qi and Fan, "Gucheng langzhong fengshui geju," 48–50.

38. Cited in March, "An Appreciation of Chinese Geomancy," 256.

39. *Dongxuan lingbao wuyue*, 6: 740–41.

40. For comparison, see Richard Smith, *Fortune-Tellers and Philosophers*, figs. 4.2–4.4.

41. Chavannes, *Le T'ai Chan*, 415–24.

42. See Despeux, "Talismans and Diagrams," 503–5; and Kroll, "Verses from on High," 244.

43. Zha, *Dai shi, j.* 1, p. 25; Jin, *Taishan zhi*, 4.4b, 5b; Xu, *Tai'anxian zhi*, 首、圖.2a.

44. For examples of spring source maps, see Jin, *Taishan zhi*, 4.33b–34a; and Xu, *Tai'anxian zhi*, 首、圖.8b–9a.

45. For examples of star maps, see Zha, *Dai shi, j.* 1, p. 15; Xu, *Tai'anxian zhi*, 首、圖.1b; and Ren, *Tai'anzhou zhi, j. 序*, p. 7.

46. See, e.g., Richard Smith, *Fortune-Tellers and Philosophers*, 146.

47. SDS, 152.

48. Li Jisheng, *Gulao de Taishan*, 24. For additional springs recognized for their healing and mystical properties, see Appendix nos. 64, 67, 68,

and 73. Contemporary residents of Tai'an, the city at the mountain's base, still believe in the efficacy of the mountain's springs. They make regular trips to collect water at a spring adjacent to the Martyrs' Shrine (no. 14). This water is believed to have restorative properties and to be especially good for brewing tea.

49. Nie, *Taishan daoli ji*, 13.

50. Chavannes, *Le T'ai Chan*, 76–77.

51. At the time of my visit in April 1995, there was a small altar to the God of Caves and Rocks (Dongfu shi shen 洞府石神) beside the rock.

52. Nie, *Taishan daoli ji*, 21. For further discussion of this stone, see the "History" section below.

53. Keightley, "The Late Shang State," 551–52.

54. Wechsler, *Offerings of Jade and Silk*, 161.

55. *Shang shu*, 99–100 (舜典).

56. Munakata, *Sacred Mountains in Chinese Art*, 4–5.

57. *Zhushu jinian*, 1.4a, 4b, 5b. Yao was a legendary, ideal leader who passed over his own son as heir to hand over the throne to Shun. Traditionally Yao was supposed to have lived around 2300 BCE.

58. See Cui and Ji, *Tai Dai shiji*, 16; and Liu Hui, *Taishan zongjiao yanjiu*, 32.

59. Sima, *Shi ji, j.* 28, p. 1355; trans. Burton Watson, *Records of the Grand Historian*, 2: 4.

60. Lewis, "The *feng* and *shan* Sacrifices of Emperor Wu of the Han," 52.

61. See ibid., 54; and Wechsler, *Offerings of Jade and Silk*, 172.

62. Lewis, "The *feng* and *shan* Sacrifices of Emperor Wu of the Han," 55.

63. Ibid., 54.

64. See ibid.; and Wechsler, *Offerings of Jade and Silk*, 172.

65. Lewis, "The *feng* and *shan* Sacrifices of Emperor Wu of the Han," 54.

66. Wechsler, *Offerings of Jade and Silk*, 172–73.

67. *Mencius*, 7A: 24, p. 187.

68. For the "Eastern Mount" at the base of Mount Tai, see Appendix no. 9. For the location near Qufu, see Baker, *T'ai Shan*, 31.

69. Sima, *Shi ji, j.* 28, p. 1361.

70. Chavannes, *Le T'ai Chan*, 16–17.

71. Sima, *Shi ji, j.* 28, p. 1355.

72. Ibid., p. 1361.

73. Ibid. Mount Yunyun is about 45 kilometers southeast of Tai'an. Several of the leaders in this list, according to Sima Qian, performed the *shan* sacrifices at other small mountains or hills in the general vicinity of Mount Tai. The legendary Yellow Emperor supposedly performed the

shan sacrifices at Mount Tingting (亭亭山, about 25 kilometers south of Tai'an). Yu performed the *shan* sacrifices at Mount Guiji 會稽山, which, according to Chavannes, is in Zhejiang province (*Les mémoires historiques de Se-ma Ts'ien*, 1: 162n4). The last of these twelve rulers, King Cheng of Zhou, performed the *shan* sacrifices at Mount Sheshou 社首山, a small hill at the base of Mount Tai, just southwest of the traditional city wall surrounding Tai'an (no. 62) (Sima, *Shi ji, j.* 28, p. 1361). For a map showing these mountains (except Mount Guiji), see Fig. 22.

Sima Qian's text is somewhat confusing here, since he began by stating that the *shan* sacrifices took place at Mount Liangfu, but the subsequent list does not include any ceremonies at this site. One possibility is that perhaps Mount Yunyun (18 kilometers east of Mount Liangfu) could be viewed as an extension of Mount Liangfu, or that the name Liangfu refers to the chain of hills including Mount Liangfu and Mount Yunyun. Chavannes suggests that Liangfu is an alternative name for Mount Sheshou (*Le T'ai Chan*, 168n, 186n). Kroll also refers to Mount Liangfu as a foothill of Mount Tai ("Verses from on High," 227).

74. Ren, *Tai'anzhou zhi*, 19 (1.2a).

75. Sima, *Shi ji, j.* 28, pp. 1366–67. Sima Qian also stated that the emperor set up a stone on top of Mount Tai "praising the virtue of the First Emperor of Qin, making clear his achievement of the *feng* [sacrifice]" (ibid.). Chavannes, however, argued that although Qin Shihuangdi did climb Mount Tai, he did not perform the *feng* and *shan* sacrifices because these ceremonies are not mentioned in the text of this inscription (*Le T'ai Chan*, 18).

The discrepancy between Sima's account of the text and the actual inscription can be explained in at least two ways. First, Sima Qian had access to oral traditions and historical documents no longer extant. He may have projected solid evidence of Qin Shihuangdi's performance of the rituals into his account and erroneously tied that evidence to the inscription, which did not actually mention the *feng* sacrifice. Another explanation derives from the fact that Sima Qian's chapter on the *feng* and *shan* sacrifices (*juan* 28) "has traditionally been interpreted as a veiled attack . . . upon Emperor Wu [Han Wudi 武帝 (r. 140–87 BCE)]" (Burton Watson, *Records*, 2: 3n). Much of the attack involves indirect comparisons between Han Wudi and Qin Shihuangdi. It is possible that in order to heighten the comparison and thus the criticism, Sima Qian projected Han Wudi's performances of the *feng* and *shan* sacrifices back on Qin Shihuangdi. Most recent scholarship accepts that Qin Shihuangdi did indeed perform sacrifices that he and his officials called *feng* and *shan* (see, e.g., Lewis's chapter

"The *feng* and *shan* Sacrifices of Emperor Wu of the Han"; and Liu Hui, *Taishan zongjiao yanjiu*, 75–77).

76. Sima, *Shi ji*, *j*. 28, pp. 1366–67; trans. Burton Watson, *Records*, 2: 12.

77. Sima, *Shi ji*, *j*. 6, p. 242. *Wudafu* was an official rank during the Qin dynasty; see Hucker, *A Dictionary of Official Titles in Imperial China*, no. 7824. Hucker translates the term as "Grandee of the Ninth Order, [it was the] 12th highest of 20 titles of honorary nobility" (573).

Here Sima Qian stated that Qin Shihuangdi encountered the wind and rain storm as he was descending (下) (*Shi ji*, *j*. 6, p. 242). In two other references to the incident, however, Sima had Qin Shihuangdi encountering the storm on the way up (上) the mountain (*Shi ji*, *j*. 28, pp. 1367, 1371).

78. Sima, *Shi ji*, *j*. 28, p. 1367; trans. Burton Watson, *Records*, 2: 12–13.

79. Sima, *Shi ji*, *j*. 28, p. 1371; trans. Burton Watson, *Records*, 2: 15.

80. For example, see Sima, *Shi ji*, *j*. 28, pp. 1369, 1370.

81. See ibid., pp. 1385, 1393, 1397; and Lewis, "The *feng* and *shan* Sacrifices of Emperor Wu of the Han," 59, 67.

82. Wechsler, *Offerings of Jade and Silk*, 173. See also Ch'en P'an, "Taishan zhu sheng yi zhu si shuo"; and Liu Zenggui, "Tiantang yu diyu."

83. Sima, *Shi ji*, *j*. 28, p. 1367; trans. Burton Watson, *Records*, 2: 12; see also Wechsler, *Offerings of Jade and Silk*, 193.

84. The source for Han Wudi's visits through 98 BCE is Sima, *Shi ji*, *j*. 28, pp. 1398, 1399, 1401–3. For the 93 BCE visit, see Ban Gu, *Han shu*, *j*. 6, p. 207. In 110 BCE Han Wudi performed the *shan* sacrifice at Mount Suran 肅然山, a foothill on the northeast side of Mount Tai. In 102 and 93 BCE, he performed the *shan* ceremony at Mount Shilü 石閭山, located about 23 kilometers south of Tai'an. Mount Gaoli 高里山, also known as Mount Haoli 蒿里山, is a foothill located just south and a little west of Tai'an (no. 63 in the Appendix). All three of these foothills are labeled in Fig. 22.

85. Sima, *Shi ji*, *j*. 28, pp. 1385, 1393, 1397; trans. Burton Watson, *Records*, 2: 26, 36, 41.

86. Sima, *Shi ji*, *j*. 28, p. 1398.

87. Lewis, "The *feng* and *shan* Sacrifices of Emperor Wu of the Han," 54.

88. See Burton Watson, *Records*, 2: 3n; and Lewis, "The *feng* and *shan* Sacrifices of Emperor Wu of the Han," 64.

89. Ying-shih Yü, "O Soul, Come Back!," 387.

90. Wechsler, *Offerings of Jade and Silk*, 174; see also Ch'en P'an, "Taishan zhu sheng yi zhu si shuo."

91. Kleeman, "Mountain Deities in China," 238.

92. Lewis, "The *feng* and *shan* Sacrifices of Emperor Wu of the Han," 63–64.

93. The founder of the Sui dynasty, Sui Wendi (r. 589–604), was urged by some of his officials to perform the *feng* and *shan* sacrifices. He at first rejected these suggestions but then became more inclined toward them. In the end, however, although he did visit Mount Tai in 594, he did not perform the *feng* and *shan* sacrifices (Wechsler, *Offerings of Jade and Silk*, 175–76). Tang Gaozong 高宗 (r. 649–83) scheduled a performance of the *feng* and *shan* sacrifices to be held at the Central Sacred Peak, Mount Song, on three occasions (676, 679, and 684) but did not follow through with the plans (Wechsler, *Offerings of Jade and Silk*, 188–89). Empress Wu 武后 (624–705; also known as Wu Zhao 武曌), the empress of Tang Gaozong who ascended the throne and founded her own dynasty (Zhou 周 690–705) after his death, performed the *feng* and *shan* sacrifices previously planned by her late husband at Mount Song in 697 (Chavannes, *Le T'ai Chan*, 194*n*).

94. Cited in Wechsler, *Offerings of Jade and Silk*, 194.

95. Ibid., 175.

96. See ibid.

97. Chavannes, *Le T'ai Chan*, 22.

98. Lewis, "The *feng* and *shan* Sacrifices of Emperor Wu of the Han," 67.

99. See Bokenkamp, "Record of the Feng and Shan Sacrifices," 251.

100. Ibid., 252.

101. Chavannes, *Le T'ai Chan*, 20–26. For a detailed description of early Tang plans for the sacrifices, see Wechsler, *Offerings of Jade and Silk*, 179–81, 185–86.

102. Chavannes, *Le T'ai Chan*, 21–26. The jade tablets from Song Zhenzong's *feng* ceremony of 1008 were uncovered and reburied in 1482 (Nie, *Taishan daoli ji*, 23; see Appendix, no. 54). They were again uncovered in 1747 and became part of the Qianlong emperor's personal collection (Chavannes, *Le T'ai Chan*, 60; SDS 187). In 1931 the tablets from the *shan* ceremonies of both Tang Xuanzong's ceremony of 725 and Song Zhenzong's ceremony of 1008 were discovered during the process of repairing a shrine on Mount Sheshou and are now held in the National Palace Museum in Taibei (see Na et al., "Tang Song yuce zhuanji").

103. For the various boxes, see Wechsler, *Offerings of Jade and Silk*, 180; and Chavannes, *Le T'ai Chan*, 22–24, figs. 5–7. In the *sealing* of the boxes and the burial in a *raised altar mound*, we see two of the meanings of the term *feng*. Indeed, Wechsler (*Offerings of Jade and Silk*, 179–80) notes that Tang ritual experts emphasized both these meanings in their explication of the rites.

104. Chavannes, *Le T'ai Chan*, 25.

105. Wechsler, *Offerings of Jade and Silk*, 190–91.

106. Cao Xueqin, *The Story of the Stone*, 1: 328 (chap. 17).

107. Zha, *Dai shi, j.* 8, p. 111; Xiao, *Taishan xiaoshi*, 50.

108. Nie, *Taishan daoli ji*, 21; Tang, *Dai Lan*, 8.5b–6a; also see Chavannes, *Le T'ai Chan*, 57–58.

109. I am indebted to Professor Cho-yun Hsu for this interpretation of the Wordless Stele as a prehistoric megalith.

110. Liu Wenzhong, "Annotations," 49.

111. Han Wudi, whose title means "martial emperor," is renowned for his substantial expansion of Chinese territory.

112. For more on this inscription, see Harrist, "Record of the Eulogy on Mt. Tai"; for a translation of the text into French, see Chavannes, *Le T'ai Chan*, 318–28.

113. Ouyang, *Songshi, j.* 7, p. 136. For more on the Heavenly Text, see Cahill, "Taoism at the Sung Court."

114. Nie, *Taishan daoli ji*, 20.

115. Xiao, *Taishan xiaoshi*, 25.

116. Baker, *T'ai Shan*, 64.

117. *Li ji* (*Book of Rites*), 716 (檀弓下第四).

118. From *Quan Tang shi, j.* 216, p. 2253.

119. Wang Chong, *Lun heng, j.* 4, 書虛篇, p. 56.

120. *Analects*, 3.6, pp. 67–68.

121. Ibid., 67*n*.

122. Translated in Kroll, "Verses from on High," 224.

123. Sima, *Shi ji, j.* 28, p. 1398.

124. *Liezi*, 天瑞篇: 10.

125. *Chuang-tzu: Basic Writings*, trans. Burton Watson, 27; see also Ying-shih Yü, "O Soul, Come Back!," 386.

126. Song Shou, *Taishan jishi*, 115.

127. Kong, *Taishan jisheng*, 9a.

128. Mount Tai "TLV" mirror inscription, reproduced in Chavannes, *Le T'ai Chan*, 424, fig. 59.

129. Trans. Kroll, "Verses from on High," 228.

130. Excerpt from poem 1, trans. ibid, 249.

131. Excerpt from poem 4, trans. ibid., 254.

132. Excerpt from poem 6, trans. Cahill, *Transcendence and Divine Passion*, 1. The whole series of Li Bo's six poems in Chinese is found in *Quan Tang shi, j.* 179, pp. 1823–24.

133. Cahill, "Performers and Female Taoist Adepts," 155, 157.

134. Liu Zenggui, "Tiantang yu diyu," 196, 205.

135. Ibid., 196–97, 201; and Lü, "Kunlun Taishan."

136. Cahill, *Transcendence and Divine Passion*, 48–53.

137. Tang, *Dai Lan*, 12.2a.

138. Cahill, *Transcendence and Divine Passion*, 59.

139. See Bujard, *Le sacrifice au Ciel*, 12, 138, and map no. 1 (p. 242).

140. Sima, *Shi ji, j.* 28, p. 1367.

141. Ying-shih Yü, "O Soul, Come Back!," 388–89. For more on Taishan fujun, see Sawada, *Jigoku hen*, 45–48.

142. Chavannes, *Le T'ai Chan*, 398–99.

143. Sima, *Shi ji, j.* 28, p. 1361.

144. Ibid., p. 1403; trans. Burton Watson, *Records*, 2: 50.

145. Ying-shih Yü, "O Soul, Come Back!," 392.

146. Chavannes, *Le T'ai Chan*, 104, 106.

147. Cited in Ying-shih Yü, "O Soul, Come Back!," 393; see also Sawada, *Jigoku hen*, 49.

148. Ying-shih Yü, "O Soul, Come Back!," 391; Sawada, *Jigoku hen*, 43–44.

149. Chavannes, *Le T'ai Chan*, 400.

150. "Zhu zhao ren hunpo, . . . zhi ren shengming de changduan" 主召人魂魄, . . . 知人生命的長短; cited in Liu Hui, *Taishan zongjiao yanjiu*, 123; see also Liu Zenggui, "Tiantang yu diyu," 197.

151. See Sawada, *Jigoku hen*, 44; Ying-shih Yü, "O Soul, Come Back!," 394; and Teiser, "The Scripture on the Ten Kings," 176.

152. For more on the Ten Kings see Sawada, *Jigoku hen*, 22–30; and Teiser, "The Scripture on the Ten Kings."

153. Teiser, "The Scripture on the Ten Kings," 1, 48.

154. Ibid., 176, 223, 226; and Sawada, *Jigoku hen*, 26–27.

155. See Hansen, *Changing Gods in Medieval China*, 181; Anne Goodrich, *The Peking Temple of the Eastern Peak*, 16; and Eberhard, *Guilt and Sin in Traditional China*, 55–57.

156. See Naquin, *Peking: Temples and City Life*, 516; idem, "The Peking Pilgrimage to Miao-feng Shan," 335–37; Anne Goodrich, *Chinese Hells*; and idem, *The Peking Temple of the Eastern Peak*. The Eastern Sacred Peak Temple (Dongyue dian 東嶽殿) in Tainan, Taiwan (the former provincial capital), is still a popular temple for spirit mediums (Donald Sutton, pers. comm., 1997).

157. See Sawada, *Jigoku hen*, 50–51.

158. See TenBroeck, "Appendix: Description of the Tung-yüeh Miao of Peking in 1924," 241–55; and Chavannes, *Le T'ai Chan*, 109, 135, 364–69.

159. The information for this paragraph comes from a series of sources reproduced in Zong Li and Liu Qun, *Zhongguo minjian zhushen*, 413–17; and from *Ji shuoquan zhen xubian*, 24: 99–102.

160. Zong Li and Liu Qun (*Zhongguo minjian zhushen*, 417) cite a source that mentions a plaque from the Kangxi period (1662–1722) in Guangdong province. William Geil photographed one in Guangxi in 1909 (*The Sacred Five of China*, opposite p. 8). Aleksei M. Pozdneyev, writing in 1892, described one erected by Chinese living in Mongolia (*Mongolia and the Mongols*, 1: 206). In 1995, I saw a highly weathered stone with this inscription facing outwards near the edge of the Kong family graveyard in Qufu (the Konglin 孔林). Also in 1995, I saw one imbedded in a wall of a house compound at the edge of a village in rural Shandong.

161. Summary of the tale recorded in *Taishan chuanshuo gushi*, 99–101. The ability of the plaque, as a proxy of the real person, to scare away evil spirits is like that of the images of powerful warriors used to scare away evil spirits. Small, rectangular stones engraved with the phrase "Taishan Shi Gandang" were popular souvenirs on Mount Tai in 1994, 1995, and 2000.

162. See, e.g., Idema, "The Pilgrimage to Taishan," 33–34.

163. Ibid., 31–35.

164. Ibid., 41–54. Idema cites a case from 1313 in which a man burned his son alive at Mount Tai (23). It is quite likely that the play was based on this historical event (26).

165. Nie, *Taishan daoli ji*, 23; Baker, *T'ai Shan*, 144–45.

166. See, e.g., Edward Davis, *Society and the Supernatural in Song China*; Teiser, *"The Scripture on the Ten Kings"*; idem, *The Ghost Festival in Medieval China*; and Johnson, *Ritual Opera, Operatic Ritual*.

167. Cited in Idema, "The Pilgrimage to Taishan," 23.

168. Wang Zhigang, "Yunü zhuan," 154; see also Che, "Taishan nüshen de shenhua."

169. Cahill, "Performers and Female Daoist Adepts," 157.

170. *Hanyu dacidian*, 7: 1066–67.

171. Liu Hui, *Taishan zongjiao yanjiu*, 142.

172. Trans. Cahill, *Transcendence and Divine Passion*, 1.

173. Trans. Cahill, "Performers and Female Daoist Adepts," 159.

174. *Hanyu dacidian*, 11: 718.

175. Liu Hui, *Taishan zongjiao yanjiu*, 142.

176. *Hanyu dacidian*, 7: 1075.

177. Ibid., 2: 211.

178. Bixia Yuanjun translates awkwardly into English. Scholars studying this goddess have translated her name differently, but recent scholarship has tended to use the romanized Chinese name. Most of the translations leave out one of the three main attributes of the name (i.e., "green," "clouds of dawn," and "goddess"). Some of the translations are "Princesse des nuages colorés" (The Princess of Colored Clouds; Chavannes, Le T'ai Chan, 29); "Sovereign of the Clouds of Dawn" (Naquin, "The Peking Pilgrimage to Miao-feng Shan," 334); and "Goddess of Green Clouds" (Pei-yi Wu, "An Ambivalent Pilgrim," 78).

179. See Gu Jiegang, Miaofengshan; Luo, "Bixia Yuanjun"; Dudbridge, "A Pilgrimage in Seventeenth-Century Fiction"; Naquin, "The Peking Pilgrimage to Miao-feng Shan"; and Pomeranz, "Power, Gender, and Pluralism."

180. For a discussion of this tax, see the "Economics of Attaining the Summit" section below.

181. Liu Xiuchi, Taishan daquan, 665.

182. Zha, Dai shi, j. 9, p. 139; Liu Xiuchi, Taishan daquan, 669.

183. Nie, Taishan daoli ji, 8; Chavannes, Le T'ai Chan, 87.

184. Cited in Pei-yi Wu, "An Ambivalent Pilgrim," 76.

185. Ibid., 76–77.

186. Jin, Taishan zhi, 10.15b; Chavannes, Le T'ai Chan, 71.

187. Zha, Dai shi, j. 9, pp. 150–51.

188. SDS, 193.

189. Chavannes, Le T'ai Chan, 85, 102–3.

190. Pomeranz, "Power, Gender, and Pluralism," 188, 193, 200–203.

191. Overmyer, Precious Volumes, 273.

192. See Watson, "Standardizing the Gods."

193. Chün-fang Yü, Kuan-yin, 491.

194. See Arthur Wolf, "Gods, Ghosts and Ancestors."

195. Sangren, "Female Gender in Chinese Religious Symbols," 23.

196. Ibid., 20–21.

197. Pomeranz, "Power, Gender, and Pluralism," 204.

198. Other relationships mentioned were granddaughter of the God of Mount Tai, daughter of the Jade Emperor, younger sister of the Jade Emperor, and daughter of Taishan Shi Gandang. See, e.g., Zong Ruji, Zhuding yuwen, 93 (1.44a); Bredon and Mitrophanow, The Moon Year, 281; Ji, "Taishan Bixia," 54; and Zong Li and Liu Qun, Zhongguo minjian zhushen, 321–26.

199. Gu Yanwu, Shandong kaogu lu, 7; see also Wang Zhigang, "Yunü zhuan," 153. For more on this style of scholarship, see p. 308n42.

200. The name Shi Shoudao 石守道 can also be read as a phrase meaning "the stone that protects the path." This name of Bixia Yuanjun's father is reminiscent of the Mount Tai demon queller Shi Gandang. Mei-
Hui Shiau ("The Cult of Mount T'ai in the Ming," 56) believes that the
name derives from the style name of Song scholar Shi Jie 石介, who lived
and lectured in the area of Mount Tai in the eleventh century.

201. The source for this story is the *Yunü juan* 玉女卷 (Volume of the
Jade Maiden); this text is no longer extant, but it is cited in many late imperial period essays. This summary comes from the earliest known cita-
tion, from around 1572: Wang Zhigang, "Yunü zhuan," 153–54.

202. See Cahill, "Performers and Female Daoist Adepts," 165.

203. *Lingying Taishan Niangniang baojuan, pin* 1: 14–15. Citations are
given with the original chapter number or *pin* (品), followed by the page
number in the reprinted version; cited hereafter as *Baojuan*.

204. Eliade, *The Sacred and the Profane*, 20–25, 35–37.

205. Bernbaum, *Sacred Mountains of the World*, 206.

206. Eade and Sallnow, *Contesting the Sacred*, 15.

207. Coleman and Elsner, *Pilgrimage*, 209.

208. Bernbaum, *Sacred Mountains of the World*, 214; Morinis, "Introduction," 18; and Park, *Sacred Worlds*, 251.

209. Preston, "Spiritual Magnetism," 33.

210. Ibid.

211. Reproduced in Chavannes, *Le T'ai Chan*, 424.

212. Preston, "Spiritual Magnetism," 35.

213. See, e.g., Mullikin, "Tai Shan," 715; and Dudbridge, "A Pilgrimage
in Seventeenth-Century Fiction," 227.

214. For one such tale, see Pomeranz, "Power, Gender, and Pluralism," 200.

215. *Mencius*, 7A.24, p. 187.

216. Reproduced in Chavannes, *Le T'ai Chan*, 424.

217. From poem 4, trans. Kroll, "Verses from on High," 254.

218. From poem 6, trans. Cahill, *Transcendence and Divine Passion*, 1.

219. *Mencius*, 4A.26, p. 127.

220. Cited in Pei-yi Wu, "An Ambivalent Pilgrim," 76.

221. See Po and Johnson, *Domesticated Deities*, 11–12.

222. Morinis, "Introduction," 10.

223. Ibid., 10, 11, 12, 13.

224. The mountain did, however, become a national cultural and historical symbol beginning in the Republican period. Many Chinese
throughout the world today believe that a visit to Mount Tai, like a visit

to Confucius' ancestral home in Qufu, is essential to being well educated in Chinese culture and history. See, e.g., Wang Lianru, *Taishan zhinan*, preface 1a–1b; and Shandong dianshitai, *Zhonghua Taishan*, a twelve-episode documentary on VCD, which aired on Central Chinese Television during the summer of 2000. For modern appropriations of Mount Tai, see my "Signifying Mount Tai."

225. Nie, *Taishan daoli ji*, 8; Chavannes, *Le T'ai Chan*, 87.

226. Cited in Pei-yi Wu, "An Ambivalent Pilgrim," 76.

227. Chavannes, *Le T'ai Chan*, 72.

228. Pei-yi Wu, "An Ambivalent Pilgrim," 76–77.

229. Morinis, "Introduction," 18.

230. If available, records of the incense tax receipts collected at Mount Tai from 1516 until 1736 would be the best source for estimating a minimum number of pilgrims per year. Unfortunately, precise figures no longer exist. The most solid figure available comes from the *Ming shi* (Standard history of the Ming): the average amount remitted to Beijing was a little over 20,000 taels per year (Zhang Tingyu et al., *Ming shi*, 7: 2006 [*j*. 82]). This was only a portion of the overall tax intake, since the funds also went to local temple repairs and Shandong provincial coffers, and a certain amount was no doubt lost to graft. In addition, some pilgrims undoubtedly managed to avoid paying the tax. Based on the tax rate set in 1580 of 8 *fen* per person, the sum of 20,000 taels (2,000,000 *fen*) works out to 250,000 pilgrims. The total number of pilgrims traveling to the mountain each year would be significantly higher.

An inscription dated 1593, erected in the main Bixia temple, gives an estimate of "several hundred thousand" as the number of pilgrims offering incense at that temple every year (reproduced in Song Enren, *Taishan shuji*, 14: 350–54 [*j*. 6]).

Another annual estimate for the number of pilgrims dates from the mid-seventeenth century: "Before the year *chi-ssu* 己巳 of Ch'ung-chen 崇禎 [1629] the annual number of pilgrims would come to as many as 800,000, and never fewer than 600,000. Today the figure is less than 400,000" (cited in Dudbridge, "A Pilgrimage in Seventeenth-Century Fiction," 226). The decrease was almost certainly a result of the Ming decline, which was expressed in the neglect of flood-control dikes, rampant banditry and unrest, and eventually the Manchu invasion. From the time the Manchus gained firm control on inner China in the late seventeenth century until the mid-nineteenth century, the numbers of pilgrims would have returned to pre-1629 levels. Another sharp decline undoubtedly occurred during the Taiping Rebellion (1850–64) and probably again during the Boxer Uprising (1899–1900). A. C. Moule, writing in 1912, was informed that in earlier times pilgrims "came in hundreds of thousands if not millions, and from all parts of the empire" ("T'ai Shan," 7).

A number of Chinese and foreign writers recorded estimates of daily averages for the number of pilgrims. For the peak pilgrimage season, the first four lunar months, these range from 3,000 to 10,000 per day, and on peak days, such as New Year's day or the fifteenth of the first lunar month, from 10,000 to 20,000 (see Zhang Dai, "Dai zhi," 37; Mateer, "T'ai San," 414; Mullikin, "Tai Shan," 701; Williamson, *Old Highways in China*, 184; and Franck, *China: A Geographical Reader*, 89). Since round numbers tend to be favored, there is a distinct possibility that these numbers were rounded up from actual figures. However, the conservative daily estimates result in a figure of around 400,000 people per year. Pomeranz ("Power, Gender, and Pluralism," 182) proposes 400,000 as a minimum.

In more recent times the People's Republic of China severely limited pilgrimages from 1965 to 1985 and forced all monks and nuns to leave their temples and take up nonreligious lives elsewhere. However, since 1985 the government has relaxed restrictions against pilgrimages, and monks and nuns are again living on the mountain. Official tallies from 1990 recorded three million visitors to Mount Tai (Zhang Zeyu, "An Open City at the Foot of Mt Tai," 16).

231. Zha, *Dai shi*, *j*. 13, p. 189.

232. The most common date was the eighteenth of the fourth lunar month. A wondrous scripture (*miaojing* 妙經) about Bixia Yuanjun gives this date as the day the goddess obtained enlightenment and determined to help people in this world (*Bixia Yuanjun huguo bimin puji baosheng miaojing*, 34: 744; cited hereafter as *Miaojing*). Naquin ("The Peking Pilgrimage to Miao-feng Shan," 337) notes that in Beijing, by the Wanli reign (1574–1619), celebrations were held instead on the eighth day of the fourth month, which was already a Buddhist holiday.

The lunar dates for special celebrations in honor of Bixia Yuanjun drawn from a compilation of local Shandong gazetteers are listed below (Ding et al., *Zhongguo difangzhi minsu ziliao*). Each page cited below is from a different gazetteer from a different county; all pages are from vol. 1 of the collection:

3/28	(131)
4/8	(172, 277, 291, 324, 331)
4/15	(254)
4/18	(181, 217, 221, 222, 230, 288, 317, 335)

In 1995 Bixia Yuanjun's birthday was celebrated on the fifteenth day of the third lunar month at Mount Tai. This date is apparently a recent adaptation with no particular precedent.

233. Mateer, "T'ai San," 414. One *li* is about a third of a mile or half of a kilometer. An inscription from 1593 erected in the main temple claims that "[those from] nearby [travel] several hundred *li*, [and those from] far away [travel up to] several thousand *li*" (reproduced in Song Enren, *Taishan shuji*, 14: 351 [*j.* 6]).

234. Baker, *T'ai Shan*, 9.

235. Both these stelae were erected in the Mother of the Big Dipper Temple (no. 15). They date from 1779 and 1789. Both societies were from Wen'an County (文安縣) in Shuntian prefecture 順天府, in Zhili.

236. The term "catchment," used in studies of pilgrimages, is borrowed from physical geography, where it refers to a watershed—the area of land that drains into the same stream or river. Larger rivers, like more popular pilgrimage sites, have larger catchment areas (see Turner, *Dramas, Fields, and Metaphor*, 178–79).

237. See Arthur Smith, *Village Life in China*, 141–45.

238. Naquin, "The Peking Pilgrimage to Miao-feng Shan," 361, 371*n*. These numbers come from two studies conducted by Chinese researchers in the 1920s and 1930s.

239. Idema, "The Pilgrimage to Taishan," 23.

240. For an analysis and translation of these chapters, see Dudbridge "A Pilgrimage in Seventeenth-Century Fiction"; and idem, "Women Pilgrims to T'ai Shan."

241. See Mateer, "T'ai San," 414; Moule, "T'ai Shan," 7; Hubbard, "The Pilgrims of Taishan," 324; Baker, *T'ai Shan*, 9; and Bergen, "A Visit to T'ai Shan," 541.

242. Arthur Smith, *Village Life in China*, 142, 144.

243. Bergen, "A Visit to T'ai Shan," 541.

244. See Mateer, "T'ai San," 414; Bergen, "A Visit to T'ai Shan," 541; and Moule, "T'ai Shan," 7.

245. Reproduced in Tang, *Dai Lan*, 6.25a–b.

246. See Idema, "The Pilgrimage to Taishan," 23.

247. Turner and Turner, *Image and Pilgrimage in Christian Culture*, 250.

248. Coleman and Elsner, *Pilgrimage*, 201.

249. See Bergen, "A Visit to T'ai Shan," 541; and Hubbard, "The Pilgrims of Taishan," 326.

250. See C. K. Yang, *Religion in Chinese Society*, 87; and Naquin and Yü, "Introduction: Pilgrimage in China," 12.

251. For examples, see Bergen, "A Visit to T'ai Shan," 541.

252. Ibid.

253. Baker, *T'ai Shan*, 17; a photograph of the temple near Dongping faces p. 20.

254. Chavannes, *Le T'ai Chan*, 32–34 (includes a photograph).

255. Cited in Dudbridge, "A Pilgrimage in Seventeenth-Century Fiction," 226.

256. See Baker, *T'ai Shan*, 17.

257. Cited in Idema, "The Pilgrimage to Taishan," 36.

258. Zhang Dai, "Dai zhi," 37; trans. Pei-yi Wu, "An Ambivalent Pilgrim," 74.

259. Zhang Dai, "Tai'an zhou kedian," 60; trans. Pei-yi Wu, "An Ambivalent Pilgrim," 75.

260. Chapter 69 of *Xingshi yinyuan zhuan* also includes a less detailed description of one of these inns. For further discussion of these inns, see Pei-yi Wu, "An Ambivalent Pilgrim"; and Dudbridge, "A Pilgrimage in Seventeenth-Century Fiction."

261. Hubbard, "The Pilgrims of Taishan," 326.

262. See, e.g., Mullikin and Hotchkis, *The Nine Sacred Mountains of China*, 4.

263. See Dudbridge, "A Pilgrimage in Seventeenth-Century Fiction," 227; and Mullikin, "Tai Shan," 715.

264. See Ayscough, "Shrines of History," 68; Dransmann, *T'aishan-Küfow Guide*, 218; and Mullikin, "Tai Shan," 703.

265. Around 1628, Zhang Dai's inn collected eighteen *fen* from each pilgrim for the tax, but the actual tax at that time was only twelve *fen* (Zhang Dai, "Tai'an zhou kedian," 59). For a recent detailed study of the Taishan incense tax, see Sawada, *Chūgoku no minkan shinkō*, 298–316.

266. Zha, *Dai shi, j.* 13, pp. 188–90.

267. The tael (*liang* 兩), the official monetary unit during the Ming and Qing dynasties, was a Chinese ounce of silver. One tael, at least in theory, was the equivalent of 100 *fen* (分), or 1,000 *li* (厘).

268. Zha, *Dai shi, j.* 13, pp. 188–90.

269. Zhang Dai, "Dai zhi," 37.

270. *QLSL*, 1: 299 (7.25b).

271. Hubbard, "The Pilgrims of Taishan," 324.

272. Zhang Dai, "Dai zhi," 38; trans. Pei-yi Wu, "An Ambivalent Pilgrim," 77.

273. Franck, *China: A Geographical Reader*, 91.

274. Mateer, "T'ai San," 403.

275. See Sawada, *Chūgoku no minkan shinkō*, 301–2, 307–11.

276. Franck, *Wandering in Northern China*, 274.

277. See Liu Hui, *Taishan miaohui yanjiu*.

278. Mateer, "T'ai San," 368–69.

279. Wechsler, *Offerings of Jade and Silk*, 174.

280. Chavannes, *Le T'ai Chan*, 400.

Chapter 1

1. Huang Liu-hung, *A Complete Book Concerning Happiness*, j. 26, p. 551 (trans. modified).

2. *Analects*, 6.20; trans. Chan, *Source Book*, 30.

3. Huang Liu-hung, *A Complete Book Concerning Happiness*, j. 26, p. 551 (trans. modified).

4. Furth, "The Patriarch's Legacy," 187.

5. Hui-chen Wang Liu, "An Analysis of Chinese Clan Rules," 91.

6. Cited in Furth, "The Patriarch's Legacy," 187.

7. Huang Liu-hung, *A Complete Book Concerning Happiness*, j. 31, p. 608.

8. Cited in Furth, "The Patriarch's Legacy," 187.

9. Hui-chen Wang Liu, "An Analysis of Chinese Clan Rules," 91.

10. Furth, "The Patriarch's Legacy," 196.

11. Huang Liu-hung, *A Complete Book Concerning Happiness*, j. 26, p. 551, j. 31, p. 608.

12. Hanan, "Introduction," xi.

13. Li Yu, *The Carnal Prayer Mat*, 77–78.

14. Hanan, "Introduction," viii.

15. Huang Liu-hung, *A Complete Book Concerning Happiness*, j. 31, p. 609.

16. Furth, "The Patriarch's Legacy," 196.

17. Ibid., 197.

18. Dudbridge, "Women Pilgrims to Ta'i Shan," 39.

19. Xizhousheng, *Xingshi yinyuan zhuan*, 68: 526; trans. Dudbridge, "Women Pilgrims to Ta'i Shan," 50 (trans. modified).

20. Xizhousheng, *Xingshi yinyuan zhuan*, 69: 532; trans. Dudbridge, "Women Pilgrims to Ta'i Shan," 60.

21. Dudbridge, "A Pilgrimage in Seventeenth-Century Fiction," 252.

22. Naquin, "The Peking Pilgrimage to Miao-feng Shan," 365, 372n. Naquin bases this figure on names from stelae, a field study from 1925, and photographs from the time.

23. Wang Shizhen, writing in 1576, observed a "train of men and women on their way to pay homage" (cited in Pei-yi Wu, "An Ambivalent Pilgrim," 69). Although a male observer from this time might have

been prone to mention women even if they made up well under 10 percent of those present, Wang does establish that women were climbing
Mount Tai in the sixteenth century. A mid-seventeenth-century Chinese
source noted that "each year in the third and fourth months men and
women from all parts climb in hundreds of thousands to offer sacrifice"
(cited in Dudbridge, "A Pilgrimage in Seventeenth-Century Fiction," 226).
Mateer wrote in 1879 that "the men generally walk, and a few of the
women. . . . The women and officers and rich men were carried up by
professional carriers. . . . While in the city we saw every day strings of
wheelbarrows thumping over the stones loaded with women, mostly old
women" ("T'ai San," 414). Ayscough commented that the courts of the
temple to the Goddess of Mount Tai "were thronged with women"
("Shrines of History," 68). See also Bergen, "A Visit to T'ai Shan," 541;
and King-Salmon, *House of a Thousand Babies*, 41.

24. See Pomeranz, "Power, Gender, and Pluralism," 185, 189. He cites
three sources as support (405n31). One source is by a magistrate whose
purpose in writing about the pilgrimage was to condemn it because
women were involved, and his figures on the number of women participants are hence suspect. The second source is the novel *Xingshi yinyuan
zhuan*. Again, however, the author was extremely critical of the pilgrimage, and inferences based on this novel about the number of women are
unreliable. The third source is an article by G. E. Hubbard written in 1925.
Hubbard, however, never stated that the majority of the pilgrims were
women. Hubbard observed that pilgrims "arrive mostly in parties, sometimes of men alone striding along with the easy gait of the peasant, sometimes accompanied by women who stumble up the steps and frequently
have to be helped along by a man on either side" ("The Pilgrims of
Taishan," 326). In 1994, 1995, and 2000, women made up well over half of
the people I observed burning incense and spirit money to the Goddess
of Mount Tai.

25. Societies that erected stelae were likely to have been among the more
affluent of the pilgrimage groups and may have been more influenced by
elite mores. Thus it is possible that the number of women included in these
inscriptions is lower than the actual number of women who participated
in these groups. For example, although some men may have been quite
willing to acknowledge their mothers (especially if she were a respectable widow), they may not have recorded the name of an accompanying
daughter-in-law.

26. Sangren, "Female Gender in Chinese Religious Symbols," 15–16.

27. *Baojuan, pin* 1: 31.

28. *Miaojing*, 744. This *miaojing* is included in the *Supplement to the Daoist Canon*, which was compiled in 1607. There are several other *miaojing* about Bixia Yuanjun. Although the text differs, all versions convey the same overall tone, information, and message. Below are abbreviated bibliographic citations for four *miaojing*; the complete entries can be found in the bibliography.

A. *Bixia Yuanjun huguo bimin puji baosheng miaojing*. Included in the 1607 *Supplement to the Daoist Canon*.
B. *Tianxian yunü Bixia Yuanjun zhenjing*. 1611. Copy kindly provided by Zhou Shaoliang.
C. *Taishanglaojun shuo tianxian yunü Bixia Yuanjun hushi hongji miaojing*. 1874. Printed at a Bixia temple just west of Tai'an. Some of the funds for the printing were donated by the Dai Temple. Held in the library of the Tai'an Municipal Museum.
D. *Taishanglaojun shuo tianxian yunü Bixia Yuanjun hushi hongji miaojing*. Probably mid-nineteenth century. Held in the library of the Tai'an Municipal Museum.

29. Unfortunately none of the collections of myths state when the stories were written down. It is quite likely, however, that similar stories were told at least as early as the beginning of the twentieth century. Following is a list of versions of this origin myth about Bixia Yuanjun's gaining control of Mount Tai:

"The Legend of Bixia Yuanjun," in *Taishan chuanshuo*, 1–3.
"History of the Origin of Bixia Yuanjun," in *Taishan chuanshuo gushi*, 1–4.
"History of the Origin of Bixia Yuanjun," in Chen Qinghao and Wang Qiugui, *Shandong minjian gushi ji*, 11–15 (identical to the previous version).
"Bixia Yuanjun Takes Mount Tai," in Zhao Yufeng et al., *Tai'an minjian gushi jicui*, 9–11.
"Bixia Yuanjun Takes Mount Tai," in Tao Yang et al., *Taishan minjian gushi*, 164–66.
"History of the Origin of the Female Deity of Mount Tai, Bixia Yuanjun," in Tao Yang et al., *Taishan minjian gushi*, 10–14.
"Legend of the Old Mother of Mount Tai," *Zibo gushi zhuan*, 166–70.

Tik-Sang Liu ("Festival Site, Museum, and Tourist Attraction") recounts nearly identical stories about the southern goddess Mazu gaining control of sites near Hong Kong.

30. Apte, *Humor and Laughter*, 30–33.

31. Remensnyder, "Un problème de cultures ou de culture?"

32. Arthur Wolf, "Gods, Ghosts and Ancestors," 160.

33. Cited in Hui-chen Wang Liu, "An Analysis of Chinese Clan Rules," 72.

34. Mann, "The Male Bond in Chinese History," 1603.

35. *Mencius*, 4A: 26.

36. Eastman, *Family, Field, and Ancestors*, 15.

37. Furth, "The Patriarch's Legacy," 196, 190, 192.

38. Chavannes, *Le T'ai Chan*, 14–15, 107–8; the quotation is on 107.

39. Reproduced in ibid., 108.

40. Reproduced in ibid., 107.

41. Xizhousheng, *Xingshi yinyuan zhuan*, end of chap. 69; see also Dud-bridge, "Women Pilgrims to T'ai Shan," 60–62.

42. Mullikin, "Tai Shan," 715.

43. Bergen, "A Visit to T'ai Shan," 541.

44. DuBose, *The Dragon, Image and Demon*, 274.

45. Margery Wolf, *Women and the Family*, 32.

46. See ibid., esp. 32–41. Although Margery Wolf's formulation of the concept of the "uterine family" came from anthropological work in mid-twentieth-century Taiwan, it has been widely used by Chinese historians for earlier periods. For example, Alan Cole, in his 1998 book *Mothers and Sons in Chinese Buddhism*, asserts that he is "convinced that uterine family politics were present in seventh-century China in a form comparable to twentieth-century anxieties described in anthropological accounts" (130).

47. Margery Wolf, *Women and the Family*, 160.

48. Hsiung, "Constructed Emotions," 97–98.

49. Martin, "Gender and Ideological Differences in Representations of Life and Death," 174.

50. *Lingying Taishan Niangniang baojuan*. For more on this text, see Overmyer, *Precious Volumes*, 361–63.

51. *Baojuan, pin* 10: 160, 163, 164; *pin* 11: 172, 174, 180; *pin* 21: 319.

52. Ibid., *pin* 10: 159, 161–62; *pin* 12: 194–95.

53. Ibid., *pin* 20: 312; *pin* 21: 318.

54. Huang Liu-hung, *A Complete Book Concerning Happiness, j.* 31, p. 608.

55. *Miaojing*, 744.

56. Ibid.

57. Judd, "*Niangjia*: Chinese Women and Their Natal Families"; and Falk, "Of Bricks, Baskets and Steamed Buns."

58. Margery Wolf, "Beyond the Patrilineal Self," 263.

59. Hsiung, "Constructed Emotions."

60. Although the Queen Mother of the West is not discussed in detail, she is included in a list of goddesses at the beginning of a precious scroll about Bixia Yuanjun (*Baojuan, pin* 1: 11). The Myriad Transcendents Tower near the base of Mount Tai included statues of the Queen Mother as well as Bixia Yuanjun and her two main assistants (see Appendix, no. 13). In addition, two recent studies of Chinese popular religion list both Bixia Yuanjun and the Queen Mother among the deities usually found in goddess temples (*niangniang miao* 娘娘廟) (Wang Yude et al., *Zhonghua shenmi wenhua*, 331; and Ma Shutian, *Quanxiang zhongguo sanbai shen*, 39).

Nine goddesses: Goodrich print collection 1931, Columbia University, C. V. Starr East Asian Library: Goddess of Mount Tai, Goddess of Eyesight, Goddess of Descendants, Goddess Who Hastens Birth, Goddess of Conception, Goddess of Smallpox, Goddess of Guidance, Goddess of Healthy Upbringing, Goddess of Nursing.

Seven goddesses: images at the beginning of *Baojuan*: Goddess of Mount Tai, Goddess of Eyesight, Goddess of Descendants, Goddess Who Hastens Birth, Goddess of Smallpox, Goddess of Conception, Goddess Who Determines Time of Birth.

Five goddesses: statues in the Goddess Hall (Yuanjun dian 元君殿) in the White Cloud Temple (Baiyun guan 白雲觀) in Beijing: Goddess of Mount Tai, Goddess of Eyesight, Goddess of Conception, Goddess of Smallpox, Goddess Who Hastens Birth.

61. In Chinese cosmology the Big Dipper was associated with Mount Tai (Chavannes, *Le T'ai Chan*, 66; see Appendix, nos. 15, 42).

62. Zhongguo daojiao xiehui and Suzhou daojiao xiehui, *Daojiao da cidian*, 215, 218, 221.

63. Furth, "From Birth to Birth," 175.

64. Modern immunizations seem to have made the Goddess of Smallpox obsolete in contemporary China. There are no images of her in any temple on Mount Tai. There is a statue of her in the Goddess Hall in the White Cloud Temple in Beijing, but, at the times I visited, she did not seem to be receiving any special prayers.

65. According to Po Sung-nien and David Johnson, pantheon prints "were not displayed throughout the year, but were set up for one ceremony and burned at the end of it" (*Domesticated Deities*, 84). Listed below are references to a number of pantheon prints which contain Bixia Yuanjun.

A. Print with forty-nine deities, from the Qing period from Shandong. Bixia Yuanjun appears on the left side in the second of five rows and balances Guanyin on the right side (Po and Johnson, *Domesticated Deities*, no. 33).

B. Print with twenty-six deities, not dated, from Tianjin. Bixia Yuan-jun appears as the central deity in the third of four rows (Wang Shucun, *Zhongguo gudai minsu banhua*, no. 75).

C. Print with forty-four deities, not dated, from Shandong. Bixia Yuanjun appears on the left in the third of five rows (Shu Ding, *Minjian yishu*, no. 45).

D. Print with thirty-one deities, not dated, from Shandong. Bixia Yuanjun appears in the third of five rows. The third row consists of three goddesses: Guanyin in the center, Bixia Yuanjun on the right, and an unidentified goddess on the left (Shu Ding, *Minjian yishu*, no. 52).

E. Print with over a hundred deities, 1931, from Beijing or Tianjin. Bixia Yuanjun and four assistants appear in the fifth of seven rows. They are balanced on the left by the gods of the Five Sacred Peaks (see Fig. 16) (Anne Goodrich, *Peking Paper Gods*, 414).

F. Print with 154 deities, early twentieth century, probably Beijing or Tianjin. This print is very similar to the one in Goodrich's collection. It also has Bixia Yuanjun with four assistants and the gods of the Five Sacred Peaks in the fifth of seven rows (from the Alexeyev collection in the Hermitage in St. Petersburg, reproduced in Rudova, *Chinese Popular Prints*, no. 9).

66. See Po and Johnson, *Domesticated Deities*, 11–12; Lust, *Chinese Popular Prints*, 248.

67. Po and Johnson, *Domesticated Deities*, 18; Anne Goodrich, *Peking Paper Gods*, 23; Lowe, *The Adventures of Wu*, 2: 141.

68. See Po and Johnson, *Domesticated Deities*, 76, 80; and Anne Goodrich, *Peking Paper Gods*.

69. Anne Goodrich's collection contained Bixia Yuanjun and at least six of the assistant goddesses (see *Peking Paper Gods*, 107–25). In a semi-autobiographical account of life in Beijing in the 1910s through the 1930s, Lowe (*The Adventures of Wu*, 1: 18–19) describes a set of thirteen images burned as part of a ceremony held at a baby's ritual third-day bath. Nine of the thirteen images were of Bixia Yuanjun and eight of her assistants.

70. The doll in the ritual represents the desired child. The Chinese word *wawa* 娃娃 works well in this context because it can mean either baby or doll.

71. The most detailed explanation of the more complex ritual was explained to Sally Bormann and Kimberley Falk at a women's table at a wedding in a Shandong village. The conversation took place in January 1995 where Kimberley Falk was conducting her dissertation fieldwork. Kimberley Falk helped with translation of the local Shandong dialect.

72. This is the Beijing temple to the God of Mount Tai in his guise as a judge in purgatory. The Eastern Sacred Peak Temple was located just outside the eastern city wall, close to Chaoyang Gate (Chaoyang men 朝陽門). The large, popular temple also contained shrines to Bixia Yuanjun and her assistant goddesses.

73. Lowe, *The Adventures of Wu*, 1: 6.

74. Margery Wolf, "Beyond the Patrilineal Self," 264, 265.

75. "Dajie shuan wawa" 大姐拴娃娃 (Oldest sister ties a baby doll), in Wang Shucun, *Yangliuqing nianhua*, pl. 64.

76. See Lowe, *The Adventures of Wu*, 2: 141; and Lust, *Chinese Popular Prints*, 127.

77. See Anne Goodrich, *The Peking Temple of the Eastern Peak*, plates XII, XIII.

78. The date for a special temple festival in honor of Bixia Yuanjun's birthday, particularly in the Beijing area. This was the most efficacious day on which to visit the temple.

79. "Dajie shuan wawa."

80. Jin, *Taishan zhi*, 3.38b.

81. Maspero, *Taoism and Chinese Religion*, 166; Eberhard, *A Dictionary of Chinese Symbols*, 264. Pomeranz points out that unlike Guanyin and Mazu, Bixia Yuanjun is often portrayed as having bound feet and argues that Bixia Yuanjun's bound feet and her embroidered shoes "seem to call particular attention to . . . her femininity" ("Power, Gender, and Pluralism," 195).

82. Eberhard, *A Dictionary of Chinese Symbols*, 264.

83. Mathews, *Mathews' Chinese-English Dictionary*, nos. 2545 and 2005.

84. Rao, *Guangzhou yin zidian*, 243, 469.

85. Bynum, *Holy Feast and Holy Fast*, 191.

86. Wang Jun and Wang Feng, *Tai'an & Mt. Tai*, 66.

87. Ma Changyi and Liu Xicheng, *Shi yu shishen*, 87.

88. Of the thirty-eight pilgrimage society stelae on Mount Tai for which I have figures on the membership, seven list women as leaders (see Table 1). Some of the stelae do not label the leaders, and it is quite possible that other groups had women leaders as well. A stele from the Bixia Yuanjun Travel Palace in Boshan (75 kilometers east of Tai'an) erected in 1829 also lists women leaders: 1,985 members, 1,024 women. 51 leaders, 40 women ("Chongxiu fenghuang'a Bixia Yuanjun xinggong beiji").

89. Judd, "*Niang jia*: Chinese Women and Their Natal Families."

90. Ibid., 541.

91. Sangren, "Female Gender in Chinese Religious Symbols," 9.

92. Stenz, *Beiträge zur Volkskunde Süd-Schantungs*, 37.

93. Judd, "*Niangjia*: Chinese Women and Their Natal Families," 531.

94. This information comes from personal observations and conversations with pilgrims, as well as from communications with Kimberley Falk, who did anthropological fieldwork in rural Shandong.

95. I am indebted to Sally Bormann for drawing my attention to this modification of ritual practice.

96. Bynum, *Fragmentation and Redemption*, 33–36.

97. Judd, "*Niangjia*: Chinese Women and Their Natal Families," 531.

98. Doumu (斗母) or Doulao (斗姥) was a multiarmed female deity. She was the mother of the God of the Big Dipper (Beidou 北斗). Mount Tai was closely associated with this constellation. Doumu was associated with the elixir of longevity created by the rabbit in the moon. She "dispensed this medicine to the world, curing illnesses and ensuring safe births" (Little, *Taoism and the Arts of China*, 283).

99. The lower temple to Bixia Yuanjun was the Numinous Palace (no. 61).

100. This is a title for Bixia Yuanjun not found in any other source.

101. Liu Yihou, "Liufang gujin."

102. Turner and Turner, *Image and Pilgrimage*, 250.

103. For similar comparisons, see Pomeranz, "Power, Gender, and Pluralism."

104. Judd, "*Niangjia*: Chinese Women and Their Natal Families," 538–39.

105. Ko, *Teachers of the Inner Chambers*, 8.

Chapter 2

1. The trips by these two emperors to Mount Tai were more than just stops on the way to worship Confucius at nearby Qufu. Kangxi visited Mount Tai three times but stopped at Qufu on only one of those occasions, in 1684 (references for all three trips: *KXSL*, 1563–79, 1865–75, 2829–40). On that tour, the emperor stopped at Mount Tai on the outward or south-bound leg of the trip, and at Qufu on the return leg of the trip (*KXSL*, 1563–79). The Kangxi emperor made three other southern tours during his reign, in 1699, 1705, and 1707. On these trips he did not stop at either Mount Tai or Qufu (*KXSL*, 2576–94, 2938–58, 3048–68). On the Qianlong emperor's nine trips to Mount Tai, he stopped at Qufu six times, in 1748, 1762, 1771, 1776, 1784, 1790 (references for all nine trips: *QLSL*, 4484–507, 5722–93, 7698–789, 9552–619, 12564–79, 14792–809, 16148–

56, 17488–93, 20034–45). In 1765, the Qianlong emperor did not stop at either Mount Tai or Qufu during his southern tour (*QLSL*, 10424–505).

2. Although while still a prince, Yinzhen, the future Yongzheng emperor (r. 1723–35), a son of the Kangxi emperor and father of the Qianlong emperor, accompanied his father up Mount Tai during the Kangxi emperor's 1703 tour, he did not visit the mountain while he was emperor (Spence, *Ts'ao Yin and the K'ang-hsi Emperor*, 131–32). During his reign, the Yongzheng emperor did order significant repairs to temples on the mountain, but these actions do not add to our knowledge of the nature of Qing rulership.

3. China proper, or Inner China, is a term used to distinguish the core of the Qing empire from the outer regions. China proper was the territory of the Ming dynasty. It was populated predominantly by Han Chinese, and the vast majority of Han Chinese resided in this territory. Outer China, namely Manchuria, Mongolia, Xinjiang, Qinghai, and Tibet, was populated mostly by non-Han groups.

4. Rawski, "Presidential Address: Reenvisioning the Qing," 831.

5. Elliot, *The Manchu Way*, 3.

6. Chia, "The Lifanyuan and the Inner Asian Rituals," 87.

7. Rawski, *The Last Emperors*, 2, 10; Crossley, "*Manzhou yuanliu kao* and the Formalization of the Manchu Heritage," 780.

8. Farquhar, "Emperor as Bodhisattva in the Governance of the Ch'ing Empire."

9. Rawski, *The Last Emperors*, 10.

10. See Guy, *The Emperor's Four Treasuries*; Crossley, "*Manzhou yuanliu kao* and the Formalization of the Manchu Heritage"; and idem, *A Translucent Mirror*.

11. See Wechsler, *Offerings of Jade and Silk*, 176–83.

12. Ibid., 178, 191, 183.

13. Ibid., 177–78, 181, 182.

14. Cited in ibid., 178.

15. See ibid., 183–84, 187.

16. Cahill, "Taoism at the Sung Court," 35, 37.

17. See Ouyang, *Songshi*, j. 7, p. 135–38; also see Cahill, "Taoism at the Sung Court."

18. Cahill, "Taoism at the Sung Court."

19. Ibid., 29, 30.

20. See Chavannes, *Le T'ai Chan*, 266–302; and SDS, 432–35.

21. This prayer is reproduced and translated into French in Chavannes, *Le T'ai Chan*, 266–68.

22. Zha, *Dai shi, j.* 6, p. 73.

23. See L. Carrington Goodrich and Chaoying Fang, *Dictionary of Ming Biography*, 940.

24. Jin, *Taishan zhi*, 10.17a.

25. Zha, *Dai shi, j.* 9, p. 148; and Tang, *Dai lan*, 9.22b.

26. See *Hanyu dacidian*, 11: 1191. According to Moule ("T'ai Shan," 17), this pavilion was originally gilt.

27. The bronze pavilion and statue were subsequently moved to other temples on the mountain; see Appendix, no. 58.

28. Chavannes, *Le T'ai Chan*, 104.

29. For more on the association between this empress and the Nine Lotus Bodhisattva, see Chün-fang Yü, "P'u-t'o Shan," 238–39*n*; and Thomas Shiyu Li and Naquin, "The Baoming Temple," 160–62.

30. The source for the information about the statues of the two empresses is a short essay by Gu Yanwu reproduced in Jin, *Taishan zhi*, 10.28b–29a. The origins of the Bodhisattva of Wisdom are uncertain. It is possible that this name also comes from a sectarian scripture. The statues of these empresses were moved to the Numinous Palace in the mid-nineteenth century (see the Appendix, nos. 61, 73).

31. *Tianxian yunü Bixia Yuanjun zhenjing*. See also Zhou Shaoliang, "Mingdai huangdi, guifei, gongzhu yinshi de jiben fojing."

32. SDS, 193.

33. Hearn, "Document and Portrait," 92.

34. See Spence, *Ts'ao Yin and the K'ang-hsi Emperor*, 124–34.

35. Wechsler, *Offerings of Jade and Silk*, 161–62.

36. Spence, *Ts'ao Yin and the K'ang-hsi Emperor*, 125–26.

37. Ibid., 126.

38. Garrett, *Mandarin Squares*, 19–20.

39. Hearn, "Document and Portrait," 96–97.

40. Most of this chart is reproduced in Cao Wanru et al., *Zhongguo gudai ditu ji: Qingdai* (pl. 57). The Number One Historical Archives dates this map to the Qing dynasty, but not more precisely. It is cataloged under the title "Taishan ditu" 泰山地圖 within documents held by the Imperial Household Department (Neiwufu 內務府). There is a small seal in the lower left corner of the map. Unfortunately I have been able to see only photo-reproductions of the original, and they do not give enough detail to be able to read the seal. Nor has the Number One Archives transcribed the seal. However, it had to have been painted at least by 1761, because it is listed in an imperially commissioned catalog from that year (Cao Wanru et al., *Zhongguo gudai ditu ji: Qingdai*, notes on plates: 7, 36).

Since it is quite detailed, elements on the map itself provide some basis for its dating. Within the city walls are the Temple for Paying Homage from Afar (Fig. 5, no. 1) and the large Dai Temple (no. 2). Between these two temples is the Dai Temple Arch, which was erected in 1672. This then limits the dates for the map to between 1672 and 1761. The compound within the city walls just to the right of the large Dai Temple is labeled as the seat of the Tai'an departmental government (Tai'an zhou 泰安州). In 1735 Tai'an was upgraded from a department to a prefecture. Therefore, maps made after 1735 (including the one used for Fig. 5) label this compound the yamen of the Tai'an prefectural government (Tai'an fu 泰安府). This supports a date between 1672 and 1735.

Two characteristics about this map make it extremely likely that it was either offered to or commissioned by an emperor. First, it was stored in the archives of the Imperial Household Department. As Jonathan Spence notes, "The term 'Imperial Household,' the common translation of *nei-wu-fu*, is not really adequate; a nearer translation would be the 'Emperor's personal bureaucracy,' since this would show more clearly the scope of this large and complex organization" (*Ts'ao Yin and the K'ang-hsi Emperor*, 32). In addition, the labels used to name sites on the map are made of yellow paper—the imperial color. While adhering labels on separate pieces of paper to a map is not unique to imperial maps, to the best of my knowledge yellow labels are found only on maps commissioned by or presented to emperors (see, e.g., Harley and Woodward, *The History of Cartography*, color plates 6 and 7 for imperial maps with yellow labels, color plates 3 and 11 for nonimperial maps with red labels; see also Cao Wanru et al., *Zhongguo gudai ditu ji: Qingdai*, color plates 15, 26, 27, and 48 for imperial maps with yellow labels and color plates 102, 121, 122, 123, and 124 for nonimperial maps with red labels).

If we accept that this map was either presented to or commissioned by a Qing emperor, then it is extremely unlikely that it was produced after the Kangxi emperor's visit in 1684. While on the top of the mountain, the emperor issued an edict stating: "Having taken and moistened my brush, the completed calligraphy of the four characters 'Illumines all Heaven and Earth' can be placed on a plaque in a pavilion to be built at the Place Where Confucius Saw the World Was Small" (*KXQZ*, 2: 1239). This building, the Pavilion of Heaven and Earth, is not depicted on the Number One Archives map. It is extremely unlikely that an imperial map made after 1684 would not show a building commissioned by imperial decree and containing a plaque inscribed with the imperial hand. Therefore, a tentative date of 1684 for the Number One Archives map seems well founded.

41. See Yee, "Chinese Maps in Political Culture," 77.

42. Evidential learning, or *kaozhengxue* 考證學, at the most generalized level, combined searching out the earliest sources for a particular issue with a keen interest in philology. For a detailed study of evidential learning see Elman, *From Philosophy to Philology*.

43. The Changbai Mountains are sometimes translated as the Continuously White or Ever White Mountains. For the foundation myths, see Crossley, "An Introduction to the Qing Foundation Myth."

44. A proclamation from 1709 states that "Li Guangdi memorialized, saying 'The majority [of the mountains in Shandong] come from Shaanxi and Henan.' [To which] the emperor said 'No, instead, the mountains of Shandong come from the Changbai Mountains. . . . The veins of all the mountains in Shandong, [including] Mount Taidai (泰岱), all come from the Changbai Mountains'" (*KXSX*, 70). From this statement by the Kangxi emperor, it appears he had already written this essay on Mount Tai's mountain veins by 1709. The emperor had ordered a survey of the Changbai Mountains in 1677 (Rawski, *The Last Emperors*, 73). It seems likely that he used this survey when composing his essay and that he would have made timely use of these data in order to legitimate his newly consolidated empire. His triumphant first southern tour would have been a logical occasion for him to bolster the information from the survey with his own experience.

45. Wula 烏喇 is in the southern part of modern Guyuan 固遠 county, Inner Mongolia.

46. Qing-period name for Shenyang (also known as Mukden), the present capital of Liaoning province. Shengjing was the Manchu capital from 1625 until 1644. It remained an important imperial site throughout the Qing dynasty.

47. Ban Gu (32–92 CE) was the author of the *Book of the [Former] Han*.

48. *KXYW*, 4: 2373–74 (27.10a–12b). This essay was reproduced in most of the mountain gazetteers, usually under the title "Taishan longmai lun" 泰山龍脈論 (A discussion of Mount Tai's dragon veins). See, e.g., Jin, *Taishan zhi*, 1.1a–2a.

49. For a discussion of an increase in literati travels to remote mountains and rivers to discover their roots during the late Ming, see Pei-yi Wu, *The Confucian's Progress*, 98.

50. Wu Hung, "Beyond Stereotypes," 307.

51. Ibid., 358.

52. Wu Hung, "Emperor's Masquerade," 28.

53. Wakeman, *The Great Enterprise*, 15–16, 225.

54. Clunas, *Superfluous Things*, 169.

55. Zhaozhen Temple is an older name for the Bixia Temple on top of Mount Tai (no. 58). The Tianxian Hall is the main hall of this temple.

56. *KXQZ*, 2: 1238–39.

57. Fong, "Chinese Art and Cross-Cultural Understanding," 36.

58. Hearn, "Document and Portrait," 112.

59. Ibid.

60. Stuart, "Imperial Pastimes," 56.

61. Hearn, "Document and Portrait," 93–94; idem, pers. comm., June 2004.

62. Munakata, *Sacred Mountains in Chinese Art*, 63.

63. *KXQZ*, 3: 1826. Although this and other official sources do not name the exact site of the first set of rituals, they were conducted "at the base of Mount Tai," and, since the emperor subsequently entered the city "through the north gate," it is likely that they were conducted somewhere north of the city wall and south of where the steeper ascent begins (no. 8 in Fig. 5). If the temporary altar was set up before an arch, as it is in the painting, then the Daizong Arch (no. 3) is the most likely candidate for the site of these ceremonies.

64. Wang Hui, "Disanjuan," colophon.

65. Wu Hung, "Emperor's Masquerade," 28.

66. Fong, "The Imperial Cult," 104.

67. See Yee, "Chinese Maps in Political Culture."

68. See Wu Hung, "Beyond Stereotypes."

69. Trans. Chan, *Source Book*, 79, 81.

70. *KXQZ*, 2: 1239.

71. *KXQZ*, 2: 1238–39.

72. *KXQZ*, 2: 1239.

73. Ibid.

74. Fong, "Some Cultural Prototypes," 107.

75. Stuart, "Imperial Pastimes," 56.

76. *KXQZ*, 2: 1239.

77. Tschepe, *Der T'ai Schan*, 118; Baker, *T'ai Shan*, 139.

78. *KXQZ*, 2: 1240.

79. See Hearn, "Document and Portrait."

80. See Nie, *Taishan daoli ji*, 23. For further information about this site, see the Appendix, no. 57.

81. This is a well-known phrase from Chapter One of the *Classic of Filial Piety* (*Xiaojing* 孝經); see Makra and Sih, *Hsiao Ching*, 2–3.

82. Zengzi曾子 (505–ca. 436 BCE) was one of Confucius' disciples. He was well known for his filial piety and was traditionally believed to have been the author of the *Classic of Filial Piety*. Here the Kangxi emperor seems to be referring to the careful attention Zengzi paid to loyalty and respect, as recorded in the *Analects*: "Tseng-Tzu [Zengzi] said, 'Every day I examine myself on three points: whether in counseling others I have not been loyal; whether in intercourse with my friends I have not been faithful; and whether I have not repeated again and again and practiced the instructions of my teacher'" (trans. Chan, *Source Book*, 20).

83. *KXQZ*, 2: 1239.

84. Mair, "Language and Ideology in the Written Popularization of the *Sacred Edict*," 325.

85. Trans. from ibid., 325, 326.

86. That the passage from the *Classic of Filial Piety* was the obvious one to quote in this situation is seen in the fact that Kong Zhenxuan's (*Taishan jisheng*, 7a) 1673 travelogue entry for the Abandon Life Cliff also uses the same line to condemn the practice of suicide.

87. See Jin, *Taishan zhi*, 3.24b–28b; Chavannes, *Le T'ai Chan*, 392; and Jiang, *Taishan lidai shike xuanzhu*, 432–33.

Cao He was from Jiangsu and passed the *jinshi* exam in 1664. His first appointment was as a secretary of the Grand Secretariat (BH, no. 137; rank 7b). In 1679 he participated in the special examination conducted to recruit scholars to compile the Ming History (the *boxue hongru* 博學鴻儒 competition; see Hucker, *A Dictionary of Official Titles in Imperial China*, 388; and Struve, "The Hsü Brothers and Semiofficial Patronage of Scholars in the K'ang-hsi Period," 237, 244). Cao He became a second-class compiler in the Hanlin Academy (BH, no. 200B; rank 7a). In 1681 his rank remained the same, but he was appointed a diarist for the *Diary of Action and Repose* (BH, no. 204). The highest position he held was libationer of the Imperial Academy (BH no. 412A; rank 4b; Hucker, *A Dictionary of Official Titles in Imperial China*, translates this position as "chancellor of the Directorate of Education," no. 542). All biographical information on Cao He comes from *Qingshi leizhuan*, 104: 802–3 (71.9b–10a); and *Qing shi jishi chubian*, 20: 477 (j. 4, p. 455).

88. Wechsler, *Offerings of Jade and Silk*, 171.

89. *KXQZ*, 2: 1239.

90. Ibid., 1239–40.

91. *Yujian jinni* 玉劍金泥 is a phrase commonly used in Qing discussions of the *feng* and *shan* sacrifices. *Yujian* refers to the jade covers placed

around the jade tablets and *jinni* refers to the clay mixed with gold dust used to seal the boxes (see e.g. Wechsler, *Offerings of Jade and Silk*, 180).

92. *KXQZ*, 2: 1240.

93. *KXYW*, 1: 538 (39.12a–b).

94. "Chongxiu daimiao beiji" 重修岱廟碑記 (Repairing the Dai Temple inscription), reproduced in Jiang, *Taishan lidai shike xuanzhu*, 429–36. Also reproduced and translated into French in Chavannes, *Le T'ai Chan*, 387–97.

95. Reproduced in Jin, *Taishan zhi*, 2.7a.

96. Liu Wenzhong, "Annotations," 49.

97. "Nanxun biji" 南巡筆記 (Miscellaneous notes from the southern tour), in *KXYW*, 1: 317 (20.5b). Also in Jin, *Taishan zhi*, 1.2b.

98. KXYW, 1: 317 (20.6a). Also in Jin, *Taishan zhi*, 1.2b.

99. See Crossley, "*Manzhou yuanliu kao* and the Formalization of the Manchu Heritage"; and Guy, *The Emperor's Four Treasuries*.

100. Jin Qi's *Taishan zhi* contains the texts of eight poems by the Kangxi emperor, none of which were inscribed on the mountain. The second *juan* of this gazetteer contains 139 poems about Mount Tai by the Qianlong emperor, 43 of which were inscribed onto the mountain or on stelae placed on the mountain.

101. Wu Hung, "Emperor's Masquerade," 35.

102. See, e.g., Farquhar, "Emperor as Bodhisattva in the Governance of the Ch'ing Empire"; Wu Hung, "Emperor's Masquerade"; Yu Hui, "Naturalism in Qing Imperial Group Portraiture"; and Kahn, "A Matter of Taste."

103. *QLSL*, 1: 299 (7.25b–26a).

104. See Naquin, "The Peking Pilgrimage to Mount Miao-feng," 335; Pomeranz, "Power, Gender, and Pluralism," 182–86.

105. *Qinding daqing huidian shili*, 415.1a–b.

106. Ibid., 441.1a–b, 442.1a.

107. Ibid., 444.5b.

108. See, e.g., *QLQZ*, reel 36: QL13.2.29, reel 42: QL16.4.19, QL22.4.11 [not on microfilm], reel 72: QL45.1.27, reel 77: QL49.2.6; and *QLSL* 13: 9617, 17: 12566, 20: 14803.

109. Rawski, *The Last Emperors*, 257–58.

110. Chow, *The Rise of Confucian Ritualism in Late Imperial China*, 44.

111. Tai'anshi bowuguan, *Taishan jiqi*, 12. "The Eight Auspicious Symbols represent the offerings that are presented to Shakyamuni Buddha. They are the Wheel of Dharma, the White Conch Shell, the Precious Parasol, the Lotus Flower, the Banner of Victory, the Vase of Great

Treasures, the Two Golden Fish, and the Knot of Eternity" (Palace Museum, *Cultural Relics of Tibetan Buddhism*, 245).

112. See Palace Museum, *Cultural Relics of Tibetan Buddhism*, figs. 108-1, 109-1, 110, and 114.

113. See Tai'anshi bowuguan, *Taishan jiqi*. "The Seven Royal Treasures . . . consist of [the] golden wheel, divine pearls, jewels of women, able ministers of the Treasury, white elephants, dark swift horses, and loyal generals. The Seven Treasures can be traced to an Indian myth. According to the story, only Cakravarti (the ruler the wheel of whose chariot rolls everywhere without hindrance) possessed the Seven Treasures. Then, the Seven Royal Treasures were inherited by Buddhism and taken as offerings presented to Shakyamuni Buddha" (Palace Museum, *Cultural Relics of Tibetan Buddhism*, 245).

114. See Tai'anshi bowuguan, *Taishan jiqi*, 13, 27.

115. Ibid., 19.

116. SDS, 334.

117. Fong, "Chinese Art and Cross-cultural Understanding," 35.

118. See Clunas, *Superfluous Things*; Wai-yee Li, "The Collector, The Connoisseur, and Late-Ming Sensibility"; and Zeitlin, *Historian of the Strange*.

119. Zeitlin, *Historian of the Strange*, 73.

120. Ibid., 70.

121. Stuart, "Imperial Pastimes," 58, 59, 61.

122. Kohara, "The Qianlong Emperor's Skill in Connoisseurship of Chinese Paintings," 66.

123. Kahn, "A Matter of Taste," 291.

124. Kuo, *Word As Image*, 17.

125. Kahn, "A Matter of Taste," 295.

126. Stuart, "Imperial Pastimes," 61.

127. Kahn, *Monarchy in the Emperor's Eyes*, 136.

128. Kohara, "The Qianlong Emperor's Skill in Connoisseurship," 60, 72.

129. See Stuart, "Imperial Pastimes."

130. Zeitlin, *Historian of the Strange*, 70.

131. Kahn, "A Matter of Taste," 296.

132. Stuart, "Imperial Pastimes," 61.

133. This line contains a phrase found in a poem by Du Fu (see Ma Mingchu, *Taishan lidai shi xuan*, 119).

134. Ibid., 118. The phrase "to wait for things to come one's way" (*zhushou* 株守) derived from the writings of Han Feizi (see ibid., 119).

135. Wu Hung, "Emperor's Masquerade," 40.

136. "Gongsong huangzu le yai er dazi" 恭頌皇祖勒崖二大字, in Jin, *Taishan zhi*, 2.7a–b.

137. *KXQZ*, 2: 1240.

138. Nie, *Taishan daoli ji*, 23.

139. SDS, 187.

140. *QLSL*, 27: 20035.

Chapter 3

1. For a biography of Ye Fen, see Zhu, *Ming shi zong*, 846 (44.30a).

2. Yi 沂 is a name of a series of streams to the southeast of Mount Tai.

3. A grotto abode (*dong fu* 洞府) is a dwelling place of immortals and a site for reflective meditation leading to immortality, similar to the more common Daoist term "grotto-heavens" (*dong tian* 洞天) (see Hahn, "Daoist Sacred Sites," 695; and Li Shuhai, *Daojiao da cidian*, 412–13).

4. Auspicious site (*fu di* 福地) is another Daoist term for sacred sites where one can see the immortals and obtain immortality (see Hahn, "Daoist Sacred Sites," 695; and Li Shuhai, *Daojiao da cidian*, 494).

5. Shilü 石閭 was the site of Han Wudi's 102 BCE performance of the *shan* ceremony. According to Sima Qian, the emperor chose this site because his *fangshi* advisors informed him that Shilü was "the gateway to the village of the immortals" (Sima, *Shi ji, j.* 28, p. 1403; trans. Burton Watson, *Records of the Grand Historian*, 2: 50).

6. The exact meaning of this line is ambiguous. Given its context in the poem, it should be a positive reference to a historical event. According to Sima Qian, King Cheng of the Zhou dynasty performed the *feng* sacrifices at a Mingtang 明堂 altar at the base of Mount Tai to honor his ancestors who had overthrown the Shang dynasty (Sima, *Shi ji, j.* 28, pp. 1357, 1361, 1364; Jin, *Taishan zhi*, 7.18b–20a; Baker, *T'ai Shan*, 143).

7. This is a reference to the seventy-two venerable rulers, who, according to a passage recorded by Sima Qian, had performed the *feng* and *shan* sacrifices in antiquity (*Shi ji, j.* 28, p. 1361). Ye probably rounded the number to seventy in order to maintain the five-character line.

8. This line refers to Tang Xuanzong's inscription on top of the mountain commemorating his performance of the *feng* and *shan* sacrifices in 726 (see Appendix, no. 45).

9. Ying is short for Yingzhou 瀛洲, island-residence of immortals. According to Qin Shihuangdi's *fangshi* advisors, it, along with Penglai and Fangzhang 方丈, was located in the Gulf of Bohai (Sima, *Shiji, j.* 28, p. 1369).

10. The phrase also has a possible secondary meaning. *Fengyue* can mean "soothing wind and bright moon" or, by extension, "amorous relations between a man and woman" (*Hanyu dacidian*, 12: 594). With this meaning, the full four-character phrase would mean "an amorous affair without limits." I found only one source that supports this interpretation of the phrase. Chang Yinuo (*Taishan wuqian nian*, 32) claims that Liu was making a scathing comment about the nuns in the Mother of the Big Dipper Temple. This pun is inscribed on a rock near this temple. In 1906 the resident nuns were expelled, apparently for running a brothel (see Appendix, no. 15). The author may have intended a double entendre, but the predominant interpretation is that he was praising the natural scenery. Indeed, one source claims that the author took the phrase from the name of a famous nature-viewing pavilion in Hangzhou (see *Mount Taishan*, 37). For the full four-character phrase, the *Hanyu dacidian* (12: 594) notes only its usage as a superlative for natural scenery.

11. While the doubling of the population is accepted, there are debates about the exact numbers. The traditional figures, derived from official Ming and Qing sources, place the population of Inner China at 65 million in 1400 and at 150 million in 1600 (see, e.g., Ho, *Studies on the Population of China*, 277). The highest figures, proposed by Martin Heijdra and accepted by F.W. Mote, are 85 million in 1393 and 231 million in 1600 (cited in Mote, *Imperial China 900-1800*, 745).

12. Strassberg, *Inscribed Landscapes*, 56.

13. See Brook, *Geographical Sources*; Strassberg, *Inscribed Landscapes*; Pei-yi Wu, *The Confucian's Progress*; and idem, "An Ambivalent Pilgrim."

14. Brook, *Geographical Sources*, 15.

15. Ibid., 19.

16. Ibid., 5.

17. For a detailed study of evidential learning, see Elman, *From Philosophy to Philology*.

18. Brook, *Geographical Sources*, 52.

19. The biographical information on these three authors comes from Ma Mingchu, *Taishan lidai wenshi cuibian*, 232, 238, 242; and Lü Yunfang, *Taishan lidai zhushu tiyao*, 33, 40.

20. In Jin, *Taishan zhi*, *xu*.1a–4a.

21. In Ma Mingchu, *Taishan lidai wenshi cuibian*, 237–40.

22. For more on these two travelers, see Pei-yi Wu, "An Ambivalent Pilgrim."

23. For example, a conference entitled "After Secularism/Religion: Interpretation, History, and Politics" was held at the University of Minnesota in May 2000.

24. Strassberg, *Inscribed Landscapes*, 20.

25. Victor Turner, *Dramas, Fields, and Metaphors*, 197.

26. Morinis, "Introduction," 4.

27. Strassberg, *Inscribed Landscapes*, 21–22.

28. Brook, *Geographical Sources*, 55, 58.

29. Pei-yi Wu, *The Confucian's Progress*, 96–97.

30. Tang, *Dai lan*, 10.8a.

31. Jin, "Taishan zhong baishu ji."

32. Ibid.

33. Jin, *Taishan zhi*, 4.14b–19b.

34. Wu Shikai, "Chongxiu Yaocanting bei," 148.

35. SDS, 293.

36. Yao Nai, "Deng Taishan ji," 123.

37. Waltner, "T'an-Yang-tzu and Wang Shih-chen," 105.

38. Wang Shizhen, "You Taishan ji," 287–88; trans. Pei-yi Wu, "An Ambivalent Pilgrim," 70.

39. Kong, *Taishan jisheng*, foreword.1a.

40. Pei-yi Wu, *The Confucian's Progress*, 106–7.

41. Wu Hung, "Tiananmen Square," 86.

42. Yu Shu, "Sheng xian fang," 6.17b.

43. Lai belonged to the Mongol Yellow Banner. He received his *jinshi* degree during the Daoguang period (1821–50). He assumed the post of prefect in 1857 (Ma Mingchu, *Taishan lidai wenshi cuibian*, 148n).

44. Lai, "Chongxiu yaocanting beiji."

45. A prefect who assumed the post in 1760 (Ma Mingchu, *Taishan lidai wenshi cuibian*, 148n).

46. Wu Shikai, "Chongxiu Yaocanting bei," 147.

47. Makra and Sih, *Hsiao ching*, 2–3.

48. Nie, *Taishan daoli ji*, 20.

49. See Liu Wenzhong, "Annotations," 63; and SDS, 186.

50. Ironically, Lin's name, like the text he effaced, has not been clearly preserved. Xiao Xiezhong (*Taishan xiaoshi*, 61) gives the name Lin Tun 林焞. Zhang Dai ("Dai zhi," 42), however, gives the name as Lin Fu 林焞. The discrepancy is almost certainly due to an editorial or typesetting error.

51. Zhang Dai, "Dai zhi," 42.

52. Ibid., 38; trans. Pei-yi Wu, "An Ambivalent Pilgrim," 77–78.

53. Zhang Dai, "Dai zhi," 42.

54. Jin, "Taishan zhong baishu ji."

55. Huang Liu-hung, *A Complete Book Concerning Happiness*, j. 3, p. 129.

56. Wu Shikai, "Chongxiu Yaocanting bei," 147.

57. *Analects*, 13: 3; trans. Wing-tsit Chan, *Source Book*, 40.

58. Nie, *Taishan daoli ji*, 12; Jin, *Taishan zhi*, 6.13a.

59. Xiao, *Taishan xiaoshi*, 25; see also Nie, *Taishan daoli ji*, 13.

60. Reproduced in Liu Xiuchi, *Taishan daquan*, 1002–3.

61. Nie, *Taishan daoli ji*, 13.

62. Eberhard, *A Dictionary of Chinese Symbols*, 237.

63. Li Huan, *Guochao qixian lei zheng chubian*, 159: 713 (219.29a).

64. Kong, *Taishan jisheng*, foreword.1a; for the Queen Mother Pool, see 9b, and for the Dai Temple, 14a.

65. Nie, *Taishan daoli ji*, 10.

66. See, e.g., SDS, 153. None of the sources identify whether this destruction was perpetrated by a person or by nature.

67. *Sheng jing* usually referred to the works of Confucius.

68. Li Bangzhen, "Jing zheng." The passage is from *Mencius* 7B: 37.

69. In translating Buddhist texts into Chinese, Buddhists borrowed *jing* 經 to translate the Sanskrit term *sūtra*.

70. Zha, *Dai shi*, j. 10, p. 166. Yan was Confucius' favorite disciple, Yan Yuan 顏淵. According to legend, he ascended Mount Tai with Confucius. Zengzi 曾子 was another of Confucius' disciples; authorship of the *Classic of Filial Piety* is traditionally ascribed to him. Si refers to Zi Si 子思, Confucius' grandson.

71. Zha, *Dai shi*, j. 10, p. 168. Zha, an inspector in the Salt Administration, was given special orders to write an updated gazetteer about Mount Tai and to investigate conditions on the mountain (see Zha, *Dai shi*, 1).

72. Chu, "The Appropriation and Contestation of Sacrificial Ritual," 6–9.

73. Zha, *Dai shi*, j. 10, p. 169.

74. "Green range" refers to Mount Tai.

75. "Taiping Summit" was another name for the highest point on Mount Tai.

76. Reproduced in Ma Mingchu, *Taishan lidai shi xuan*, 105.

77. See Tang, *Dai lan*, 12.20b–21a; and Baker, *T'ai Shan*, 19.

78. *KXQZ*, 2: 1238–39.

79. Zhang Pengge (1649–1725) had ample reasons for praising the Kangxi emperor. Zhang obtained the *jinshi* degree in 1670 during the Kangxi emperor's reign. In 1703 the emperor praised Zhang in a poem.

Also in 1703 Zhang was granted the honorary title of Grand Guardian of the Heir Apparent (Hummel, *Eminent Chinese of the Ch'ing Period*, 49–50).

80. Victor Turner, *Dramas, Fields, and Metaphors*, 197.

81. Kong, *Taishan jisheng*, foreword.1a.

82. Anderson, *Imagined Communities*.

83. For an important study of how early Qing literati used monuments and place to construct identity and maintain a transregional elite, see Meyer-Fong, *Building Culture in Early Qing Yangzhou*.

Conclusion

1. Sewell, "The Concept(s) of Culture," 55–56.

2. Ibid., 56–57.

3. I examine this topic in "Signifying Mount Tai."

4. Duara, *Culture, Power, and the State*, 148.

5. Dransman, *T'aishan-Küfow Guide*, 222, pl. 10.

6. Mullikin, "Tai Shan," 712.

7. Ibid., 705.

8. See Appendix, nos. 14, 19, 55, 76–82.

9. *Taishan zhi tu shei gan dong*.

10. Wagner, "Reading the Chairman Mao Memorial Hall," 408.

11. Dong Ruicheng, *Zhong hua zhi hun, wuyue duzun: Taishan*, 4.

12. Taishan fengjing mingsheng guanli weiyuanhui, *Zhongguo Taishan*, 4.

13. Li Peng, inscription on top of Mount Tai; also reproduced in Taishan fengjing mingsheng guanli weiyuanhui, *Zhongguo Taishan* [vii].

Appendix

1. Chavannes began his numbering system at the top of the mountain, whereas this appendix begins at the bottom, following the route of the pilgrims.

2. See Nie, *Taishan daoli ji*, 2; Jin, *Taishan zhi*, 13.2a; and Tan, *Zhongguo lishi ditu ji*, 1: 39–40, 2: 19–20, 44–45, 4: 48–49. The towns and cities mentioned in this section are labeled in Fig. 22. With the exception of "county" instead of "district" for *xian* 縣, the English translations of the administrative regions follow Hucker, *A Dictionary of Official Titles in Imperial China*.

3. See Tang, *Dai lan*, 1.11b; and Jin, *Taishan zhi*, 13.2b.

4. Nie, *Taishan daoli ji*, 3; Jin, *Taishan zhi*, 13.2b; Tang, *Dai lan*, 1.11b; Chavannes, *Le T'ai Chan*, 257. Both Jin Qi and Tang Zhongmian state

that the new city was thirty *li* (15 kilometers) southeast of the old city. This, however, would place it where Bocheng was located. Geil (*The Sacred Five of China*, 16) translates a long passage from an unidentified source that gives the distance as only three *li*. Moule ("T'ai Shan," 19) also gives the distance as three *li*. This seems much more likely and also corresponds with the map in Huang Qian's 1782 *Tai'an xianzhi* (see Fig. 22).

5. Geil, *The Sacred Five of China*, 16.

6. Lai, "Chongxiu Yaocanting beiji."

7. Li Jisheng, *Gulao de Taishan*, 24; and SDS, 143.

8. Mi, "Taishan shenci," 6–15.

9. Chavannes, *Le T'ai Chan*, 135; Baker, *T'ai Shan*, 157.

10. SDS, 295.

11. Tang, *Dai lan*, 12.2a; Chavannes, *Le T'ai Chan*, 88.

12. My source for the provenance of this statue is a personal conversation with Jiang Fengrong in April 1995. At that time Jiang was director of the Religion Department of the Mount Tai Scenic and Historic Site Administration Committee of the City of Tai'an.

13. Chavannes, *Le T'ai Chan*, 87; Liu Xiuchi, *Taishan daquan*, 665.

14. Kong, *Taishan jisheng*, 9a.

15. Nie, *Taishan daoli ji*, 9; SDS, 295.

16. Nie, *Taishan daoli ji*, 9; SDS, 295; Liu Maolin, *Shandong mingsheng yinglian*, 258; *Mencius* 7A.24.

17. Nie, *Taishan daoli ji*, 9; Xiao, *Taishan xiaoshi*, 6.

18. Chavannes, *Le T'ai Chan*, 85 and fig. 28; Liu Wenzhong, "Annotations," 121; personal conversation with Jiang Fengrong in April 1995.

19. Nie, *Taishan daoli ji*, 9; SDS, 149–50.

20. Jin, *Taishan zhi*, 10.14a; Chavannes, *Le T'ai Chan*, 84.

21. Yan, *Taishan fengjing mingsheng daoyou*, 27.

22. Liu Wenzhong, "Annotations," 10–11; Chavannes, *Le T'ai Chan*, 83; SDS, 83.

23. Chavannes, *Le T'ai Chan*, fig. 28; Liu Wenzhong, "Annotations," 121; personal conversation with Jiang Fengrong in April 1995. The new *Mount Tai Gazetteer* misidentifies this statue as the Bodhisattva Dizang (SDS, 152).

24. Chavannes, *Le T'ai Chan*, 84; SDS, 152; Baker, *T'ai Shan*, 48; Chang, *Taishan wuqian nian*, 32.

25. Liu Wenzhong, "Annotations," 14; SDS, 309.

26. Nie, *Taishan daoli ji*, 10; SDS, 153. None of the sources identify whether the destruction of this inscription was perpetrated by a person or by nature.

27. Li Bangzhen, "Jing zheng."

28. SDS, 293.

29. Yan, *Taishan fengjing mingsheng daoyou*, 31.

30. Ibid., 32.

31. Chavannes, *Le T'ai Chan*, 80; Nie, *Taishan daoli ji*, 11; Liu Wenzhong, "Annotations," 19.

32. SDS, 364.

33. Baker, *T'ai Shan*, 64; Xiao, *Taishan xiaoshi*, 25.

34. Chavannes, *Le T'ai Chan*, 76–77; Nie, *Taishan daoli ji*, 13.

35. Liu Wenzhong, "Annotations," 23.

36. Baker, *T'ai Shan*, 68.

37. Xiao, *Taishan xiaoshi*, 28.

38. Ibid., 25.

39. SDS, 334.

40. Nie, *Taishan daoli ji*, 13.

41. Ma Dibo, "Fengshan yiji," 3167; SDS, 160.

42. SDS, 160.

43. Tang, *Dai lan*, 11.3b.

44. SDS, 180.

45. SDS, 181, 293; Nie, *Taishan daoli ji*, 15.

46. Cited in Baker, *T'ai Shan*, 75.

47. Ma Dibo, "Fengshan yiji," 3168; Wang Chong, *Lun heng, j. 4,* 書虛篇: 56.

48. Tang, *Dai lan*, 10.8a.

49. Zha, *Dai shi, j.* 10, p. 166.

50. Liu Wenzhong, "Annotations," 53.

51. Nie, *Taishan daoli ji*, 21; Chavannes, *Le T'ai Chan*, 64.

52. Chavannes, *Le T'ai Chan*, 66; Liu Wenzhong, "Annotations," 61.

53. Chavannes, *Le T'ai Chan*, 59; and Nie, *Taishan daoli ji*, 22.

54. Liu Xiuchi, *Taishan daquan*, 669.

55. Baker, *T'ai Shan*, 103.

56. Ibid., 102.

57. Chavannes, *Le T'ai Chan*, 72.

58. SDS, 186.

59. SDS, 185; Jiang, *Taishan lidai shike xuanzhu*, 78. For a reproduction and translation into French of the text of this inscription, see Chavannes, *Le T'ai Chan*, 315–28. For more on this inscription, see Harrist, "Record of the Eulogy on Mt. Tai."

60. Nie, *Taishan daoli ji*, 20. For a reproduction and translation into French of the text of this inscription, see Chavannes, *Le T'ai Chan*, 329–43.

61. Baker, *T'ai Shan*, 107; Chavannes, *Le T'ai Chan*, 69–70, 120–21; *QLQZ*, reel 36: QL13.2.29.

62. Nie, *Taishan daoli ji*, 21.

63. Jiang, "Taishan wuzibei kaobian." I am indebted to Professor Cho-yun Hsu for the interpretation of the Wordless Stele as a prehistoric megalith.

64. Chavannes, *Le T'ai Chan*, 48–49.

65. Liu Wenzhong, "Annotations," 49; Jin, *Taishan zhi*, 2.7a.

66. Nie, *Taishan daoli ji*, 23.

67. Ibid.; Chavannes, *Le T'ai Chan*, 60; SDS, 187.

68. Nie, *Taishan daoli ji*, 23; Chavannes, *Le T'ai Chan*, 63; Baker, *T'ai Shan*, 144–45.

69. Wang Zhigang, "Yunü zhuan," 154; Tang, *Dai lan*, 9.22b–23a; Jin, *Taishan zhi*, 10.15b; Chavannes, *Le T'ai Chan*, 70–71; Zha, *Dai shi, j. 9*, pp. 147–51; Nie, *Taishan daoli ji*, 16.

70. Ma Mingchu and Yan Dengfei, "Annotations," 148.

71. See *Hanyu dacidian*, 11: 1191. According to Moule ("T'ai Shan," 17), this pavilion was originally gilded.

72. Nie, *Taishan daoli ji*, 43.

73. Chavannes, *Le T'ai Chan*, 66, 69.

74. Wang Zhigang, "Yunü zhuan," 153.

75. SDS, 193; personal correspondence with Jiang Fengrong from December 1995. Geil (*The Sacred Five of China*, 104) reproduces four drawings related to the Jade Woman's life before her apotheosis; one shows a monkey or gibbon offering a peach of immortality to the Jade Woman, who is sitting in the entrance to a cave. Unfortunately Geil gives no clue as to the origins of these drawings.

76. SDS, 193.

77. Chavannes, *Le T'ai Chan*, 103; SDS, 147–48.

78. See Na, "Tang Song yuce zhuanji."

79. Chavannes, *Le T'ai Chan*, 398–99.

80. Yanluo or Yan wang 閻王 is the Chinese name for the Vedic deity who ruled the land of the dead, Yama rāja. Yanluo eventually became the judge in the fifth court of the Chinese purgatory (Teiser, "*The Scripture on the Ten Kings*," 2). The Bodhisattva Dizang (Sanskrit Kṣitigarbha, Japanese Jizō) vowed to rescue all beings suffering in the underworld and is found in proximity to the Ten Kings.

81. Nie, *Taishan daoli ji*, 44; Chavannes, *Le T'ai Chan*, 13–15, 107–8; Liu Wenzhong, "Annotations," 125.

82. Tang, *Dai lan*, 12.20b–21a; Baker, *T'ai Shan*, 19; Chavannes, *Le T'ai Chan*, 91; Hubbard, "The Pilgrims of Taishan," 323; Franck, *Wandering in Northern China*, 278–79.

83. Baker, *T'ai Shan*, 17.

84. Jin, *Taishan zhi*, 10.13b; Tschepe, *Der T'ai Schan*, 55.

85. Tschepe, *Der T'ai Schan*, 55.

86. Chavannes, *Le T'ai Chan*, 99.

87. Jiang, *Taishan lidai shike xuanzhu*, 130.

88. Ibid., 119. For a reproduction and translation into French of this text, see Chavannes, *Le T'ai Chan*, 329–43.

89. Baker, *T'ai Shan*, 17.

90. Moule, "T'ai Shan," 18; Cahill, "Taoism at the Song Court," 28; Nie, *Taishan daoli ji*, 32; Jin, *Taishan zhi*, 10.28b–29a; Ma Mingchu and Yan Dengfei, "Annotations," 156.

91. SDS, 282.

92. Chavannes, *Le T'ai Chan*, 121; Yan, *Taishan fengjing mingsheng daoyou*, 77–80.

93. Sheridan, *Chinese Warlord*, 44–48; Yan, *Taishan fengjing mingsheng daoyou*, 80–81.

94. Yan, *Taishan fengjing mingsheng daoyou*, 76.

95. Ibid.

96. Ibid., 75.

97. The information about Qiu Huanwen comes from the marker at his grave.

Works Cited

Analects. Trans. D. C. Lau. Middlesex, Eng.: Penguin Books, 1979.

Anderson, Benedict R. *Imagined Communities: Reflections on the Origin and Spread of Nationalism.* London: Verso, 1983.

Apte, Mahadev L. *Humor and Laughter: An Anthropological Approach.* Ithaca: Cornell University Press, 1985.

Ayscough, F. "Shrines of History: Peak of the East—T'ai Shan!" *Journal of the North China Branch of the Royal Asiatic Society* 48 (1917): 57–70.

Baker, Dwight C. *T'ai Shan: An Account of the Sacred Eastern Peak of China.* Shanghai: Commercial Press, 1925.

Ban Gu 班固. *Han shu* 漢書 (Book of the [Former] Han). Reprinted in 8 vols. Beijing: Zhonghua shuju, 1962.

Baojuan, see *Lingying Taishan Niangniang baojuan.*

Bergen, Paul D. "A Visit to T'ai Shan." *Chinese Recorder and Missionary Journal* 19, no. 12 (1888): 541–46.

Bernbaum, Edwin. *Sacred Mountains of the World.* 2nd ed. Berkeley: University of California Press, 1997.

Biernacki, Richard. "Method and Metaphor After the New Cultural History." In *Beyond the Cultural Turn: New Directions in the Study of Society and Culture,* ed. Victoria E. Bonnell and Lynn Hunt, 62–92. Berkeley: University of California Press, 1999.

Bixia Yuanjun huguo bimin puji baosheng miaojing 碧霞元君護國庇民普濟保生妙經 (Wondrous scripture of Bixia Yuanjun, who protects the nation, shelters the people, saves all and preserves life). In *Xu Daozang* 續道藏 (Supplement to the Taoist Canon), 34: 744–46. Ca.

1607. Reprinted—Beijing: Wenwu chubanshe, 1988. (HY no. 1433; Schipper no. 1445.) Cited as *Miaojing*.

Bokencamp, Stephen. "Record of the Feng and Shan Sacrifices." In *Religions of China in Practice*, ed. Donald S. Lopez, Jr., 251–60. Princeton Readings in Religions. Princeton: Princeton University Press, 1996.

Bonnell, Victoria E., and Lynn Hunt. "Introduction." In *Beyond the Cultural Turn: New Directions in the Study of Society and Culture*, ed. Victoria E. Bonnell and Lynn Hunt, 1–32. Berkeley: University of California Press, 1999.

Bonnell, Victoria E., and Lynn Hunt, eds. *Beyond the Cultural Turn: New Directions in the Study of Society and Culture*. Studies on the History of Society and Culture, no. 34. Berkeley: University of California Press, 1999.

Book of Changes, see *Zhou yi*.

Book of History, see *Shang shu*.

Book of Odes, see *Mao shi*.

Book of Rites, see *Li ji*.

Bredon, Juliet, and Igor Mitrophanow. *The Moon Year: A Record of Chinese Customs and Festivals*. Shanghai: Kelly & Walsh, 1927.

Brook, Timothy. *Geographical Sources of Ming-Qing History*. Michigan Monographs in Chinese Studies, no. 58. Ann Arbor: University of Michigan, Center for Chinese Studies, 1988.

Brunnert, H. S., and V. V. Hagelstrom. *Present Day Political Organization of China*. Trans. A. Beltchenko and E. E. Moran. Reprinted—Taibei: Ch'eng Wen Publishing, 1978.

Bujard, Marianne. *Le sacrifice au Ciel dans la Chine ancienne: théorie et pratique sous les Hans occidentaux*. Ecole française d'Extrême-Orient monographies, no. 187. Paris: Ecole française d'Extrême-Orient, 2000.

Bynum, Caroline Walker. *Fragmentation and Redemption: Essays on Gender and the Human Body*. New York: Zone, 1991.

———. *Holy Feast and Holy Fast: The Religious Significance of Food to Medieval Women*. The New Historicism: Studies in Cultural Poetics, no. 1. Berkeley: University of California Press, 1987.

Cahill, Suzanne E. "Performers and Female Taoist Adepts: Hsi Wang Mu as the Patron Deity of Women in Medieval China." *Journal of the American Oriental Society* 106, no. 1 (1986): 155–68.

———. "Taoism at the Sung Court: The Heavenly Text Affair of 1008." *Bulletin of Sung-Yüan Studies* 16 (1980): 23–44.

———. *Transcendence and Divine Passion: The Queen Mother of the West in Medieval China*. Stanford: Stanford University Press, 1993.

Cao Wanru 曹婉如 et al., eds. *Zhongguo gudai ditu ji: Qingdai* 中国古代地图集: 清代 (An atlas of ancient maps in China: Qing dynasty). Beijing: Wenwu chubanshe, 1997.

Cao Xueqin. *The Story of the Stone [Dream of the Red Chamber]*. Trans. David Hawkes and John Minford. 5 vols. Middlesex, Eng.: Penguin Books, 1973–86.

Chan, Wing-tsit. *A Source Book in Chinese Philosophy*. Princeton: Princeton University Press, 1963.

Chang Yinuo 常一诺. *Taishan wuqian nian* 泰山五千年 (*A Picture Album of Five Thousand Years of Mt. Taishan*). Bilingual Chinese-English ed. Ji'nan: Shandong wenyi chubanshe, 1989.

Chavannes, Edouard. *Le T'ai Chan: Essai de monographie d'un culte chinois*. Annales du Musée Guimet. Paris: Ernest Leroux, 1910.

Chavannes, Edouard, trans. and annot. *Les mémoires historiques de Se-ma Ts'ien*. 6 vol. Paris: Ernest Leroux, 1895–1905. Reprinted—Paris: Adrien-Maisonneuve, 1967.

Che Yanglun 车锡伦. "Taishan nüshen de shenhua xinyang yu zongjiao" 泰山女神的神话信仰与宗教 (Religious myths and beliefs about the female deities of Mount Tai). In *Taishan yanjiu luncong: san* 泰山研究论丛:三 (Third collection of essays on the study of Mount Tai), ed. Li Zhengming 李正明 and Zhang Jie 张杰, 15–32. Qingdao: Qingdao haiyang daxue chubanshe, 1991.

Ch'en P'an 陳槃. "Taishan zhu si yi zhu sheng shuo" 泰山主死亦主生説 (Taishan controls not only death but also life). *Zhongyang yanjiuyuan, Lishi yuyan yanjiusuo jikan* 51, no. 3 (1980): 407–12.

Chen Qinghao 陳慶浩 and Wang Qiugui 王秋桂, eds. *Shandong minjian gushi ji* 山東民間故事集 (Collection of Shandong folktales). Zhongguo minjian gushi quanji (Complete collection of Chinese folktales), no. 26. Taibei: Yuanliu, 1989.

Chia, Ning. "The Lifanyuan and the Inner Asian Rituals in the Early Qing (1644–1795)." *Late Imperial China* 14, no. 1 (June 1993): 60–92.

"China Historical GIS, Version: 2.0." Cambridge, Mass: Harvard Yenching Institute, Oct. 2003.

"Chongxiu fenghuang'a Bixia Yuanjun xinggong beiji" 重修鳳凰阿碧霞元君行宮碑記 (Record of repairing the Phoenix Pillar Bixia Yuanjun Travel Palace). Inscription in the Bixia Temple in Boshan 博山, Shandong, 1829.

Chow, Kai-wing. *The Rise of Confucian Ritualism in Late Imperial China: Ethics, Classics, and Lineage Discourse*. Stanford: Stanford University Press, 1994.

Chu, Ron Guey. "The Appropriation and Contestation of Sacrificial Ritual of the Confucian Temple in Ming China." Paper presented at the Conference on State and Ritual in East Asia, Paris, 1995.

Chuang-tzu: Basic Writings. Trans. Burton Watson. Columbia College Program of Translations from the Oriental Classics. New York: Columbia University Press, 1964.

Clunas, Craig. *Superfluous Things: Material Culture and Social Status in Early Modern China.* Urbana: University of Illinois Press, 1991.

Cole, Alan. *Mothers and Sons in Chinese Buddhism.* Stanford: Stanford University Press, 1998.

Coleman, Simon, and John Elsner. *Pilgrimage: Past and Present in the World Religions.* Cambridge, Mass.: Harvard University Press, 1995.

Crossley, Pamela Kyle. "An Introduction to the Qing Foundation Myth." *Late Imperial China* 6, no. 2 (Dec. 1985): 13–24.

——. "*Manzhou yuanliu kao* and the Formalization of the Manchu Heritage." *Journal of Asian Studies* 46, no. 4 (Nov. 1987): 761–89.

——. *A Translucent Mirror: History and Identity in Qing Imperial Ideology.* Berkeley: University of California Press, 1999.

Cui Xiuguo 催秀国 and Ji Aiqin 吉爱琴. *Tai Dai shiji* 泰岱史迹 (Historical traces of Tai Dai [Mount Tai]). Ji'nan: Shandong youyi shushe, 1987.

"Dajie shuan wawa" 大姐拴娃娃 (Oldest sister ties a baby doll). In *Yangliuqing nianhua ziliaoji* 楊柳青年画資料集 (A collection of Yangliuqing New Year's prints), ed. Wang Shucun 王術村, pl. 64. Beijing: Renmin meishu, 1959.

Davis, Edward L. *Society and the Supernatural in Song China.* Honolulu: University of Hawai'i Press, 2001.

Davis, Natalie Zemon. "From 'Popular Religion' to Religious Cultures." In *Reformation Europe: A Guide to Research*, ed. Steven Ozment, 321–41. St. Louis: Center for Reformation Research, 1982.

de Bary, Wm. Theodore, Wing-tsit Chan, and Burton Watson, eds. *Sources of Chinese Tradition.* 2 vols. Introduction to Oriental Civilizations. New York: Columbia University Press, 1960.

Despeux, Catherine. "Talismans and Diagrams." In *Daoism Handbook*, ed. Livia Kohn, 498–540. Leiden: Brill, 2000.

Ding Shiliang 丁世良, Zhao Fang 赵放, et al., eds. *Zhongguo difangzhi minsu ziliao huibian: huadong juan* 中国地方志民俗资料汇编:华东卷 (Collected data on folk practices from Chinese local gazetteers: eastern China). 3 vols. Beijing: Shumu wenxian chubanshe, 1995.

Dong Ruicheng 董瑞成 et al., eds. *Zhong hua zhi hun, wuyue duzun: Tai-shan* 中华之魂,五岳独尊:泰山 (*Mount Tai: Symbol of the Chinese Spirit*). Beijing: Zhongguo luyou chubanshe, 1995.

Dong Shenbao. "Metamorphic and Tectonic Domains of China." *Journal of Metamorphic Geology* 1993, no. 11: 465–81.

Dongxuan lingbao wuyue guben zhenxing tu 洞玄靈寶五嶽古本眞形圖 (Plans of the ancient origins of the true forms of the obscure, numinous, precious caverns of the five sacred peaks). In *Daozang* 道藏 (Daoist canon), 6: 735–44. Reprinted—Beijing: Wenwu chubanshe, 1988. (HY no. 441, Schipper no. 441.)

Doré, Henri. *Researches into Chinese Superstitions*. Trans. M. Kennelly. 11 vols. Reprinted—Taibei: Ch'eng-wen Publishing, 1966–67.

Dott, Brian Russell. "Ascending Mount Tai: Social and Cultural Interactions in Eighteenth Century China." Ph.D. diss., University of Pittsburgh, 1998.

———. "Signifying Mount Tai: Modern Meanings of an Ancient Site." Forthcoming.

Dransmann, F. *T'aishan-Küfow Guide*. Bilingual English-German ed. Yen-chowfu, Shandong: Catholic Mission Press, 1934.

Duara, Prasenjit. *Culture, Power, and the State: Rural North China, 1900–1942*. Stanford: Stanford University Press, 1988.

DuBose, Hampden C. *The Dragon, Image and Demon. Or the Three Religions of China: Confucianism, Buddhism, and Taoism*. Richmond: Presbyterian Committee of Publication, 1899.

Dudbridge, Glen. "A Pilgrimage in Seventeenth-Century Fiction: T'ai-shan and the *Hsing-shih yin-yüan chuan*." *T'oung Pao* 77, no. 4–5 (1991): 226–52.

———. "Women Pilgrims to T'ai Shan: Some Pages from a Seventeenth-Century Novel." In *Pilgrims and Sacred Sites in China*, ed. Susan Naquin and Chün-fang Yü, 39–64. Berkeley: University of California Press, 1992.

Eade, John, and Michael J. Sallnow, eds. *Contesting the Sacred: The Anthropology of Christian Pilgrimage*. London: Routledge, 1991.

Eastman, Lloyd E. *Family, Field, and Ancestors: Constancy and Change in China's Social and Economic History, 1550–1949*. Oxford: Oxford University Press, 1988.

Eberhard, Wolfram. *A Dictionary of Chinese Symbols: Hidden Symbols in Chinese Life and Thought*. Trans. G. L. Campbell. London: Routledge, 1986.

————. *Guilt and Sin in Traditional China*. Berkeley: University of California Press, 1967.

Eliade, Mircea. *The Sacred and the Profane: The Nature of Religion*. Trans. Willard Trask. New York: Harcourt, Brace, 1959.

Elliot, Mark C. *The Manchu Way: The Eight Banners and Ethnic Identity in Late Imperial China*. Stanford: Stanford University Press, 2001.

Elman, Benjamin A. *From Philosophy to Philology: Intellectual and Social Aspects of Change in Late Imperial China*. Harvard East Asian Monographs, no. 110. Cambridge, Mass.: Harvard University, Council on East Asian Studies, 1984.

Falk, Kimberley Charlesworth. "Of Bricks, Baskets and Steamed Buns: Gender and the Reproduction of Family in Contemporary Rural North China." Ph.D. diss., University of Pittsburgh, forthcoming.

Farquhar, David M. "Emperor as Bodhisattva in the Governance of the Ch'ing Empire." *Harvard Journal of Asiatic Studies* 38, no. 1 (1978): 5–34.

Fong, Wen C. "Chinese Art and Cross-Cultural Understanding." In *Possessing the Past: Treasures from the National Palace Museum, Taipei*, ed. Wen C. Fong, James C. Y. Watt, et al., 27–36. New York: Metropolitan Museum of Art, 1996.

————. "The Imperial Cult." In *Possessing the Past: Treasures from the National Palace Museum, Taipei*, ed. Wen C. Fong, James C. Y. Watt, et al., 99–105. New York: Metropolitan Museum of Art, 1996.

————. "Some Cultural Prototypes." In *Possessing the Past: Treasures from the National Palace Museum, Taipei*, ed. Wen C. Fong, James C. Y. Watt, et al., 107–19. New York: Metropolitan Museum of Art, 1996.

Franck, Harry A. *China: A Geographical Reader*. Dansville, N.Y.: F. A. Owen, 1927.

————. *Wandering in Northern China*. New York: Century, 1923.

Furth, Charlotte. "From Birth to Birth: The Growing Body in Chinese Medicine." In *Chinese Views of Childhood*, ed. Anne Behnke Kinney, 157–91. Honolulu: University of Hawai'i Press, 1995.

————. "The Patriarch's Legacy: Household Instructions and the Transmission of Orthodox Values." In *Orthodoxy in Late Imperial China*, ed. Kwang-ching Liu, 187–211. Berkeley: University of California Press, 1990.

Garrett, Valery M. *Mandarin Squares: Mandarins and Their Insignia*. Images of Asia. Oxford: Oxford University Press, 1990.

Geil, William E. *The Sacred Five of China*. Boston: Houghton Mifflin, 1926.

Goodrich, Anne Swann. *Chinese Hells: The Peking Temple of Eighteen Hells and Chinese Conceptions of Hell*. St. Augustin, Germany: Monumenta Serica, 1981.

———. *Peking Paper Gods: A Look at Home Worship*. Monumenta Serica Monograph Series, no. 23. Nettatal, Germany: Steyler Verlag, 1991.

———. *The Peking Temple of the Eastern Peak: The Tung-yüeh Miao in Peking and Its Lore*. Nagoya: Monumenta Serica, 1964.

Goodrich, L. Carrington, and Chaoying Fang, eds. *Dictionary of Ming Biography, 1368–1644*. New York: Columbia University Press, 1976.

Gu Jiegang 顧頡剛, ed. *Miaofengshan* 妙峰山 (Marvelous Peak Mountain). Canton: Zhongshan daxue, Yuyan lishi xuehui yanjiusuo, 1928. Reprinted: Zhongshan daxue minsu congshu, no. 29. Taibei: Fulu tushu gongsi, 1969.

Gu Yanwu 顧炎武. *Shandong kaogu lu* 山東考古錄 (Record of Shandong antiquities). 1661. Reprinted in Congshu jicheng chubian, vol. 3144. Beijing: Zhonghua shuju, 1985.

Guy, R. Kent. *The Emperor's Four Treasuries: Scholars and the State in the Late Ch'ien-lung Era*. Harvard East Asian Monographs, no. 129. Cambridge, Mass.: Harvard University, Council on East Asian Studies, 1987.

Hahn, Thomas H. "Daoist Sacred Sites." In *Daoism Handbook*, ed. Livia Kohn, 683–708. Leiden: Brill, 2000.

Han Dezhou 韩德洲, ed. *Mount Taishan* 泰山 (*Taishan*). Bilingual Chinese-English ed. Beijing: Foreign Languages Press, 1981.

Hanan, Patrick. "Introduction." In Li Yu, *The Carnal Prayer Mat (Rou Putuan)*. Trans. Patrick Hanan, v–xiv. New York: Ballantine, 1990.

Hansen, Valerie. *Changing Gods in Medieval China, 1127–1276*. Princeton: Princeton University Press, 1990.

Hanyu dacidian bianji weiyuanhui 汉语大词典编辑委员会. *Hanyu dacidian* 汉语大词典 (Comprehensive dictionary of Chinese words). 12 vols. Shanghai: Hanyu dacidian chubanshe, 1988–1994.

Hanyu dazidian bianji weiyuanhui 汉语大字典编辑委员会. *Hanyu dazidian, suoyinben* 汉语大字典, 缩印本 (Comprehensive dictionary of Chinese characters, condensed edition). Chengdu: Sichuan cishu chubanshe, 1993.

Harley, J. B., and David Woodward, eds. *The History of Cartography*, vol. 2, book 2, *Cartography in the Traditional East and Southeast Asian Societies*. Chicago: University of Chicago Press, 1994.

Harrist, Robert E., Jr. "Record of the Eulogy on Mt. Tai and Imperial Autographic Monuments of the Tang Dynasty." *Oriental Art* 46, no. 2 (2000): 68–79.

Hearn, Maxwell K. "Document and Portrait: The Southern Tour Paintings of Kangxi and Qianlong." In *Chinese Painting Under the Qianlong
Emperor: The Symposium Papers in Two Volumes*, ed. Ju-hsi Chou and
Claudia Brown, 91–131. Phœebus, no. 6.1. Tempe: Arizona State University, 1988.

Ho, Ping-ti. *Studies on the Population of China, 1368–1953*. Harvard East
Asian Studies, no. 4. Cambridge, Mass.: Harvard University Press, 1959.

Hsiung Ping-chen. "Constructed Emotions: The Bond Between Mothers
and Sons in Late Imperial China." *Late Imperial China* 15, no. 1 (June
1994): 87–117.

Huang Liu-hung 黃六鴻. *A Complete Book Concerning Happiness and Benevolence "Fu-hui ch'üan-shu": A Manual for Local Magistrates in Seventeenth-Century China* 福惠全書. Trans. and ed. Djang Chu 章楚. Tuc-
son: University of Arizona Press, 1984.

Huang Qian 黃鈐, comp. *Tai'anxian zhi* 泰安縣志 (Gazetteer of Tai'an
county). 14 *juan*. 1782.

Hubbard, G. E. "The Pilgrims of Taishan." *China Journal of Sciences and
Arts* 3, no. 6 (1925): 322–30.

Hucker, Charles O. *A Dictionary of Official Titles in Imperial China*. Stanford: Stanford University Press, 1985.

Hummel, Arthur W., ed. *Eminent Chinese of the Ch'ing Period*. 2
vols. Washington, D.C.: Government Printing Office, 1943, 1944.
Reprinted—Taibei: Southern Materials Center, 1991.

Idema, Wilt L. "The Pilgrimage to Taishan in the Dramatic Literature of
the Thirteenth and Fourteenth Centuries." *Chinese Literature: Essays,
Articles, Reviews* 19 (1997): 23–57.

Ji Naifu 姬乃甫. "Taishan Bixia / yunli jindian" 泰山碧霞 / 云里金殿
(Mount Tai Bixia / golden hall among the clouds). In *Zhongguo simiao
zhanggu yu chuanshuo* 中国寺庙掌故与传说 (Anecdotes and legends
about China's temples), 54–61. N.p., n.d. (ca. 1985).

Ji shuoquan zhen xubian 集説詮眞續編 (Supplement to the collection ex-
pounding the truth). 1880. Reprinted in *Zhongguo minjian xinyang
ziliao huibian* 中國民間信仰資料彙編 (Collection of materials on
Chinese folk beliefs), ed. Wang Qiugui 王秋桂 and Li Fengmao 李豐
楙, vol. 24. Taibei: Xuesheng shuju, 1989.

Jiang Fengrong 姜丰荣. "Taishan wuzibei kaobian" 泰山无字碑考辨 (An
examination of the Wordless Stele of Mount Tai). In *Taishan yanjiu
luncong: wu* 泰山研究论丛:五 (Fifth collection of essays on the study
of Mount Tai), ed. Dai Youkui 戴有奎 and Zhang Jie 张杰, 179–88.
Qingdao: Qingdao haiyang daxue chubanshe, 1992.

Jiang Fengrong 姜丰荣, ed. *Taishan lidai shike xuanzhu* 泰山历代石刻选注 (Annotated selections of Mount Tai stone inscriptions from past dynasties). Taishan wenhua congshu. Qingdao: Qingdao haiyang da-xue, 1993.

Jin Qi 金棨, comp. *Taishan zhi* 泰山志 (Gazetteer of Mount Tai). 20 *juan*. 1801.

———. "Taishan zhong baishu ji" 泰山種柏樹記 (Record of planting cy-press trees on Mount Tai). Stele on Mount Tai, near Red Gate, erected in 1797.

Johnson, David. "Communication, Class, and Consciousness in Late Im-perial China." In *Popular Culture in Late Imperial China*, ed. David Johnson, Andrew J. Nathan, and Evelyn S. Rawski, 34–72. Berkeley: University of California Press, 1985.

Johnson, David, ed. *Ritual Opera, Operatic Ritual: "Mu-lien Rescues His Mother" in Chinese Popular Culture*. Publications of the Chinese Popu-lar Culture Project, no. 1. Berkeley: Chinese Popular Culture Project, 1989.

Johnson, David, Andrew J. Nathan, and Evelyn S. Rawski. "Preface." In *Popular Culture in Late Imperial China*, ed. David Johnson, Andrew J. Nathan, and Evelyn S. Rawski, ix–xvii. Studies on China, no. 4. Berke-ley: University of California Press, 1985.

Judd, Ellen R. "*Niangjia*: Chinese Women and Their Natal Families." *Journal of Asian Studies* 48, no. 3 (Aug. 1989): 525–44.

Kahn, Harold L. "A Matter of Taste: The Monumental and Exotic in the Qianlong Reign." In *The Elegant Brush: Chinese Painting Under the Qianlong Emperor 1735–1795*, ed. Ju-hsi Chou and Claudia Brown, 288–302. Phoenix: Phoenix Art Museum, 1985.

———. *Monarchy in the Emperor's Eyes: Image and Reality in the Ch'ien-lung Reign*. Cambridge, Mass.: Harvard University Press, 1971.

Keightley, David N. "The Late Shang State: When, Where and What?" In *The Origins of Chinese Civilization*, ed. David N. Keightley, 523–64. Berkeley: University of California Press, 1983.

King-Salmon, Frances W. *House of a Thousand Babies: Experiences of an American Woman Physician in China (1922–1940)*. New York: Exposi-tion Press, 1968.

Kleeman, Terry F. "Mountain Deities in China." *Journal of the American Oriental Society* 114, no. 2 (Apr.–June 1994), 226–38.

Ko, Dorothy. *Teachers of the Inner Chambers: Women and Culture in Seventeenth-Century China*. Stanford: Stanford University Press, 1994.

Kohara Hironobu. "The Qianlong Emperor's Skill in Connoisseurship of Chinese Paintings." In *Chinese Painting Under the Qianlong Emperor: The Symposium Papers in Two Volumes*, ed. Ju-hsi Chou and Claudia Brown, 56–73. Phœbus, no. 6.1. Tempe: Arizona State University, 1988.

Kohn, Livia, ed. *Daoism Handbook*. Handbook of Oriental Studies: IV China, no. 14. Leiden: Brill, 2000.

Kong Zhenxuan 孔貞瑄. *Taishan jisheng* 泰山紀勝 (Record of the beautiful scenery of Mount Tai). 1673. Reprinted: Baibu congshu jicheng, no. 32. Taibei: Yiwen yinshuguan, 1968.

Kroll, Paul W. "Verses from on High: The Ascent of T'ai Shan." *T'oung Pao* 69, no. 4–5 (1983): 223–60.

Kuo, Jason C. *Word As Image: The Art of Chinese Seal Engraving*. New York: China House Gallery, 1992.

KXQZ. *Kangxi qiju zhu* 康熙起居注 (Diaries of activity and repose of the Kangxi reign). Qing. Reprint comp. Zhongguo diyi lishi dang'an guan. 3 vols. Beijing: Zhonghua shuju, 1984.

KXSL. *Da Qing Shengzu ren (Kangxi) huangdi shilu* 大清聖祖仁 (康熙) 皇帝實錄 (Veritable records of the great Qing emperor Shengzu ren [Kangxi]). 6 vols. Reprinted—Taibei: Taiwan huawen shuju, 1964.

KXSX. *Shengzu ren huangdi [Kangxi] shengxun* 聖祖仁皇帝聖訓 (Sacred instructions and edicts of the emperor Shengzu ren [Kangxi]). In *Da Qing shichao shengxun* 大清十朝聖訓 (Sacred instructions and edicts of the ten Qing emperors), vol. 1. Reprinted—Taibei: Wenhai chubanshe, 1965.

KXYW. *Kangxidi yuzhi wenji* 康熙帝御製文集 (Collection of the writings of the Kangxi emperor). 4 vols. Reprinted—Taibei: Taiwan xuesheng shuju, 1969.

Lai Xiu 來秀. "Chongxiu yaocanting beiji" 重修遙參亭碑記 (Record of repairing the Temple for Paying Homage from Afar). Inscription in Temple for Paying Homage from Afar, ca. 1858.

Lewis, Mark Edward. "The *feng* and *shan* Sacrifices of Emperor Wu of the Han." In *State and Court Ritual in China*, ed. Joseph P. McDermott, 50–80. University of Cambridge Oriental Publications, no. 54. Cambridge, Eng: Cambridge University Press, 1999.

Li Bangzhen 李邦珍. "Jing zheng" 經正 (The Classics rectify). Inscription in the Stone Sūtra Vale, 1578.

Li Huan 李桓. *Guochao qixian lei zheng chubian* 國朝耆獻類徵出編 (Verification of virtuous elders of this dynasty, first register). In *Qingdai zhuanji congkan* 清代傳記叢刊 (Collection of Qing dynasty biographies), ed. Zhou Junfu 周駿富, vol. 159. Taibei: Mingwen shuju, 1985.

Li Jisheng 李继生. *Gulao de Taishan* 古老的泰山 (Ancient Mount Tai). Beijing: Xinshijie chubanshe, 1987.

Li Shuhai 李叔還, ed. *Daojiao da cidian* 道教大辭典 (Dictionary of Daoism). Taibei: Juliu tushu gongsi, 1979.

Li, Thomas Shiyu 李世瑜, and Susan Naquin. "The Baoming Temple: Religion and the Throne in Ming and Qing China." *Harvard Journal of Asiatic Studies* 48, no. 1 (1988): 131–88.

Li, Wai-yee. "The Collector, The Connoisseur, and Late-Ming Sensibility." *T'oung Pao* 81, no. 4–5 (1995): 269–302.

Li Yu. *The Carnal Prayer Mat (Rou Putuan).* Trans. Patrick Hanan. New York: Ballantine, 1990.

Liezi, yizhu 列子譯注 (*Liezi*, annotated). Ed. Yan Jie 嚴捷 and Yan Beiming 嚴北溟. Hong Kong: Zhonghua shuju, 1987.

Li ji 禮記 (Book of rites). In *Shisan jing* 十三經 (The Thirteen Classics), ed. Wu Shuping 吳樹平. Beijing: Beijing yanshan chubanshe, 1991.

Lingying Taishan Niangniang baojuan 靈應泰山娘娘寶卷 (Precious volume of the divinely efficacious Goddess of Mount Tai). 17th c. 2 *juan*. Reprinted in *Baojuan* 寶卷 (Precious volumes), ed. by Zhang Xishun 張希舜 et al., 1st collection, vol. 13. Taiyuan: Shanxi renmin chubanshe, 1994. Cited as *Baojuan*.

Little, Stephen, with Shawn Eichman. *Taoism and the Arts of China*. Chicago: Art Institute of Chicago, 2000.

Liu Hui 刘慧. *Taishan miaohui* 泰山庙会 (Mount Tai temple festivals). Ji'nan: Shandong jiaoyu chubanshe, 1999.

———. *Taishan zongjiao yanjiu* 泰山宗教研究 (Study of Mount Tai religions). Beijing: Wenwu chubanshe, 1994.

Liu, Hui-chen Wang. "An Analysis of Chinese Clan Rules: Confucian Theories in Action." In *Confucianism in Action*, ed. David S. Nivison and Arthur F. Wright, 63–96. Stanford: Stanford University Press, 1959.

Liu Maolin 刘茂林 et al., eds. *Shandong mingsheng yinglian* 山东名胜楹联 (Famous Shandong couplets). Ji'nan: Shandong renmin chubanshe, 1993.

Liu Tik-sang. "Festival Site, Museum, and Tourist Attraction: A Rebuilt Tian Hou Temple in South China." Paper presented at the Association for Asian Studies meeting, Chicago, 2001.

Liu Wenzhong 刘文仲. "Annotations." In Xiao Xiezhong 蕭協中, *Taishan xiaoshi jiaozhu* 泰山小史校注 (Short history of Mount Tai, punctuated and annotated), punct. and annot. Liu Wenzhong 刘文仲. Tai'an: Tai'anshi xinwen chubanju, 1992.

Liu Xiuchi 刘秀池, ed. *Taishan daquan* 泰山大全 (Complete Mount Tai).
Ji'nan: Shandong youyi chubanshe, 1995.

Liu Yihou 劉義厚 et al. "Liufang gujin" 流芳古今 (Be honored for all
generations). Inscription in the Mother of the Big Dipper Temple, 1789.

Liu Zenggui 劉增貴. "Tiantang yu diyu: Handai de Taishan xinyang"
天堂與地獄: 漢代的泰山信仰 (Heavenly Hall and the underworld:
Han period beliefs about Mount Tai). *Dalu zazhi* 94, no. 5 (1997): 193-205.

Lowe, H. Y. 盧興源. *The Adventures of Wu: The Life Cycle of a Peking
Man*. 2 vols. Beijing: Peking Chronicle Press, 1940-41. Reprinted—
Princeton: Princeton University Press, 1983.

Lü Jixiang 呂继祥. "Kunlunshan Taishan zhi wenhua tezheng ji qi bijiao"
昆仑山泰山之文化特征及其比较 (The cultural features of Mount
Kunlun and Mount Tai and a comparison of them). In *Taishan yanjiu
luncong: san* 泰山研究论丛:三 (Third collection of essays on the study
of Mount Tai), ed. Li Zhengming 李正明 and Zhang Jie 张杰, 33-46.
Qingdao: Qingdao haiyang daxue chubanshe, 1991.

———. *Taishan Niangniang xinyang* 泰山娘娘信仰 (Beliefs about the
Goddess of Mount Tai). Zhonghua minsu wencong, no. 8. Beijing: Xueyuan chubanshe, 1995.

Lü Yunfang 呂蕓芳. *Taishan lidai zhushu tiyao* 泰山历代著述提要 (Summary of historical writings on Mount Tai). Taishan wenhua congshu.
Qingdao: Qingdao haiyang daxue chubanshe, 1991.

Luo Xianglin 羅香林. "Bixia Yuanjun" 碧霞元君. *Minsu* 69-70 (July 1929):
1-67.

Lust, John. *Chinese Popular Prints*. Leiden: E. J. Brill, 1996.

Ma Changyi 马昌仪 and Liu Xicheng 刘锡诚. *Shi yu shishen* 石与石神
(Stones and stone spirits). Zhonghua minsu wencong, no. 4. Beijing:
Xueyuan chubanshe, 1994.

Ma Dibo 馬第伯. "Fengshan yiji" 封禪儀記 (Record of the *feng* and *shan*
rites). In *Hou Han shu* 後漢書, comp. Fan Ye 范曄, 11: 3166-68 (志第
七: 祭祀上). Beijing: Zhonghua shuju, 1963.

Ma Mingchu 马铭初, ed. *Taishan lidai shi xuan* 泰山历代诗选 (Selected
poems on Mount Tai from past dynasties). Ji'nan: Shandong renmin
chubanshe, 1985.

———. *Taishan lidai wenshi cuibian* 泰山历代文史粹编 (Collection of
the best literary and historical works on Mount Tai from past dynasties). Ji'nan: Shandong youyi shushe, 1989.

Ma Mingchu 马铭初 and Yan Dengfei 严澄非. "Annotations." In Zha
Zhilong 查志隆, comp. *Dai shi jiao zhu* 岱史校注 (*A History of Dai*
[Mount Tai], punctuated and annotated), punct. and annot. Ma Ming-

chu 马铭初 and Yan Dengfei 严澄非. Qingdao: Qingdao haiyang daxue chubanshe, 1992.

Ma Shutian 马书田. *Quanxiang zhongguo sanbai shen* 全像中国三百神 (300 Chinese gods with portraits). Nanchang: Jiangxi meishu chubanshe, 1992.

Mair, Victor H. "Language and Ideology in the Written Popularization of the *Sacred Edict*." In *Popular Culture in Late Imperial China*, ed. David Johnson, Andrew J. Nathan, and Evelyn S. Rawski, 325–59. Berkeley: University of California Press, 1985.

Makra, Mary Lelia, trans. and Paul K. T. Sih, ed. *The Hsiao Ching*. Asian Institute Translations, no. 2. New York: St. John's University Press, 1961.

Mann, Susan. "The Male Bond in Chinese History and Culture." *American Historical Review* 105, no. 5 (Dec. 2000): 1600–614.

Mao shi 毛詩 (Mao's [edition of the *Book of*] Odes). In *Shisan jing* 十三經 (The Thirteen Classics), ed. Wu Shuping 吳樹平. Beijing: Beijing yanshan chubanshe, 1991.

March, Andrew L. "An Appreciation of Chinese Geomancy." *Journal of Asian Studies* 27, no. 2 (Feb. 1968): 253–67.

Marcus, George E. *Ethnography Through Thick and Thin*. Princeton: Princeton University Press, 1998.

Martin, Emily. "Gender and Ideological Differences in Representations of Life and Death." In *Death Ritual in Late Imperial and Modern China*, ed. James L. Watson and Evelyn S. Rawski, 164–79. Berkeley: University of California Press, 1988.

Maspero, Henri. *Taoism and Chinese Religion*. Trans. Frank A. Kierman, Jr. Amherst, Mass.: University of Massachusetts Press, 1981.

Mateer, C. W. "T'ai San–Its Temples and Worship." 2 pts. *Chinese Recorder and Missionary Journal* 10, no. 5 (Sept.–Oct. 1879): 361–69; 10, no. 6 (Nov.–Dec. 1879): 403–15.

Mathews, R. H. *Mathews' Chinese-English Dictionary*. Rev. American ed. Cambridge, Mass.: Harvard University Press, 1943.

Mencius. Trans. D. C. Lau. New York: Penguin, 1970.

Meyer-Fong, Tobie. *Building Culture in Early Qing Yangzhou*. Stanford: Stanford University Press, 2003.

Mi Yunchang 米运昌. "Taishan shenci–Daimiao 泰山神祠—岱庙 (Mount Tai temples—Dai Temple)." In *Daimiao* 岱庙 (Dai Temple), ed. Tai'anshi bowuguan 泰安市博物馆, 3–28. Beijing: Wenwu chubanshe, 1992.

Miaojing, see *Bixia Yuanjun huguo bimin puji baosheng miaojing*.

Morinis, Alan. "Introduction: The Territory of the Anthropology of Pilgrimage." In *Sacred Journeys: The Anthropology of Pilgrimage*, ed. Alan Morinis, 1–28. Westport, Conn.: Greenwood Press, 1992.

Morinis, Alan, ed. *Sacred Journeys: The Anthropology of Pilgrimage*. Westport, Conn.: Greenwood Press, 1992.

Mote, F. W. *Imperial China 900–1800*. Cambridge, Mass.: Harvard University Press, 1999.

Mou Zhongjian 牟钟监 and Zhang Jian 张践. *Zhongguo zongjiao tongshi* 中国宗教通史 (A general history of Chinese religion). Zongjiao xuewen ku. 2 vols. Beijing: Shehui kexue wenxian chubanshe, 2000.

Moule, A. C. "T'ai Shan." *Journal of the North China Branch of the Royal Asiatic Society* 43 (1912): 1–31.

Mount Taishan 泰山 (Taishan). Beijing: Foreign Language Press, 1981.

Mullikin, Mary Augusta. "Tai Shan, Sacred Mountain of the East." *National Geographic* June 1945: 699–719.

Mullikin, Mary Augusta, and Anna M. Hotchkis. *The Nine Sacred Mountains of China: An Illustrated Record of Pilgrimages Made in the Years 1935–1936*. Hong Kong: Vetch & Lee, 1973.

Munakata, Kiyohiko. *Sacred Mountains in Chinese Art*. Urbana-Champaign: Krannert Art Museum and University of Illinois Press, 1991.

Na Zhiliang 那志良 et al. "Tang Song yuce zhuanji" 唐宋玉册專輯 (Special collection of the Tang and Song jade tablets). *Gugong wenwu yuekan* 9, no. 10 (1992): 4–62.

Naquin, Susan. "The Peking Pilgrimage to Miao-feng Shan: Religious Organizations and Sacred Site." In *Pilgrims and Sacred Sites in China*, ed. Susan Naquin and Chün-fang Yü, 333–77. Berkeley: University of California Press, 1992.

———. *Peking: Temples and City Life, 1400–1900*. Berkeley: University of California Press, 2000.

Naquin, Susan, and Chün-fang Yü. "Introduction: Pilgrimage in China." In *Pilgrims and Sacred Sites in China*, ed. Susan Naquin and Chün-fang Yü, 1–38. Berkeley: University of California Press, 1992.

Naquin, Susan, and Chün-fang Yü, eds. *Pilgrims and Sacred Sites in China*. Studies on China, no. 15. Berkeley: University of California Press, 1992.

Nie Jianguang 聶劍光 (Nie Wen 聶鈫). *Taishan daoli ji* 泰山道里記 (An itinerary of Mount Tai), punct. and ed. Dai Lin 岱林 et al. 1 *juan*. 1763. Reprinted—Ji'nan: Shandong youyi shushe, 1987.

"Oldest Sister Ties a Baby Doll," see "Dajie shuan wawa."

Ouyang Xuan 歐陽玄. *Songshi* 宋史 (History of the Song). 1345. Reprinted—Beijing: Zhonghua shuju, 1977.

Overmyer, Daniel L. *Precious Volumes: An Introduction to Chinese Sectarian Scriptures from the Sixteenth to Seventeenth Centuries.* Harvard-Yenching Institute Monograph Series, no. 49. Cambridge, Mass.: Harvard University Asia Center, 1999.

Palace Museum 故宮博物院 (Gugong bowuyuan). *Cultural Relics of Tibetan Buddhism Collected in the Qing Palace* 清宮藏传佛教文物 (*Qinggong zangchuan fojiao wenwu*). Bilingual Chinese-English ed. Beijing: Zijincheng chubanshe, Forbidden City Press, 1992.

Park, Chris C. *Sacred Worlds: An Introduction to Geography and Religion.* London: Routledge, 1994.

Po Sung-nien and David Johnson. *Domesticated Deities and Auspicious Emblems: The Iconography of Everyday Life in Village China. Popular Prints and Papercuts from the Collection of Po Sung-nien.* Publications of the Chinese Popular Culture Project, no. 2. Berkeley: Chinese Popular Culture Project, 1992.

Pomeranz, Kenneth. "Power, Gender, and Pluralism in the Cult of the Goddess of Taishan." In *Culture and State in Chinese History: Conventions, Accommodations, and Critiques*, ed. Theodore Huters, R. Bin Wong, and Pauline Yu, 182–204. Irvine Studies in the Humanities. Stanford: Stanford University Press, 1997.

Pozdneyev, Aleksei M. *Mongolia and the Mongols.* Trans. John Roger Shaw and Dale Plank. Uralic and Altaic series, no. 61. Bloomington: Indiana University Press, 1971.

Preston, James J. "Spiritual Magnetism: An Organizing Principle for the Study of Pilgrimage." In *Sacred Journeys: The Anthropology of Pilgrimage*, ed. Alan Morinis, 31–46. Westport, Conn.: Greenwood Press, 1992.

Qi Heng 戚珩 and Fan Wei 范为. "Gucheng langzhong fengshui geju: qianshi fengshui lilun yu gucheng huanjing yixiang" 古城阆中风水格局: 浅释风水理论与古城环境意象 (The *fengshui* pattern of ancient Langzhong: a preliminary explanation of *fengshui* theory and the environmental form of ancient cities)." In *Fengshui lilun yanjiu* 风水理论研究 (Study of *fengshui* theory), ed. Wang Qixiang 王其享, 41–69. Tianjin: Tianjin daxue chubanshe, 1992.

Qinding da Qing huidian shili 欽定大清會典事例 (Collected statutes of the great Qing, with precedents). 19 vols. Guangxu ed., 1899.

Qing shi jishi chubian 清詩紀事出編 (Initial volume of a chronicle of Qing poetry). In *Qingdai zhuanji congkan* 清代傳記叢刊 (Collection of Qing dynasty biographies), ed. Zhou Junfu 周駿富, vol. 20. Taibei: Mingwen shuju, 1985.

Qingshi liezhuan 清史列傳 (Collected biographies from the Qing history). Reprinted in *Qingdai zhuanji congkan* 清代傳記叢刊 (Collection of Qing dynasty biographies), ed. Zhou Junfu 周駿富, vol. 104. Taibei: Mingwen shuju, 1985.

QLQZ. Qianlong qiju zhu 乾隆起居注 (Diaries of activity and repose of the Qianlong reign). Held in the Number One Historical Archives, Beijing.

QLSL. Da Qing Gaozong chun (Qianlong) huangdi shilu 大清高宗純(乾隆) 皇帝實錄 (Veritable records of the great Qing emperor Gaozong chun [Qianlong]). 30 vols. Reprinted—Taibei: Taiwan huawen shuju, 1964.

Quan Tang shi 全唐詩 (Complete poems of the Tang). Reprinted—Beijing: Zhonghua shuju, 1979.

Rao Bingcai 饒秉才, ed. *Guangzhou yin zidian* 广州音字典 (Dictionary of Guangzhou [Cantonese] pronunciation). [Guangzhou]: Guangdong renmin chubanshe, 1983.

Rawski, Evelyn S. "A Historian's Approach to Chinese Death Ritual." In *Death Ritual in Late Imperial and Modern China*, ed. James L. Watson and Evelyn S. Rawski, 20–34. Berkeley: University of California Press, 1988.

———. *The Last Emperors: A Social History of Qing Imperial Institutions*. Berkeley: University of California Press, 1998.

———. "Presidential Address. Reenvisioning the Qing: The Significance of the Qing Period in Chinese History." *Journal of Asian Studies* 55, no. 4 (Nov. 1996): 829–50.

Remensnyder, Amy G. "Un problème de cultures ou de culture?: la statue-reliquaire et les joca de sainte Foy de Conques dans le *Liber miraculorum* de Bernard d'Angers." *Cahiers de Civilisation Médiévale* 33, no. 4 (1990): 351–79.

Ren Honglie 任弘烈, comp. *Tai'anzhou zhi* 泰安州志 (Gazetteer of Tai'an subprefecture). 1603. Reprinted—Zhongguo fangzhi congshu: huabei difang, no. 10. Taibei: Chengwen chubanshe, 1968.

Rudova, Maria. *Chinese Popular Prints*. Leningrad: Aurora Art Publisher, 1988.

Sangren, P. Steven. "Female Gender in Chinese Religious Symbols: Kuan Yin, Ma Tsu, and the 'Eternal Mother.'" *Signs: Journal of Women in Culture and Society* 9, no. 1 (1983): 4–25.

Sawada Mizuho 澤田瑞穗. *Chūgoku no minkan shinkō* 中国の民間信仰 (Chinese folk beliefs). Tokyo: Kōsakusha, 1982.

―――. *Jigoku hen: Chūgoku no meikai setsu* 地獄変：中国の冥界説 (Transformations of the underworld: commentary on the Chinese realm of the dead). Ajia no shūkyō bunka, no. 3. Kyoto: Hōzōkan, 1968.

Schafer, Edward H. *Pacing the Void: T'ang Approaches to the Stars.* Berkeley: University of California Press, 1977.

Schipper, Kristofer Marinus. *Concordance du Tao-tsang: titres des ouvrages.* Publications de l'Ecole française d'Extrême-Orient, no. 102. Paris: Ecole française d'Extrême-Orient, 1975.

SDS, *see* Shandongsheng difangshizhi bianzuan weiyuanhui.

Sewell, William H., Jr. "The Concept(s) of Culture." In *Beyond the Cultural Turn: New Directions in the Study of Society and Culture,* ed. Victoria E. Bonnell and Lynn Hunt, 35–61. Berkeley: University of California Press, 1999.

Shandong dianshitai 山东电视台 (Shandong Television). *Zhonghua Taishan* 中华泰山 (China's Mount Tai). 12–episode VCD. Ji'nan: Qilu Audio & Video Publishing, 1998. Aired on Central Chinese Television, Summer 2000.

Shandongsheng difangshizhi bianzuan weiyuanhui 山东省地方史志编纂委员会. *Taishan zhi* 泰山志 (Mount Tai gazetteer). Shandongsheng zhi, no. 72. Beijing: Zhonghua shuju, 1993. Cited as SDS.

Shang shu 尚書 (Book of history). In *Shisan jing* 十三經 (The Thirteen Classics), ed. Wu Shuping 吳樹平. Beijing: Beijing yanshan chubanshe, 1991.

Sheridan, James E. *Chinese Warlord: The Career of Feng Yü-hsiang.* Stanford: Stanford University Press, 1966.

Shiau, Mei-hui. "The Cult of Mount T'ai in the Ming: Beliefs, Practices and Historical Developments." M.A. thesis, University of British Columbia, 1994.

Shi jing, see *Mao shi.*

Shu Ding 述鼎. *Minjian yishu: caihui* 民間藝術：彩繪 (Art of folk painting). Minjian yishu, no. 3. Taibei: Yishu tushu gongsi, 1993.

Sima Qian 司馬遷. *Shi ji* 史記 (Records of the Grand Historian). 10 vols. Reprinted—Beijing: Zhonghua shuju, 1959.

Smith, Arthur H. *Village Life in China: A Study in Sociology.* New York: Fleming Revell, 1899.

Smith, Richard J. *Fortune-Tellers and Philosophers: Divination in Traditional Chinese Culture.* Boulder, Colo.: Westview Press, 1991.

Song Enren 宋恩仁. *Taishan shuji* 泰山述記 (Records of Mount Tai). In *Taishan congshu* 泰山叢書 (Collected works on Mount Tai), ed. Wang

Jiefan 王介藩 et al., vols. 11–16. 1790. Reprinted—Qufu: Qufu shifan daxue tushuguan, 1989.

Song Shou 宋壽. *Taishan jishi* 泰山紀事 (Records of Mount Tai). 16th c. Reprinted in *Taishan congshu* 泰山叢書 (Collected works on Mount Tai), ed. Wang Jiefan 王介藩 et al., vol. 8. Qufu: Qufu shifandaxue tushuguan, 1989.

Spence, Jonathan D. *Ts'ao Yin and the K'ang-hsi Emperor, Bondservant and Master.* Yale Historical Publications, no. 85. 2nd ed. New Haven: Yale University Press, 1988.

Stenz, Georg M. *Beiträge zur Volkskunde Süd-Schantungs.* Leipzig: R. Voigtländers Verlag, 1907.

Strassberg, Richard E., trans. and annot. *Inscribed Landscapes: Travel Writing from Imperial China.* Berkeley: University of California Press, 1994.

Struve, Lynn A. "The Hsü Brothers and Semiofficial Patronage of Scholars in the K'ang-hsi Period." *Harvard Journal of Asiatic Studies* 42, no. 1 (June 1982): 231–66.

Stuart, Jan. "Imperial Pastimes: Dilettantism as Statecraft in the 18th Century." In *Life in the Imperial Court of Qing Dynasty China*, ed. Chuimei Ho and Cheri A. Jones, 55–65. Proceedings of the Denver Museum of Natural History, vol. 3, no. 15. Denver: Denver Museum of Natural History, 1998.

Tai'anshi bowuguan 泰安市博物馆. *Taishan jiqi* 泰山祭器 (Sacrificial utensils from Mount Tai). N.p.: Shandong huabao chubanshe, 1995.

Taishan chuanshuo 泰山传说 (Legends of Mount Tai). Ji'nan: Shandong renmin chubanshe, 1985.

Taishan chuanshuo gushi 泰山传说故事 (Traditional stories of Mount Tai). Beijing: Zhongguo minjian wenyi chubanshe, 1981.

"Taishan ditu" 泰山地圖 (Chart of Mount Tai). Neiwufu yutu 內務府輿圖, ca. 1684. Held in the Number One Historical Archives, Beijing.

Taishan fengjing mingsheng guanli weiyuanhui 泰山风景名胜管理委员会. *Zhongguo Taishan* 中国泰山 (*Mount Taishan in China*). Beijing: Wenwu chubanshe, 1993.

Taishanglaojun shuo tianxian yunü Bixia Yuanjun hushi hongji miaojing 太上老君説天仙玉女碧霞元君護世弘濟妙經 (Laozi announces the wondrous scripture of the Heavenly Immortal, Jade Woman, Bixia Yuanjun, who protects the world with capacious aid). 1874. Held in the Tai'an Municipal Museum.

Taishanglaojun shuo tianxian yunü Bixia Yuanjun hushi hongji miaojing 太上老君説天仙玉女碧霞元君護世弘濟妙經 (Laozi announces the wondrous scripture of the Heavenly Immortal, Jade Woman, Bixia

Yuanjun, who protects the world with capacious aid). N.d. Held in the Tai'an Municipal Museum.

Taishan zhi tu shei gan dong 泰山之土谁敢动 (Mount Tai's territory, who dares move it?). Dajia lai chang xin min'ge, no. 1. Shanghai: Shanghai wenyi chubanshe, 1958.

Tan Qixiang 谭其骧, ed. *Zhongguo lishi ditu ji* 中国历史地图集 (Historical atlas of China). 8 vols. Shanghai: Ditu chubanshe, 1982–87.

Tang Zhongmian 唐仲冕. *Dai lan* 岱覽 (An overview of Dai [Mount Tai]). 33 *juan*. N.p., 1793.

Tao Yang 陶阳, Xu Jimin 徐纪民, and Wu Mian 吴绵, eds. *Taishan minjian gushi daguan* 泰山民间故事大观 (Overview of Taishan folktales). Beijing: Wenhua yishu, 1984.

TenBroeck, Janet R. "Appendix: Description of the Tung-yüeh Miao of Peking in 1924." In Anne Swann Goodrich, *The Peking Temple of the Eastern Peak: The Tung-yüeh Miao in Peking and Its Lore*, 232–81. Nagoya: Monumenta Serica, 1964.

Teiser, Stephen F. *The Ghost Festival in Medieval China*. Princeton: Princeton University Press, 1988.

———. *"The Scripture on the Ten Kings" and the Making of Purgatory in Medieval Chinese Buddhism*. Honolulu: University of Hawai'i Press, 1994.

Tianxian yunü Bixia Yuanjun zhenjing 天仙玉女碧霞元君眞經 (True scripture of the Heavenly Immortal, Jade Woman, Bixia Yuanjun). N.p., 1611.

Tschepe, P. A. *Der T'ai Schan und seine Kultstatten*. Jentschoufu: Katholischen Mission, 1906.

Turner, Victor. *Dramas, Fields, and Metaphors: Symbolic Action in Human Society*. Ithaca: Cornell University Press, 1974.

———. *Process, Performance and Pilgrimage: A Study in Comparative Symbology*. New Delhi: Concept, 1979.

———. *The Ritual Process: Structure and Anti-Structure*. Chicago: Aldine, 1969.

Turner, Victor, and Edith Turner. *Image and Pilgrimage in Christian Culture: Anthropological Perspectives*. New York: Columbia University Press, 1978.

Wagner, Rudolf G. "Reading the Chairman Mao Memorial Hall in Peking: The Tribulations of the Implied Pilgrim." In *Pilgrims and Sacred Sites in China*, ed. Susan Naquin and Chün-fang Yü, 378–423. Berkeley: University of California Press, 1992.

Wakeman, Frederic E., Jr. *The Great Enterprise: The Manchu Reconstruction of Imperial Order in Seventeenth-Century China*. 2 vols. Berkeley: University of California Press, 1985.

Walters, Derek. *Chinese Astrology: Interpreting the Revelations of the Celestial Messengers*. 2nd ed. London: Aquarian Press, 1992.

Waltner, Ann. "T'an-Yang-tzu and Wang Shih-chen: Visionary and Bureaucrat in the Late Ming." *Late Imperial China* 8, no. 1 (June 1987): 105-33.

Wang Chong 王充. *Lun heng* 論衡 (Balanced discourses). Reprinted—Shanghai: Shanghai renmin chubanshe, 1974.

Wang Hui 王翬 and assistants. "Disanjuan: cong Ji'nanfu jing Tai'anzhou, zhi li Taishan 第三卷: 從濟南府經泰安州, 致禮泰山 (The third scroll: from Ji'nan prefecture through Tai'an department, [with] performance of ceremonies at Mount Tai)." Part of *Nanxuntu* 南巡圖 (Pictures of the Southern Tour). 1691-98. 12 handscrolls. Metropolitan Museum of Art, New York. The Dillon Fund Gift, 1979. 68.7 cm x 1393 cm.

Wang Jiefan 王介藩 et al., eds. *Taishan congshu* 泰山叢書 (Collected works on Mount Tai). 48 vols. Qufu: Qufu shifandaxue tushuguan, 1989.

Wang Jun 王军 and Wang Feng 汪锋. *Tai'an & Mt. Tai*. Beijing: New World Press, 1987.

Wang Lianru 王連儒. *Taishan zhinan* 泰山指南 (Guide to Mount Tai). N.p., 1922.

Wang Qixiang 王其享, ed.. *Fengshui lilun yanjiu* 风水理论研究 (Study of Fengshui theory). Tianjin: Tianjin daxue chubanshe, 1992.

Wang Shizhen 王世貞. "You Taishan ji" 遊泰山記 (Record of Mount Tai travels). In *Taishan lidai wenshi cuibian* 泰山历代文史粹编 (Collection of the best literary and historical works on Mount Tai from past dynasties), ed. Ma Mingchu 马铭初, 285-92. Ji'nan: Shandong youyi shushe, 1989.

Wang Shucun 王樹村, ed. *Zhongguo gudai minsu banhua* 中國古代民俗版畫 (Ancient Chinese folk prints). Beijing: xin shijie, 1992.

———. *Yangliuqing nianhua ziliao ji* 楊柳青年畫資料集 (A collection of Yangliuqing New Year's prints). Beijing: Renmin meishu, 1959.

Wang Yude 王玉德 et al. *Zhonghua shenmi wenhua* 中华神秘文化 (The culture of Chinese mysticism). Changsha: Hunan chubanshe, 1993.

Wang Zhigang 王之綱. "Yunü zhuan" 玉女傳 (Biography of the Jade Woman). In *Dai shi* 岱史 (A history of Dai [Mount Tai]), ed. Zha Zhilong 查志隆, *juan* 9: 153-54. Ca. 1572. Reprinted—Qingdao: Qingdao haiyang daxue chubanshe, 1992.

Wang Ziqing 汪子卿, comp. *Taishan zhi* 泰山志 (Gazetteer of Mount Tai). 4 *juan*. 1555.

Watson, Burton, trans. and annot. *Records of the Grand Historian: Han Dynasty*. Rev. ed. 2 vols. New York: Columbia University Press, 1993.

Watson, James L. "Standardizing the Gods: The Promotion of T'ien Hou ('Empress of Heaven') Along the South China Coast, 960–1960." In *Popular Culture in Late Imperial China*, ed. David Johnson, Andrew J. Nathan, and Evelyn S. Rawski, 292–324. Berkeley: University of California Press, 1985.

Watson, James L., and Evelyn S. Rawski, eds. *Death Ritual in Late Imperial and Modern China*. Berkeley: University of California Press, 1988.

Wechsler, Howard J. *Offerings of Jade and Silk: Ritual and Symbol in the Legitimation of the T'ang Dynasty*. New Haven: Yale University Press, 1985.

Werner, E. T. C. *Dictionary of Chinese Mythology*. Shanghai: Kelly and Walsh, 1932.

Williamson, Isabelle. *Old Highways in China*. New York: American Tract Society, 1884.

Wolf, Arthur. "Gods, Ghosts and Ancestors." In *Religion and Ritual in Chinese Society*, ed. Arthur Wolf, 131–82. Stanford: Stanford University Press, 1974.

Wolf, Margery. "Beyond the Patrilineal Self: Constructing Gender in China." In *Self as Person in Asian Theory and Practice*, ed. Roger T. Ames, Wimal Dissanayake, and Thomas P. Kasulis, 251–67. Albany: SUNY Press, 1994.

———. *Women and the Family in Rural Taiwan*. Stanford: Stanford University Press, 1972.

Wu Hung. "Beyond Stereotypes: The Twelve Beauties in Qing Court Art and the *Dream of the Red Chamber*." In *Writing Women in the Late Imperial Period*, ed. Ellen Widmer and Kang-I Sun Chang, 306–65. Stanford: Stanford University Press, 1997.

———. "Emperor's Masquerade—'Costume Portraits' of Yongzheng and Qianlong." *Orientations* 26, no. 7 (July-Aug. 1995): 25–41.

———. "Tiananmen Square: A Political History of Monuments." *Representations* 35 (1991): 84–117.

Wu, Pei-yi. "An Ambivalent Pilgrim to T'ai Shan in the Seventeenth Century." In *Pilgrims and Sacred Sites in China*, ed. Susan Naquin and Chün-fang Yü, 65–88. Berkeley: University of California Press, 1992.

———. *The Confucian's Progress: Autobiographical Writings in Traditional China*. Princeton: Princeton University Press, 1990.

Wu Shikai 吳士愷. "Chongxiu Yaocanting bei" 重修遙參亭碑 (Stele inscription on repairing the Temple for Paying Homage from Afar). In
Taishan lidai wenshi cuibian 泰山历代文史粹编 (Collection of the best
literary and historical works on Mount Tai from past dynasties), ed.
Ma Mingchu 马铭初, 147–49. Ji'nan: Shandong youyi shushe, 1989.

Xiao Xiezhong 蕭協中. *Taishan xiaoshi jiaozhu* 泰山小史校注 (Short history of Mount Tai, punctuated and annotated), punct. and annot. Liu
Wenzhong 刘文仲, with 1922 annotations by Zhao Xinru 趙新儒. Ca.
1640. Reprinted—Tai'an: Tai'anshi xinwen chubanju, 1992.

Xingshi yinyuan zhuan, see Xizhousheng.

Xizhousheng 西周生, pseud. *Xingshi yinyuan zhuan* 醒世姻緣傳 (Marriage destinies that will bring society to its senses). 17th c. Reprinted—
Ji'nan: Qilu shushe, 1993.

Xu Zonggan 徐宗幹, comp. *Tai'anxian zhi* 泰安縣志 (Gazetteer of Tai'an
county). 14 *juan*. 1828.

Yan Jingsheng 顏景盛. *Taishan fengjing mingsheng daoyou* 泰山风景名胜
导游 (Guide to Mount Tai's scenic and famous sites). Ji'nan: Shandong
wenyi chubanshe, 1993.

Yang, C. K. *Religion in Chinese Society: A Study of Contemporary Social
Functions of Religion and Some of Their Historical Factors*. Berkeley:
University of California Press, 1961.

Yao Nai 姚鼐. "Deng Taishan ji" 登泰山記 (Record of climbing Mount
Tai). In *Taishan gujin youji xuanzhu* 泰山古今游记选注 (Annotated selections of ancient and modern Mount Tai travelogues), ed. Zhou Qian
周谦 and Lü Jixiang 吕继祥, 123–27. Ji'nan: Shandong renmin chubanshe, 1987.

Yee, Cordell D. K. "Chinese Maps in Political Culture." In *The History of
Cartography*, vol. 2, book 2, *Cartography in the Traditional East and
Southeast Asian Societies*, ed. J. B. Harley and David Woodward, 71–95.
Chicago: University of Chicago Press, 1994.

Yi jing (Book of changes), see *Zhou yi*.

Ying Shao 應劭. *Fengsu tongyi* 風俗通義 (Comprehensive explanations of
customs). Reprinted—Zhuzi baijia congshu. Shanghai: Shanghai guji
chubanshe, 1990.

Yu Hui. "Naturalism in Qing Imperial Group Portraiture." *Orientations*
26, no. 7 (July–Aug. 1995): 42–50.

Yu Shu 余恕. "Sheng xian fang" 昇仙坊 (Promoted to transcendent arch).
In *Taishan zhi* 泰山志 (Gazetteer of Mount Tai), comp. Jin Qi 金棨,
6.17b. 1801.

Yü, Chün-fang. *Kuan-yin: The Chinese Transformation of Avalokiteśvara.* Institute for Advanced Studies of World Religions. New York: Columbia University Press, 2001.

———. "P'u-t'o Shan: Pilgrimage and the Creation of the Chinese Potalaka." In *Pilgrims and Sacred Sites in China*, ed. Susan Naquin and Chün-fang Yü, 190–245. Berkeley: University of California Press, 1992.

Yü, Ying-shih. "O Soul, Come Back! A Study in the Changing Conceptions of the Soul and Afterlife in Pre-Buddhist China." *Harvard Journal of Asiatic Studies* 47, no. 2 (1987): 363–95.

Zeitlin, Judith T. *Historian of the Strange: Pu Songling and the Chinese Classical Tale.* Stanford: Stanford University Press, 1993.

Zha Zhilong 查志隆, comp. *Dai shi jiao zhu* 岱史校注 (A history of Dai [Mount Tai], punctuated and annotated), punct. and annot. Ma Mingchu 马铭初 and Yan Dengfei 严澄非. 18 *juan*. 1587. Reprinted—Qingdao: Qingdao haiyang daxue chubanshe, 1992. Also in *Xu Daozang* 續道藏 (Supplement to the Daoist Canon), 35: 675–826. Beijing: Wenwu chubanshe, 1988. (HY no. 1460; Schipper no. 1472.)

Zhan Yinxin 詹鄞鑫. *Shenling yu jisi: Zhongguo chuantong zongjiao zonglun* 神灵与祭祀: 中国传统宗教综论 (Deities and sacrifices: A summary of Chinese traditional religions). Zhongguo guwenxian yanjiu congshu. Nanjing: Suzhou guji chubanshe, 1992.

Zhang Dai 張岱. "Dai zhi" 岱志 (Annals of Dai [Mount Tai]). In idem, *Langxuan wenji* 瑯嬛文集 (Collected works of Zhang Dai), 36–44. Reprinted—Taibei: Danjiang shuju, 1954.

———. "Tai'anzhou kedian" 泰安州客店 (Guest inns of Tai'an subprefecture). In idem, *Taoan mengyi* 陶庵夢憶 (Dream memories of Taoan), 59–60. Ca. 1640. Reprinted—Taibei: Kaiming shudian, 1972.

Zhang Tingyu 張廷玉, et al., eds. *Ming shi* 明史 (Standard history of the Ming). Reprinted—Beijing: Zhonghua shuju, 1959.

Zhang Zeyu. "An Open City at the Foot of Mt. Tai." *Beijing Review* 34, no. 35 (1991): 15–20.

Zhao Xinggen 赵杏根. *Zhongguo baishen quanshu: minjian shenling yuanliu* 中国百神全书: 民间神灵源流 (Complete book of Chinese deities: complete details of folk spirits). Haikou: Nanhai chuban gongsi, 1994.

Zhao Xinru 趙新儒. "Annonations." In Xiao Xiezhong 蕭協中, *Taishan xiaoshi jiaozhu* 泰山小史校注 (Short history of Mount Tai, punctuated and annotated), punct. and annot. Liu Wenzhong 刘文仲. 1922. Reprinted—Tai'an: Tai'anshi xinwen chubanju, 1992.

Zhao Yufeng 赵玉峰, Zhang Zhang 张章, and Zhu Liangfu 朱良富, eds. *Tai'an minjian gushi jicui* 泰安民间故事集粹 (Collection of the best folktales of Tai'an). Tai'an: Tai'anshi xinwen, 1992.

Zhongguo daojiao xiehui 中国道教协会 and Suzhou daojiao xiehui 苏州道教协会. *Daojiao da cidian* 道教大辞典 (Dictionary of the Daoist religion). Beijing: Huaxia chubanshe, 1994.

Zhou Junfu 周骏富, ed. *Qingdai zhuanji congkan* 清代傳記叢刊 (Collection of Qing dynasty biographies). 205 vols. Taibei: Mingwen shuju, 1985–86.

Zhou Qian 周谦 and Lü Jixiang 吕继祥, eds. *Taishan gujin youji xuanzhu* 泰山古今游记选注 (Annotated selections of ancient and modern Mount Tai travelogues). Ji'nan: Shandong renmin chubanshe, 1987.

Zhou Shaoliang 周绍良. "Mingdai huangdi, guifei, gongzhu yinshi de jiben fojing" 明代皇帝, 贵妃, 公主印施的几本佛经 (Commissions to print several Buddhists scriptures by Ming dynasty emperors, imperial concubines, and princesses). *Wenwu* 1987, no. 8: 8–11.

Zhou yi 周易 (Zhou dynasty [Book of] changes). In *Shisan jing* 十三經 (The Thirteen Classics), ed. Wu Shuping 吴樹平. Beijing: Beijing yanshan chubanshe, 1991.

Zhu Yizun 朱彝尊. *Ming shi zong* 明詩綜 (Summary of Ming poets). 2 vols. Reprinted—Shanghai: Shanghai guji chubanshe, 1993.

Zhu Yunjing 朱雲燦. *Daizong ji* 岱宗記 (A record of Daizong [Mount Tai]). 1752.

Zhuangzi, see *Chuang-tzu*.

Zhushu jinian bazhong 竹書紀年八種 (Eight bamboo annals). Reprinted—Taibei: Shijie shuju, 1963.

Zibo gushi juan 淄博故事卷 (Zibo stories). Ji'nan: Shandong wenyi, 1990.

Zong Li 宗力 and Liu Qun 刘群, eds. *Zhongguo minjian zhushen* 中国民间诸神 (Chinese folk deities). Shijiazhuang: Hebei renmin chubanshe, 1986.

Zong Ruji 宗汝濟. *Zhuding yuwen* 鑄鼎餘聞. In *Zhongguo minjian xinyang ziliao huibian* 中國民間信仰資料彙編 (Collection of materials on Chinese folk beliefs), ed. Wang Qiugui 王秋桂 and Li Fengmao 李豐楙, vol. 20. Qing. Reprinted—Taibei: Xuesheng shuju, 1989.

Index

Numbers in boldface refer to pages with figures, maps, or tables. References in parentheses following an entry (no. 29), correspond to the numbers marked on Fig. 5 (p. 16) and to the numbers in the Appendix.

Harvard East Asian Monographs
(* out-of-print)

Harvard East Asian Monographs

Harvard East Asian Monographs

Harvard East Asian Monographs

Harvard East Asian Monographs

Harvard East Asian Monographs

Harvard East Asian Monographs

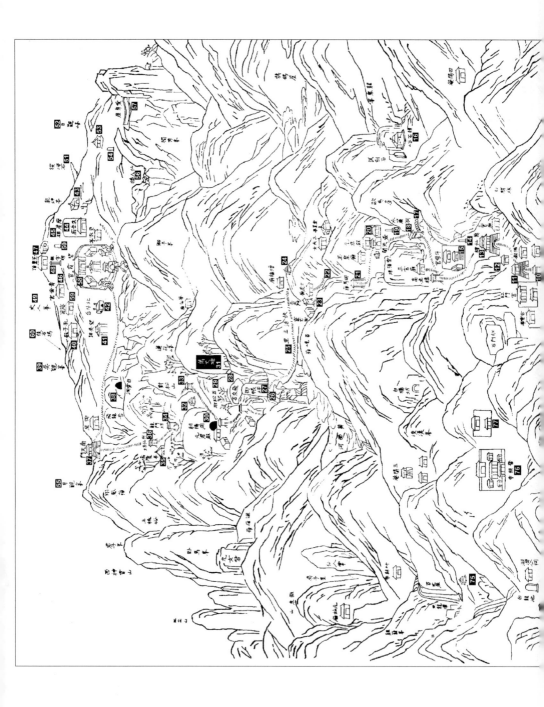